Making the Law of the Sea

The law of the sea is an important area of international law that must be able to adapt to the changing needs of the international community. *Making the Law of the Sea* examines how various international organizations have contributed to the development of this law and what kinds of instruments and law-making techniques have been used. Each chapter considers a different international institution – including the International Maritime Organization and the United Nations – and analyzes its functions and powers. Important questions are posed about the law-making process, including what actors are involved and what procedures are followed. Potential problems for the development of the law of the sea are considered and solutions are proposed. In particular, James Harrison explores and evaluates the current methods employed by international institutions to coordinate their law-making activities in order to overcome fragmentation of the law-making process.

DR JAMES HARRISON is a lecturer at the University of Edinburgh where he teaches public international law and public law.

CAMBRIDGE STUDIES IN INTERNATIONAL AND COMPARATIVE LAW

Established in 1946, this series produces high-quality scholarship in the fields of public and private international law and comparative law. Although these are distinct legal sub-disciplines, developments since 1946 confirm their interrelation.

Comparative law is increasingly used as a tool in the making of law at national, regional and international levels. Private international law is now often affected by international conventions, and the issues faced by classical conflicts rules are frequently dealt with by substantive harmonization of law under international auspices. Mixed international arbitrations, especially those involving state economic activity, raise mixed questions of public and private international law, while in many fields (such as the protection of human rights and democratic standards, investment guarantees and international criminal law) international and national systems interact. National constitutional arrangements relating to "foreign affairs," and to the implementation of international norms, are a focus of attention.

The Board welcomes works of a theoretical or interdisciplinary character, and those focusing on the new approaches to international or comparative law or conflicts of law. Studies of particular institutions or problems are equally welcome, as are translations of the best work published in other languages.

A list of books in the series can be found at the end of this volume.

Making the Law of the Sea
A Study in the Development
of International Law

James Harrison

CAMBRIDGE
UNIVERSITY PRESS

CAMBRIDGE UNIVERSITY PRESS
Cambridge, New York, Melbourne, Madrid, Cape Town,
Singapore, São Paulo, Delhi, Mexico City

Cambridge University Press
The Edinburgh Building, Cambridge CB2 8RU, UK

Published in the United States of America by Cambridge University Press, New York

www.cambridge.org
Information on this title: www.cambridge.org/9781107668737

First published 2011
Reprinted 2012
First paperback edition 2013

A catalogue record for this publication is available from the British Library

Library of Congress Cataloguing in Publication Data
Harrison, James, 1979–
  Making the law of the sea : a study in the development of international law /
  [James Harrison].
  p.   cm. – (Cambridge studies in international and comparative law)
  Includes bibliographical references and index.
  ISBN 978-0-521-19817-2 (hardback)
  1. Law of the sea.   I. Title.   II. Series.
  KZA1145.H375 2011
  341.4′5–dc22
  2010054308

ISBN 978-1-107-66873-7 Paperback

Contents

Acknowledgements

Much of the research contained in this book was conducted as part of my PhD at the University of Edinburgh. Throughout this process I was lucky to have Professor Alan Boyle as my PhD supervisor. I am indebted to his constructive comments on my work, which have assisted my understanding of the intricacies of the law of the sea and international law more generally. I would also like to acknowledge the guidance and support of other members of the academic staff at the University of Edinburgh. I would particularly like to thank Professor Chris Himsworth for his advice and encouragement in carrying out my research. I am grateful that since I completed by PhD, I have been able to count these individuals as colleagues and I have continued to be able to benefit from their immeasurable experience. Finally, I would like to thank Katie Pekot for all her support, as well as her patience in proofreading and editing earlier versions of this work.

Table of treaties

Table of cases

Abbreviations

APFC	Asia-Pacific Fisheries Commission
CCAMLR	Commission on the Conservation of Antarctic Marine Living Resources
CECAF	Fishery Committee for the Eastern Central Atlantic
CITES	Convention on International Trade in Endangered Species
COP	Conference of the Parties
ECOSOC	Economic and Social Council
EEZ	Exclusive Economic Zone
FAO	Food and Agriculture Organization
GFCM	General Fisheries Commission for the Mediterranean
IATTC	Inter-American Tropical Tuna Commission
ICCAT	International Commission for the Conservation of Atlantic Tunas
ICJ	International Court of Justice
ICNT	Informal Composite Negotiating Text
ICP	Open-Ended Informal Consultative Process on the Law of the Sea
ILA	International Law Association
ILC	International Law Commission
ILO	International Labour Organization
IMO	International Maritime Organization
IOTC	Indian Ocean Tuna Commission
ISNT	Informal Single Negotiating Text
IUCN	International Conservation Union
IUU	Illegal, Unreported and Unregulated
MOU	Memorandum of Understanding
NAFO	North West Atlantic Fisheries Organization

NEAFC	North East Atlantic Fisheries Commission
NGO	Nongovernmental Organization
PSSA	Particularly Sensitive Sea Area
RECOFI	Regional Committee for Fisheries
SEAFO	South East Atlantic Fisheries Organization
UN	United Nations
UNCED	United Nations Conference on Environment and Development
UNCITRAL	United Nations Commission on International Trade Law
UNCLOS I	First United Nations Conference on the Law of the Sea
UNCLOS II	Second United Nations Conference on the Law of the Sea
UNCLOS III	Third United Nations Conference on the Law of the Sea
WCPFC	Western and Central Pacific Fisheries Commission
WECAFC	Western Central Atlantic Fishery Commission

1   Making the modern law of the sea: challenges and opportunities

1 The challenges of international law-making

The law of the sea is an important area of international law that regulates the uses of the world's seas and oceans. The law of the sea defines the jurisdiction of states over all kinds of maritime activities, including navigation, the exploitation of living and nonliving resources, the laying of cables and pipelines, and the conduct of marine scientific research. This book is not intended to explain in detail what substantive rights and obligations arise in this area of international law.[1] Rather, it is concerned with explaining and analyzing the process of how the law of the sea is created and how it can be adapted to meet modern challenges facing the international community.

Since very early in the history of the law of the sea, it has been recognized that no single state has an exclusive claim to the vast expanses of the oceans. Rather all states, whether they are coastal or landlocked, have been seen as having an interest in the sea and its resources.[2] Thus, McDougal and Burke describe how "the historic function of the law of the sea has long been recognized as that of protecting and balancing the common interests, inclusive and exclusive, of all peoples in the use and enjoyment of the oceans, while rejecting all egocentric assertions of special interests in contravention of the general community interest."[3] This remains true today. Modern attempts at making

---

[1] In this regard, see e.g. R. Churchill and V. Lowe, *The Law of the Sea* (3rd edn., Manchester University Press, 1997).

[2] The oceans could be classified as, what Weiler has called, a "common asset" of the international community; see J. Weiler, "The geology of international law – governance, democracy and legitimacy" (2004) 64 *ZaöRV* 547, at 556.

[3] M. S. McDougal and W. T. Burke, *Public Order of the Oceans* (Yale University Press, 1962) at 1.

the law of the sea have sought to establish an international regime of a truly global character that would be applicable to all states. This is perhaps clearest from the decision of the UN General Assembly in 1970 to convene the Third United Nations Conference on the Law of the Sea, where it was stressed that the conference should aim to "accommodate the interests and needs of all states"[4] and the results of the conference should ultimately be "generally acceptable"[5] to all members of the international community.

Yet creating a universal regime for the seas and oceans is complicated by the decentralized nature of the international legal system. Charney observes that "the traditions of the international legal system appear to work against the ability to legislate universal norms."[6] There is no global legislature that can impose rules on all relevant actors. As Pauwelyn notes, the international legal system has "essentially as many law-makers as there are states."[7]

The importance of states as law-makers is underlined by the fact that each of them is independent and sovereign. The sovereign equality of states is "a fundamental axiomatic premise of the international legal order"[8] and it follows from this principle that individual states cannot have rules or principles of international law imposed on them without their consent. The significance of consent in the international legal order was emphasized by the Permanent Court of International Justice in its judgment in the 1927 *SS Lotus Case* when it said:

International law governs relations between independent States. The rules of law binding upon States therefore emanate from their own free will ...[9]

The centrality of consent in the law-making process means that states can resist the imposition of rules that they perceive to be at variance

---

[4] *Reservation exclusively for peaceful purposes of the sea-bed and the ocean floor, and the subsoil thereof, underlying the high seas beyond the limits of present national jurisdiction and use of their resources in the interests of mankind, and convening of a conference on the law of the sea,* UNGA Resolution 2750C, December 17, 1970, preamble.

[5] Law of the Sea Convention, preamble.

[6] J. Charney, "Universal international law" (1993) 87 *Am. J. Int'l L.* 529, at 530.

[7] J. Pauwelyn, *Conflict of Norms in Public International Law* (Cambridge University Press, 2003) at 13.

[8] J. Kokott, "States, sovereign equality," in R. Wolfrum *et al.* (eds.), *Max Planck Encyclopedia of Public International Law* (Oxford University Press, Online Edition Updated August 2007) at para. 1.

[9] *The SS Lotus Case* (1927) PCIJ Reports, Series A, No. 10, at 18.

with their sovereign interests. This makes it much more difficult to establish regimes that create a common set of rules for all states.

At the beginning of the twenty-first century states are still retaining a tight grip on international law-making.[10] Yet the law of the sea presents an interesting example of the successful emergence of an international regime that is, to a large extent, accepted by all states. It is suggested that the creation of a universal legal order of the oceans has been significantly facilitated by the use of increasingly sophisticated law-making procedures involving international institutions. In this area of international law, as in others, international institutions of various kinds have played a central role in the law-making process. The growth in international institutions has not, however, led to new sources of international law. Few of these organizations have formal legislative powers that allow them to override the consent of individual states.[11] Rather, the significance of international institutions in this context lies in their ability to bring states together in a single forum and to facilitate the creation of the traditional sources of international law, namely treaties and customary international law.

In order to understand the contribution that international institutions have made to developing the law of the sea, it is first necessary to comprehend the potential for the traditional sources of international law to create universal norms. The following sections will provide a basic introduction to treaties and customary international law and their ability to create rules and principles that are binding on all states. The analysis will also consider what influence international institutions can have on law-making activities and how they can contribute to the creation of universal legal regimes.

2 Treaties as law-making instruments

Treaties are generally defined as international agreements in written form and governed by international law, whatever its particular designation.[12] Today, treaties are one of the most common tools for

---

[10] See generally A. E. Boyle and C. Chinkin, *The Making of International Law* (Oxford University Press, 2007) at 95.

[11] There may be some exceptional cases such as the United Nations Security Council, on which see e.g. E. Rosand, "The Security Council as global legislature: ultra-vires or ultra-innovator?" (2005) 28 *Fordham Int'l L. J.* 10.

[12] 1969 Vienna Convention on the Law of Treaties, Article 2(1)(a); 1986 Vienna Convention on the Law of Treaties between States and International Organizations or between International Organizations, Article 2(1)(a).

international law-making.[13] Hundreds of treaties are concluded every year by states and other international actors. What all treaties have in common is that they have been specifically negotiated to meet a particular need. As Tomuschat observes, "law-making by treaty is the only organized procedure for the conscious, rational positing of legal rules, at least at the universal level."[14]

The majority of multilateral treaties are today concluded under the auspices of international organizations or other institutional frameworks such as intergovernmental conferences. The increased involvement of international organizations in the negotiation of treaties has arguably had an impact on the treaty negotiation process by increasing the number of states and non-state actors involved in the process.[15] Moreover, international institutions are able to provide "a relatively stable negotiation forum that permits negotiators to continue their interaction beyond a single round of negotiations."[16] Indeed, the existence of a permanent organization means that delegates can build up relationships of mutual trust and respect, which may increase the chances of reaching agreement. The involvement of the secretariat of an international organization in the negotiation of a treaty may also offer advantages to the treaty-making process. The secretariat of an international organization can carry out what Alvarez calls "leadership functions" by:[17]

(1)   promoting areas or topics on which collective treaty-making would be beneficial;
(2)   mobilizing potential collaborators from both within and outside the organization;
(3)   shaping the agenda by providing productive frameworks for negotiations;
(4)   building consensus; and
(5)   brokering compromise.

---

[13] Boyle and Chinkin, *The Making of International Law*, at 233.
[14] C. Tomuschat, "Obligations arising for states without or against their will" (1993) 241 *Recueil des Cours* 194, at 239. See also B. Simma, "From bilateralism to community interest in international law" (1994) 250 *Recueil des Cours* 221, at 323; A. D. McNair, "The functions and differing legal character of treaties" (1930) *Brit. Ybk Int'l L.* 100, at 101; Boyle and Chinkin, *The Making of International Law*, at 233.
[15] J. E. Alvarez, *International Organizations as Law-Makers* (Oxford University Press, 2005) at 276.
[16] *Ibid.*, at 339.   [17] *Ibid.*, at 342.

These tasks can also be carried out not only by the secretariat, but also by other individuals working in an institutional capacity, such as the members of the bureau appointed by an international conference or the elected chair of an organ of an international institution.[18]

Although international institutions offer advantages to the treaty-making process, they cannot overcome the inherent limitations of treaties when it comes to the creation of universal international law. One cannot escape the fact that treaties are contractual instruments that depend upon the express consent of states before they become binding. According to the fundamental doctrine of *pacta tertiis nec nocent prosunt*, a treaty creates legal obligations only for states that become a party to it.[19] Thus, even if a state has been involved in the negotiation of a treaty, it will not become bound by its contents until it has individually consented. The International Law Commission has described the doctrine of *pacta tertiis* as "one of the bulwarks of the independence and equality of States,"[20] emphasizing its fundamental character as a principle of international law. The importance of the *pacta tertiis* principle is also stressed by McNair in his well-known work on the law of treaties where he says that "both legal principle and common sense are in favour of the rule ... because as regards States which are not parties ... a treaty is res inter alios acta."[21] It is therefore clear that treaties, regardless of their purpose, are not legislative instruments as the legal force of a treaty stems not from their adoption, but from the subsequent acceptance of states through signature, ratification or accession.[22]

There are some exceptions to the principle of *pacta tertiis* that may facilitate the wider application of a treaty beyond those states that have formally consented to be bound. When negotiating a treaty, states can, in certain circumstances, create rights and obligations for third states that are not formally a party to the treaty.[23] These exceptions to the

---

[18] See further Chapter 2.
[19] Article 34 of the Vienna Convention on the Law of Treaties provides that "a treaty does not create either obligations or rights for a third State without its consent." There are exceptions to this rule which will be discussed below.
[20] International Law Commission, "Draft articles on the law of treaties: report of the Commission to the General Assembly" (1966–II) *Ybk Int'l Law Commission* at 227.
[21] A. D. McNair, *The Law of Treaties* (Oxford University Press, 1961) at 309. See also Tomuschat, "Obligations arising for states without or against their will," at 242.
[22] See Vienna Convention on the Law of Treaties, Articles 11–17.
[23] The Vienna Convention defines a "third state" as "a State not party to a treaty"; Vienna Convention on the Law of Treaties, Article 2(1)(h).

pacta tertiis principle are recognized by Articles 35 and 36 of the Vienna Convention on the Law of Treaties.

Article 36 of the Vienna Convention provides that "a right arises for a third State from a provision of a treaty if the parties to the treaty intend the provision to accord that right either to the third State, or to a group of States to which it belongs, or to all States, and the third State assents thereto." According to this provision, there are two conditions that must be satisfied for a treaty to effectively create a right for a third state.

First, it must be shown that the parties to the treaty intended to create such a right. The principal means of identifying intention should be the text of the treaty itself and the normal rules of treaty interpretation apply.[24] It may also be appropriate to consider the *travaux préparatoires* where the text itself is ambiguous or obscure.[25] In either case, there should be a clear intention to confer a legally enforceable right on a third state, rather than simply bestow a benefit to that state. In the words of the Permanent Court of International Justice in the *Free Zones Case*, "it cannot be lightly presumed that stipulations favourable to a third State have been adopted with the object of creating an actual right in its favour."[26]

Secondly, it is made absolutely clear in Article 36 that the consent of the third state is still a necessary condition for the conferral of a right on it. At the same time, Article 36 says that consent shall be "presumed so long as the contrary is not indicated."[27] In other words, the third state will possess a right conferred on it by a treaty unless it expressly repudiates the right.[28] Thus, consent becomes a legal fiction insofar

---

[24] See C. Chinkin, *Third Parties in International Law* (Clarendon Press, 1993) at 33.

[25] Vienna Convention on the Law of Treaties, Article 32.

[26] *Free Zones of Upper Savoy and District of Gex Case* (1932) PCIJ Reports, Series A/B, No. 46, at 147. The Court goes on to say that "the question of the existence of a right acquired under an instrument drawn between other States is therefore one to be decided in each particular case: it must be ascertained whether the States which have stipulated in favour of a third State meant to create for that State an actual right which the latter has accepted as such."

[27] Vienna Convention on the Law of Treaties, Article 36.

[28] The commentary to Article 35 notes that the issue of consent in relation to third party rights is controversial and a treaty cannot impose a right on a third state because "a right can always be disclaimed or waived." According to the commentary, the text of Article 35 is intended to leave open the question of whether juridically the right is created by the treaty or by the beneficiary state's act of acceptance; International Law Commission, "Draft articles on the law of treaties: report of the Commission to the General Assembly," at 228–9.

as the conferral of rights on third states is concerned. If rights are claimed by a third state, Article 36(2) of the Vienna Convention specifies that the third state must comply with any conditions attached to that right.

Article 35 of the Vienna Convention governs the creation of obligations for third states under a treaty. It provides that "an obligation arises for a third state from a provision of a treaty if the parties to the treaty intend the provision to be the means of establishing the obligation and the third state expressly accepts that obligation in writing."

Once again, the importance of the intention of the parties to the treaty to create an obligation for a third state is stressed. As with the conferral of rights, intention can be deduced from the text of the treaty itself, or in the case of ambiguity or obscurity, from the *travaux préparatoires.*

Consent of the third state to that obligation is also a necessary requirement under Article 35. Yet, unlike the presumption of consent for the conferral of rights on third states, Article 35 specifies that a third state must expressly accept an obligation imposed on it by the treaty in writing.[29] This is a much stricter requirement that underlines the practical difference between conferring a right and an obligation on a third state. In practice, this means that the conferral of the obligation is itself the subject of a second "collateral" treaty between the third state on the one hand and the parties to the original treaty on the other hand.[30]

Whereas these two exceptions to the *pacta tertiis* principle allow some leeway for the application of treaties to third states, they are not without their own problems. For example, Chinkin notes that while the Vienna Convention draws a clear distinction between rights and obligations, "treaties, like any other form of agreement, characteristically incorporate both rights and duties as part of an interlocking bargain."[31] She

---

[29] There was much discussion about the form of consent to an obligation in the discussions of the ILC; see 733rd meeting to 735th meeting (1964-I) *Yearbook of the International Law Commission*, at 64–80. The condition that acceptance must be in writing was added at the Vienna Conference following a proposal by Vietnam; see I. Sinclair, *The Vienna Convention on the Law of Treaties* (Manchester University Press, 1984) at 101.

[30] International Law Commission, "Draft articles on the law of treaties: report of the Commission to the General Assembly," at 227.

[31] Chinkin, *Third Parties in International Law*, at 40.

therefore concludes that the application of these exceptions is often impracticable.[32]

A further exception to the *pacta tertiis* principle does not draw such a rigid distinction between rights and obligations for third states. The doctrine of objective regimes concerns the application of treaty regimes, comprising a number of interrelated provisions, to third states.[33] Early support for the existence of this doctrine is found in the judgment of the Permanent Court of International Justice in the *The SS Wimbledon Case*.[34] This case concerned a claim by the United Kingdom, France, Italy and Japan that Germany was under a duty to guarantee free access through the Kiel Canal under the terms of Part XII, Section VI of the 1919 Treaty of Versailles. The Court classified Part XII of the 1919 Treaty as a "self-contained regime"[35] and it held that its provisions, and in particular Article 380, created an international waterway "intended to provide easier access to the Baltic for the benefit of all nations of the world."[36] According to this decision, the effect of this part of the Treaty of Versailles was to create a set of rules that were applicable to all states, whether or not they were party to the treaty.

A version of the doctrine of objective regimes was originally included in the draft articles on the law of treaties prepared by Waldock, the fourth and final special rapporteur on the law of treaties to the International Law Commission (ILC). Waldock described a treaty as creating an objective regime:

when it appears from its terms and from the circumstances of its conclusion that the intention of the parties is to create in the general interest general obligations and rights relating to a particular region, State, territory, locality, river, waterway, or to a particular area of sea, sea-bed, or air-space; provided

---

[32] *Ibid.*

[33] For a historical account of the doctrine, see P. Subedi, "The doctrine of objective regimes in international law and the competence of the United Nations to impose territorial or peace settlements on states" (1994) 37 *German Ybk Int'l L.* 162.

[34] *The SS Wimbledon Case* (1923) PCIJ Reports, Series A, No. 1.

[35] In *The SS Wimbledon Case*, the Permanent Court of International Justice held that the drafters of the Treaty of Versailles took care to place the provisions on the Kiel Canal in a special section, and in this sense the Court describes it as a "self-contained" regime; *ibid.*, at 23–4.

[36] *Ibid.*, at 22; the Court continues, "under its new regime, the Kiel Canal, must be open, on a footing of equality, to all vessels, without making any distinction between war vessels and vessels of commerce, but on one express condition, namely, that these vessels must belong to nations at peace with Germany." For a comment on this case, see M. Ragazzi, *The Concept of International Obligations Erga Omnes* (Clarendon Press, 1997) at 24–7.

that the parties include among their number any State having territorial competence with reference to the subject matter of the treaty, or that any such State has consented to the provision in question.[37]

It can be seen from this explanation of the doctrine that it shares many common characteristics with the other exceptions to the *pacta tertiis* principle discussed above. The intention of the parties to create general rights and obligations, as well as the consent of any third states, are both requirements for the doctrine of objective regimes, as described by Waldock. In his proposed scheme, Waldock suggested that consent to an objective regime could be express or implied. His draft articles also suggested that a failure to oppose a treaty within a certain time limit amounted to tacit acceptance of an objective regime contained therein.[38]

Yet, the doctrine of objective regimes is not found in the Vienna Convention on the Law of Treaties. The ILC ultimately decided not to include the doctrine in its draft articles because it was unlikely to meet with the general acceptance of states.[39] One reason for this position was that the Commission considered that the doctrine implied a form of majoritarian law-making which is not easy to reconcile with the central role for consent in the law of treaties, as expressed through the principle of *pacta tertiis*.

Despite its absence from the Vienna Convention on the Law of Treaties, it does not follow that the doctrine of objective regimes no longer has any validity in international law. Sinclair, who acted as the independent expert to the Vienna Conference on the Law of Treaties, insists that "it must not be assumed that the deliberate decision of the Commission and the Conference not to make special provision for treaties creating 'objective regimes' in the series of articles on treaties and third states in the Vienna Convention on the Law of Treaties

---

[37] H. Waldock, "Third Report on the Law of Treaties" (1964-II) *Ybk Int'l L. Commission*, at 26.

[38] Draft Article 63(2). The idea of a deadline was only tentatively proposed by Waldock in order to remove doubts over the acceptance of an objective regime; see *ibid.*, at 33.

[39] International Law Commission, "Draft articles on the law of treaties: report of the Commission to the General Assembly," at 231. Chinkin suggests that the doctrine of objective regimes was particularly controversial at the time of the ILC discussions because of the situation in Antarctica and the drafting of the Antarctic Treaty; see Chinkin, *Third Parties in International Law*, at 36.

constitutes a denial of the existence of this category of treaty."[40] Indeed, the doctrine can still find support in the writings of many commentators on the law of treaties.[41]

Nevertheless, it is clear from the writings on the subject that the doctrine of objective regimes was never intended to circumvent the ordinary requirements of treaty acceptance. In his commentary on the draft article, Waldock stresses that the doctrine does not cover "cases where the parties have a general treaty-making competence with respect to the subject-matter of the treaty but no greater competence than any other state; in other words, it excludes law-making treaties concerned with general international law or with areas not subject to the exclusive jurisdiction of any state."[42] Thus, the doctrine of objective regimes would not facilitate the creation of universal norms in a field of international law such as the law of the sea, which by definition is concerned with areas that are largely beyond the jurisdiction of any single state and where no state possesses any special competence.

Indeed, it can be asked whether any of these exceptions to the *pacta tertiis* principle can be applied to treaties that have been negotiated through multilateral institutions. The exceptions to the *pacta tertiis* principle evolved in the context of treaties concluded in the late nineteenth and early twentieth centuries. This was an era in which the most powerful states wielded significant authority and they were able to impose international settlements that affected many states, even though these other states may not necessarily have been involved in the negotiation process. For instance, in the *Free Zones Case* considered above, the Court was concerned with whether or not the small number of important states at the 1815 Congress of Vienna and later diplomatic gatherings had intended to confer on Switzerland a right to the withdrawal of the French customs barrier behind the political frontier. These conferences had largely excluded the smaller states. Thus, the exceptions to the *pacta tertiis* principle were necessary in order to give full effect to the treaty for third states. In contrast, as

---

[40] Sinclair, *The Vienna Convention on the Law of Treaties*, at 105–6. Cf. G. M. Danilenko, *Law-making in the International Community* (Martinus Nijhoff Publishers, 1993) at 63.

[41] See e.g. J. Brierly, *The Law of Nations* (Oxford University Press, 1963) at 326–7; Simma, "From bilateralism to community interest in international law," at 358–64; M. Shaw, *International Law* (6th edn., Cambridge University Press, 2008) at 930; Subedi, "The doctrine of objective regimes in international law"; A. Aust, *Modern Treaty Law and Practice* (Cambridge University Press, 2nd edn., 2007) at 258.

[42] Waldock, "Third Report on the Law of Treaties," at 33.

noted above, most modern treaty-making taking place through international institutions includes all states in the law-making process. Indeed, most states would today consider that they had a right to participate in a treaty that affected their interests. As Tunkin pointed out during the ILC discussions on the exceptions to the *pacta tertiis* principle, "if a state had a legitimate interest in the subject-matter of a treaty, it should be invited to the Conference formulating the treaty or at least consulted during its formulation."[43] This point was also supported by Fitzmaurice when he was special rapporteur on the law of treaties to the ILC:

it seems clear that when a treaty itself makes provision for the admission of third states, then the correct method of procedure, if those third States wish to benefit from, or to enjoy the rights provided by the treaty or if they are prepared to assume obligations, it is for them to avail themselves of the faculty of becoming parties.[44]

It can therefore be argued that the participation of all states in the treaty-making process and the possibility for them to become full parties to the treaty may render these exceptions to the *pacta tertiis* principle redundant. It would be incredibly difficult to maintain the position that the drafters of a treaty intended to confer rights or obligations on third states if those third states are expressly permitted to become a party to the treaty. It follows that the exceptions to the *pacta tertiis* principle will have limited application in the context of modern international law-making, which generally takes place in international fora that are open to all states.

It would seem from this discussion that the limitations of treaties as instruments for the creation of universal law are obvious. From the strict perspective of the law of treaties, it is necessary for all states to

---

[43] 736th meeting (1964-I) *Ybk Int'l L. Commission*, at 85.

[44] G. Fitzmaurice, "Fifth report on the law of treaties" (1960-II) *Ybk Int'l L. Commission*, at 89. See also the comments of Bartos (1964-I) *Ybk Int'l L. Commission*, at 67; Lachs, *ibid.*, at 70; Tabibi, *ibid.*, at 74; El-Erian, *ibid.*, at 75. Contrast the comments of Rosenne who "agreed with Mr Lachs that all interested States should, as a matter of principle, be given the opportunity of participating in negotiations on matters of interest to them" but went on to say that "even if this desirable state of affairs were achieved, a provision of the kind set out in paragraph 1 would still be needed because, without wishing to become parties to an instrument, states might nonetheless wish to assume certain obligations in regard to it." Yet, even Rosenne deemed that there may be some difficulty in determining how the principles on third states apply to general multilateral treaties; *ibid.*, at 75.

become party to the convention in order for it to successfully create universal norms. This is possible, although very rare.[45]

It is in this context that international institutions can offer another advantage to the treaty-making process. Following the adoption of an instrument, international organizations are able to play an important role in promoting the acceptance of a newly negotiated treaty by states. In addition, an international organization may be able to provide technical and financial support for countries that desire to become a party but cannot do so without assistance. An example of an international organization carrying out this role is the International Labor Organization (ILO). The International Labour Conference, the plenary organ of the ILO, adopted the Maritime Labour Convention in 2006. At the same time, the Conference also adopted a resolution calling on the ILO to "give due priority in the allocation of resources of the Organization's technical cooperation program to promoting ratification of the Convention and to assisting countries which request assistance in its implementation."[46] In furtherance of the resolution, the ILO has adopted an action plan "to help ensure rapid entry into force of the Convention and widespread ratification by countries with major maritime interests, and in particular flag states and port states."[47] The Action Plan lists a number of activities that will be undertaken by the secretariat of the ILO in order to promote the widespread ratification of the Convention, including promotional campaigns, diplomatic missions to target countries, developments of guidelines on implementation, and individual assistance to governments. The ILO predicts that "a sufficient number of ratifications will be achieved by the end of 2010 or early 2011, ideally by the fifth anniversary of adoption of the [Convention], to allow for entry into force in early 2012." [48]

[45] The Charter of the United Nations offers an example of one of the few instruments that comes close to achieving universality of participation. At the time of writing, there were 192 Members of the United Nations; see www.un.org/en/members/ growth.shtml <checked July 22, 2010>.

[46] *Resolution concerning the promotion of the Maritime Labour Convention*, Resolution No. 1 of the 94th (Maritime) Session of the International Labour Conference, adopted February 22, 2006, available at www.ilo.org/global/What_we_do/ InternationalLabourStandards/MaritimeLabourConvention/Resolutions/lang – en/ index.htm#P19_1578 <checked July 22, 2010>.

[47] Maritime Labour Convention 2006 Action Plan 2006–2011, at 16; available at www.ilo.org/wcmsp5/groups/public/---ed_norm/---normes/documents/publication/ wcms_088034.pdf <checked December 3, 2010>.

[48] *Background paper for the Preparatory Tripartite Maritime Labour Convention 2006 Committee*, Document PTMLC/2010, at para. 21.

Yet, an international organization can only do so much to persuade states to accept a treaty. Moreover, promotional campaigns, such as that undertaken by the ILO, can be a time-consuming and resource-intensive process. Ultimately the success of a treaty as a law-making instrument depends on the political will of states to formally consent to be bound.

3 International institutions and customary international law

Given the inherent limitations of treaties as law-making instruments, customary international law is the primary source for the creation of universal international law. Custom is defined in Article 38(1) of the International Court of Justice (ICJ) Statute as "general practice accepted as law." This definition reflects what are generally considered as being the two aspects of customary international law, namely state practice and *opinio juris*.[49] State practice consists of what states do in their relations with each other.[50] *Opinio juris*, sometimes called the subjective element of customary international law, is the belief that a particular action or inaction is permitted or required by international law. Both elements must be proven in order to establish that a rule of customary international law exists.

Not all rules of customary international law are binding on all states. The ICJ has recognized customary rules of a regional[51] and indeed a bilateral[52] character. However, it is also clear that it is possible that rules of customary international law can have a universal character.

It would appear from the case law of the ICJ that for the creation of rules of general application, it is not necessary to show that all states have actively participated in the creation of customary international

---

[49] See, however, Higgins who says "Article 38 could more correctly have been phrased to read 'international custom as *evidenced* by a general practice accepted as law'"; R. Higgins, *Problems and Process – International Law and How We Use It* (Oxford University Press, 1994) at 18.

[50] See e.g. International Law Commission, "Ways and means for making the evidence of customary international law more readily available" (1950–II) *Ybk Int'l Law Commission* 367.

[51] *Asylum Case* (1950) ICJ Reports 266.

[52] *Rights of Passage over Indian Territory* (1960) ICJ Reports 6, at 37 where the Court held that: "It is difficult to see why the number of States between which a local custom may be established on the basis of long practice must necessarily be larger than two. The Court sees no reason why long continued practice between two States accepted by them as regulating their relations should not form the basis of mutual rights and obligations between the two States."

law. In the *North Sea Continental Shelf Cases* the ICJ held that state practice must be "extensive and virtually uniform."[53] While this certainly
sets a high threshold for participation in state practice, it falls short of
universality. As one study observes, "no international court or tribunal
has ever refused to hold that a State was bound by a rule of alleged
general customary international [law] merely because it had not itself
actively participated in the practice in question or deliberately acquiesced in it."[54] Often passive acquiescence in a rule will be sufficient for
a state to be bound.[55] Only positive objection to a rule can definitively
prevent its application to a particular state.[56]

At the same time, it is still necessary to show clear trends of state
practice and *opinio juris* of a large number of states in order to prove
customary international law of general application. This may be particularly challenging when the only source of evidence is the unilateral actions of numerous states, as is illustrated by some early cases on
the law of the sea.

The Paquete Habana Case, decided by the United States Supreme Court
in 1899, provides a good example of the challenges faced by judges
in deciding on the content of customary international law. The Court
had to answer the question whether there was a rule of international
law prohibiting small coastal fishing vessels that were flying the flag
of an enemy state from being captured as prize. In order to identify
the applicable legal norms, the Court traced the history of prize jurisdiction from 1403 onwards, examining several international treaties,
the work of scholars and prize court decisions of various countries.[57]
Although the justices seemingly agreed on the material sources that
contribute to the formation of customary international law, they pro-
foundly disagreed on their assessments of the prevailing state practice
and *opinio juris*. Faced with a mass of, often contradictory, evidence, the
majority of the Court concluded that the available evidence supported

---

[53] *North Sea Continental Shelf Cases* (1969) ICJ Reports 3, at para. 73.
[54] International Law Association, "Final Report of the Committee on the Formation of
Customary (General) International Law: Statement of Principles Applicable to the
Formation of General Customary International Law," in *Report of the 69th Conference of
the International Law Association*, London, 2000, at 24.
[55] See *Anglo-Norwegian Fisheries Case* (1951) ICJ Reports 116, at 138.
[56] The so-called persistent objector principle. See *ibid.*, at 131 where the Court held
that "in any event, the ten-mile rule would appear to be inapplicable as against
Norway inasmuch as she has always opposed any attempt to apply it to the
Norwegian coast."
[57] *The Paquete Habana Case* (1899) 175 US Reports 677.

the existence of an exemption for small coastal fishing vessels. Yet this view was not shared by all the judges. A minority of the Court, led by Chief Justice Fuller, dissented, arguing that the available state practice was inconclusive and that "in truth, the exemption of fishing craft is essentially an act of grace, and not a matter of right and it is extended or denied as the exigency is believed to demand."[58] In other words, they disagreed with the precise characterization of the state practice and whether or not it was supported by sufficient *opinio juris*.

Similar difficulties in identifying conclusive trends of state practice can be seen in *The SS Lotus Case*.[59] This was one of the first contentious cases to come before the Permanent Court of International Justice. The dispute concerned the enforcement jurisdiction of states over activities taking place on the high seas. In a decision adopted by the casting vote of the President, the majority of the Court denied the existence of a principle of international law prohibiting Turkey from prosecuting the Master of a French vessel that had collided with a Turkish ship on the high seas. The majority reasoned that the applicable rules of customary international law "must be ascertained by examining precedents offering a close analogy to the case under consideration; for it is only from precedents of this nature that the existence of a general principle applicable to the particular case may appear."[60] Yet the evidence of state practice was itself ambiguous and there were precedents pointing in both directions. In the words of Judge Weiss, the record of the case demonstrated "controversial doctrine and contradictory judicial decisions ... invoked by both parties."[61] The actual result of the case largely turns on the assumption made by the majority of the Court that states may exercise jurisdiction unless there is a positive rule that prohibits such action.[62] As France was not able to adduce sufficient evidence of such a rule, its arguments failed. Moreover, the Court was unwilling to treat the lack of prosecutions of ships on the high seas as evidence of a rule of customary international law prohibiting such action because of a lack of *opinio juris*. The Court reasoned that "only if such abstention

---

[58] *Ibid.*, at 719.
[59] *The SS Lotus Case* (1927) PCIJ Reports, Series A, No. 10.
[60] *Ibid.*, at 21.
[61] *Ibid.*, Dissenting Opinion of Judge Weiss.
[62] *Ibid.*, at 19. See also D. P. O'Connell, *The International Law of the Sea* (Oxford University Press, 1982) at 31.

were based on their being conscious of having a duty to abstain would it be possible to speak of an international custom."[63]

Weiler describes these cases as presenting "a very sedate, almost 'magisterial,' and backward looking practice of customary law."[64] Indeed, they clearly illustrate that traditional conceptions of customary international law, based upon piecing together individual state practice and *opinio juris*, suffer from a number of weaknesses as a means of regulating the activities of a large number of states. First, divergences in the numerous instances of state practice taken into account by the courts mean that it is often difficult to identify the applicable law at any one time. The more states there are, the more difficult this task is. Secondly, the reliance on claims and counter-claims advanced by states at different times and in different contexts leaves much to be desired in terms of the precise formulation of rules and principles. These problems are inherent in a system with a lack of any institutional structures. It is perhaps in recognition of this fact that states have increasingly turned to international institutions when seeking to develop rules and principles of international law.

A central argument of this book is that international institutions present new opportunities for creating customary international law by offering a single forum in which states can exchange views on emerging norms. Making this point, Judge Tanaka argued in his individual opinion in the *South West Africa Cases* that "in the contemporary age of highly developed techniques of communication and information, the formation of custom through the medium of international organizations is greatly facilitated and accelerated."[65]

The role of instruments adopted by international institutions in the development of customary international law can be seen in the jurisprudence of the ICJ. In the *North Sea Continental Shelf Cases* the ICJ was concerned with whether or not certain rules contained in the 1958 Convention on the Continental Shelf could be relied on as evidence of customary international law. The 1958 Convention had been adopted

---

[63] *The Case of the SS Lotus*, at 28.
[64] Weiler, "The Geology of International Law," at 549.
[65] Dissenting Opinion of Judge Tanaka, in *The South West Africa Cases (Second Phase)* (1966) ICJ Reports 3, at 177. See also Q. Wright, "Custom as a basis for international law in the post-world war world" (1966) *Texas Int'l L. Forum* 147, at 157–8; I. Brownlie, *Principles of Public International Law* (6th edn., Oxford University Press, 2003) at 6; R. Baxter, "Custom and treaty" (1970) 129 *Recueil des Cours* 27; A. Weisburd, "Customary international law: the problem of treaties" (1988) 21 *Vanderbilt J. Transnational L.* 1.

by the First United Nations Conference on the Law of the Sea following extensive preparatory work by the ILC.[66] The Court recognized that treaties negotiated through diplomatic conferences could have a significant impact on the creation of customary international law. The Court distinguished three different ways in which a treaty can do so.[67]

First, the Court stated that treaties could codify customary international law. Codification involves recording the existing rules of the customary rules in the text of a treaty. Occasionally a treaty itself will expressly declare itself to be a codification treaty, although on most occasions it will be necessary to consider the drafting history of the instrument to identify whether or not a treaty was intended to be codificatory.[68] Where this is the case, the treaty will contain rules that are binding on all states, whether or not they are a contracting party, unless they can claim to be a persistent objector.[69]

Secondly, the Court accepted that treaties could generate news norms of customary international law by influencing the practice of states which were not a party to the treaty. In his individual opinion, Judge Sørenson described how treaties can serve as "a nucleus around which a new set of generally recognized rules may crystallize."[70] In this situation, it is the accumulation of subsequent state practice and *opinio juris* that creates the new rules of customary international law, not the conclusion of the treaty per se. Nevertheless, the rules contained in the treaty become binding on all states as a result of their transition into customary international law.

Thirdly, the Court stated that a treaty may "crystallize" customary international law. It is the process of crystallization that demonstrates the most dynamic interaction between a treaty and customary international law. The Court referred to crystallization as "the process of the definition and consolidation of the emerging customary law [that]

---

[66] See Chapter 2.

[67] *North Sea Continental Shelf Cases*, at para. 60.

[68] Baxter notes that "it is only exceptionally that a so-called 'codification treaty' concluded under United Nations auspices on the basis of a draft prepared by the International Law Commission asserts on its face that it codifies existing international law"; R. Baxter, "Multilateral treaties as evidence of customary international law" (1967) *Brit. Ybk Int'l L.* 275, at 287. An example is the 1958 High Seas Convention which recognizes in the preamble the desire of the parties "to codify the rules of international law relating to the high seas."

[69] See above, at footnote 56.

[70] Dissenting Opinion of Judge Sørenson in *North Sea Continental Shelf Cases*, at 244. His use of the term "crystallize" is somewhat confusing in this context and it should not be confused with crystallization as will be discussed below.

took place through the work of the International Law Commission, the reaction of governments to that work and the proceedings of the Geneva Conference ... [T]his emerging customary law became crystallized in the adoption of the Continental Shelf Convention."[71] The reasoning of the Court suggests that the negotiation of a treaty can itself count towards state practice. Moreover, it is clear that the institutions involved in the negotiation process play a crucial role in facilitating the crystallization process. This proposition is made more explicit in the pleadings of the Netherlands and Denmark from where the concept of crystallization originates:

Throughout the period during which the codification and progressive development of the law of the sea was under consideration by the International Law Commission, the whole doctrine of the coastal State's rights over the continental shelf was still in course of formation. The unilateral claims which had been made by individual States varied in their nature and extent; and many coastal States, including all Parties to the present dispute, had not yet promulgated any claim. The work of the Commission both helped to consolidate the doctrine in international law and to clarify its content ... Thus, just as the work of the Commission and the contribution to that work made by governments were important factors in developing a consensus as to the acceptability of the doctrine and its nature and extent, so also were they important factors in developing a consensus as to the acceptability of the equidistance principle as the general rule for the delimitation of continental shelf boundaries.[72]

From this extract it can be clearly seen that the concept of crystallization stresses that the practice of states taking part in the negotiation of an international treaty can sometimes count towards the creation of customary international law, if it is supported by *opinio juris*. Indeed, it is through the process of crystallization that international institutions can perhaps have the greatest impact on customary international law.

The judgment of the ICJ in the *North Sea Continental Shelf Cases* was only concerned with the impact of a treaty on customary international law. However, it is not just treaties that can influence customary international law in this way. Arguably any instrument adopted by an international institution could potentially have the effect of influencing the

---

[71] *North Sea Continental Shelf Cases*, at para. 61.
[72] *Counter-Memorial of the Netherlands*, North Sea Continental Shelf Cases, ICJ Pleadings, 1968, Vol. 1, at 336–7.

development of customary international law.[73] What is important is how the instrument was negotiated and whether it is supported by enough states.

There are certain advantages to this conception of customary international law-making. Being able to rely upon the proceedings of international institutions to identify rules of customary international law is simpler than having to piece together individual instances of state practice and *opinio juris*.[74] This is particularly true when one is considering the creation of universal international law that is binding on all states. It is also the case that customary international law can develop more rapidly through international institutions. This was recognized by the ICJ in the *North Sea Continental Shelf Cases* when it said that "the passage of only a short period of time is not necessarily, or of itself, a bar to the formation of a new rule of customary international law."[75] One could go further and argue that the institutionalization of customary international law-making also makes the process fairer and more transparent as it permits "broader and more effective participation by all states" in the law-making process.[76] Indeed, by taking into account the practice of states acting through international institutions, customary international law-making no longer appears as an inchoate and informal process. Rather, it comes to resemble an organized procedure through which states, acting collectively through international institutions, can set out to consciously create new legal rules that will be binding on them all.[77]

This conception of customary international law is, however, not without its critics.[78] For example, some argue that taking into

---

[73] For instance, the International Court of Justice considered the impact of General Assembly Resolutions on customary international law in the *Advisory Opinion on the Legality of the Threat or Use of Nuclear Weapon* (1996) ICJ Reports 226.

[74] See Charney, "Universal international law," at 543–5; R. Higgins, *The Development of International Law through the Political Organs of the United Nations* (Oxford University Press, 1963) at 2; Danilenko, *Law-making in the International Community*, at 79; R. Jennings and A. Watts (eds.), *Oppenheim's International Law, Vol. 1, Peace* (9th edn., Longman, 1992), at 46.

[75] *North Sea Continental Shelf Cases*, at para. 60.

[76] Charney, "Universal international law," at 547.

[77] In this context, the point has been made by Jennings that the nomenclature of customary international law is seriously outmoded; R. Jennings, "The identification of international law," in B. Cheng (ed.), *International Law: Teaching and Practice* (Stevens, 1982) at 6.

[78] See criticism concerning terminology, in Jennings, "The identification of international law," at 6.

account the practice of states acting through international institutions attributes legislative powers to institutions that have not been expressly conferred on them.[79] Yet this analysis is arguably misconceived. Recognizing what states do within international institutions as potential evidence of state practice does not automatically convert all decisions of international institutions into binding rules of customary international law. Formal adoption of a rule by an international institution is by itself meaningless.[80] The negotiation and adoption of an international instrument will only count as relevant state practice if it can be shown that states intended to lay down a rule of customary international law. In other words, it is also necessary to look for *opinio juris* in support of the purported customary rule. This point is stressed by the ICJ in the *North Sea Continental Shelf Cases*, where it accepted that although crystallization is possible, it did not agree that it had occurred in the case of Article 6 of the 1958 Continental Shelf Convention.[81] Article 6 concerned the delimitation of the continental shelf among opposite and adjacent coastal states. As the Court stressed, the negotiation of Article 6 was "impromptu" and the subject of "long continued hesitations."[82] Thus, the evidence available to the Court did not support the contention that there was sufficient support for the rule found in Article 6 of the Convention in order to crystallize customary international law. A similar attitude is seen in the *Legality of Nuclear Weapons Advisory Opinion* where the Court held that the simple adoption of an instrument is not sufficient to invest it with potential normative force: "it is necessary to look at its content and the conditions of its adoption."[83] In that case, the opposition of a number of nuclear states to a General Assembly resolution condemning the possession of nuclear weapons illustrated the lack of sufficient state practice and *opinio juris* for the creation of customary international law. The identification of *opinio juris* therefore becomes the litmus test to distinguish those elements of state practice

---

[79] See A. D'Amato, "Trashing customary international law" (1987) 91 *Am. J. Int'l L.* 657, at 102.

[80] J. Brunee, "Coping with consent: law-making under multilateral environmental agreements" (2002) 15 *Leiden J. Int'l L.* 1, at 37.

[81] *North Sea Continental Shelf Cases*, at paras. 61–2.

[82] *North Sea Continental Shelf Cases*, at paras. 49–53.

[83] *Advisory Opinion on the Legality of the Threat or Use of Nuclear Weapons*, at para. 70; see also Higgins, *Problems and Process*, at 24.

through international institutions that can and cannot contribute to the creation of customary international law.[84]

The difficulty of establishing sufficient evidence of state practice and *opinio juris* in this context should not be underestimated. In the *North Sea Continental Shelf Cases*, the Court stressed that the creation of customary international law through the negotiation of an international instrument "is not lightly to be regarded as having been attained."[85] It cannot be presumed that a treaty or other instrument adopted by an international institution creates a customary norm without "clear-cut and unequivocal" evidence of widespread support of a rule, as well as evidence that states consider the rule to be binding.[86] Moreover, the burden of meeting this threshold rests on the state alleging the creation of a customary rule.[87] One must consider carefully the language of the rule that is being proposed, as well as the individual statements made by states in the context of negotiations.

It is also important to remember that the proceedings of international institutions should not be considered in isolation from other evidence of state practice and *opinio juris*.[88] It is rare that institutional practice exists in a vacuum. Unilateral state practice will continue to be relevant. In some cases, other forms of state practice will support and consolidate the practice that is evidenced through the proceedings of an international institution. On the other hand, any contradictory state practice will tend to contradict the assertion that the proceedings of an international institution have codified or crystallized a rule of customary international law. Yet, in the *Nicaragua Case* the Court noted that lack of uniformity in unilateral state practice may not always undermine the assertion of a customary rule by an international

---

[84] See B. Cheng, "United Nations resolutions on outer space: instant customary international law?" in B. Cheng (ed.), *International Law: Teaching and Practice* (Stevens, 1982). Whereas Cheng concluded that only *opinio juris* is necessary for the creation of customary international law, it is suggested that the contributions of states to debates within international organizations can itself constitute state practice which, if supported by evidence that states believe the rules being discussed are customary international law, can show that a rule of customary international law has crystallized.

[85] *North Sea Continental Shelf Cases*, at para. 71.

[86] International Law Association, "Statement of principles applicable to the formation of general customary international law," at 42; see also Cheng, "United Nations resolutions on outer space," at 251 and 254; M. Akehurst, "Custom as a source of international law" (1974–75) *Brit. Ybk Int'l L.* 1, at 6–7.

[87] See *Asylum Case* (1950) ICJ Reports 266, at 276.

[88] See Higgins, *Problems and Process*, at 24.

institution. It noted that there may be other reasons that can explain contradictory state practice:

> The Court does not consider that, for a rule to be established as customary, the corresponding practice must be in rigorous conformity with the rule. The Court deems it sufficient that the conduct of States should, in general, be consistent with such rules, and that instances of State conduct inconsistent with a given rule should generally have been treated as breaches of that rule, not as indications of the recognition of a new rule.[89]

In these circumstances, it is necessary to choose which of the competing trends of state practice and *opinio juris* carries the most weight. As Akehurst suggests, "it may be that a claim supported by physical acts carries greater weight than a claim not supported by physical acts [although] that is not the same as saying that the latter claim carries no weight at all."[90]

It can be seen from this analysis that "custom can and often does dovetail neatly with the complicated mechanisms now operating for the identification and progressive development of the principles of international law."[91] What is important for present purposes is that the institutionalization of customary international law-making described above clearly presents new opportunities for states to create universal rules and principles. Indeed, this conception of customary international law can make up for deficiencies in treaty law as state practice may crystallize around certain provisions of a treaty, even if the treaty as a whole, for a variety of reasons, may not have attracted widespread support.[92] However, it must always be remembered that the availability of an international institution as a forum in which to discuss and debate the development of international law does not obviate the need to show extensive evidence of state practice supported by *opinio juris*. Thus, modern law-making still falls short of an international legislative process.[93]

---

[89] *Case Concerning Military and Paramilitary Activities in and against Nicaragua (Merits)* (1986) ICJ Reports 14, at para. 186.

[90] Akehurst, "Custom as a source of international law," at 2, footnote 1.

[91] M. Shaw, *International Law* (5th edn., Cambridge University Press, 2003) at 58. See also A. Jiminez de Arechaga, "Custom," in A. Cassese and J. J. Weiler (eds.), *Change and Stability in International Law-Making* (Walter de Gruyter, 1988) at 2–4.

[92] See A. N. Pronto, "Some thoughts on the making of international law" (2008) 19 *Euro. J. Int'l L.* 601, at 611.

[93] Cf. H. Chodosh, "Neither treaty nor custom: the emergence of declarative international law" (1991) 26 *Texas J. Int'l L.* 87.

4 The development of the law of the sea through international institutions

It can be seen from the preceding discussion that international institutions help to facilitate international law-making. It is suggested that this has been particularly the case in the context of the law of the sea where a large number of international institutions operate. It is the purpose of this study to consider how institutions have contributed to the development of this area of international law. To what extent have they been able to facilitate the creation of a universal legal order of the oceans?

The law of the sea provides an interesting case study of law-making by international institutions because of the different types of institutions involved in this field. In few cases does the significance of international institutions stem from their formal status and powers. Rather, their importance lies in their ability to act as a forum in which states can meet and agree upon mutually acceptable approaches to common problems. The study will consider the ways in which institutions have sought to promote agreement on new rules and principles of international law and what types of instruments are used for this purpose.

One of the most important law-making events in this field was the Third United Nations Conference on the Law of the Sea.[94] Although the Conference was only an ad hoc institution, it had a significant impact on the modern law of the sea through its ability to garner widespread support for the 1982 United Nations Convention on the Law of the Sea. Today, this instrument is widely considered as providing the legal basis for the modern law of the sea. While the Convention still falls short of universal participation, it is nevertheless considered by many to create a universal legal order for the oceans. The arguments in support of this conclusion will be analyzed in Chapter 2 where it will be seen that the process of negotiating the Convention was a major factor in its subsequent impact on the law of the sea.

Chapter 3 will look at the procedures contained in the Convention itself for the development of the law of the sea regime. In particular, it will consider the appropriateness of the amendment procedures in the Convention and the role that can be played by the Meeting of the States Parties in the progressive development of the Convention regime.

---

[94] Hereinafter, UNCLOS III.

Chapter 4 will analyze the two implementing agreements which have been adopted since the conclusion of the 1982 Convention in order to modify the Convention regime, namely the 1994 Agreement Relating to the Implementation of Part XI of the 1982 Convention on the Law of the Sea of 10 December 1982, and the 1995 Agreement for the Implementation of the Provisions of the United Nations Convention on the Law of the Sea of 10 December 1982 relating to the Conservation and Management of Straddling Fish Stocks and Highly Migratory Fish Stocks. These treaties were adopted to address particular problems with the original text of the Convention and they now form a central part of the law of the sea framework. It is therefore important to consider how they were negotiated and their legal status for parties and non-parties.

Chapters 5 to 7 will consider the role of several international institutions that have a special interest in particular aspects of the law of the sea regime. Chapter 5 looks at the role of the International Seabed Authority in relation to seabed mining. Chapter 6 analyzes the law-making activities of the International Maritime Organization in relation to shipping. Chapter 7 considers the Food and Agriculture Organization and its contribution to international fisheries law. These institutions have been selected both because of the importance of the subject matter with which they are concerned and because they demonstrate a diverse range of law-making roles that can be played by international organizations.

Of all of the institutions considered in this work, the International Seabed Authority comes the closest to an international legislator, as it is able to adopt decisions that are binding on its members without further consent. In recognition thereof, its decision-making procedures are carefully designed to ensure that all major interests are protected. Chapter 5 examines in detail these decision-making procedures and the safeguards that are applied in the context of the law-making powers of the Authority.

By contrast, the International Maritime Organization (IMO) has no formal law-making powers. Rather the IMO is only able to adopt treaties or nonbinding instruments containing technical rules and regulations. Nevertheless, the standards adopted by the IMO can become binding on states through the operation of so-called rules of reference found in the 1982 United Nations Convention on the Law of the Sea[95] if they are generally accepted by states. Chapter 6 analyzes the concept of

[95] Hereinafter, the Law of the Sea Convention.

"generally accepted international rules and regulations" and how the decision-making procedures of the IMO facilitate the general acceptance of states. This chapter also considers the extent to which the IMO has the potential to modify the Law of the Sea Convention by adopting and approving navigational measures that are not foreseen in the Convention's navigational regime.

The Food and Agriculture Organization (FAO) also has no formal law-making powers. Rather its influence on international law is exercised through the negotiation of general principles in the form of treaties or nonbinding codes of conduct or guidelines. Chapter 7 looks at the way in which the FAO negotiates international instruments and how it seeks to work with fishing states and regional fisheries bodies involved in the regulation of particular fish stocks in order to promote the application of these instruments.

All of these institutions have contributed to the development of the law of the sea in different ways. The existence of a number of institutions offering themselves as a forum for law-making also presents problems of its own however. Given the decentralized nature of the international legal order, none of these institutions has the exclusive authority to adopt rules and principles on a particular issue. In practice, it is common that the mandates of several organizations will overlap. In this regard, international law-making is inherently fragmented and eclectic. As Boyle and Chinkin point out, "the choice of process depends upon context, political preference and purpose."[96]

In this context, Chapter 8 looks at the interrelationship between rules and principles adopted by the various institutions described in this book and to what extent there is any hierarchical structure between them. The chapter also investigates ways in which individual international organizations formally and informally cooperate with each other in order to promote a coherent approach to regulating the oceans. In practice, these institutions have developed a complex relationship that demonstrates the possibilities for a coherent and integrated approach to international law-making.

The availability of several law-making institutions may also lead to fragmentation in the substantive law if divergent rules are developed in distinct international fora. This threat has increased with the creation of ever more specialized regimes with a narrow perspective on a particular area of international law. According to a study conducted

[96] Boyle and Chinkin, *The Making of International Law*, at 9.

by the International Law Commission, "the result is the emergence of regimes of international law that have their basis in multilateral treaties and acts of international organizations, specialized treaties and customary patterns that are tailored to the needs and interests of each network but rarely take account of the outside world."[97] Overall, fragmentation of the law-making process poses a challenge to the coherent development of international law that no study of international law-making can ignore. Several questions arise in this context. What happens when two institutions produce inconsistent and conflicting rules? Are there any formal mechanisms through which a hierarchy of norms can be established at the international level if a conflict of law does arise? These questions will also be addressed in Chapter 8.

[97] *Fragmentation of international law: difficulties arising from the diversification and expansion of international law*, Report of the Study Group of the International Law Commission, Document A/CN.4/L.682, April 13, 2006, at para. 482.

2   The United Nations Convention on the Law of the Sea

1 Introduction

The 1982 United Nations Convention on the Law of the Sea[1] was described at the time of its adoption as "the greatest international legislative effort undertaken by the United Nations and probably the greatest ever undertaken in the annals of international law as a whole."[2] The Convention sets out the rules and principles governing all ocean activities, from navigation to fishing, including marine scientific research and deep seabed mining. It was the product of several years of intense negotiations.

The conclusion of the Law of the Sea Convention was not the first time that the international community had sought to codify and progressively develop the law of the sea. The twentieth century saw a number of international conferences that were dedicated to this task. These attempts to codify the law of the sea illustrate the increasing institutionalization of law-making described in the previous chapter.

This chapter will trace the progression of several international conferences dedicated to the codification and progressive development of the law of the sea. It will start with a short overview of initial attempts at codification by the League of Nations and by the United Nations before turning to a more detailed look at the promulgation of the Law of the Sea Convention itself. Given its importance to the modern law of the sea, it is appropriate to consider in detail how the Law of the Sea Convention was negotiated and to what extent it has met its drafters' hopes of creating a single, coherent framework for the law of the sea.

---

[1] Hereinafter, Law of the Sea Convention.
[2] Statement of Norway, 186th Meeting, *Official Records of the Third United Nations Conference on the Law of the Sea*, Vol. 17, 27, at para. 42.

This chapter will analyze the procedures of the Third United Nations Conference on the Law of the Sea,[3] which was responsible for drafting and adopting the Law of the Sea Convention. It will also consider the normative impact of the Convention. It will be seen that the way in which the Convention was negotiated has increased the impact of the Convention on customary international law. This is important given that many of the innovations in international law-making techniques trialed at UNCLOS III have been adopted by other international institutions involved in developing the law of the sea.

2 Early attempts at the codification of the law of the sea

2.1 The origins of codification

From the late nineteenth century it was widely believed that the codification of international law on significant areas of international law would contribute to the maintenance of international peace and security by promoting clarity in the applicable law, thereby avoiding the causes of international conflict.[4] Furthermore, it was hoped that codification would ultimately enhance the authority of international law and make states more willing to submit their disputes to international courts and tribunals.[5]

One of the first proposals for the codification of international law is found in a resolution adopted by the Second Hague Peace Conference held in 1907, which called for the codification of topics that were "ripe for embodiment in international regulation."[6] The outbreak of the First World War delayed this initiative from being further pursued for a number of years. Nevertheless, this resolution has been identified as "the seed which was ultimately to burgeon forth, first as the Committee of Experts for the Progressive Codification of International Law, and later as the International Law Commission of the United Nations."[7] When codification once again appeared on the international agenda, various

---

[3] Hereinafter, UNCLOS III.
[4] S. Rosenne, *Committee of Experts for the Progressive Codification of International Law (1925–1928)* (Oceana Publications, 1972) at xxix.
[5] *Survey of international law in relation to the work of the codification of international law*, Memorandum submitted by the Secretary-General, Document A/CN.4/1/Rev.1, February 10, 1949, at 8, 61.
[6] Rosenne, *Committee of Experts for the Progressive Codification of International Law (1925–1928)*, at xxix.
[7] *Ibid.*, at xxx.

aspects of the law of the sea were among the topics that were considered "ripe for embodiment in international regulation."

2.2 Codification of the law of the sea by the League of Nations

The first major multilateral attempt by states to codify international law took place after the First World War.[8] In 1924 the Council of the League of Nations initiated a process for the codification of international law. The Council established a Committee of Experts for the Progressive Codification of International Law, which was to be "a body representing the main forms of civilization and the principal legal systems of the world."[9] The Committee of Experts was charged with investigating which topics or fields of law were suitable for codification.[10]

Codification in this context was not understood as simply recording existing agreement over what constituted customary international law. It was recognized that if the rules of customary international law were already clear and unambiguous, their codification would be of little assistance. Rather, codification was conceived of as clarifying state practice and in making suggestions about how ambiguities or disagreements could be overcome.[11] This understanding of codification is reflected in a resolution of the League of Nations Assembly of September 27, 1927 which provided that codification "should not confine itself to the mere registration of the existing rules, but should aim at adapting them as far as possible to the contemporary conditions of international life."[12]

The law of the sea was one of the topics considered for codification by the Committee of Experts. The initial list of subjects identified by the Committee of Experts for potential codification included the status of territorial waters, the status of government ships engaged in commerce, the suppression of piracy and the exploitation of the products of the sea.[13] Following a series of debates, the Committee of Experts

---

[8] Prior to this time, several nongovernmental attempts at codification had taken place; see R. Churchill and V. Lowe, *The Law of the Sea* (3rd edn., Manchester University Press, 1997) at 13–14.

[9] Rosenne, *Committee of Experts for the Progressive Codification of International Law (1925–1928)*, at xxxv.

[10] For a copy of the resolution, see *ibid.*, at vii.

[11] *Survey of International Law in Relation to the Work of the Codification of International Law*, at 12.

[12] Resolution adopted by the League of Nations on 27 September 1927 available in (1947) 41 *Am. J. Int'l L. Supp.* 105.

[13] Rosenne, *Committee of Experts for the Progressive Codification of International Law (1925–1928)*, at lxi.

narrowed down the list to those topics of international law which it considered were "sufficiently ripe" for codification by a general international conference. Of those aspects of the law of the sea listed in the preliminary report, only the subject of territorial waters was considered to meet this criterion.[14]

Following the preliminary report, work on the legal regime of territorial waters was carried out by the Committee of Experts. On the basis of information and views submitted by governments, the Committee of Experts prepared Bases of Discussion and a series of proposals for deliberation by a diplomatic conference.

The Hague Codification Conference was convened in 1930 to consider the materials prepared by the Committee of Experts. The Codification Conference was attended by delegates from forty-seven governments, including several states that were not at that time members of the League of Nations. While the preparatory work had been undertaken by the Committee of Experts, it was recognized that it was the views of governments that would dictate the success or failure of the codification process.

The proceedings of the Second Committee of the Conference were dedicated to the topic of territorial waters. Despite prolonged discussions, delegates were unable to agree on some of the fundamental issues that were necessary to conclude a treaty on territorial waters. A resolution adopted by the Conference noted that "the discussions have revealed, in respect of certain ... divergence of views which for present renders the conclusion of a [treaty on the] territorial sea impossible." In particular, the issue of the breadth of the territorial sea was a major point of contention between those states represented at the Conference.[15] Although it was not possible to conclude a treaty, the Second Committee did agree upon a set of draft articles on the legal status of the territorial sea. These draft articles were appended to the Conference resolution cited above and subsequently circulated to governments by the Secretariat of the League of Nations.[16] While this text did not create legally binding obligations in the same way that a treaty would have done, it was not without legal significance. It is generally accepted that the draft articles agreed by the Second Committee "later

[14] *Ibid.*, at lxx.
[15] See "Report of the Second Committee: Territorial Sea," in S. Rosenne, *League of Nations Conference for the Codification of International Law (1930)*, Vol. 4 (Oceana Publications, 1975) at 210.
[16] See "Conference Resolution on the Territorial Sea," in *ibid.*, at 1423.

exerted influence to the extent that Governments accepted them as a statement of existing international law."[17] This conclusion is supported by the fact that many of the rules found in the draft articles are reproduced in almost identical form in later codification treaties on the law of the sea. Thus, the draft articles adopted by the 1930 Codification Conference are an early example of the influence that a written text adopted by a diplomatic conference can have on the formation of customary international law if they garner sufficient support from states.

2.3 The First and Second United Nations Conferences on the Law of the Sea

The codification of international law was to become a much more prominent and permanent feature of the international system following the Second World War and the creation of the United Nations. In 1947 the UN General Assembly established the International Law Commission (ILC) for the purposes of advancing the "progressive development of international law and its codification" in accordance with Article 13 of the UN Charter.[18] The ILC, which is composed of a number of independent legal experts, was charged with identifying topics that were suitable for codification or progressive development and making proposals to the General Assembly.[19] In line with previous practice, codification is understood as "the more precise formulation and systematization of rules of international law."[20] However, the task of the ILC went beyond mere codification to include progressive development, which is defined in the Statute of the Commission as "the preparation of draft conventions on subjects which have not yet been regulated by international law or in regard to which the law has not yet been sufficiently developed in the practice of States."[21] Despite this clear distinction between codification and progressive development in the Statute, the ILC has in practice found it inherently problematic to separate its two functions and it has tended to avoid making strong distinctions between the two.[22] Indeed, the ILC has used a single consolidated procedure

---

[17] United Nations, *The Work of the International Law Commission* (United Nations, 1988) at 3–4. See also Churchill and Lowe, *The Law of the Sea*, at 14–15.

[18] *Establishment of an International Law Commission*, UNGA Resolution 174 (II), November 21, 1947, to which is annexed the Statute of the International Law Commission. The first members of the International Law Commission were elected in 1948.

[19] See the Statute of the International Law Commission.

[20] *Ibid.*, Article 15.   [21] *Ibid.*

[22] I. Sinclair, *The International Law Commission* (Grotius Publications, 1987) at 46.

for carrying out its work that does not distinguish between the two aspects of its mandate.[23]

At its first meeting in 1949, the ILC identified a provisional list of fourteen topics as suitable for codification.[24] The regime of high seas and the regime of territorial seas were both identified as key issues that were worthy of the attention of the Commission.[25] Initially, the ILC agreed to prioritize the codification of only three topics, one of which was the regime of the high seas. J. P. A. François, the Dutch Commissioner who had previously served as rapporteur at the 1930 Codification Conference, was appointed as special rapporteur on the subject.[26] However, when considering the first report of the International Law Commission, the UN General Assembly noted that the topics of the high seas and the territorial seas were "closely related" and it recommended that the Commission also include the latter subject on its work program.[27] This is an early example of the General Assembly taking an active interest in the codification and progressive development of the law of the sea. Following this resolution, the ILC subsequently started work on the regime of the territorial sea at its 1951 session, appointing J. P. A. François as special rapporteur on this topic as well.[28] The ILC proceeded with these two topics simultaneously, although it continued to treat them as separate items on its work program.

The work of the ILC on the territorial sea built upon the previous attempts at codification by the 1930 Hague Codification Conference. Like its predecessor, the Commission sought to solve questions concerning the breadth of the territorial sea and the rights and privileges to be exercised by the coastal state in their adjacent waters. The topic of the high seas covered a range of issues that had not previously been the subject of codification. These included rights of navigation, fisheries

---

[23] International Law Commission, "Report of the Working Group on review of the multilateral treaty-making process" (1979-II) *Ybk Int'l Law Commission* 18, at para. 16.

[24] International Law Commission, "Report of the International Law Commission covering its first session 12 April–9 June 1949" (1949 II) *Ybk Int'l Law Commission* 3, at para. 16.

[25] *Survey of International Law in Relation to the Work of the Codification of International Law,* at 40–4.

[26] International Law Commission, "Report of the International Law Commission covering its first session, 12 April–9 June 1949," at paras. 20–1.

[27] *Recommendation to the International Law Commission to include the regime of the territorial waters in its list of topics to be given priority,* UNGA Resolution 374 (IV), December 6, 1949.

[28] International Law Commission, "Report of the International Law Commission covering its third session, 16 May–27 July 1951" (1951-II) *Ybk Int'l Law Commission* 140, at para. 86.

on the high seas and the legal regime concerning the use of seabed resources. However, as with its work on other subjects, the ILC struggled to maintain a clear distinction between codification and progressive development. It noted in one report to the General Assembly that:

in preparing rules on the law of the sea, the Commission has become convinced that, in this domain at any rate, the distinction established in the statute between these two activities can hardly be maintained. Not only may there be wide differences of opinion as to whether a subject is already "sufficiently developed in practice" but also several of the provisions adopted by the Commission, based on a "recognized principle of international law," have been framed in such a way as to place them in the progressive development category. Although it tried at first to specify which articles fell into one or the other category, the Commission has had to abandon the attempt, as several do not wholly belong to either.[29]

In furtherance of its work on the high seas, the ILC submitted sets of draft articles on the continental shelf and on fisheries to the General Assembly in 1953. In its report to the General Assembly, the Commission recommended that the General Assembly adopt the articles on the continental shelf in the form of a resolution.[30] In addition, the Commission proposed that the articles on fisheries should be forwarded to the United Nations Food and Agriculture Organization for adoption.[31] The General Assembly, however, refused to follow these recommendations from the Commission. Citing "the physical, as well as the juridical, linking of the problems related to the high seas, territorial waters, contiguous zones, the continental shelf and the superjacent waters," the General Assembly resolved that "it would not deal with any aspect of the regime of the high seas or of the regime of territorial waters until all problems involved have been studied by the Commission and reported by it to the General Assembly."[32]

The ILC therefore continued its work on the law of the sea until it was in a position to submit a single set of draft articles on the topic to

[29] International Law Commission, "Report of the International Law Commission covering the work of its eighth session, 23 April–4 July 1956" (1956-II) Ybk Int'l Law Commission 254, at para. 26.

[30] International Law Commission, "Report of the International Law Commission covering the work of its fifth session, 1 June–14 August 1953" (1953-II) Ybk Int'l Law Commission 217, at para. 91.

[31] Ibid., at para. 102.

[32] Regime of the High Seas, UNGA Resolution 798(VIII), December 7, 1953, cited in Sinclair, The International Law Commission, at 45–6. This stance was confirmed in 1954 when nine states once again brought the issue before the General Assembly, asking for it not to delay its consideration of the topic of the continental shelf. In its

the General Assembly in 1956.[33] These draft articles formed the basis for discussions at the First United Nations Conference on the Law of the Sea,[34] which was convened by the General Assembly in order to "examine the law of the sea, taking account not only of the legal but also of the technical, biological, economic and political aspects of the problem, and to embody the results of its work in one or more international conventions or such other instruments that the conference may deem appropriate."[35] The mandate of the conference is important in a number of respects. First, the General Assembly recognized that the law of the sea raised issues of a political or technical nature, as well as questions of law. Secondly, the General Assembly also abandoned its previous insistence on treating the law of the sea as a coherent whole. The mandate of the Conference foresaw the adoption of more than one international treaty if necessary. Indeed, the General Assembly left open the question of whether the outcome of the Conference would be legally binding at all by indicating that the Conference could adopt any instruments that it deemed appropriate.

UNCLOS I took place in Geneva from February 24 to April 27, 1958. The final list of participants included eighty-six states[36] as well as observers from seven specialized agencies.[37] While the draft articles of the International Law Commission provided the initial basis for discussions at the Conference, it was clear that states did not consider themselves bound by the work of the Commission. Many of the draft articles were the subject of renegotiation at the Conference in order to achieve as broad support as possible among states. All substantive decisions of the Conference were subject to a vote of a two-thirds majority and the final texts were adopted provision by provision.[38]

resolution *Draft articles on the continental shelf*, UNGA Resolution 899(IX), December 14, 1954, the General Assembly again deferred the issue until the International Law Commission had submitted its final reports on the law of the sea; see United Nations, *The Work of the International Law Commission*, at 40.

[33] International Law Commission, "Report of the International Law Commission covering the work of its eighth session, 23 April–4 July 1956," at 254–300.

[34] Hereinafter, UNCLOS I.

[35] *International conference of plenipotentiaries to examine the law of the sea*, UNGA Resolution 1105(XI), February 21, 1957.

[36] At the time, only eighty-two states were members of the United Nations.

[37] See Final Act of the Conference, Document A/CONF.13/L.58, in *Official Records of the United Nations Conference on the Law of the Sea*, Vol. 2, at 146.

[38] Rule 35, Rules of Procedure, in *Official Records of the United Nations Conference on the Law of the Sea*, Vol. 2, at xxxiii. See L. Sohn, "Voting procedures in United Nations Conferences for the codification of international law" (1975) 69 *Am. J. Int'l L.* 310, at 317.

Four principal treaties were negotiated at the Conference, dealing with the territorial sea and the contiguous zone, the continental shelf, the high seas and fishing.[39] The Conference also adopted an optional protocol on dispute settlement. The conclusion of these treaties was a significant step forward. Where there had been previously only customary rules based upon trends of unilateral state practice, there were now four substantive treaties on the law of the sea. Nevertheless, the results of the Conference were not necessarily satisfactory from the perspective of creating a universal regime for the law of the sea. Although the draft articles had been prepared by the ILC as a single and coherent text, the four substantive treaties were not in any way linked, so that a state could choose which instruments it would accept. Whereas this created a certain amount of flexibility, O'Connell notes it also "opened up the possibility for States to adhere to parts only of what was intended to be an over-all scheme, and so distortions and exaggerations became inevitable."[40] Thus, the balance of rights and obligations crafted by the ILC was weakened at UNCLOS I. Only those states that had accepted all four Conventions were subject to the package of rights and obligations as it was initially intended to apply. Indeed, the reception of the 1958 Conventions among states was distinctly underwhelming.[41] The High Seas Convention, with sixty-two ratifications, was the most widely accepted of the four treaties. The Fisheries Convention, on the other hand, only managed to attract thirty-seven contracting parties. Even for those states that had consented to be bound, it was possible to make reservations to some of the articles upon ratification.[42]

---

[39] See D. P. O'Connell, *The International Law of the Sea* (Oxford University Press, 1982) at 22. The work of the fifth committee on free access to the sea by landlocked states did not result in a separate convention but aspects of its work are contained in the Territorial Sea Convention and the High Seas Convention; see United Nations, *The Work of the International Law Commission*, at 42. The Continental Shelf Convention was adopted by 57 votes to 3, with 8 abstentions. The Fisheries Convention was adopted by 45 votes to 1, with 18 abstentions. The High Seas Convention was adopted by 65 votes to none, with 2 abstentions. The Territorial Sea Convention was adopted by 61 votes to none, with 2 abstentions.

[40] O'Connell, *The International Law of the Sea*, at 22.

[41] For a list of ratifications and accessions, see Churchill and Lowe, *The Law of the Sea*, Appendix 2, Table B.

[42] See 1958 Continental Shelf Convention, Article 12; 1958 Fisheries Convention, Article 19.

That is not to say that the Geneva Conventions did not have some normative impact. The High Seas Convention, which was the most widely accepted of the four treaties, claimed in its preamble to be "generally declaratory of rules of established principles of international law."[43] Insofar as it was codificatory of custom, it represented rules that were binding on all states. For example, the Convention codified the principle of the freedom of the high seas, providing that "every state, whether coastal or landlocked, has the right to sail ships under its flag on the high seas."[44] Even some relatively new aspects of the law of the sea that had been the subject of analysis by the ILC for the first time were successfully incorporated into the corpus of customary international law. In the *North Sea Continental Shelf Cases*, the International Court of Justice held that Articles 1 to 3 of the Continental Shelf Convention, setting out the basic principles of the continental shelf, had crystallized into customary international law.[45] However, other articles of the Convention did not make this transition.[46] In their submissions in the *North Sea Continental Shelf Cases*, the Netherlands and Denmark had attempted to rely upon Article 6 of the Convention that applied the so-called equidistance rule to the delimitation of the continental shelf. Yet the Court did not accept these arguments, finding that the rule in Article 6 had been "proposed by the Commission with considerable hesitation, somewhat on an experimental basis, at most de lege ferenda and not at all de lege lata or an emerging rule of customary international law."[47]

Not only did the four conventions adopted at UNCLOS I receive varying degrees of support among states, but the Conference also failed to solve several key issues in the law of the sea. In particular, no agreement was forthcoming on the breadth of the territorial sea or on the rights of states to regulate fish stocks in their coastal waters. A second United Nations Conference on the Law of the Sea[48] was convened in 1960 for the purpose of trying to reach agreement on these outstanding issues, although this too failed.[49] UNCLOS II was only able to conclude that "the development of international law affecting fishing may lead to changes in practices and requirements of many states."[50] As a

[43] 1958 Convention on the High Seas, preamble.
[44] Convention on the High Seas, Article 4.
[45] *North Sea Continental Shelf Cases* (1969) ICJ Reports 3, at para. 63.
[46] Ibid., at para. 62.   [47] Ibid.   [48] Hereinafter, UNCLOS II.
[49] *Convening of a second United Nations conference on the law of the sea*, UNGA Resolution 1307 (XIII), December 10, 1958.
[50] Resolution II adopted at the thirteenth plenary meeting on April 26, 1960.

result, unilateral state practice in this area continued to be a significant factor in the development of the law following UNCLOS I and II.[51]

3 The Third United Nations Conference on the Law of the Sea

3.1 Convening of the Third United Nations Conference on the Law of the Sea

Technological advances kept the issue of the law of the sea on the international agenda throughout the 1960s. In 1967 the Maltese ambassador Arvid Pardo addressed the First Committee of the UN General Assembly, demanding urgent action to ensure the peaceful development of the law of the sea and in particular the legal regime relating to the deep seabed. This was a new issue that had not been considered by any of the previous conferences on the law of the sea. In response to this speech, the General Assembly established the Committee on the Peaceful Uses of the Seabed,[52] whose initial mandate was to prepare a survey of state practice on the deep seabed and the ocean floor, an account of the scientific, technical, economic, legal and other aspects of the issue, and an indication of practical means of promoting international cooperation in the exploration, conservation and exploitation of the ocean floor.[53] The work of the Committee led to the adoption by the General Assembly of the 1970 Declaration of Deep Seabed Principles.[54] In the words of one author, these principles "obviously filled a void created by the rampant technological revolution in this rampant area."[55] The promulgation of the

---

[51] State practice continued to develop to the degree that the ICJ held in 1974 that coastal states could claim a twelve-mile exclusive fisheries zone, a "tertium genus between the territorial sea and the high seas," as well as preferential fishing rights on the high seas, despite the principle of freedom of fishing as found in the 1958 High Seas Convention. See *Fisheries Jurisdiction Case* (1974) ICJ Reports 3, at para. 54.

[52] Hereinafter, the Seabed Committee.

[53] *Examination of the question of the reservation exclusively for peaceful purposes of the sea-bed and the ocean floor, and the subsoil thereof, underlying the high seas beyond the limits of present national jurisdiction, and the use of their resources in the interests of mankind*, UNGA Resolution 2340 (XXII), December 18, 1967, at para. 2.

[54] *Declaration of principles governing the sea-bed and the ocean floor, and the subsoil thereof, beyond the limits of national jurisdiction*, UNGA Resolution 2749 (XXV), December 17, 1970. At the twenty-fifth session, the General Assembly also adopted a Treaty on the Prohibition of the Emplacement of Nuclear Weapons and Other Weapons of Mass Destruction on the Sea-Bed and the Ocean Floor and in the Sub-Soil Thereof, appended to UNGA Resolution 2660 (XXV), December 7, 1970.

[55] J. Evensen, "Working methods and procedures in the Third United Nations Conference on the Law of the Sea" (1986) 199 *Recueil des Cours* 414, at 436.

Declaration differed drastically from the process of codification because the Committee was faced with completely new issues where there was no settled state practice.[56] In other words, this was clearly a case of progressive development of international law. Moreover, the process was being carried out by a political body composed of state representatives, as opposed to a technical body of independent legal experts. Nevertheless, the Declaration can be said to have had a significant impact on international law. The Declaration was negotiated by all interested states and it was adopted without objections by the General Assembly.[57] The principles contained in the Declaration were widely accepted by states and the principle that the deep seabed is the common heritage of mankind arguably made a rapid transition into customary international law.[58]

The Declaration was not intended to be an end in itself and it foresaw the establishment of an international regime to implement the principles in a more concrete form.[59] Therefore, at the same time as adopting the 1970 Declaration, the General Assembly also decided to convene another conference on the law of the sea.[60] The mandate of the Third

---

[56] In this aspect, the 1970 Declaration has much in common with the previous activities of the General Assembly in the field of space law, where states were creating the applicable legal principles from scratch; *Declaration of legal principles governing the activities of states in the exploration and uses of outer space*, UNGA Resolution 1962 (XVIII), December 13, 1963; see B. Cheng, "United Nations resolutions on outer space: instant customary international law?" in B. Cheng (ed.), *International Law: Teaching and Practice* (Stevens, 1982).

[57] The resolution was adopted by 108 votes in favour and 14 abstentions. There were no negative votes. Cf. the so-called "moratorium resolution," *Question of the reservation exclusively for peaceful purposes of the sea-bed and the ocean floor, and the subsoil thereof, underlying the high seas beyond the limits of present national jurisdiction, and the use of their resources in the interests of mankind*, UNGA Resolution 2574D (XXIV), December 15, 1969, whose adoption could only be secured by a majority vote of sixty-two votes in favour to twenty-eight against, with twenty-eight abstentions.

[58] See Churchill and Lowe, *The Law of the Sea*, at 234–5. Cf. Jennings, who accepts that the principles are international law but he would not classify them as customary international law: "the idea is surely that the 1970 principles governing 'the area' (sic) as found in General Assembly resolution 2749 (XXV) are now general law even apart from the question of any treaty; and if they are, this is no custom, for there is no practice at all, and they are not treaty. I am not suggesting that the 1970 principles are not law; I am suggesting that our orthodox categories need revision"; R. Jennings, "The identification of international law," in B. Cheng (ed.), *International Law: Teaching and Practice* (Stevens, 1982) at 7. This objection, however, is less persuasive if one considers the actions of states within international institutions to constitute state practice. See also D. W. Arrow, "Seabeds, sovereignty and objectives regimes" (1983–84) 7 Fordham Int'l L. J. 169, at 205.

[59] UNGA Resolution 2749 (XXV), at para. 9.

[60] *Reservation exclusively for peaceful purposes of the sea-bed and the ocean floor, and the subsoil thereof, underlying the high seas beyond the limits of present national jurisdiction and use of*

United Nations Conference on the Law of the Sea[61] was not to be limited to the deep seabed, however. Rather, UNCLOS III was instructed to "adopt a convention dealing with all matters relating to the law of the sea."[62] In other words, the General Assembly sanctioned further reform of the whole law of the sea, including those issues that had already been dealt with at UNCLOS I. According to one study, "nothing was now to be taken for granted; everything was to be looked at again in the light of new political, economic and technological realities."[63] Indeed, the agenda of the Conference was much broader than previous attempts at law-making in this area; deep seabed mining, the marine environment and the transfer of marine technology were all now key issues in the discussions.

As with previous attempts at codification and progressive development of the law of the sea, it was recognized that the widespread involvement of as many states as possible was a vital factor. General Assembly Resolution 3067 (XXVIII) called for universality of participation at the Conference and it mandated the UN Secretary-General to invite all Members States of the United Nations or its specialized agencies, members of the International Atomic Energy Agency, contracting parties to the ICJ Statute, as well as Guinea–Bissau and North Vietnam, who at the time were not yet UN members.[64] In addition, invitations were sent to a variety of intergovernmental and nongovernmental organizations.[65] The number of states involved in the negotiations had dramatically increased since earlier conferences. Whereas 86 states had attended the 1958 Conference, over 160 states participated at various stages of UNCLOS III.[66]

Perhaps more important than the increase in the number of states was the diversity of state interests represented at UNCLOS III. A large number of participants were newly independent states that

---

their resources in the interests of mankind, and convening of a conference on the law of the sea, UNGA Resolution 2750 C (XXV), December 17, 1970, at para. 2.

[61] Hereinafter, UNCLOS III.

[62] *Reservation exclusively for peaceful purposes of the sea-bed and the ocean floor, and the subsoil thereof, underlying the high seas beyond the limits of present national jurisdiction and use of their resources in the interests of mankind, and convening of the 3rd United Nations Conference on the Law of the Sea-Bed and the Ocean Floor beyond the Limits of National Jurisdiction,* UNGA Resolution 3067 (XXVIII), November 16, 1973, at para. 3. The Conference did not deal with military issues.

[63] C. Sanger, *Ordering the Oceans* (Zed Books, 1986) at 40.

[64] UNGA Resolution 3067 (XXVIII), at para. 7. The UN Council for Namibia was also invited.

[65] *Ibid.*, at para. 8.

[66] For a full list, see the Final Act of the Conference.

had emerged as a result of decolonization in the 1960s. Among these developing states there was a widespread dissatisfaction with the existing law of the sea as many felt that the 1958 Conventions did not sufficiently take into account their interests. As a consequence, UNCLOS III took place in a much more politically charged atmosphere than previous attempts at law-making. Throughout the Conference the polarization of developed and developing countries continued to be one of the major dynamics, which would influence the ultimate fate of the negotiations. Clearly there was a lot at stake for all states concerned and UNCLOS III was "as much a daring venture of international politics and international relations as an exercise in international law."[67]

3.2 Decision-making procedures at the Third United Nations Conference on the Law of the Sea

The intense politicization of the issues also affected the methods of law-making that were adopted by UNCLOS III. From the outset, the Conference was a drastically different process from previous attempts at codifying the law of the sea.

One key difference was that the task of preparing for the conference was not delegated to the International Law Commission. It was the view of some states that the balancing of competing state interests could not be undertaken by a body of independent legal experts. As one commentator says, "states were simply unwilling to leave the promotion of their vital interests to the International Law Commission because they reasoned that only governmental representatives could effectively formulate solutions."[68] In particular, developing countries doubted the representativeness of the Commission and they had serious reservations about its conservative approach to codification.[69] This view perhaps underestimated the role that governments had in fact taken in previous attempts at codification. Nevertheless, it meant that governments would take the lead in the law-making process at UNCLOS III from the very beginning.

---

[67] J. Evensen, "Keynote address," in B. Oxman and A. W. Koers (eds.), *The 1982 Law of the Sea Convention* (Law of the Sea Institute, 1983) at xxi.

[68] T. Koh and S. Jayakumar, "An overview of the negotiating process of UNCLOS III," in M. Nordquist *et al.* (eds.), *United Nations Convention on the Law of the Sea 1982 – A Commentary*, Vol. 1 (Martinus Nijhoff Publishers, 1985) at 50.

[69] *Ibid.*; Sinclair, *The International Law Commission*, at 28.

The preparatory work for the Conference was entrusted to the Seabed Committee, which had been previously established by the General Assembly. The membership of the Seabed Committee was increased in size to ninety-one members for this purpose in order to permit broader participation in the preparatory process.[70] General Assembly Resolution 2750 (XXV) mandated the Committee to prepare draft treaty articles embodying the international regime for the deep seabed area and resources of the seabed beyond the limits of national jurisdiction, as well as a comprehensive list of subjects and issues relating to the law of the sea to be dealt with by the Conference, including draft articles on such subjects and issues.[71] The Seabed Committee met for six sessions between 1971 and 1973. Its final report consisted of six volumes of proposals and counterproposals submitted by states, as well as a number of studies prepared by the UN Secretariat at the behest of the Committee.[72] However, unlike the International Law Commission, the Committee failed to produce a single draft text for consideration by the Conference.[73] Thus, the promulgation of an acceptable treaty text was left to the Conference itself.

The procedures for decision-making would clearly be a vital component in the ability of the Conference to reconcile the conflicting claims and counterclaims of states. In the words of one participant, "from the outset it was acknowledged that it would be an exercise in futility to draw up a draft convention unacceptable to one or more of the major groupings within the United Nations."[74] General Assembly Resolution 2750 stressed that the conference should "seek to accommodate the interests and needs of all States, whether landlocked or coastal."[75] Universal agreement was therefore the aim and it was the negotiating process and procedures that would facilitate its achievement.

It was no surprise then that questions of procedure dominated the first session of the Conference in 1973 and it was only after intense intersessional negotiations that the second session was able to reach

---

[70] UNGA Resolution 2750 C (XXV), at para. 5.
[71] *Ibid.*, at para. 6.
[72] For a study of the work of the Seabed Committee, see S. Oda, *The Law of the Sea in our Time: The United Nations Seabed Committee 1968–1973* (Sijthoff, 1977).
[73] See B. H. Oxman and J. R. Stevenson, "The preparations for the Law of the Sea Conference" (1974) 68 *Am. J. Int'l L.* 1.
[74] Evensen, "Keynote address," at xxvi.
[75] UNGA Resolution 2750 C (XXV), preamble.

agreement on an acceptable formula.[76] It was clear that majority voting would not be an appropriate method of decision-making as the developing countries would be able to outvote the industrialized states on matters of substance. Even the two-thirds majority employed at UNCLOS I would not safeguard the interest of all states. As noted by the United States representative in the negotiation of the rules of procedure, "this particular Conference, as so many delegates have pointed out, is so comprehensive in scope and so important to the vital interests of so many countries that we must make a maximum effort to achieve the maximum of general agreement before we move to a voting stage."[77] The compromise reached at the second session of the Conference was on a process of consensus decision-making. According to Buzan, the formalization of the consensus decision-making procedures was one of the most important innovations of UNCLOS III.[78]

The Rules of Procedure themselves do not mention consensus;[79] rather they require procedural decisions to be made by a simple majority while substantive decisions required a two-thirds majority.[80] However, the so-called Gentlemen's Agreement, adopted as an annex to the Rules of Procedure, mediates the use of the voting procedures and explicitly calls for consensus decision-making. The Gentlemen's Agreement provided:[81]

the Conference should make every effort to reach an agreement on substantive matters by way of consensus and there should be no voting on such matters until all efforts at consensus have been exhausted.

Evensen describes the consensus principle embodied in the Gentleman's Agreement as "the cornerstone of the Conference ... it

---

[76] See J. R Stevenson and B. H. Oxman, "The Third United Nations Conference on the Law of the Sea: the 1974 Caracas Session" (1975) 69 *Am. J. Int'l L.* 1; Sohn, "Voting procedures in United Nations Conferences for the Codification of International Law," at 333–52.

[77] Cited in Sohn, "Voting procedures in United Nations Conferences for the Codification of International Law," at 338.

[78] B. Buzan, "Negotiating by consensus: developments in technique at the United Nations Conference on the Law of the Sea" (1981) 75 *Am. J. Int'l L.* 324, at 328. See also G. Plant, "The Third United Nations Conference on the Law of the Sea and the Preparatory Commission: models for United Nations law-making?" (1987) 36 *Int'l & Comp. L. Q.* 525, at 526–7.

[79] Plant, "The Third United Nations Conference on the Law of the Sea and the Preparatory Commission," at 532–3.

[80] The Rules of Procedure are reproduced by Buzan, "Negotiating by consensus," at 347–8.

[81] See *ibid.*

meant the adoption of articles – and the text of the Convention as a whole – by general agreement (or understanding) without resorting to a vote and, in effect, without requiring an unanimous decision."[82] In other words, the consensus decision-making procedure was concerned with achieving an outcome that would balance the interests of all the states involved. In this sense, consensus is to be distinguished from unanimity, which requires the affirmative vote of all negotiating states. Rather, consensus simply requires that there is "a very considerable convergence of opinions and the absence of any delegations in strong disagreement."[83]

Consensus did not stand alone as a decision-making procedure at the Conference. Rather, it was linked to a majority vote, which served the purpose of acting "as a threat [or] an inducement to achieve consensus."[84] In other words, the possibility of calling for a vote meant that a small number of recalcitrant states would not be able to block an emerging consensus. Nevertheless, several procedural safeguards were agreed in order to ensure that a vote could not be taken before efforts at consensus had been exhausted. These safeguards included the deferral of the vote, during which time the President of the Conference would make every effort to facilitate an agreement. A deferral of up to ten days could be requested by fifteen delegates of the Conference and a further deferral could be agreed by a majority vote of the plenary.[85] It should be noted that these safeguards did not apply to the adoption of the Convention as a whole. Rather, in this situation, the Rules provided that "the Convention shall not be put to the vote less than four working days after the adoption of its last article."[86] This additional safeguard gave some breathing space to allow a last attempt at bringing reluctant states on board. Even with the procedural safeguards, there is an obvious tension between the voting procedures and the principle of consensus.[87] In the end, effective implementation of the consensus procedures relies to a certain extent on the good faith of the negotiators and a strong political will to reach a compromise.

The Gentlemen's Agreement was only one aspect of the consensus decision-making procedure adopted at UNCLOS III. Buzan also

---

[82] Evensen, "Keynote address," at xxvi.
[83] D. Vignes, "Will the Third Conference on the Law of the Sea work according to consensus rule?" (1975) 69 *Am. J. Int'l L.* 119, at 124.
[84] *Ibid.*, at 120.   [85] Rule 37.   [86] Rule 39(2).
[87] Vignes, "Will the Third Conference on the Law of the Sea work according to consensus rule?" at 120.

identifies what he calls an "active consensus procedure" that was intended to push forward the process of consensus formation by removing the role of proposing solutions from the participants themselves and seeking to prevent the hardening of negotiating positions.[88] Following a failure to make progress in the initial negotiations, the Conference agreed at its third session in 1975 to mandate the chairs of the three main committees to produce what were known as the Informal Single Negotiating Texts (ISNT). As its name suggests, the ISNT had no official status and it simply acted as a focus for the negotiations. In the words of the President of UNCLOS III, "the texts would not prejudice the position of any delegation, and would not represent any negotiated text or accepted compromise."[89]

As well as the official negotiation process, a number of unofficial negotiating groups operated on the sidelines of the Conference, contributing to its success.[90] These informal groups brought together the important delegations from special interest groups in a private forum that was more conducive to fruitful negotiations. The best known of these was the Evensen Group, which dealt with a variety of issues including the exclusive economic zone, the protection of the marine environment, marine scientific research and the continental shelf. Many of the compromises produced in this group were to substantially influence the official negotiating texts.[91]

3.3 The package deal

The interrelatedness of the law of the sea was an important factor during the Conference negotiations where the need to identify compromises between competing state interests was vital to its success. The interrelationship was expressly recognized in General Assembly resolutions from 1969 onwards and ultimately in the preamble to the Law of the Sea Convention itself, which says, "the problems of ocean space are closely related and need to be considered as a whole." On the other hand, how this interrelationship was to be achieved in practice was not clear

---

[88] Buzan, "Negotiating by consensus," at 328–9.
[89] *Third United Nations Conference on the Law of the Sea, Official Records*, Vol. IV, at 26, at paras. 92–3.
[90] See B. Buzan, "'United we stand...' – informal negotiating groups at UNCLOS III" (1980) 4 *Marine Policy* 183.
[91] See Koh and Jayakumar, "An overview of the negotiating process of UNCLOS III," at 106–7.

when the Conference opened in 1973. UNCLOS III continued the organ-izational set-up adopted by the Sea-Bed Committee so that the work was divided into three main committees, covering the seabed regime, the general law of the sea, and the marine environment and marine scientific research. While the work was split on thematic grounds, the issues discussed in the three committees continued to be interlinked. As Paul Bamela Engo, chair of the First Committee, explained, "some matters under consideration in other Main Committees had significant repercussions in the First Committee"[92] and the same was clearly true for the other two committees.[93] Given these de facto linkages, states were only willing to make compromises in one committee contingent on the outcome of debates in other committees.

While linkages between particular provisions of a treaty are common,[94] it is the linking of the Convention as a whole that charac-terizes the package deal concept that arose at UNCLOS III.[95] Evensen, a key participant in the Conference, described the package deal as "the notion that all the main parts of the Convention should be looked upon as an entity, as a single negotiated package, where the laws of give and take presumably had struck a reasonable balance between participating states considered as a whole."[96] It was the objective of the Conference to resolve the outstanding issues in the law of the sea to the satisfaction of as many states as possible and it became clear that compromises between the principal protagonists would be crucial to its success.

In a significant step, the ISNTs that had been individually produced by the committee chairs were combined in 1977 into a single docu-ment, the so-called Informal Composite Negotiating Text (ICNT). Evensen explains the significance of the ICNT: "for the first time, the Conference prepared a treaty text where the different parts were coor-dinated and where obvious contradictions and unnecessary repetitions

---

[92] P. Engo, "Issues of the First Committee," in B. H. Oxman and A. W. Koers (eds.), *The 1982 Law of the Sea Convention* (Law of the Sea Institute, 1983) at 40.

[93] A. Yankov, "The significance of the 1982 Convention for the protection of the marine environment – Third Committee Issues," in B. H. Oxman and A. W. Koers (eds.), *The 1982 Law of the Sea Convention* (Law of the Sea Institute, 1983) at 72.

[94] L. T. Lee, "The Law of the Sea Convention and third states" (1983) 77 *Am. J. Int'l L.* 541, at 567.

[95] What Plant calls the "grand-package"; Plant, "The Third United Nations Conference on the Law of the Sea and the Preparatory Commission," at 528.

[96] Evensen, "Keynote address," at xxvii.

had been remedied."[97] All the same, the ICNT remained a negotiating text subject to further compromise. Delegates continued to refine the issues over which there were disagreements. In order to aid this process, seven specific negotiating groups were formed at the seventh session in 1978 to concentrate on key divisive topics.[98]

In another significant step taken at the 1977 session of the Conference, it was agreed that:

Any modifications to be made in the [ICNT] should emerge from the negotiations themselves and should not be introduced on the initiative of any single person, whether it be the President or a Chairman of a Committee, unless presented to the Plenary and found, from the widespread and substantial support prevailing in Plenary, to offer a substantially improved prospect of a consensus ... the revision of the [ICNT] should be the collective responsibility of the President and the Chairmen of the main committees, acting together as a team headed by the President."[99]

This move made it much more difficult to change the negotiating text and it was, according to one author, "a recognition that a heavy burden of proof [was] necessary for any proposal to change any one of the large majority of articles that already [enjoyed] widespread and substantial support."[100] At the close of the ninth session in 1980, the title of the document was changed to a "draft convention," although its status as a negotiating text remained unaffected until its final adoption in 1982.

3.4 Adoption of the Law of the Sea Convention

The package deal, combined with the consensus decision-making procedures described above, were important negotiating tools that were aimed at achieving a treaty text that was acceptable to as many states as possible. In other words, these procedures were intended to achieve a compromise over all aspects of the law of the sea that had not been possible in previous attempts at law-making in this field. If this was achieved, the outcome would be a major advancement in the law of the sea and it was more likely to influence customary international law on the topic.

---

[97] Evensen, "Working methods and procedures in the Third United Nations Conference on the Law of the Sea," at 471.

[98] See B. H. Oxman, "The Third United Nations Conference on the Law of the Sea: The Seventh Session (1978)" (1979) 73 Am. J. Int'l L. 1, at 3–24.

[99] Cited by Buzan, "Negotiating by consensus," at 337.

[100] Oxman, "The Third United Nations Conference on the Law of the Sea: the Seventh Session (1978)," at 5.

Yet all of these procedural innovations did not necessarily guarantee a successful outcome of the negotiations. In the end, factors outside the control of the Conference were to dictate its success or failure. A turning point was the election of Ronald Reagan as President of the United States in 1980, which heralded a new political order in the United States. President Reagan immediately ordered a root and branch review of the draft convention. This review identified a number of perceived problems with the treaty text. The principal objection of the United States and other associated industrialized states was to the provisions on the International Seabed Area in Part XI of the Convention.[101] Determined to oppose the treaty, the United States demanded a vote on the adoption of the treaty at the final session of the Conference on April 30, 1982. As a result, the final text of the Law of the Sea Convention was adopted by 130 votes in favor, 4 against, and 17 abstentions.[102] The list of those countries that did not vote in favor of the Convention includes most industrialized states and Soviet states.[103] Despite last-minute efforts to persuade them to participate, many industrialized states resolved that they would not consent to be bound by the Convention as it stood in 1982.[104]

Buzan argued before the final session of the Conference that "actual resort to [a vote] would in all likelihood have indicated a breakdown of the negotiations ... [and] the only sensible conclusion to the negotiating techniques evolved at UNCLOS is to adopt the final revision by consensus."[105] On this view, the recourse to a vote by UNCLOS III indicates the failure to accommodate a number of important interests. Nonetheless, the results of the Conference cannot be discounted as a failure. It did manage to produce a clear and comprehensive set of rules and principles on the law of the sea. Indeed, apart from Part XI, most other sections of the Law of the Sea Convention garnered the support

---

[101] See D. Larson, "The Reagan rejection of the UN Convention" (1985) 14 *Ocean Dev. & Int'l L.* 337.
[102] The principal objection of the USA was to the provisions on the International Seabed Area in Part XI of the Convention. Turkey, Israel and Venezuela also voted against the Convention, albeit for different reasons. Turkey and Venezuela both objected to the methods outlined in the Convention for delimiting the continental shelf and the EEZ. Israel, on the other hand, principally opposed the provisions on straits contained in Part III of the Convention.
[103] The Soviet and Eastern European states changed their position and signed the Convention when it was opened for signature in December 1982.
[104] Churchill and Lowe, *The Law of the Sea*, at 23.
[105] Buzan, "Negotiating by consensus," at 332.

of an overwhelming majority of states. In the final speech to the Conference, the United States delegate stressed that while the deep sea-bed mining regime was largely unacceptable, those parts dealing with the traditional aspects of the law of the sea reflected prevailing international practice.[106] The Conference was therefore successful in forging a consensus on many aspects of the law of the sea, including many issues that had evaded settlement since the first attempts at codification. It is this consensus that can perhaps explain the impact that the Convention has had on customary international law of the sea.

4 The Law of the Sea Convention

4.1 An overview of the Law of the Sea Convention

The Law of the Sea Convention has been hailed as "a constitution for the oceans."[107] The treaty has 320 articles, arranged in 15 parts, and 9 annexes, which together deal with "practically every aspect of the use and resources of the seas and the oceans."[108] The following section will provide a brief overview of the Convention before we turn to consider its impact on international law.

First and foremost, the Convention sets out the jurisdictional regime for the seas and oceans. It empowers coastal states to establish a number of zones of maritime jurisdiction in which they may claim certain rights. Beyond these areas of national jurisdiction lie the high seas, and the Convention confirms the principle of the freedom of the high seas for peaceful purposes.[109]

UNCLOS III was able to solve some of the controversies that had plagued earlier attempts at codifying the law of the sea. Part II of the Convention defines the legal status of the territorial sea and the contiguous zone. Coastal states are able to claim a territorial sea of up to 12 nautical miles from baselines drawn in accordance with the

---

[106] See statement of the United States, 192nd meeting, *Official Records of the Third United Nations Conference on the Law of the Sea*, Vol. 17, at 116–17. See also the statement of the United Kingdom, 189th meeting, *ibid.*, at 79–80.

[107] T. B. Koh, "A Constitution for the Oceans," available at www.un.org/depts/los/convention_agreements/texts/koh_english.pdf <checked July 6, 2010>. See also S. V. Scott, "The LOS Convention as a constitutional regime for the oceans," in A. G. Oude Elferink (ed.), *Stability and Change in the Law of the Sea: The Role of the LOS Convention* (2006, Martinus Nijhoff Publications).

[108] *Ibid.*

[109] Law of the Sea Convention, Part VII.

Convention.[110] While coastal states have sovereignty over the territorial sea, ships in this zone retain a right of innocent passage.[111] In straits used for international navigation, coastal states have fewer powers of regulation and ships and aircraft have a right of unimpeded transit passage as defined in Part III of the Convention. A coastal state may also designate a contiguous zone up to 24 nautical miles from their baselines. In the contiguous zone, the coastal state may "exercise control necessary to prevent infringement of its customs, fiscal, immigration, or sanitary laws and regulations within its territory or territorial sea and punish infringements of [those] laws and regulations committed within its territory or territorial sea."[112]

The Convention also creates a number of new maritime zones that did not exist prior to the start of negotiations. Perhaps most important of all, the Convention introduces the concept of the Exclusive Economic Zone (EEZ) which extends up to 200 nautical miles from the baselines of a coastal state. Within this area, a coastal state may claim sovereign rights over living and nonliving resources and it may exercise functional jurisdiction over the establishment and use of artificial islands, installations and structures, marine scientific research, and the protection and preservation of the marine environment.[113]

A coastal state also has sovereignty over the seabed up to at least 200 nautical miles from its shores. Moreover, the Convention provides that a coastal state may claim sovereign rights to the seabed throughout its natural prolongation to the outer edge of the continental margin as delineated in accordance with Article 76 of the Convention, thereby replacing the ambiguous exploitability test found in the 1958 Convention on the Continental Shelf. The Commission on the Outer Limits of the Continental Shelf is established to verify claims to an outer continental shelf by coastal states and it operates in accordance with Article 76 and Annex III of the Convention.

Perhaps the most innovative and certainly the most controversial aspect of the Convention is the designation of the deep seabed as the common heritage of mankind and the creation of international machinery in order to oversee its management. Part XI of the Convention establishes the International Seabed Authority with

---

[110] *Ibid.*, Article 3.
[111] *Ibid.*, Articles 2 and 17. Note that the sovereignty of a coastal state extends to the air space above the territorial sea but there is no corresponding right of innocent passage for aircraft under the Convention.
[112] *Ibid.*, Article 33.   [113] Law of the Sea Convention, Article 56.

powers to regulate mining for minerals found in the International Seabed Area.[114]

The Convention was negotiated at a time when the protection of the environment had just become a prominent issue in international relations. Shortly before the convening of UNCLOS III, the United Nations had adopted the Stockholm Declaration on the Human Environment which had called on states to inter alia "take all possible steps to prevent pollution of the seas by substances that are liable to create hazards to human health, to harm living resources and marine life, to damage amenities or to interfere with other legitimate uses of the sea."[115] The Law of the Sea Convention was an opportunity to set out a comprehensive framework for the protection of the marine environment. Part XII of the Convention deals with all sources of marine pollution, including pollution from ships, pollution from land-based sources, pollution from seabed activities and pollution from the atmosphere.

Parts XIII and XIV, containing almost 100 articles or about one third of the Convention, deal with the marine scientific research and transfer of marine technology respectively. The importance attached to these issues recognizes that "without marine science and technology, we would be blatantly unable to explore, exploit, manage or conserve marine resources or navigate safely or to protect our coasts."[116] The Convention also recognizes that marine scientific research and marine technology are costly and developing countries may need assistance in order to obtain access to them. The Convention therefore stresses the need for international cooperation in these areas.

Part XV of the Convention creates a sophisticated and complex dispute settlement mechanism.[117] Judicial settlement of disputes arising under the Convention is compulsory unless States Parties can agree on some other form of nonbinding settlement.[118] The dispute settlement procedures are vital to the overall balance of the Convention by

---

[114] See Chapter 5.
[115] Stockholm Declaration on the Human Environment, Principle 7; available at www. unep.org/Documents.Multilingual/Default.asp?documentid=97&articleid=1503 <checked July 6, 2010>.
[116] E. Mann Borgese, *The Oceanic Circle: Governing the Seas as a Global Resource* (United Nations University Press, 1998) at 114.
[117] See e.g. N. Klein, *Dispute Settlement in the UN Convention on the Law of the Sea* (Cambridge University Press, 2005); Churchill and Lowe, *The Law of the Sea*, Chapter 19; A. E. Boyle, "Dispute settlement and the Law of the Sea Convention: problems of fragmentation and jurisdiction" (1997) 46 *Int'l & Comp. L. Q.* 37.
[118] Law of the Sea Convention, Article 286.

providing a means through which states can ensure its proper and effective implementation.

As noted above, the Convention was negotiated as a package deal. This is reflected in Article 309 of the Convention, which provides that "no reservations or exceptions may be made to this Convention unless expressly permitted by other Articles of this Convention." In practice, only a handful of limited exceptions are permitted to the compulsory settlement of disputes under the Convention.[119] In reality, therefore, states must accept all of the substantive provisions of the Convention as an integral whole.

4.2 The impact of the Law of the Sea Convention on international law

The Law of the Sea Convention was opened for signature on December 10, 1982. It is open to formal acceptance by all states, as well as a range of non-state actors that had attended UNCLOS III.[120] States can consent to be bound by the Convention through ratification or accession.[121] The Convention required sixty ratifications or accessions in order to come into force. For many years, owing to the opposition to Part XI, the Convention remained a limping treaty. It finally entered into force on November 16, 1994.[122] States accepting the Convention following its entry into force will become bound thirty days after indicating their acceptance.[123] As of March 1, 2010, there were 160 States Parties to the Convention.[124] While this includes a significant proportion of the international community, it still falls short of the 192 states that are currently members of the United Nations.

Although the Law of the Sea Convention has not yet achieved universal participation among all states, it is undeniable that it has had a significant impact on the law of the sea, so much so that it is possible to argue that, for a large part, it has created a universal legal framework for the regulation of the oceans. Such arguments are premised upon

---

[119] See ibid., Article 298.   [120] Ibid., Article 305.   [121] Ibid., Articles 306–7.

[122] Guyana deposited the sixtieth ratification on November 16, 1993. The Convention entered into force as modified by the 1994 Part XI Agreement, which was necessary to ensure the participation in the Convention of the group of industrialized states which objected to the deep seabed provisions of the original Convention. See Chapter 4.

[123] Law of the Sea Convention, Article 308(2).

[124] See www.un.org/depts/los/reference_files/chronological_lists_of_ratifications. htm#The%20United%20Nations%20Convention%20on%20the%20Law%20of%20 the%20Sea <checked July 14, 2010>.

the influence that the Convention has had on customary international law.

Some commentators have denied that the Convention can influence customary international law at all due to the fact that it was adopted as a package deal. Adopting this position, Caminos and Molitor argue that "the package nature of the 1982 Convention links nearly all of its provisions together, rendering them indivisible and thus modifying the application of the traditional treaty-custom rules identified by [the International Court of Justice]."[125] As a consequence, these authors conclude that "if one assumes that the package deal was solidified at the time that the Convention was formally adopted, then those of its provisions that had not attained customary status by that date may have been precluded from ever doing so."[126] They cite numerous declarations and statements made by participants at UNCLOS III to support their argument. Perhaps the most striking illustration is the speech given by Deputy Foreign Minister Gouzhenko of the Soviet Union to UNCLOS III in which he asserts that "the Convention is not a basket of fruit from which one can pick only those one fancies. As is well known, the new comprehensive Convention has been elaborated as a single and indivisible instrument, as a package of closely interrelated compromise decisions."[127]

On closer inspection, however, the package deal argument is not particularly convincing. The most obvious objection is that this view does not explain how one identifies the customary international law of the sea if one cannot rely on the state practice and *opinio juris* that coincides with the Convention. In this regard, Vasciannie notes that "it would ... require States to deny the independent status of custom as a source of obligations in matters falling within the purview of the [Law of the Sea Convention]: as this requirement has no basis in law, it cannot be supported."[128] Nor is it an argument that has been accepted by states or by international courts and tribunals. Indeed, it may have been this argument that a chamber of the ICJ had in mind when it

---

[125] H. Caminos and M. R. Molitor, "Progressive development of international law and the Package Deal" (1985) 79 *Am. J. Int'l L.* 871, at 886-7.

[126] *Ibid.*, at 888.

[127] Cited in *ibid.*, at 877. A similar statement by Ambassador Tommy Koh of Singapore, acting as President of UNCLOS III, is also cited in support of this argument; *ibid.*, at 886.

[128] S. Vasciannie, "Part XI of the Law of the Sea Convention and Third States: some general observations" (1989) 48 *Cambridge L. J.* 85, at 94.

said that certain provisions of the Law of the Sea Convention, "even if they in some respects bear the mark of compromise surrounding their adoption, may nevertheless be regarded as consonant at present with general international law on the question."[129]

Even Caminos and Molitor accepted that some parts of the Convention had the effect of codifying preexisting rules of customary international law.[130] During the negotiations many states had noted the codifying effect of certain provisions. For instance, the United Kingdom stated at the closing session of UNCLOS III that "many of the Convention's provisions are a restatement or codification of existing conventional or customary international law and state practice."[131] Indeed, several parts of the Convention incorporate provisions found in the 1958 Conventions on the Law of the Sea without substantial change. This is particularly true of provisions relating to the territorial sea and the high seas.

Yet codification cannot account for the entire impact of the Convention on customary international law. Many provisions in the Convention, including important concepts such as the exclusive economic zone, were almost without precedent in law or state practice prior to UNCLOS III. Of these new norms, some have undoubtedly inspired subsequent state practice, which has contributed to their transition into customary international law. In some cases state practice began to coalesce around certain rules before the whole regime had been finally agreed.[132]

It can also be argued that the process of negotiating the Convention itself contributed to the development of customary international law in this area by leading to the crystallization of new rules and principles accepted by all states. As Moore suggested shortly after the conclusion of the Convention, "no description of ... the customary international law-making process as applied to oceans law would be complete without noting that for the last seventeen years the UNCLOS process and

---

[129] *Delimitation of the Maritime Boundary in the Gulf of Maine Area* (1984) ICJ Reports 246, at 294.
[130] Caminos and Molitor, "Progressive development of international law and the Package Deal," at 887.
[131] Statement of United Kingdom, 189th meeting, *Official Records of the Third United Nations Conference on the Law of the Sea*, Vol. 17, at 79, at para. 200. See also Statement of Indonesia, 186th meeting, *ibid.*, at 25, at paras. 23–5. Cf. Statement by Cameroon, 185th meeting, *Official Records of the Third United Nations Conference on the Law of the Sea*, Vol. 17, at 16, at para. 84.
[132] Koh and Jayakumar, "An overview of the negotiating process of UNCLOS III," at 60-1.

patterns of practices have been a central feature in the customary international law-forming process."[133]

A number of judicial decisions on the law of the sea would seem to attribute weight to the negotiation of the Convention in the formation of customary international law. The most explicit reference to the negotiating techniques employed at UNCLOS III is found in the *Gulf of Maine Case*, where a Chamber of the ICJ confirmed that the fact that the Law of the Sea Convention had not entered into force "in no way detracts from the consensus reached on large portions of the instrument and, above all, cannot invalidate the observation that certain provisions of the Convention, concerning the continental shelf and the exclusive economic zone, which may, in fact, be relevant to the present case, were adopted without any objections."[134] Although not expressing itself explicitly in terms of crystallization, the Court nevertheless appears to attach importance to the consensus underlying the Convention as a critical factor in determining its impact on customary international law. Other decisions also appear to attribute a significant weight to the manner in which the Convention was adopted and negotiated. In the *Continental Shelf Case between Libya Arab Jamahiriya and Malta*, the Court stressed the adoption of the Convention by "an overwhelming majority of states." It continued to find that the institution of the EEZ is also shown, "by the practice of states," to be part of customary international law.[135] Yet, as noted by one author, "the most

---

[133] J. Moore, "Customary international law after the Convention," in R. B. Krueger and S. A. Riesenfeld (eds.), *The Developing Order of the Oceans* (Law of the Sea Institute, 1984) at 42; see also L. Sohn, "Implications of the Law of the Sea Convention regarding the protection of the marine environment," in R. B. Krueger and S. A. Riesenfeld (eds.), *The Developing Order of the Oceans* (Law of the Sea Institute, 1985) at 189.

[134] *Delimitation of the Maritime Boundary in the Gulf of Maine Area*, at para. 94.

[135] *Continental Shelf Case between Libya Arab Jamahiriya and Malta* (1985) ICJ Reports 13, at para. 34. The Court has in other cases held that parts of the Law of the Sea Convention are declaratory of custom. In the *Case Concerning Maritime Delimitation and Territorial Questions between Qatar and Bahrain (Merits)*, the Court found that both parties agreed that most of the provisions of the Convention relevant to the case reflected customary international law; *Case Concerning Maritime Delimitation and Territorial Questions between Qatar and Bahrain (Merits)* (2001) ICJ Reports 40, at para. 167. In its reasoning, the Court refers to Articles 5, 7(4), 15 and 121. The parties to the dispute disagreed over the customary status of Part IV of the Convention on archipelagic states, although the Court did not find it necessary to make a determination on this point in its decision; see paras. 181–3. In the *Nicaragua Case*, the Court held that the Law of the Sea Convention provisions on the sovereignty of the coastal state over its territorial sea codifies one of the "firmly established and longstanding tenets of customary international law"; *Case Concerning Military and*

striking element in this reasoning is not that provisions of an international agreement are qualified as customary international law but that this was done without embarking upon any empirical research as to whether the respective rules were recognized as law and reflected in State practice."[136]

It is important for these purposes that the Convention was negotiated by consensus and that the majority of its provisions were widely accepted by states, including those who were not prepared to become a party.[137] As argued by Boyle and Chinkin, "once there is international consensus on the basic rule, it is highly unlikely that any state will object if it is then implemented, however rarely, in state practice."[138]

It should not be thought that this argument dismisses the relevance of subsequent state practice in the law of the sea. Such state practice can and must be taken into account. In this regard, some authors have argued that the diversity of state practice on certain aspects of the law of the sea undermines the argument that the Convention has crystallized customary international law. For instance, Orrego Vicuña says: "while the basic elements of the regime of the territorial sea, including the twelve mile limit, can be considered to have been transformed into customary law, ... not every detail of the Convention will have followed the same path."[139] In the context of the EEZ, Churchill and Lowe similarly conclude that:

it would seem that what is part of customary international law are the broad rights of coastal and other States enumerated in Articles 56 and 58 of the

Paramilitary Activities in and against Nicaragua (Merits) (1986) ICJ Reports 14, at para. 212. It also noted the customary right of innocent passage for ships, reflected in Article 18(1)(b) of the Law of the Sea Convention, as well as freedom of navigation in the EEZ and on the high seas; *ibid.*, at para. 214.

[136] R. Wolfrum, "The legal order for the seas and the oceans," in M. Nordquist and J. Moore (eds.), *Entry into Force of the Law of the Sea Convention* (Kluwer Law International, 1995) at 174. See similar comments by C. Tomuschat, "Obligations arising for states without or against their will" (1993) 241 *Recueil des Cours* 195, at 258.

[137] "United States Ocean Policy" (1983) 77 *Am. J. Int'l L.* at 620. In the *Gulf of Maine Case*, the ICJ took into account the presidential statement in deciding what weight to confer on the Convention as a material source of customary international law; *Delimitation of the Maritime Boundary in the Gulf of Maine Area*, at para. 94.

[138] A. E. Boyle and C. Chinkin, *The Making of International Law* (Oxford University Press, 2007) at 237.

[139] F. Orrego Vicuña, "The Law of the Sea experience and the corpus of international law: effects and interrelationships," in R. B. Krueger and S. A. Riesenfeld (eds.), *The Developing Order of the Oceans* (The Law of the Sea Institute, 1984) at 15.

Convention. It is much more doubtful whether the detailed obligations in the articles relating to the exercise of coastal State jurisdiction over fisheries, pollution and research have passed or are likely quickly to pass into customary international law.[140]

In contrast, however, O'Connell argues that "it is possible that State practice will depart from [the rules in the Convention] but the whole is in the nature of a 'package,' and, presumptively, at least, the new concept [of the EEZ] includes the incidents and details which the Conference has attached to it."[141] It is suggested that this latter view is preferable as it recognizes the strength of the consensus that underlies many of the rules in the Convention. While it may be the case that the unilateral practice of some states deviates from the Convention, it does not follow these states are thereby seeking to assert rules which are different from those contained in the Convention. Rather their actions can be understood as deviations from customary international law rules.[142] This argument is possible because the Convention continues to be the benchmark against which state actions are judged in the law of the sea. The international community regularly reaffirms its commitment to the Law of the Sea Convention, proclaiming that it contains the "legal framework within which all activities in the oceans and the seas must be carried out."[143] Such pronouncements arguably provide continuing evidence of the acceptance of many of the rules concerning maritime jurisdiction found in the Law of the Sea Convention. Thus, the ongoing consensus that underpins much of the Convention arguably makes up for the lack of complete uniformity in the practice of states.[144]

---

[140] Churchill and Lowe, *The Law of the Sea*, at 161–2. See also O. Schachter, *International Law in Theory and Practice* (Martinus Nijhoff Publishers, 1991) at 283; F. Orrego Vicuña, *The Exclusive Economic Zone* (Cambridge University Press, 1989) at 252.

[141] O'Connell, *The International Law of the Sea*, at 49.

[142] See *Case Concerning Military and Paramilitary Activities in and against Nicaragua (Merits)*, at para. 186 in which the Court held that "the Court deems it sufficient that the conduct of States should, in general, be consistent with such rules, and that instances of State conduct inconsistent with a given rule should, generally, have been treated as breaches of that rule, not as indications of the recognition of a new rule."

[143] E.g. *Oceans and law of the sea*, UNGA Resolution 55/7, October 30, 2000, preamble. This statement is regularly repeated in General Assembly resolutions on oceans and the law of the sea.

[144] In this vein Treves concludes, "In view of the high number of States bound by it and of its influence on practice, it seems correct to say that there is a presumption that the noninstitutional provisions correspond to customary law, unless the contrary is proven"; T. Treves, "The United Nations Convention on the Law of the Sea," 2008, United Nations Audio Visual Library, available at www.un.org/law/avl <checked July 21, 2010>.

Even if the negotiation of the Convention by consensus led to the crystallization of many rules and principles of customary international law, it does not follow that the whole Convention has become customary international law. From the records of UNCLOS III, it is clear that many of the provisions on deep seabed mining in Part XI of the Convention were not supported by consensus and there has not been sufficient state practice and *opinio juris* for their translation into customary international law. Whereas the designation of the International Seabed Area as the common heritage of mankind is reaffirmed by Part XI of the Convention, the details of the legal regime through which this principle was to be applied did not receive the support of all states. Applying the words of the ICJ from a different context, these provisions were the subject of "long continued hesitations."[145] The industrialized states consistently raised objections to the regime for deep seabed mining both before and after the conclusion of the Convention. The verbal protests of the industrialized states presented at the Conference itself were further supplemented by state practice that conflicted with the detail of the treaty text. Several states, including the United States, the United Kingdom, the Soviet Union, Germany, France and Italy, passed unilateral legislation permitting their nationals to undertake mining without authorization from the international machinery created by the Convention. Further to these unilateral acts, Germany, France, the United States and the United Kingdom entered into an Agreement concerning Interim Arrangements relating to Polymetallic Nodules of the Deep Seabed in 1982.[146] These actions do not undermine the argument that the deep seabed is designated as the common heritage of mankind. The objections of the industrialized nations were aimed at the details of institutional design of the International Seabed Authority. Indeed, much of the legislation adopted by these states was explicitly said to be of an interim character pending the negotiation of an international regime based upon the common heritage of mankind that was generally acceptable to all

---

[145] *North Sea Continental Shelf Cases*, at paras. 49–53.
[146] See E. Brown, *The International Law of the Sea* (Dartmouth Publishing Company, 1994) at 457. Note that in August 1985 the Preparatory Commission passed a resolution condemning the actions of these states and affirming that the Convention was the only legal regime applicable to the Area; see Churchill and Lowe, *The Law of the Sea*, at 234.

states.[147] For example, section 1402 of the United States Deep Seabed Hard Minerals Resources Act provided that:

The Secretary of State is encouraged to negotiate successfully a comprehensive Law of the Sea Treaty which, among other things, provides assured and nondiscriminatory access to the hard mineral resources of the deep seabed for all nations, gives legal definition to the principle that the resources of the deep seabed are the common heritage of mankind, and provides for the establishment of requirements for the protection of the quality of the environment as stringent as those promulgated pursuant to this [Act].

Unilateral national legislation also reflected certain aspects of the principle of the common heritage of mankind. For instance, the United Kingdom legislation established a deep sea mining fund, the proceeds of which were to be paid to the International Seabed Authority.[148]

It is not only lack of consensus that prevents certain parts of the Convention from making the transition into customary international law. Several parts of the Convention are also of an institutional nature. Yet the creation of institutions can only occur through the conclusion of a treaty.[149] As Jennings explains, "a treaty is not capable of becoming a general rule of custom in a form which belongs essentially to the particular treaty context. This is without prejudice to whether that rule, in abstracto or in another context, would be capable of becoming a rule of general law."[150]

This is another reason why the majority of Part XI cannot be considered as customary international law as it is largely concerned with creating and maintaining an international institution to manage the International Seabed Area. This argument is reinforced by the fact that many of the provisions in this Part of the Convention are specifically directed at "States Parties" to the Convention, stressing their foundation

---

[147] See Arrow, "Seabeds, sovereignty, and objective regimes," at 202.
[148] Deep Sea Mining (Temporary Provisions) Act 1981, s. 10. See V. Lowe, "The United Kingdom and the Law of the Sea," in T. Treves (ed.), *The Law of the Sea: The European Union and its Member States* (Martinus Nijhoff Publishers, 1997) at 547: "The United Kingdom Government took the view that unilateral interim deep sea mining and interim legislation to regulate it was lawful and compatible with the 1970 Declaration on Principles."
[149] See T. Treves, "UNCLOS as a non-universally ratified instrument," in B. H. Oxman and A. W. Koers (eds.), *The 1982 Convention on the Law of the Sea* (Law of the Sea Institute, 1982) at 685.
[150] R. Jennings, "The discipline of international law," in *Report of the 57th Conference of the International Law Association* (Madrid, 1976) 620, at 626.

in treaty law. The same considerations also apply to the provisions on dispute settlement found in Part XV of the Convention.[151]

Finally, it should be mentioned that individual states that objected to particular provisions of the Convention at the time of its adoption could claim to be persistent objectors to the extent that they have maintained their objections. For instance, Israel voted against the adoption of the Convention because it could not accept the provision on international straits in Part III of the Convention. Similarly, Turkey and Venezuela voted against the Convention because of their objection to the methods outlined in the Convention for delimiting the continental shelf and the EEZ. None of these states have become a party to the Convention, which suggests that their objections still stand. Such objections can prevent the application of customary rules to the state concerned. However, it does not prevent the emergence of customary international law for all other states that have acquiesced in these rules.

Regardless of the substantial influence that the Convention has had on the customary international law of the sea, it does not completely mitigate the need for states to consent to be bound by the Convention. This explains why the UN General Assembly continues to call on all states that have not done so to become a State Party to the Law of the Sea Convention.[152] Only with universal participation will the Convention be fully effective for all states.

5 Conclusion

This chapter has sought to trace the attempts at the codification and progressive development of the law of the sea through international conferences. It has highlighted a trend towards formal, institutional procedures for law-making starting with the Hague Codification Conference in 1930. Many lessons have been learned over the years that have been applied to successive codification attempts.

---

[151] Therefore, apart from the duty to settle law of the sea disputes peacefully, non-parties would not be bound by the provisions to submit disputes to arbitration or other courts or tribunals. Of course, states could accept these obligations without becoming a party to the Convention and many law of the sea disputes have been settled by adjudication or arbitration.

[152] E.g. *Oceans and law of the sea*, UNGA Resolution 61/222, December 20, 2006, at para. 3.

Out of all of the attempts at law-making described in this chapter, there is no doubt that UNCLOS III was the most successful. UNCLOS III managed to settle many of the outstanding controversies that had precipitated the collapse of previous efforts at codifying the law of the sea. As a consequence, the Law of the Sea Convention is hailed as a milestone in the international legal order. It has been described by one author as "a shining example of international cooperation, diplomacy and the role of international law in the regulation of international affairs and is considered to be one of the most complex and ultimately successful international diplomatic negotiations that took place in the twentieth century."[153]

Yet the success of the Conference was not only in concluding a treaty, but also in its influence over the modern customary international law of the sea. These achievements can largely be ascribed to the innovative decision-making techniques that were developed by the Conference in order to promote consensus. It was the process of negotiating the Law of the Sea Convention that allowed new rules of customary international law to crystallize. Today, the Convention can be said to provide the bedrock for the modern law of the sea. Although state practice may not be uniform, the Convention is nevertheless accepted as providing a "legal framework within which all activities in the oceans and the seas must be carried out."[154]

The argument in favor of crystallization should not, however, be taken to suggest that the law of the sea is fixed and rigid. While the Law of the Sea Convention has had huge success in stabilizing state claims to jurisdiction over the oceans, it is also true that "the law needs to be flexible and able to change to reflect new circumstances whether it be increased national sovereignty, greater environmental protection, or enhanced global security."[155] How the law of the sea evolves in light of the ever-changing challenges facing the international community will be considered in the following chapters. It is suggested that institutionalized processes of law-making will continue to play a central role in the development of the law of the sea. Most issues that arise over the development of the law of the sea are dealt with through one of the

---

[153] D. Rothwell, "Oceans management and the law of the sea in the twenty-first century," in A. Oude Elferink and D. Rothwell (eds.), *Oceans Management in the 21st Century: Institutional Frameworks and Responses*, (Koninklijke Brill NV, 2004) at 329.

[154] UNGA Resolution 55/7, preamble.

[155] Rothwell, "Oceans management and the law of the sea in the twenty-first century," at 350.

many international institutions that have an interest in this topic. The following chapters will look at how these institutions contribute to developing the law of the sea. What is interesting to note is the influence that UNCLOS III has had on the working practices of these institutions. It will be seen that consensus still appears to be very much the aim of states when it comes to the continuing development of the law of the sea and many of the law-making techniques utilized at UNCLOS III have been employed by other institutions in order to maintain the balance of interests in this field of law.

3   Amendment and modification of the Law of the Sea Convention by the States Parties

1 Introduction

The drafters of the Law of the Sea Convention were aware that if the Convention was to provide an enduring legal framework, it must be able to evolve to take into account legal, political, scientific and technological developments. At the closing session of UNCLOS III, the delegate from Sri Lanka summed up the transience of the Convention framework in the following words:[1]

> It is in the nature of all things that they do not remain static, that there will be growth and there will be decay. The march of technology and changing perceptions and aspirations will, in time, place pressures upon the regimes we establish today.

The purpose of this chapter is to consider the formal and informal mechanisms for the review of the law of the sea regime and the making of amendments or modifications thereto.

The need for some institutional means through which measures could be taken to implement and develop the Law of the Sea Convention was discussed by UNCLOS III on a number of occasions. The issue was raised at an early stage by the UN Secretary-General in a speech to the second session of the Conference, when he highlighted to delegates that "inevitably ... the international community would continue to evolve and its uses of the sea would continue to develop and diversify."[2] The Secretary-General went on to advocate that "the Conference ...

[1] Statement of Sri Lanka, 187th meeting, *Official Records of the Third United Nations Conference on the Law of the Sea*, Vol. 17, at 48, at para. 161.
[2] Statement by the UN Secretary-General, 14th meeting, Thursday 20 June 1974, *Official Records of the Third United Nations Conference on the Law of the Sea*, Vol. 1, 35, at 38, at para. 42.

might well consider whether some institutional means should be created whereby, within the framework of the new convention, common measures could be agreed upon and taken whenever necessary so as to avoid obsolescence under changing world conditions."[3]

Several proposals were made regarding such an institutional mechanism including the creation of a permanent commission on the law of the sea[4] and a periodic conference on international ocean affairs.[5] A similar mechanism proposed by various states was the possibility of convening a review conference after a certain period of time in order to review the implementation of the Convention and to propose revisions.[6] What all of these proposals have in common is the creation of a forum for the purpose of reviewing the implementation of the Convention.

Owing to the lack of agreement, however, the idea of a general review conference was gradually dropped from the negotiating agenda[7] and delegates concentrated their minds on designing robust amendment procedures instead. Part XVII of the Convention contains a number of amendment procedures and these are the principal means through which the drafters anticipated that changes to the Convention would be made.

At the same time, the need for some institutional mechanism to oversee the implementation of the Convention was accommodated in Article 319, which provides that the UN Secretary-General shall report to, inter alia, all States Parties to the Convention "on issues of a general nature that have arisen with respect to [the] Convention."[8] Although it was not expressly anticipated in the Convention itself, the Meeting of the States Parties has become an annual event that offers states the opportunity to oversee developments in the law of the sea regime.

---

[3] *Ibid.*

[4] Peru: Proposal regarding an international commission on the law of the sea, Document A/CONF.62/L.22, *Official records of the Third United Nations Conference on the Law of the Sea*, Vol. 9, at 180.

[5] Portugal: proposal regarding periodic conferences on international ocean affairs, Document A/CONF.62/L.23, *Official records of the Third United Nations Conference on the Law of the Sea*, Vol. 9, at 181.

[6] The idea of a review conference was included in the first set of draft articles proposed by the Chairman of the Group of Legal Experts on Final Clauses prepared in 1979. See M. Nordquist *et al.* (ed.), *United Nations Convention on the Law of the Sea – A Commentary, Vol. 5* (1989, Martinus Nijhoff Publishers) at 252–3.

[7] See *ibid.*, at 259–60.   [8] Law of the Sea Convention, Article 319(2)(a).

This chapter will consider these different mechanisms for updating the Convention regime. First, it will analyze the amendment procedures in the Convention, asking whether they offer an effective means to ensure the integrity of the law of the sea regime. Secondly, it will consider the role of the Meeting of the States Parties in overseeing the Convention. It will examine what law-making powers the Meeting of the States Parties possesses to implement, interpret or modify the Convention in order to meet contemporary challenges in the law of the sea regime.

2 Amendment of the Law of the Sea Convention

2.1 Introduction to the amendment procedures

Amendment is one of the principal ways in which a treaty can be adapted to meet the changing needs of the contracting parties. Article 39 of the Vienna Convention on the Law of Treaties lays down the fundamental principle that "a treaty may be amended by agreement between the parties."[9] While the Vienna Convention suggests a basic procedure for the adoption of amendments, it also makes clear that the drafters of a treaty may design their own amendment procedures to apply to a particular treaty.[10]

In common with most modern multilateral treaties, the Law of the Sea Convention includes its own specific amendment procedures. The formal process of amending the Law of the Sea Convention is dealt with in a series of articles found in the final provisions of the Convention. At an early stage, it was recognized by those delegates involved in drafting the amendment procedures that it would be necessary to balance the need for flexibility on the one hand with the desire to protect the integrity of the Convention on the other hand.[11] These provisions are

---

[9] Vienna Convention on the Law of Treaties, Article 39.

[10] Vienna Convention on the Law of Treaties, Article 39 says that "The rules laid down in Part II apply to such an agreement except insofar as the treaty may otherwise provide." As concluded by Aust, "it is wrong to think that the Vienna Convention is a rigid structure which places obstacles in the way of treaty modification: rather, it allows states to include in treaties such amendment provisions (good or bad) as they wish"; A. Aust, *Modern Treaty Law and Practice* (2nd edn., Cambridge University Press, 2007) at 264.

[11] See President's Note; Informal Plenary on Final Clauses (Doc. FC/4 of 1 August 1979); reproduced in R. Platzöder (ed.), *Third United Nations Conference on the Law of the Sea: Documents*, Vol. 12, (Oceana Publications, 1982–1988) at 354–5.

therefore the result of a careful compromise that seeks, as far as possible, to achieve this aim.

There is no single amendment procedure that applies to all parts of the Convention. A general distinction is drawn between amendments to the deep seabed mining provisions in Part XI of the Convention and amendments to those provisions in other parts of the Convention. Amendment of Part XI of the Convention falls within the competence of the International Seabed Authority and this procedure will be considered in a subsequent chapter. Amendments to the other parts of the Convention can be adopted using one of the two general amendment procedures contained in Articles 312 and 313, which will be discussed below.

2.2 The general amendment procedure

The first general amendment procedure is set out in Article 312 of the Convention, which provides in part:

After the expiry of a period of 10 years from the date of entry into force of this Convention, a State Party may, by written communication addressed to the Secretary-General of the United Nations, propose specific amendments to this Convention, other than those relating to activities in the Area, and request the convening of a conference to consider such proposed amendments. The Secretary-General shall circulate such communication to all States Parties. If, within 12 months from the date of the circulation of the communication, not less than one half of the States Parties reply favourably to the request, the Secretary-General shall convene the conference.

The first thing to note about this provision is that it only became available ten years after entry into force of the Convention. Freestone and Elferink speculate that "the intent of the ten-year period, which expired on 16 November 2004, could be considered to be to provide the Convention regime with a chance of proving itself in practice and prevent immediate challenges to the package deal regime."[12] In other words, the temporal limitation was aimed at preserving the integrity of the Convention for its initial period of operation. It is implicitly recognized in this view that the amendment procedures potentially

---

[12] D. Freestone and A. Oude Elferink, "Flexibility and innovation in the law of the sea – will the LOS Convention amendment procedures ever be used?" in A. Oude Elferink (ed.), *Stability and Change in the Law of the Sea: The Role of the LOS Convention* (Martinus Nijhoff Publishers, 2005) at 176.

threaten the package deal negotiated at the Third United Nations Conference on the Law of the Sea.[13]

Under Article 312, a specific proposal for an amendment is to be submitted to the UN Secretary-General who will circulate the proposal to all the States Parties.[14] States Parties will be asked to approve the convening of an amendment conference in order to discuss the proposal.[15] At least fifty percent of the States Parties must communicate their consent to the convening of an amendment conference within twelve months.

Article 312(2) says very little about how an amendment conference would be expected to operate. The amendment conference is expected to closely follow the types of decision-making procedures used at UNCLOS III, although the precise procedures to be followed would be a matter for the amendment conference itself. Nevertheless, the Convention urges that "the conference should make every effort to reach an agreement on any amendments by way of consensus and there should be no voting on them until all efforts at consensus have been exhausted."[16] In this way, the Convention seeks to promote the integrity of the law of the sea regime by ensuring, as far as possible, that all States Parties accept any amendment that is negotiated.

While the text of the Convention makes no reference to participation of non-parties at amendment conferences, it is likely that a wide range of states and international institutions would be invited to participate in its proceedings, at least as observers. Thus, it is possible that the interests of those states that are not a party to the Convention could also be taken into account in formulating amendments, in this way maintaining the wider consensus over the law of the sea regime that was achieved at UNCLOS III.

Article 312 says that the amendment conference may "consider the proposed amendment." It would appear from the ordinary meaning of this text that the amendment conference is limited to considering

---

[13] Hereinafter, UNCLOS III.

[14] Note that the International Tribunal for the Law of the Sea may propose amendments to its Statute through a written communication to the States Parties, but that the decision to invoke the amendment procedure rests with the States Parties themselves; Law of the Sea Convention, Annex VI, Article 41(3).

[15] See Freestone and Oude Elferink, "Flexibility and innovation in the law of the sea," at 176.

[16] Law of the Sea Convention, Article 312(2). However, amendments to the Statute of the International Tribunal for the Law of the Sea must be adopted by consensus; see ibid., Annex VI, Article 41(1).

a proposal that had been previously circulated by the UN Secretary-General. The rationale for this limitation would seem to be to prevent an amendment conference turning into a general review of the law of the sea regime, thereby completely unraveling the package deal agreed at UNCLOS III. However, Freestone and Elferink suggest that "the amendment conference should be considered to be allowed to adopt changes to the proposed amendments," although they also accept that "the wording seems to suggest that such a conference could not adopt amendments that are wholly unrelated to the subject matter of the specific amendments contained in the original written communication."[17] While this view is the most consistent with a literal reading of the text of the Convention,[18] it is likely that any amendment conference would take a fairly flexible attitude to its mandate in the interest of seeking to maintain a consensus over the law of the regime as a whole. This may require other aspects of the law of the sea to be considered alongside the proposed amendment.

While amendments should be adopted by consensus if possible, it is ultimately open for an amendment conference to adopt an amendment by a majority vote. However, adoption alone does not make the amendment binding and any amendments adopted under this procedure must be subject to formal acceptance in accordance with Article 316, which is discussed below.

2.3 The simplified amendment procedure

A second amendment procedure is found in Article 313 of the Convention, which sets out a simplified amendment procedure. Unlike the previous amendment procedure, Article 313 contains no temporal limits on its invocation. Thus, it has been available since the Convention entered into force in November 1994. The lack of a temporal limitation in Article 313 can be explained by the fact that any amendments must be approved by all States Parties, and so this procedure does not threaten the integrity of the law of the sea regime in the same way as Article 312.[19]

---

[17] Freestone and Oude Elferink, "Flexibility and innovation in the law of the sea," at 176.

[18] Freestone and Oude Elferink also note that it is consistent with the drafting history of the Convention; ibid., footnote 38.

[19] Freestone and Elferink say "this distinction seems to have been intended to allow amendments necessary to keep the Convention up-to-date to be made at any point"; ibid., at 177.

The simplified amendment procedure in Article 313 permits any State Party to circulate an amendment proposal to all other States Parties through the UN Secretary-General. A proposal that is circulated in this way is automatically considered to be adopted if no State Party objects to the proposal within twelve months of the date on which it was circulated. Although the simplified procedure in Article 313 provides for the tacit approval of amendments by the States Parties, it only requires the objection of a single State Party to frustrate the process of adoption. In effect, each State Party wields a veto over any proposal made under this procedure. Nevertheless, given that Article 313 does not require the States Parties to meet in formal session in order to adopt the proposed amendment, the procedure is a more efficient and cost-effective mechanism than the amendment procedure available under Article 312.[20] At the same time, there are disadvantages to the lack of institutional oversight. First, the simplified procedure does not allow for any substantive discussion of proposed amendments. As a result, it would seem that this procedure is most appropriate for technical changes of a *de minimis* character that do not affect any of the fundamental principles of the Convention. Secondly, the need to wait for one year for the adoption of a proposal make this procedure less attractive for adopting quick fixes to the Convention regime.[21] Another disadvantage stemming from the lack of any institutional oversight of proposed amendments circulated under Article 313 is that there is no opportunity for non-parties to participate in the adoption process or to express concerns over proposed amendments. Finally, amendments adopted under Article 313 also require subsequent approval by individual States Parties in accordance with Article 316.

2.4 *The entry into force of amendments*

Once amendments have been adopted under either Article 312 or Article 313, they will be notified to all States Parties by the UN Secretary-General[22] and they will be opened for signature for twelve months from the date of adoption, unless it is agreed otherwise.[23]

---

[20] Cost-effectiveness appears to be a factor that increasingly influences developments in this area; see Agreement Relating to the Implementation of Part XI of the United Nations Convention on the Law of the Sea of 10 December 1982 (Part XI Agreement), section 1, at para. 2.

[21] In practice, Article 313 has been superseded by regular Meetings of the States Parties. See below.

[22] Law of the Sea Convention, Article 319(d).

[23] Law of the Sea Convention, Article 315(1).

The entry into force of amendments adopted under either of the procedures considered above is dealt with by Article 316 of the Convention. Article 316(1) provides that an amendment will enter into force thirty days after the deposit of instruments of acceptance by two thirds of the States Parties or sixty States, whichever is greater.[24] This requirement in itself sets such a high threshold for the entry into force of amendments that Freestone and Elferink conclude it "is likely to prove an insurmountable hurdle for most amendments."[25]

The high number of acceptances is not the only problem posed by the entry into force requirements of the Convention. Another difficulty stems from the fact that amendments which have met the requirements for entry into force under Article 316(1) will nevertheless only be binding on those States Parties which have accepted them through ratification or accession; they will not be binding on other States Parties which have not submitted an instrument of ratification or accession. This reflects the principle found in Article 40(4) of the 1969 Vienna Convention on the Law of Treaties, which provides that "[an] amending agreement does not bind any State already a party to the treaty which does not become a party to the amending agreement."[26] While such a process places a high value on consent and the sovereignty of states, it poses a threat to the integrity of the law of the sea regime as it means that two different versions of the Convention could exist side by side.

The possibility of a fragmented law of the sea regime is confirmed by Article 316(4) of the Convention, which provides that:

A State which becomes a Party to this Convention after the entry into force of an amendment ... shall failing an expression of a different intention by that State:

(a)   be considered as a Party to this Convention as so amended; and
(b)   be considered as a Party to the unamended Convention in relation to any State Party not bound by the amendment.

The only way in which such fragmentation could be avoided is to require all States Parties to ratify or accede to an amendment before it

---

[24] At the time of writing, there are 160 States Parties to the Convention. Therefore, at least 107 states would need to submit instruments of acceptance in order for an amendment to enter into force.

[25] Freestone and Oude Elferink, "Flexibility and innovation in the law of the sea," at 179.

[26] See also the Vienna Convention on the Law of Treaties, Article 34.

enters into force. Article 316(2) the Convention does allow states to set a higher level of acceptance for the entry into force of an amendment at the time at which it is adopted.[27] Yet, with more than 150 States Parties to the Convention, a requirement for universal acceptance would in all likelihood paralyze the amendment process.

The Law of the Sea Convention has been in force for more than fifteen years and neither of these amendment procedures has yet been invoked.[28] Indeed, given the threat to the integrity of the law of the sea regime described above, it is questionable whether states would want to rely on them. This is particularly the case as modifications to the legal regime can be achieved in other ways that are more likely to maintain the consensus underlying the legal order of the oceans.

3 Law-making by the Meeting of the States Parties

3.1 Functions of the Meeting of the States Parties

A Conference of the Parties or COP is a common arrangement in many modern multilateral agreements. In assessing their law-making function, Werksman describes how "many COPs are empowered by the underlying treaty to take decisions or actions that may be required for the achievement of the agreement's objective or purposes."[29] The creation of a Conference of the Parties allows the contracting parties to regularly monitor the implementation of a treaty, ensuring its evolution in light of changes in the legal and political environment.

The Law of the Sea Convention does not formally establish a Conference of the Parties. Yet several important functions are ascribed to the States Parties at various points through the text. Aside from the adoption of amendments, mention of the States Parties is also made in the provisions relating to the election, administration and financing

---

[27] Article 316(2) says "an amendment may provide that a larger number of ratifications or accessions shall be required for its entry into force than are required by this Article."

[28] The possibility of invoking Article 313 was mooted by the UN Secretary-General in relation to extending the time limit for making submissions to the Commission on the Outer Limits of the Continental Shelf, but ultimately an ordinary decision of the Meeting of the States Parties was used. See below.

[29] J. Werksman, "The Conference of the Parties to Environmental Treaties," in J. Werksman (ed.), *Greening International Institutions* (Earthscan Publications, 1996) at 63.

of the International Tribunal for the Law of the Sea[30] and the election and administration of the Commission on the Outer Limits on the Continental Shelf.[31] In order to carry out these functions, the UN Secretary-General is required to "convene necessary meetings of the States Parties in accordance with the Convention."[32]

The Rules of Procedure adopted by the Meeting of the States Parties set out in more detail the circumstance in which meetings shall be convened.[33] Rule 3(1) repeats the instruction found in Article 319 of the Convention that the Secretary-General shall convene meetings of the States Parties "when he considers it necessary." Rule 4 provides more specific guidance on when meetings may be necessary by prescribing that meetings shall be held every three years for the election of members of the Tribunal, every five years for the election of members of the Commission and "as necessary in order to deal with the matters referred to in articles 18[34] and 19[35] of the [Statute of the Tribunal] and other matters concerning the organization of the International Tribunal or the Commission."

In addition to the duty of the Secretary-General to convene meetings when he considers it necessary, Rule 3(2) further provides that any State Party may request the convening of a meeting.[36] If a majority of the States Parties concurs with the request within 30 days, a meeting shall be convened.

While the Convention and the Rules of Procedure tend to give the impression that meetings of the States Parties will take place on an ad hoc basis, in practice they have taken place regularly since the Convention entered into force on November 16, 1994. The first meeting of the States Parties took place in November 1994, shortly after the entry into force of the Convention.[37] Thereafter, meetings of the States Parties have been convened annually in the spring at the headquarters of the United Nations in New York.[38] Occasionally the States Parties

---

[30] Hereinafter, Tribunal.   [31] Hereinafter, Commission.   [32] *Ibid.*, Article 319(2)(e).

[33] *Rules of procedure for meetings of the States Parties*, Document SPLOS/2/Rev.4, January 24, 2005.

[34] Article 18 deals with remuneration of members of the Tribunal.

[35] Article 19 deals with expenses of the Tribunal.

[36] Presumably, a request should be accompanied by an explanation of why that State Party considers a meeting is necessary.

[37] *Report of the meeting of States Parties*, Document SPLOS/3, February 28, 1995.

[38] In practice, Meetings of the States Parties take place immediately prior to the Informal Consultative Process; see Chapter 8.

will also meet in special session in order to deal with particular issues that demand their immediate attention.[39]

The precise competence of the Meeting of the States Parties has been the subject of some discussion. As the Convention requires the Meeting of the States Parties to undertake certain tasks in connection with the functioning of the Tribunal and the Commission, it is no surprise that its agenda has been dominated by issues relating to these bodies. Yet, there is also a question whether the Meeting of the States Parties can consider a wider range of law of the sea issues.

Following a proposal from New Zealand, a new item was included on the agenda under the title "the role of the Meeting of the States Parties in reviewing ocean and law of the sea issues."[40] Yet, in the ensuing discussion, there was disagreement on precisely what this role should be. These disagreements perpetuated for a number of sessions.[41] Since the fourteenth Meeting of the States Parties in 2004, the agenda has included an item on the "Report of the Secretary General under article 319 for the information of States Parties on issues of a general nature relevant to States Parties that have arisen with respect to the United Nations Convention on the Law of the Sea." The inclusion of this item on the agenda was not without controversy and precisely what action the Meeting of the States Parties can take in relation to this report has remained contentious.

Some argue that the Meeting of the States Parties is only competent to consider matters associated with those functions ascribed to it by the text of the treaty.[42] For instance, it has been suggested that the use of the terms "necessary" and "in accordance with this Convention" in connection with the duty of the UN Secretary-General to convene meetings of the States Parties points towards a restrictive interpretation of their powers.[43] On this view, the Meeting of the States Parties receives the report from the Secretary-General for information purposes only.

---

[39] For example, a Special Meeting of States Parties was convened on March 6, 2009 in order to elect one member of the International Tribunal for the Law of the Sea; see *Report of the special meeting of the States Parties*, Document SPLOS/190, March 6, 2009.

[40] *Report of the sixth meeting of the States Parties (10 to 14 March 1997)*, Document SPLOS/20, at paras. 33 and 36.

[41] See in particular, *Report of the ninth meeting of the States Parties (19 to 28 May 1999)*, Document SPLOS/48, at paras. 49–53.

[42] *Report of the fifteenth meeting of States Parties (16 to 23 June 2005)*, Document SPLOS/135, at para. 82.

[43] T. Treves, "The General Assembly and the Meeting of States Parties in the implementation of the LOS Convention," in A. Oude Elferink (ed.), *Stability and*

On the other hand, an argument can also be made that the Meeting of the States Parties possesses a general power to discuss and adopt decisions on any aspect of the Convention. This decision-making power can be implied in part from Article 319 of the Convention, which requires the UN Secretary-General to report to the States Parties, as well as from general international law that recognizes that the parties to a treaty are competent to discuss and make decisions on that instrument.[44]

This controversy has not yet been solved. Despite having achieved a compromise to include the report of the Secretary-General on the agenda of the Meeting of the States Parties, there nevertheless remains "a basic disagreement between States holding that the [Meeting of the States Parties] should not address questions of substance and those holding the opposite view."[45] This is not a purely legal dispute over the powers of the Meeting of the States Parties, but also a political issue about which is the most appropriate forum for considering law of the sea issues.

The fact that a number of important maritime states are not parties to the Convention is one reason why the Meeting of the States Parties is not considered as an appropriate institution to oversee the implementation of the Convention as a whole.[46] As most of the substantive rules found in the Convention are applicable to almost all states as a matter of customary international law, it is desirable that all states are able to participate in discussions concerning their development.

It should be noted that the limited membership of the Meeting of the States Parties does not mean that other states are excluded from discussions in this forum. The practice of the Meeting of the States Parties has been to permit non-parties to participate in its proceedings. Invitations to the first Meeting of the States Parties in November 1994 were addressed to all States Parties, as well as all other states and several international organizations and other non-state entities referred

Change in the Law of the Sea: The Role of the LOS Convention (Martinus Nijhoff Publishers, 2005) at 58.

[44] See Vienna Convention on the Law of Treaties, Article 31(3). See also the views expressed in Report of the twelfth meeting of the States Parties (16 to 26 April 2002), Document SPLOS/91, at para. 114: "In [the view of several delegations], the Meeting did have the competence to consider issues relating to the implementation of the Convention; to say otherwise would, in the view of one delegation, contradict article 319 of the Convention and the law of treaties."

[45] Treves, "The General Assembly and the Meeting of States Parties in the implementation of the LOS Convention," at 64.

[46] Ibid., at 62.

to in Article 305 of the Convention.[47] Moreover, at this meeting the provisional Rules of Procedure were specifically amended to allow the participation of non-parties in their proceedings. Rule 15 allowed states that had signed the Convention but were not yet parties to attend as observers.[48] The Rules of Procedure allow for extensive rights of participation for observer states, permitting them to take part in discussions and deliberations, albeit without a vote.[49] Indeed, observer states actually outnumbered States Parties for the first few sessions of the Meeting of the States Parties.[50] The rules on participation of observers were amended again at the seventh Meeting of the States Parties in May 1997, where it was agreed to further extend rights of participation to "States Members of the United Nations or members of specialized agencies of the United Nations or the International Atomic Energy Agency."[51] The purpose of this amendment was to permit the participation of states that had come into being since UNCLOS III. In other words, it allowed any state to attend and participate in the proceedings of the States Parties as observers. Nevertheless, the rights of observers are inherently limited. While they may contribute to the discussion, they are not able to participate in formal decision-making. As nonparties do not have the same rights as States Parties, it follows that there is always the threat that their interests may be overridden by the invocation of the voting procedures. It is arguably for this reason that substantive discussions on the law of the sea have taken place in other institutional frameworks such as the UN General Assembly where all states participate on an equal footing.[52] For its own part, the Meeting of the States Parties has tended to limit itself to discussing and deciding upon those aspects of the law of the sea regime for which it has been made explicitly responsible under the Convention.[53] This does

---

[47] Document SPLOS/3, at para. 1.   [48] *Ibid.*, at para. 12.

[49] Document SPLOS/2/Rev.4, Rules 18(1) and (6). An equivalent right is given to the International Seabed Authority in Rule 18(2) and (6). Other observers, that is those categories identified in Article 319(3)(b) of the Convention, may attend but may only make written statements on the invitation of the president and with the permission of the Meeting; *ibid.*, Rule 18(7).

[50] The president of the Fifth Meeting of the States Parties noted that the number of States Parties had for the first time exceeded 100 states at that meeting; *Report of the fifth meeting of the States Parties (24 July–2 August 1996)*, Document SPLOS/14, at para. 7.

[51] *Report of the seventh meeting of the States Parties (19–23 May 1997)*, Document SPLOS/24, at para. 28.

[52] See Chapter 8.

[53] When asked to give advice on the interpretation of certain provisions of the Convention by the Commission, the Meeting of the States Parties refused the

not mean that the Meeting of the States Parties has not played any role at all in developing the Convention. The Meeting of the States Parties has made some important decisions that have developed the law of the sea regime to deal with problems that have arisen in their application. The nature and extent of these decisions will be explored in the following sections.

3.2 Decision-making powers of the Meeting of the States Parties

The Convention expressly confers a number of decision-making powers on the States Parties connected with the setting up and the administration of the Tribunal and the Commission.[54] Yet, the role of the Meeting of the States Parties cannot be seen as exclusively an administrative one. The Meeting of the States Parties has used its decision-making powers to develop and in some cases modify the Convention in a number of ways.

Some parts of the Convention expressly call upon the Meeting of the States Parties to adopt rules and regulations in certain areas of its responsibility. For instance, Article 18(7) of Annex VI of the Convention provides that "regulations adopted at meetings of the States Parties shall determine the conditions under which retirement pensions may be given to members of the Tribunal and to the Registrar and the conditions under which members of the Tribunal and Registrar shall have their travelling expenses refunded." It was in pursuance of this mandate that the States Parties adopted the Pension Scheme Regulations at their ninth meeting in May 1999.[55] The Meeting of the States Parties is also charged with determining the salaries, allowances and compensation of members of the Tribunal and the salary of the Registrar.[56] Although such decisions are arguably of an administrative nature as they concern the financing and day-to-day operation of the Tribunal, they are nonetheless binding and they constitute part of the legal framework within which the Tribunal must operate.

---

request. One delegate stressed that "the Meeting of the States Parties did not have the competence to give a legal opinion." Several other delegations supported this view; see *Report of the eighth meeting of the States Parties (18–22 May 1998)*, Document SPLOS/31, at para. 52. Whether or not this view is legally accurate, it certainly reflects the desire that discussions on the interpretation of the Convention should take place in fora where all states are equally represented.

[54] See Law of the Sea Convention, Annex II, Article 2; Annex VI, Articles 4, 6, 18, 19.
[55] Document SPLOS/48, at para. 40.
[56] Law of the Sea Convention, Annex VI, Article 18(5) and (6).

The provisions that expressly confer decision-making powers on the Meeting of the States Parties may also impose limits on those powers. For instance, the Convention provides that payments to the members of the Tribunal "may not be decreased during the term of office."[57] The purpose of this limitation is to protect the independence of the Tribunal. Any decision which was designed to decrease the salary or other payments to members of the Tribunal would arguably be ultra vires and without legal effect.[58]

In the exercise of its functions, the Meeting has also adopted decisions that, although not expressly demanded by the Convention, purport to interpret the Convention text. The power of the parties to a treaty to interpret a treaty is clearly reflected in the law of treaties, which requires that a treaty interpreter take into account "any subsequent agreement between the parties regarding the interpretation of a treaty or the application of its provisions."[59]

One example of the Meeting of the States Parties exercising a power to interpret the Convention is the adoption of procedures for the election of Members of the Tribunal. This issue is regulated in part by the Convention itself, which sets out basic criteria for the election of judges to the Tribunal. The Convention says how many judges shall be elected[60] and it additionally requires that the composition of the Tribunal shall assure "representation of the principal legal systems of the world and equitable geographical distribution."[61] Moreover, it specifies that there should be no fewer than three representatives from each of the five geographical regions of the United Nations.[62]

The first election of judges to the Tribunal was due to take place at the fifth Meeting of the States Parties in 1996. Following informal consultations conducted by the president of the Meeting, it was agreed by consensus that all of the seats on the Tribunal would be allocated between the five geographical regions of the United Nations.[63] This

---

[57] Ibid., Annex VI, Article 18(5).
[58] There is of course the question of whether there is an available forum in which to challenge an ultra vires decision of the Meeting of the States Parties; see E. Osieke, "The legal validity of ultra vires decisions of international organizations" (1983) 77 Am. J. Int'l L. 239, at 242; cf. C. F. Amerasinghe, Principles of the Institutional Law of International Organizations (2nd edn., Cambridge University Press, 2005) at 178–9.
[59] Vienna Convention on the Law of Treaties, Article 31(3)(a).
[60] Law of the Sea Convention, Annex VI, Article 2.
[61] Ibid., Annex VI, Article 2(2).   [62] Ibid., Annex VI, Article 3(2).
[63] Document SPLOS/14.

decision provided for five judges to be elected from the African Group, five judges from the Asian Group, four judges from the Latin American and Caribbean Group, four judges from the Western Europe and Other Group, and three judges from the Eastern European Group.[64] While there is no explicit legal basis in the Convention for a decision of the States Parties to allocate the seats in this manner,[65] the decision has been applied and followed in subsequent elections to the Tribunal.[66]

In 2009 a new allocation of seats was agreed by consensus of the States Parties in order to reflect the growth of States Parties from the African and Asian groups of states.[67] According to the so-called "Arrangement for the allocation of seats on the International Tribunal for the Law of the Sea and the Commission on the Limits of the Continental Shelf," five members of the Tribunal would be elected by the Group of African States, five by the Group of Asian States, three by the Group of Eastern European States, four by the Group of Latin American States, and three by the Group of Western European and Other States. The remaining seat was to be elected from among the Group of African States, the Group of Asian States, and the Group of Western European and Other States.[68] This decision reflects the flexibility of interpretations adopted by the States Parties, which can be adapted over time to accommodate the changing circumstances of the Convention.

Not only have the States Parties sought to interpret the text of the Convention, they have also on occasion modified its provisions. International law can be said to support the ability of the parties to a treaty to modify its provisions through subsequent agreements. Aust,

---

[64] The decision of the States Parties resembles the understanding on the composition of the International Court of Justice which guarantees a seat to the five permanent members of the Security Council and allocates the remaining seats according to the pattern of equitable geographical distribution applied to the Security Council; see J. Merrills, *International Dispute Settlement* (4th edn., Cambridge University Press, 2005) at 147.

[65] Law of the Sea Convention, Annex VI, Article 4.

[66] Document SPLOS/48, at para. 29; Document SPLOS/135, at para. 36.

[67] For the initial proposal, see *Report of the seventeenth meeting of States Parties (14 to 23 June 2007)*, Document SPLOS/164, at para. 94. Although the arrangement was ultimately adopted by consensus, a number of African and Asian countries noted that they had only accepted the arrangement out of a spirit of cooperation and consensus; see *Report of the nineteenth meeting of the States Parties (22–26 June 2009)*, Document SPLOS/203, at para. 102.

[68] *Arrangement for the allocation of seats on the International Tribunal for the Law of the Sea and the Commission on the Limits of the Continental Shelf*, Document SPLOS/201, June 26, 2009, at paras. 1 and 2.

for instance, argues that "it is perfectly possible to supplement a treaty by an agreement which does not itself constitute a treaty, or by an oral agreement."[69] This is true even if an amendment procedure exists.[70]

An example of the Meeting of the States Parties modifying the Convention can be seen in the case of its decisions on the composition of the Commission. According to the Convention, the Commission is to be composed of twenty-one experts in the field of geology, geophysics or hydrography, elected by the States Parties.[71] In addition, the Convention provides that "no less than three members [of the Commission] shall be elected from each geographical region."[72] At the first elections for the Commission in March 1997, the Meeting of the States Parties agreed on the allocation of all of the seats on the Commission, thus supplementing the text of the Convention. Thus, the Commission would be composed of five members from the African States, five members from the Asian States, two members from the Eastern European States, four Members from the Latin American States and five members from the Western European and Other States.[73] This decision is similar to the decision on the composition of the Tribunal discussed above as it allocates seats on the Commission to particular geographical regions. However, it differs from that other decision because the composition of the Commission agreed by the States Parties in its decision of March 1997 deviates from the requirements of Annex II of the Convention. In an understanding reached through consultations between the president of the Meeting and the chairs of the regional groupings, it was agreed that the Group of Eastern European States would not fill the third seat to which it was entitled under the Convention. In describing the arrangement, it was stressed by the president of the Meeting that the arrangement was "on a purely ad hoc basis and relate[d] only to the first election of the members of the Commission."[74] He continued: "They should not be interpreted as derogating from the relevant provisions of the United Nations Convention on the Law of the Sea. They shall not prejudice arrangements for future elections and do not constitute a precedent."[75] This explanation strictly limits the validity of the modification to the

[69] See Aust, *Modern Treaty Law and Practice*, at 263.
[70] Aust gives the example of the 1973 Convention on International Trade in Endangered Species being modified by a conference resolution despite an amendment procedure having been built into the Convention; *ibid.*, at 263–4.
[71] Law of the Sea Convention, Annex II, Article 2(1).
[72] *Ibid.*, Annex II, Article 2(3).   [73] Document SPLOS/20, at para. 13.
[74] *Ibid.*   [75] *Ibid.*

composition of the Commission to the first election only. Indeed, at the second elections for members of the Commission in 2002, the distribution of seats was adjusted so that it was in conformity with the provisions of Annex II of the Convention.[76] Nevertheless, it cannot be denied that the effect of the decision was to derogate, albeit temporarily, from the text of the Convention.

There are other examples of law-making by the Meeting of States Parties where they seem to have modified the Convention.

At the first meeting of the States Parties in 1994, a question arose over the timing of elections to the Tribunal. The Convention provides that the first elections shall take place within six months of the entry into force of the Convention.[77] In other words, the elections should have been held before May 16, 1995. However, given the number of states that had indicated that their acceptance of the Convention was imminent, it was decided to postpone the first election of the Tribunal to August 1, 1996.[78] In addition, the decision extended the eligibility for election to candidates from states that were in the process of becoming a party to the Convention.[79] As with the decision on the composition of the Commission discussed above, this decision specified that it was a "one-time deferment" to the election schedule and that no further changes would be made unless the States Parties agreed by consensus.[80]

A similar decision was adopted in relation to the first election of the members of the Commission. The Convention provides that such elections shall take place within eighteen months of the entry into force of the Convention.[81] Thus, the Commission should have been elected before May 16, 1996. At the third Meeting of the States Parties, it was agreed to postpone the first election until March 1997.[82] Further

---

[76] Document SPLOS/91, at para. 97.

[77] Law of the Sea Convention, Annex VI, Article 4(3).

[78] Document SPLOS/3, at para. 16. This was based on a recommendation from the Preparatory Commission; see *Statement by the Chairman of the Preparatory Commission*, Document LOS/PCN/L.115/Rev.1, September 8, 1994, at para. 43, specifically citing the object of universal participation.

[79] Document SPLOS/3, at para. 16. For a description of the revised procedure, see *Election of members of the International Tribunal for the Law of the Sea – note by the Secretariat*, Document SPLOS/9, May 31, 2006.

[80] Document SPLOS/3, at para. 16(a) and (f).

[81] Law of the Sea Convention, Annex II, Article 2(2).

[82] *Report of the third meeting of the States Parties (27 November–1 December 1995)*, Document SPLOS/5, at para. 20.

details of how the elections would be conducted were agreed at the fifth Meeting of the States Parties in 1996 and it was again stated that "no change might be made to the [election] schedule unless the States Parties agreed by consensus."[83]

What all of these examples have in common is that they are concerned with relatively minor amendments to administrative aspects of the Convention regime. Nevertheless, the effect of them is to modify the Convention. What is interesting about these decisions is that they were adopted by a decision of the Meeting of the States Parties and not through invoking the formal amendment procedures discussed above. Indeed, in all of these examples there is a clear indication that once they were made, the decisions were deemed to be binding on the States Parties and they could not be reversed by a subsequent majority decision.

All of the examples considered above involve temporary changes to the Convention framework. Another, perhaps more significant, example of a decision by the States Parties which modifies the Convention regime is the postponement of the date from which the ten-year period for making submissions to the Commission is calculated. According to the Convention, a coastal state must submit particulars of its proposed outer continental shelf "as soon as possible, but in any case within 10 years of the entry into force of this Convention for that State."[84] From an early stage, many states, in particular developing nations, had expressed concern about complying with this deadline.[85] At the eleventh Meeting of the States Parties in 2001, a decision was adopted that the ten-year time limit should start from the date on which the Scientific and Technical Guidelines had been adopted by the Commission, that is May 13, 1999.[86] Accordingly, states for which the Convention entered into force before that date will not have to make submissions until May 13, 2009.[87] When making the decision, the Meeting of the States Parties discussed the form of any change to the text of Annex II. Possibilities included an amendment under

---

[83] Document SPLOS/14, at para. 42(e).
[84] Law of the Sea Convention, Annex II, Article 4.
[85] *Report of the tenth Meeting of the States Parties (22–26 May 2000)*, Document SPLOS/60, at para. 61.
[86] *Decision regarding the date of commencement of the ten-year period for making submissions to the Commission on the Limits of the Continental Shelf set out in Article 4 of Annex II to the United Nations Convention on the Law of the Sea (29 May 2001)*, Document SPLOS/72, May 29, 2001.
[87] *Ibid.*

Articles 312 or 313, an agreement relating to the implementation of Article 4 of Annex II or a decision of the States Parties.[88] It was decided that a decision of the States Parties, following the precedents for the postponements of elections discussed above, was appropriate to effectuate the necessary change.[89]

The issue of complying with the deadline for submissions to the Commission was not completely solved by the decision to postpone the deadline taken at the eleventh Meeting of the States Parties. The possibility of revisiting the issue of the ten-year time limit was raised at the sixteenth Meeting of the States Parties, but many states were not prepared to consider further adjustments.[90] Other options were explored in further consultations conducted by the president of the Meeting of the States Parties. The eighteenth Meeting of the States Parties duly adopted a decision according to which "the time period referred to in article 4 of annex II to the Convention and the decision contained in SPLOS/72, paragraph (a), may be satisfied by submitting to the Secretary-General preliminary information indicative of the outer limits of the continental shelf beyond 200 nautical miles and a description of the status of preparation and intended date of making a submission in accordance with the requirements of article 76 of the Convention."[91] This would appear to be another example of a decision of the Meeting of the States Parties modifying the Convention regime. Instead of requiring States Parties to submit "particulars" of their continental shelf limits along with "supporting scientific and technical data" within the ten-year period in accordance with Article 4 of Annex II of the Convention, the decision allows states to satisfy the time limit by providing much more limited information about their outer continental shelf claims. It is another demonstration of the willingness of the States Parties to modify the Convention regime through decision-making rather than through invoking the formal amendment procedures.

---

[88] *Report of the eleventh meeting of the States Parties (14–18 May 2001)*, Document SPLOS/73, at para. 78.

[89] Document SPLOS/72, supra, at para. 79.

[90] *Report of the sixteenth meeting of the States Parties (19–23 June 2006)*, Document SPLOS/148, at paras. 72–3.

[91] *Decision regarding the workload of the Commission on the Limits of the Continental Shelf and the ability of states, particularly developing states, to fulfil the requirements of article 4 of Annex II of the United Nations Convention on the Law of the Sea, as well as the decision contained in SPLOS/72, paragraph (a)*, Document SPLOS/183, June 20, 2008, at para. 1(a).

Both of these decisions concerning submissions to the Commission were intended to modify the requirements imposed by the Convention on states wanting to claim an outer continental shelf. Unlike the decisions discussed above, which were either temporary modifications or which had immediate effect, the changes had neither the same urgency nor the *de minimis* character as the previous instances and they can be said to be much more akin to a de facto amendment to the Convention.[92]

There are certainly advantages of using decisions of the States Parties to modify the Convention regime. First and foremost, this mechanism is quicker than invoking the amendment procedures, which not only require the circulation of proposed amendments to States Parties, but also formally require individual consent before amendments become binding. By contrast, decisions of the Meeting of the States Parties can have immediate effect.

A limitation on the use of decisions to modify a treaty is that they must be supported by all parties to the treaty if they are to be effective. While the rules of procedure do allow for the possibility of voting "after all efforts at achieving general agreement have been exhausted,"[93], decisions of the States Parties modifying the Convention arguably demand consensus. At most, a decision adopted by a majority could be considered as being binding on those states that had voted in its favor. Yet, it is clear that a majority decision could not be applied to any dissenting states, as it would have the effect of altering the established treaty rights of those states against their will.[94]

3.3 Treaty-making by the Meeting of the States Parties

Another way in which the States Parties have contributed to the development of the law of the sea regime is by acting as a forum for the negotiation and adoption of treaties. No formal treaty-making powers are expressly conferred on the States Parties by the Convention.

---

[92] Cf. T. Treves, "The General Assembly and the Meeting of States Parties in the implementation of the LOS Convention," at 71–2.

[93] *Rules of the procedure for the meeting of the States Parties*, Document SPLOS/2/Rev.4, Rule 52.

[94] R. Churchill, "The impact of State Practice on the jurisdictional framework contained in the United Nations Convention on the Law of the Sea," in A. Oude Elferink (ed.) *Stability and Change in the Law of the Sea: The Role of the LOS Convention* (Martinus Nijhoff Publishers, 2005) at 574.

Nevertheless, at its seventh session in May 1997, the Meeting of the States Parties adopted the Agreement on Privileges and Immunities of the International Tribunal for the Law of the Sea. In relation to privileges and immunities of the Tribunal, the Convention itself simply provides that "the members of the Tribunal, when engaged on the business of the Tribunal, shall enjoy diplomatic privileges and immunities."[95] The Agreement on Privileges and Immunities fills in the gaps in the Convention by building on this basic clause and specifying the scope of the immunities and privileges of the Tribunal itself, as well as including further provisions covering the treatment of judges, staff members, witnesses, experts and advocates appearing before the Tribunal.

Although negotiated by the Meeting of the States Parties, the Agreement is open to all states.[96] Indeed, the UN General Assembly has called on "states that have not done so to consider ratifying or acceding to the Agreement."[97] The Agreement itself also seeks to promote its application among as many states as possible by providing for a number of additional ways in which states can indicate their consent to be bound without becoming a full party. As well as formal acceptance through ratification or accession, special procedures allow for provisional application by states which intend to ratify or accede to the Agreement in the future[98] as well as the ad hoc application of the Agreement, which allows any state to accept the Agreement for the duration of a particular dispute.[99]

The adoption of the Agreement was not without objection. There was some discussion over the capacity of the Meeting of the States Parties to adopt an international treaty and several states, including Russia and Brazil, expressed reservations about whether they had the mandate to do so.[100] While this is the only occasion on which such a power has been utilized by the Meeting of the States Parties, the future negotiation of treaties cannot be completely ruled out. The Agreement on Privileges and Immunities of the International Tribunal for the Law of the Sea could be considered as having set a precedent for this type of law-making by the Meeting of the States Parties.

[95] Law of the Sea Convention, Annex VI, Article 10.
[96] Agreement on Privileges and Immunities, Articles 27 and 29.
[97] *Oceans and the law of the sea*, UNGA Resolution 61/222, December 20, 2006, at para. 33.
[98] Agreement on Privileges and Immunities, Article 31.
[99] Agreement on Privileges and Immunities, Article 32.
[100] See Document SPLOS/24, at para. 27.

4 Conclusion

In order to provide a stable framework for the law of the sea, it was recognized that the Convention would have to be able to adapt to the changing needs of the international community. This chapter has considered a variety of ways in which the law of the sea regime can be developed.

The starting point of the chapter was the formal amendment procedures found in the Law of the Sea Convention itself. It was argued that these procedures are unlikely to be used in practice as they are both time-consuming and the entry into force requirements for amendments threaten the integrity of the law of the sea regime.

In practice, there are other ways in which the Convention regime can be adapted to meet contemporary challenges. The Meeting of the States Parties offers an alternative mechanism in which changes to the Convention regime can be made. This body has adopted a number of decisions that have had the effect of interpreting or modifying the Convention. Some of these decisions are based upon express powers conferred by the Convention, whereas other decisions have been adopted using implied powers of the Meeting of the States Parties to interpret or modify the Convention. The adoption of decisions for these purposes offers the advantages of speed and efficiency. However, such decisions must be adopted by consensus if they are to maintain the universality and integrity of the law of the sea regime. In this regard, it is interesting to note that the Meeting of the States Parties has utilized many of the consensus decision-making techniques that were first developed at UNCLOS III. For instance, the President of the Meeting has taken a leading role in facilitating discussions and the use of informal consultations in order to achieve a compromise on crucial issues has been frequent. To date, the Meeting of the States Parties has managed to maintain the fragile consensus that exists in this area.

There are also limits on the role that the Meeting of the States Parties plays in the development of the Convention regime. In particular, the fact that not all states are yet States Parties to the Convention has meant that other institutional frameworks have been used to undertake major developments in the law of the sea regime. Arguably the most important developments have been the adoption of the two implementing agreements that will be considered in the following chapter.

4   Implementing agreements

1 Introduction

A large number of international treaties have been adopted in the field of maritime affairs since the conclusion of the Law of the Sea Convention in 1982. The Convention itself expressly foresees that States Parties will continue to regulate their relations through subsequent treaties.[1] Among the treaties which have been concluded on the law of the sea during this period, two in particular stand out because of their close relationship with the Convention and because of the impact they have had on the regime contained therein. These are the 1994 Agreement Relating to the Implementation of Part XI of the 1982 Convention on the Law of the Sea of December 10, 1982[2] and the 1995 Agreement for the Implementation of the Provisions of the United Nations Convention on the Law of the Sea of December 10, 1982 relating to the Conservation and Management of Straddling Fish Stocks and Highly Migratory Fish Stocks.[3] Both the Part XI Agreement and the Fish Stocks Agreement have been characterized as "implementing agreements" by the international community.[4] However, the title of the treaties does not normally have any particular significance in itself.[5] Rather, it is more important to consider their purpose and their legal effects.

It is suggested that the importance of the implementing agreements lies in the fact that they were negotiated in order to rectify problems

---

[1] Law of the Sea Convention, Article 311.
[2] Hereinafter, the Part XI Agreement.
[3] Hereinafter, the Fish Stocks Agreement.
[4] See e.g. *Oceans and the law of the sea, report of the Secretary-General*, Document A/64/66/ Add.1, at para. 3.
[5] See A. McNair, *The Law of Treaties* (Clarenden Press, 1961) at 22.

or omissions that were identified with the legal regime contained in the Law of the Sea Convention. Yet they would only be able to achieve this aim if they garnered the support of the international community in a similar way to the Law of the Sea Convention itself. Therefore, it is necessary to consider how these treaties were negotiated.

The purpose of this chapter is to consider the normative effects of the two implementing agreements on the law of the sea. The negotiating history of these two instruments will be described before considering their relationship with the Convention. In particular, it will be asked whether these instruments have managed to influence the development of the law of the sea regime for parties and non-parties alike in a similar way to the Law of the Sea Convention.

2 The Part XI Agreement

2.1 Negotiation of the Part XI Agreement

As explained in Chapter 2, it was the question of deep seabed mining that ultimately divided the delegates at UNCLOS III. Many industrialized countries, led by the United States, were unable to accept the provisions on the International Seabed Area contained in Part XI of the Convention and they made clear that they would not become a party to the Convention unless substantial changes were made. It was therefore clear that, if the Law of the Sea Convention were to attain universal participation, further negotiations would have to take place over the content of Part XI. The question was which forum should host such negotiations?

As the Convention had not entered into force at this time, the amendment procedures in the Convention could not be formally invoked in order to introduce any changes to it. The question was therefore which institution should discuss possible changes to the Convention regime and what form any changes should take.

One available forum was the Preparatory Commission for the International Seabed Authority and the International Tribunal for the Law of the Sea,[6] which had been created by Resolution 1 of the Third United Nations Conference on the Law of the Sea.[7] The Commission met from 1983 and it provided a forum within which to discuss issues relating to the International Seabed Area. Detailed discussions on

---

[6] Hereinafter, the Preparatory Commission.
[7] Hereinafter, UNCLOS III.

how to implement Part XI of the Convention were undertaken by the Preparatory Commission in accordance with its mandate to prepare draft rules and procedures for adoption by the International Seabed Authority when it was ultimately established.[8]

Despite its focus on law of the sea issues, and in particular the deep seabed regime, the Preparatory Commission was arguably not an appropriate forum in which to resolve the disputes over the regulation of the deep seabed for a number of reasons. The first limitation stemmed from the restricted powers of the Preparatory Commission. The resolution establishing the Preparatory Commission did not confer any substantive powers on the Commission that allowed it to alter the regime that was contained in Part XI of the Convention. The mandate of the Preparatory Commission was limited to producing a report for presentation to the first session of the Assembly of the International Seabed Authority on how to operationalize the regime.[9] Moreover, Resolution 1 made clear that any action proposed by the Preparatory Commission "must be in conformity with the provisions of the Convention concerning the powers and functions entrusted to the respective organs of the Assembly."[10] Thus, the Preparatory Commission was expressly prohibited from reopening discussions that had taken place at UNCLOS III. The second major obstacle to the Preparatory Commission acting as a forum to consider how to modify Part XI was its limited membership. Only those states that had signed the Convention or acceded to it were full participants in the Preparatory Commission.[11] While states that had signed the final act of the Third Conference on the Law of the Sea could participate in the deliberations of the Preparatory Commission as observers, they were expressly excluded from participating in the taking of decisions.[12] Some of the industrialized countries did take up the opportunity to become observers in the Commission, but there

[8] Final Act of the Third United Nations Conference on the Law of the Sea, Resolution 1, at para. 5.
[9] Ibid., at para. 11. The Preparatory Commission did have some substantive powers to implement the pioneer investors scheme, a last minute compromise intended to lure developed states to becoming a party to the Convention; see Final Act of the Third United Nations Conference on the Law of the Sea, Resolution 2. In implementing this regime, the Preparatory Commission did in fact undertake some significant developments of what had been initially anticipated; see e.g. R. Churchill and V. Lowe, *The Law of the Sea* (3rd edn., Manchester University Press, 1997) at 236–8.
[10] Final Act of the Third United Nations Conference on the Law of the Sea, Resolution 1, at para. 11.
[11] Ibid., at para. 2.   [12] Ibid., at para. 2.

were also some significant omissions. Despite the fact that it was able to participate as an observer, the United States did not attend any sessions of the Preparatory Commission.[13] The absence of such a major state from the discussions meant that there was little prospect for this institution to offer a forum to overcome the division among states and to achieve a consensus over the implementation of Part XI. If any progress were to be made, it would need to be through a different institutional framework.

As an institution that had been intricately involved in the conclusion of the Law of the Sea Convention, it was natural that the UN General Assembly would take an interest in the further development of the law of the sea regime. Indeed, a major advantage of the General Assembly compared to the Preparatory Commission was its quasi-universal membership. All interested states, regardless of whether they had signed the Convention, could participate in General Assembly debates on an equal basis. Since the conclusion of the Convention in 1982, the General Assembly had undertaken an annual debate on the law of the sea regime.[14] The General Assembly therefore offered an appropriate forum in which any further discussions on the future of the Part XI regime could take place.

In 1989 the General Assembly called on all states to make renewed efforts to facilitate universal participation in the Convention.[15] In furtherance of this mandate, the UN Secretary-General initiated a series of informal negotiations between interested parties in order to achieve this goal. The purpose of the informal consultations was to bridge the gap between developed and developing countries over the regulation of deep seabed mining. The aim of the negotiations was to reach a consensus solution. Between 1990 and 1994, fifteen meetings took place.[16] The negotiations proceeded in two principal stages.

---

[13] D. Anderson, "Efforts to ensure universal participation in the United Nations Convention on the Law of the Sea" (1993) 42 *Int'l & Comp. L. Q.* 654, at 656.

[14] *Third United Nations Conference on the Law of the Sea*, UNGA Resolution 37/66, December 3, 1982, at para. 10; *Third United Nations Conference on the Law of the Sea*, UNGA Resolution 38/59, December 14, 1982, at para. 9.

[15] *Law of the Sea*, UNGA Resolution 44/26, November 20, 1989, at para. 3. The preamble refers to the expressions of willingness to explore all possibilities of addressing issues in order to secure universal participation in the Convention, made at the meeting of the Preparatory Commission in August/September 1989.

[16] *Consultations of the Secretary-General on outstanding issues relating to the deep seabed mining provisions of the United Nations Convention on the Law of the Sea – report of the Secretary-General (Consultations of the Secretary-General)*, UN Document A/48/950, June 9, 1994, at para. 4.

The first phase of these negotiations involved a small number of major states that defined the key problems to be addressed.[17] These meetings resembled the informal negotiations that had taken place between key states at UNCLOS III. As a result of these initial consultations, a list of the nine perceived problems with Part XI of the Convention was agreed upon. These issues were costs to States Parties, the Enterprise, decision-making, the review conference, transfer of technology, production limitation, the compensation fund, financial terms of contracts and the environment.[18] These issues largely mirrored the concerns that had been raised by the industrialized countries in the closing stages of UNCLOS III.[19]

From 1992 all states were invited to participate in a second phase of the consultation process, which discussed solutions to these previously defined problems. Between seventy-five and ninety countries actually took part in this second round of consultations.[20] Once again, however, an informal group of states emerged as the leaders of negotiations. This informal group produced what was known as the "Boat Paper," which included a draft General Assembly resolution and a draft Agreement on the Implementation of Part XI. The Boat Paper became the main focus of negotiations and "regular revisions of the draft resolution and the draft agreement were prepared by a small group of participants in the light of discussions in the consultations and in the Boat Group."[21]

Although it was the Secretary-General who took the lead in facilitating the informal consultations, the process was overseen by the General Assembly. As part of its annual resolution on the law of the sea, the General Assembly noted with appreciation "the initiative of the Secretary General to promote dialogue aimed at addressing issues of concern to some States in order to achieve universal participation in

---

[17] *Ibid.*, at para. 4.

[18] The environment was subsequently dropped from the agenda. It was noted by one commentator that the environment was "qualitatively different from the eight other issues under consideration"; S. Nandan, "The efforts undertaken by the United Nations to ensure universality of the Convention," in E. L. Miles and T. Treves (eds.), *Law of the Sea: New Worlds, New Discoveries* (Law of the Sea Institute, 1992) at 378. Indeed, the protection of the marine environment is an issue that the Authority has focused on in the negotiation of rules and regulations for deep seabed mining; see Chapter 5.

[19] See Chapter 2.

[20] *Consultations of the Secretary-General*, at para. 9.

[21] D. Anderson, "Further efforts to ensure universal participation in the United Nations Convention on the Law of the Sea" (1994) 43 *Int'l & Comp. L. Q.* 886, at 889.

the Convention" and it encouraged all states to engage in a productive dialogue to that end.[22]

A major issue to be addressed by the consultations was the form that any instrument was to eventually take. Although it was accepted by all states that the results of the consultations had to be in the form of a legally binding instrument, no particular outcome was initially envisaged.[23] A number of possible outcomes for the negotiations were mooted, including a protocol of amendment, an interpretative agreement, and a transitional agreement that would apply until a definitive regime could be negotiated.[24] As no firm agreement could be reached on which of these options was preferable, it was decided that the outcome should take the form of an "implementing agreement."[25] When negotiations were completed, the resulting instrument was submitted to a resumed forty-eighth session of the General Assembly for adoption. The Part XI Agreement was duly adopted by the General Assembly on July 28, 1994 by 121 votes for, with no votes against, and only 7 abstentions.[26] It would seem from these figures that the Part XI Agreement was largely successful in bridging the divide between the developed and developing countries on the issue of the deep seabed. However, it remained to be seen what impact the Agreement would have on the legal regime for the oceans.

2.2 The relationship between the Part XI Agreement and the Law of the Sea Convention

The Part XI Agreement was the first treaty to be designated as an implementing agreement. It is therefore appropriate to consider what this means by analyzing the formal relationship between the Part XI Agreement and the Law of the Sea Convention. In order to understand the status of the agreement and its relationship with the Law of the Sea Convention, it is necessary to look to its substantive provisions.

From the opening text, the Part XI Agreement asserts a strong link with the Law of the Sea Convention. Article 1 of the Part XI Agreement provides that "the States Parties to this Agreement undertake to

---

[22] See *Law of the Sea*, UNGA Resolution 46/78, December 12, 1991, at paras. 3–6. See also *Law of the Sea*, UNGA Resolution 47/65, December 11, 1992, at paras. 3–6; *Law of the Sea*, UNGA Resolution 48/28, December 9, 1993, at paras. 3–7.

[23] *Consultations of the Secretary-General*, at para. 12.

[24] *Ibid.*, at para. 1.   [25] *Ibid.*, at para. 11.

[26] *Agreement relating to the Implementation of Part XI of the United Nations Convention on the Law of the Sea of 10 December 1982*, UNGA Resolution 48/263, July 28, 1994.

implement Part XI in accordance with this Agreement." This link is strengthened in Article 4 of the Agreement, which provides that "no State or entity may establish its consent to be bound by this Agreement unless it has previously established or establishes at the same time its consent to be bound by the Convention." In other words, the Part XI Agreement is only open to participation by states that have also accepted the Law of the Sea Convention. Article 2 of the Part XI Agreement confirms this interrelationship when it says that "the provisions of this Agreement and Part XI [of the Law of the Sea Convention] shall be interpreted and applied together as a single instrument."[27] In other words, the Part XI Agreement is not a freestanding instrument, but it is intimately connected with the Convention.

Nevertheless, it remains to be seen precisely how the Agreement interacts with the Convention. An answer to this question would seem to be found in Article 2, which says that "in the event of any inconsistency between this Agreement and Part XI [of the Law of the Sea Convention], the provisions of the Agreement shall prevail." This language is straightforward and uncompromising and it leaves no doubt that the "implementing agreement" is in fact intended to modify the legal regime created by the Law of the Sea Convention. This is even clearer if one analyzes the substantive provisions of the Part XI Agreement found in the Annexes. According to the Agreement, several provisions of the Convention are simply "disapplied."[28]

Several provisions of the Convention concerning applications for deep seabed mining are replaced by provisions that seek to improve the rights of investors and to ensure that production is undertaken in line with "sound commercial principles."[29] For instance, the Part XI Agreement removes the requirement on the Authority to specify a production ceiling for the amount of minerals that may be produced in the Area. The Part XI Agreement also removes the obligation on States Parties to fund a mine site of the Enterprise and it specifies that initial deep seabed mining operations by the Enterprise shall be conducted through joint ventures.[30] Overall, the Part XI places the Enterprise

[27] See also *ibid.*, at para. 4, which "affirms that the Agreement shall be interpreted and applied together with Part XI as a single instrument."
[28] Part XI Agreement, Annex section 2, at para. 3 and para. 11(b); section 3, at para. 8; section 4; section 5, at para. 2; section 6, at para. 7; section 8, at para. 2.
[29] See Part XI Agreement, Annex section 2, at para. 2 and section 6, at para. 1(a).
[30] Part XI Agreement, Annex section 2, at para. 3.

on an equal footing with other contractors and it loses many of the privileges that were originally conferred on it by the Convention.

The Part XI Agreement also introduces a number of institutional changes to the Authority in order to minimize the costs of the Members.[31] The establishment of the Economic and Planning Committee envisaged in Article 164 of the Convention is suspended and its functions are to be carried out by the Legal and Technical Commission until the approval of the first plan of exploitation.[32] In addition, the Enterprise will not initially be established as a separate organ of the Authority and its functions shall be carried out by the Secretariat instead.[33]

In spite of these changes to the original text, the provisions of the Agreement were carefully drafted to avoid any clear indication that what states were doing was amending Part XI of the Convention.[34] Indeed, participants in the informal consultations rejected the idea of a protocol of amendment that had been previously suggested in an Information Note produced by the UN Secretariat. It is suggested that the political context may go some way to explaining the importance attached to the title and formal status of the Agreement. Given the serious political capital that was attached to the issue of deep seabed mining by the opposing factions at UNCLOS III, to acknowledge an amendment to the original settlement would have been a serious concession on the part of those states that had advocated a strong international regime for the deep seabed. Yet whatever terminology is utilized, can it be seriously denied that the true impact of the 1994 Agreement is anything but a de facto amendment of the law of the sea regime? Many authors in fact take this view. As noted by Scovazzi, the "politically prudent label of an 'implementing agreement' is a euphemism for the word 'amendment' which would have been more correct from the legal point of view."[35] Nelson also observes that "this agreement goes beyond mere implementation" and he concludes that "the agreement can therefore

---

[31] Part XI Agreement, Annex section 1, at para. 2.
[32] Part XI Agreement, Annex section 1, at para. 4.
[33] Part XI Agreement, Annex section 2, at para. 1.
[34] Anderson, "Further efforts to ensure universal participation in the United Nations Convention on the Law of the Sea," at 889; see also D. Freestone and A. G. Oude Elferink, "Flexibility and innovation in the law of the sea," in A. G. Oude Elferink (ed.), *Stability and Change in the Law of the Sea: The Role of the LOS Convention* (2005, Martinus Nijhoff Publishers) at 185.
[35] T. Scovazzi, "Evolution of international law of the sea" (2000) 286 *Recueil des Cours* 39, at 125.

be considered a protocol of amendment."[36] Despite the ambiguity in its title and its language, the Part XI Agreement has undoubtedly had a considerable impact on the original provisions of Part XI of the Law of the Sea Convention. Although many of the basic principles underlying the deep seabed mining regime remain the same, the detailed provisions of Part XI have been subjected to far-reaching modification.

2.3 Legal impact of the Part XI Agreement

Even if it is accepted that the Part XI Agreement is a de facto amendment to the Convention, it must be also asked how far it has been successful in developing the legal regime in Part XI of the Convention.

As a treaty, the Agreement is of course only formally binding on those states that have accepted it. The provisions on the acceptance and entry into force of the Agreement are found in Article 4. As noted above, Article 4(2) provides that only those states or entities that are a party to the Law of the Sea Convention may become bound by the 1994 Part XI Agreement. However, Article 4(1) goes further and it provides that "after the adoption of this Agreement, any instrument of ratification or formal confirmation of or accession to the Convention shall also represent consent to be bound by this Agreement." There are obvious parallels between this provision and Article 40(5) of the 1969 Vienna Convention on the Law of Treaties, which provides that states becoming party to a treaty after entry into force will be bound by any amendments that have been made to that treaty. Yet, there is one important difference. While the Vienna Convention merely creates a presumption that a state accepts an amending agreement when it consents to be bound by a treaty, allowing a state to indicate its intent *not* to be bound, the Part XI Agreement does not give states this choice. In other words, States becoming party to the Law of the Sea Convention after July 28, 1994 will automatically be bound by the terms of the Part XI Agreement and there is no opportunity to opt out. This is a highly unusual, perhaps unprecedented provision[37], although it is a logical conclusion of treating

---

[36] D. Nelson, "The new deep sea-bed mining regime" (1995) 10 *Int'l J. Marine & Coastal L.* 189, at 192–3. See also in support of this view A. E. Boyle, "Further Development of the 1982 Law of the Sea Convention," in D. Freestone, R. Barnes and D. Ong (eds.), *The Law of the Sea – Progress and Prospects* (Oxford University Press, 2006) 40, at footnote 14; Freestone and Oude Elferink, "Flexibility and innovation in the law of the sea," at 184. Churchill and Lowe avoid saying that it amends the Convention but accept that it makes substantial changes; Churchill and Lowe, *The Law of the Sea*, at 238.
[37] Freestone and Oude Elferink, "Flexibility and innovation in the law of the sea," at 186.

the two instruments as a "single instrument."[38] It follows that states accepting the Law of the Sea Convention after the conclusion of the Part XI Agreement do not need to submit any additional instrument agreeing to accept the application of the Agreement.[39] Thus, the Agreement has modified the law of the sea regime for all those states that have since become a party to the Law of the Sea Convention, whether or not they have expressed their explicit consent to be bound by the Agreement.

The situation is more complicated for States that were already a party to the Law of the Sea Convention prior to July 28, 1994. In accordance with the law of treaties, those States that were already party to the Law of the Sea Convention must indicate their consent to be bound by the Agreement separately. The Part XI Agreement provides several alternative ways in which they can do this: signature, signature subject to ratification and accession.[40] In addition, Article 5 of the Agreement creates a so-called "simplified procedure" which aims to facilitate the acceptance of the Agreement by as many states as possible.[41] This article provides that all States Parties to the Law of the Sea Convention that have signed the Part XI Agreement are presumed to have consented to be bound, unless they notify the UN Secretary-General to the contrary within twelve months of the adoption of the Agreement. Thus, Article 5 creates a presumption in favor of consent for those states that have signed the Agreement. The simplified procedure still allows States Parties that signed the Agreement a degree of choice and they can opt out if they wish. A number of states become bound by the Agreement in this way.[42]

On the other hand, States that have not accepted the Part XI Agreement by any of the mechanisms in Articles 4 and 5 will not prima facie be bound. It follows that, as a matter of treaty law, there are a number of States Parties to the Law of the Sea Convention for which the Part XI Agreement is not yet binding. This state of affairs

---

[38] Part XI Agreement, Article 2(1).

[39] According to United Nations data, forty states became bound by the Part XI Agreement simply by "participation" in the Law of the Sea Convention. See www.un.org/depts/los/reference_files/status2010.pdf <checked April 9, 2010>.

[40] Part XI Agreement, Article 4(3)(a) (b) and (c).

[41] Cross-referenced in Part XI Agreement, Article 4(3)(c).

[42] According to data of the UN Division of Ocean Affairs and Law of the Sea, fifteen states became bound by the Agreement in this way. These states were Barbados, Côte d'Ivoire, Serbia and Montenegro, Grenada, Guinea, Iceland, Jamaica, Namibia, Nigeria, Sri Lanka, Togo, Trinidad and Tobago, Uganda, Zambia, and Zimbabwe; see www.un.org/depts/los/reference_files/status2010.pdf <checked April 9, 2010>.

has been recognized by the Secretary-General of the International Seabed Authority, who said in his 2000 report that "it continues to be a matter of concern that, as of 5 June 2000, 35 members of the Authority which became States Parties to the Convention prior to the adoption of the Agreement had not yet completed the necessary procedural steps to become parties to the Agreement."[43] While several States Parties to the Convention have heeded calls from the Authority and the General Assembly to become a party to the Agreement since this statement was made, there remain a number who have not.[44]

The question arises as to whether there are other ways in which these states could be bound by the obligations contained in the Part XI Agreement. One argument is that those states that are party to the Convention but not to the Part XI Agreement may be deemed to have consented to the Part XI Agreement through their participation in activities of the International Seabed Authority. There is widespread support for the theory that state practice can modify or amend treaties.[45] The original draft articles on the law of treaties produced by the International Law Commission originally provided for this possibility.[46] Although it was removed from the final text of the Convention on the Law of Treaties by the Vienna Conference,[47] Akehurst argues that "it is difficult to interpret the deletion of Article 38 as a clear rejection of the view that existing law allowed a treaty to be amended by subsequent practice, especially since the Vienna Convention did not exclude the possibility of termination of treaties by desuetude and expressly allowed a treaty to be interpreted in light of subsequent practice."[48] Indeed, the process of modification through institutional practice would appear to be confirmed by the ICJ in its 1971 *Namibia Advisory Opinion*, where the Court held that "the proceedings of the Security Council extending over a long period supply abundant evidence that presidential rulings and the positions taken by members of the Security Council, in particular its permanent members, have consistently and uniformly interpreted the practice of voluntary abstention by a permanent member as not constituting a bar to the adoption of resolutions."[49]

This reasoning can be applied to the situation of the International Seabed Authority.[50] All Members of the Authority, whether or not they have formally accepted the Part XI Agreement, are participating in meetings of the organization that operate according to the amended procedures set out in that instrument.[51] As noted by the Secretary-General of the Authority, "members of the Authority which are not parties to the 1994 Agreement necessarily participate in the work of the Authority under arrangements based on the Agreement."[52] No states have objected to the use of these procedures. On this basis, it is arguable that the provisions of the Part XI Agreement are binding on all Members of the Authority, regardless of whether they have formally consented to be bound by the Part XI Agreement. In other words, the Part XI Agreement has legal effects beyond its status as a treaty. At the same time, it should be added that the availability of this argument does not necessarily eliminate the desirability, expressed by the Secretary-General of the International Seabed Authority in the

---

[48] Akehurst, "The hierarchy of sources of international law," at 277.

[49] *Advisory Opinion on the Legal Consequences for States of the Continued Presence of South Africa in Namibia (South West Africa) Notwithstanding Security Council Resolution 276 (1970) (Advisory Opinion)* (1971) ICJ Reports 16, at para. 22. As Aust points out, it would seem from the *travaux préparatoires* that this situation was not originally intended by the permanent members; A. Aust, *Modern Treaty Law and Practice* (2nd edn., Cambridge University Press, 2007) at 243. It is for this reason that the decision of the Court is best seen as an example of amendment by subsequent practice, as opposed to an interpretation.

[50] Hereinafter, the Authority.

[51] For instance, Guyana had a seat on the Council, as constituted under the Part XI Agreement, despite the fact that it had not accepted the Agreement in any of the ways prescribed in Article 4.

[52] See *Report of the Secretary-General of the International Seabed Authority*, Document ISBA/15/A/2, March 22, 2009, at para. 5.

quote above, for all Members to formally become a party to the Part XI Agreement for the sake of legal certainty. Such action would "remove an incongruity that currently exists for those States"[53] and promote legal certainty as there would be no doubt about the application of the Part XI Agreement to those states as a matter of treaty law.

What about those states that have consented to be bound by neither the Law of the Sea Convention nor by the Part XI Agreement? As these states are not Members of the Authority and they therefore do not fully participate in meetings of the organization, they cannot be deemed to have accepted the provisions of the Part XI Agreement in the way that was described above.

Indeed, given that the Part XI Agreement is largely concerned with the internal functioning of an international organization, there is perhaps no need for other states to be bound. At the same time, it does not follow that the Part XI Agreement is without significance for this category of states. Even for those states that are not a Member of the Authority, the Part XI Agreement can be considered as having an important impact in a number of ways.

First, it can be argued that the negotiation and adoption of the Part XI Agreement using consensus decision-making techniques has solidified international support for the general principles relating to the International Seabed Area that were first contained in the 1970 Declaration of Principles Governing the Sea-Bed and the Ocean Floor Beyond National Jurisdiction and have since been confirmed in both the Part XI of the Law of the Sea Convention and the Part XI Agreement. These principles include the concept of the common heritage of mankind and the prohibition on claiming sovereignty or sovereign rights in the Area.[54] The preamble to both the General Assembly resolution adopting the Agreement and the Part XI Agreement itself both reaffirm that the seabed and ocean floor beyond national jurisdiction, as well as the resources thereof, are the common heritage of mankind.[55] Thus, all states which participated in this process and which voted in favor of the Agreement must be deemed to have accepted the application of these principles to the Area.

It can also be argued that the Part XI Agreement serves to affirm the exclusive role of the International Seabed Authority in regulating seabed activities in the International Seabed Area. The Part XI Agreement

---

[53] *Ibid.*, at para. 5.   [54] See Law of the Sea Convention, Article 137.
[55] UNGA Resolution 48/263, preamble; Part XI Agreement preamble.

is based upon the idea that all seabed mining activities should take place with the approval of the Authority. The acquiescence of all states in the formation of the regime to regulate seabed activities in the Area could be invoked in support of the argument that even those states which have not formally accepted the new legal regime are nevertheless prohibited from exploiting the resources of the Area outside of the framework of Part XI.[56] It should not be forgotten that all states, including those industrialized countries that had previously raised objections to the institutional provisions in Part XI of the Convention, participated in the negotiation of the Part XI Agreement. Moreover, not only did they participate in negotiations, but many of them, including the United States, signed the Part XI Agreement and also participated in setting up the Authority by virtue of the provisions on provisional application.[57] Their support for the conclusion and implementation of the Part XI Agreement could be interpreted as acceptance that Part XI provides the only applicable legal framework for carrying out seabed activities in the International Seabed Area.

This view is also reinforced by the General Assembly Resolution adopting the Part XI Agreement, which "calls upon States which consent to the adoption of the Agreement to refrain from any act which would defeat its object and purpose."[58] A similar rule is found in Article 18 of the Vienna Convention on the Law of Treaties, which provides that states are under an obligation to refrain from acts which would defeat the object and purpose of a treaty when they have, inter alia, signed the treaty. This General Assembly resolution would appear to extend the application of this rule, not only to states that have signed the Part XI Agreement, but also to those states that have consented to its adoption. The object and purpose of the Part XI Agreement is to establish an exclusive regime for the regulation of seabed activities in the Area. It follows that any states unilaterally authorizing such activities would be acting in a way that was incompatible with the object and purpose of the Agreement. Given that no states objected to the adoption of the Part XI Agreement when it came before the General

---

[56] In support of this view, see C. Tomuschat, "Obligations arising for states without or against their will" (1993) 241 *Recueil des Cours* 194, at 260–1; for a more ambiguous assessment, see R. Y. Jennings, "The identification of international law," in B. Cheng (ed.), *International Law: Teaching and Practice* (Stevens, 1982) at 7.
[57] Part XI Agreement, Article 7.
[58] UNGA Resolution 48/263, at para. 6.

Assembly, it is suggested that no states may authorize any seabed activities in the Area outside of the Part XI regime.

If these arguments are accepted, it follows that the Part XI Agreement, in combination with the Law of the Sea Convention, has created a universal regime with relevance for all states, including those that are not a party to the Convention or to the Agreement. Non-parties may not be directly bound by the Agreement and they may not be obliged to participate in the activities of the Authority, but they should respect the status of the Area and the role of the Authority in relation thereto. In other words, although not all states are directly bound by the Agreement, the instrument has had an indirect law-making impact on all states by establishing and consolidating an exclusive regime for the exploration and exploitation of minerals in the International Seabed Area.[59]

3 The Fish Stocks Agreement

3.1 Negotiation of the Fish Stocks Agreement

The history of the Fish Stocks Agreement can be traced back to UNCLOS III. The regulation of fishing was part of what Kwiatkowska calls the "unfinished business" of the Conference.[60] Although the Conference had managed to reach agreement on the previously problematic issue of the extent of a coastal state's fishing rights, further difficulties arose over what to do about fish stocks that straddled the jurisdictional zones created by the Law of the Sea Convention. Many coastal states argued that they had a special interest in the conservation and management of stocks that occurred in their exclusive economic zone as well as the adjacent high seas area.[61] They further argued that any measures adopted for high seas fisheries had to be compatible with measures taken by the coastal state.[62]

This issue had also been problematic in previous attempts at codifying the law of the sea. The 1958 Convention on Fishing and Conservation

---

[59] The operation of the regime and the law-making powers of the Authority will be considered in Chapter 5.

[60] B. Kwiatkowska, "The High Seas Fisheries Regime: at a point of no return?" (1993) 8 *Int'l J. Marine & Coastal L.* 327, at 327

[61] *Ibid.*, at 334.

[62] See for example the proposal submitted by Canada at the fifth session of UNCLOS III in 1976; M. Nordquist *et al.* (eds.), *1982 United Nations Convention on the Law of the Sea – A Commentary, Vol. 3* (Martinus Nijhoff Publishers, 1995) at 643–4.

of Living Resources of the High Seas had included a provision that "a coastal State has a special interest in the maintenance of the productivity of the living resources in any area of the high seas adjacent to its territorial sea," as well as a procedure through which disputes over the compatibility of conservation measures could be settled.[63] However, these provisions had themselves been controversial and this treaty had received the smallest number of ratifications among the 1958 conventions on the law of the sea, partly for this reason.[64]

The issue of straddling and highly migratory fish stocks continued to plague the negotiations at UNCLOS III. Disagreements over the status of straddling and highly migratory fish stocks continued until the final stages of the Conference.[65] Ultimately, delegates at UNCLOS III managed to reach a compromise, albeit at the cost of ambiguity. The solution arrived at in Articles 63 and 64 of the Convention stresses the need for cooperation in the management and conservation of highly migratory and straddling fish stocks without setting down any more detailed procedural or substantive obligations on how such cooperation was to be achieved.[66]

The question of fishing continued to occupy a prominent place on the international agenda during the 1980s, as further evidence of declining fish stocks came to light. The World Commission on Environment and Development warned in its 1987 Report that "overexploitation threatens many stocks as economic resources" and it highlighted what it considered to be "the pressing need for these resources to be managed sustainably."[67] The issue was addressed by the General Assembly which expressed similar concerns in its 1989 Resolution on Oceans and

---

[63] 1958 Convention on Fishing and the Conservation of Living Resources of the High Seas, 559 UNTS 285, Articles 6–7.

[64] The Convention received only thirty-seven ratifications; see Churchill and Lowe, *The Law of the Sea*, Appendix 2, Table B.

[65] Nordquist *et al.* (eds.), *1982 United Nations Convention on the Law of the Sea – A Commentary*, Vol. 3, at 645–6.

[66] P. Fauteux, "The Canadian Legal Initiative on High Seas Fishing" (1993) 4 *Ybk Int'l Env'l L.* 51 at 53. Nelson nevertheless suggests that Article 63(2) is "not necessarily an empty shell" given that the parties are under a duty to conduct negotiations in good faith, paying reasonable regard to the fishing rights and interests of each other; D. Nelson, "The development of the Legal Regime of High Seas Fisheries," in A. E. Boyle and D. Freestone (eds.), *International Law and Sustainable Development* (Oxford University Press, 1999) at 121.

[67] World Commission on Environment and Development, *Our Common Future* (Oxford University Press, 1987) at 267–8.

the Law of the Sea, in which it called on states and other members of the international community to "strengthen their cooperation in the conservation of marine living resources, including the prevention of fishing methods and practices that can have an adverse impact on the conservation and management of marine living resources."[68] However, it was also clear to many states that a simple duty to cooperate, as found in the Law of the Sea Convention, was not adequate in order to prevent overfishing of straddling and highly migratory fish stocks. These states recognized that further development of international fisheries law might be necessary if the challenges of overfishing were to be met.

In 1989 the General Assembly agreed to convene the UN Conference on Environment and Development (UNCED).[69] Fishing was one of the issues placed on the agenda of this conference. UNCED met in Rio de Janeiro from June 3 to 14, 1992. When it came to the protection of the marine environment and the conservation of marine living resources, delegates at UNCED accepted that the Law of the Sea Convention provided the basic framework for the discussions. This is reflected in the final text of Agenda 21, which expressly confirms the continuing relevance of the Convention by saying that "the provisions of the UN LOS Convention on the marine living resources of the high seas sets forth rights and obligations of States with respect to conservation and utilization of these resources."[70] This statement would seem to confirm that states participating in the Conference accepted that the Convention rules on fishing had codified or crystallized customary international law. At the same time, the conference also acknowledged that management of fish stocks was "inadequate"[71] and most states seemed to recognize that the legal framework provided by the Law of the Sea Convention was in need of further clarification and development. Precisely how the rules on fishing were to be developed remained a matter of controversy and the divisions that had prevented any substantive agreement at UNCLOS III continued to prevail at UNCED. Delegates were unable to reach any conclusive agreement on what was

---

[68] E.g. UNGA Resolution 44/26, at para. 19. This call was reiterated in subsequent resolutions in 1990, 1991 and 1992.

[69] *UN Conference on Environment and Development*, UNGA Resolution 44/228, December 22, 1989.

[70] Agenda 21, at para. 17.44.

[71] *Ibid.*, at para. 17.45

to be done. Instead, Agenda 21 includes a recommendation to convene a further conference dedicated to the fisheries issue.

It was on this basis that the General Assembly decided to convene the Fish Stocks Conference.[72] This conference was charged with promoting the effective implementation of the provisions of the Law of the Sea Convention relating to straddling and highly migratory fish stocks.[73] The Law of the Sea Convention remained the starting point of the negotiations and the mandate of the conference made it very clear that:

the work and results of the conference should be fully consistent with the provisions of the United Nations Convention on the Law of the Sea, in particular the rights and obligations of coastal States and States fishing on the high seas, and that States should give full effect to the high seas fisheries provisions of the Convention with regard to fisheries populations whose ranges lie both within and beyond exclusive economic zones (straddling fish stocks) and highly migratory fish stocks.[74]

In other words, the conference was not expected to revise the existing provisions of the Law of the Sea Convention. Rather, the purpose of the conference was to fill in the gaps left by the ambiguous settlement achieved in 1982 by specifying precisely what principles should govern the management and conservation of straddling and highly migratory fish stocks.

The Fish Stocks Conference met for the first time in April 1993 and it was to meet for six sessions in total over a three-year period.[75] The conference was open to all states, as well as relevant international organizations and nongovernmental organizations.[76] Doulman describes how the debate at the conference was dominated by fifty to sixty states, with the principal disagreement arising between distant water fishing states and coastal states.[77] In order to try to achieve a workable compromise

---

[72] *United Nations Conference on Straddling Fish Stocks and Highly Migratory Fish Stocks*, UNGA Resolution 47/192, December 22, 1992.

[73] Agenda 21, at para. 17.49(e).

[74] UNGA Resolution 47/192, at para. 3.

[75] April 19–23, 1993; July 12–30, 1993; March 14–31, 1994; August 15–26, 1994; March 27–April 12, 1995; July 24–August 4, 1995.

[76] UNGA Resolution 47/192, at para. 4. For a list of participants, see the Final Act of the Conference, available at www.un.org/depts/los/fish_stocks_conference/fish_stocks_conference.htm <checked November 29, 2010).

[77] D. J. Doulman, "Structure and process of the 1993–1995 United Nations Conference on Straddling Fish Stocks and Highly Migratory Fish Stocks," *FAO Fisheries Circular No. 898 FID/C898*, part 6, available at www.fao.org/docrep/v9929e/v9929e00.HTM <checked July 19, 2010>.

between these factions, working procedures based on the consensus decision-making techniques from UNCLOS III were utilized.[78] Thus, the Chairman of the Fish Stocks Conference adopted a prominent role in the negotiating process, preparing compromise texts and facilitating informal negotiations between the principal protagonists.

The Fish Stocks Agreement was adopted by consensus at the final session of the conference in August 1995. The conclusion of the Agreement was subsequently welcomed in General Assembly Resolution 50/24, which called on all states and other entities eligible to do so to ratify or accede to the Agreement and to consider applying it provisionally.[79]

3.2 The relationship between the Fish Stocks Agreement and the Law of the Sea Convention

The objective of the Fish Stocks Agreement is the "effective implementation of the relevant provisions of the Convention," in particular those relating to the management and conservation of straddling and highly migratory fish stocks.[80] Moreover, the Agreement also stresses that it should be interpreted "in the context of and in a manner consistent with the Convention."[81] Yet there are some key differences between the ways in which the Agreement implements the Convention when compared with the Part XI Agreement.

In the first place, the Fish Stocks Agreement does not go as far as saying that the Agreement and the Convention should be considered as a single instrument. Indeed, the Fish Stocks Agreement does not even require states to be a State Party to the Convention before they become a party to the Agreement. The Fish Stocks Agreement is open to participation by any state or other entities engaging in fisheries, whether or not they are a party to the Convention.[82] In other words, it is a freestanding treaty.[83] This has allowed some important fishing states to adhere to the

---

[78] See D. Anderson, "The Straddling Stocks Agreement of 1995 – an initial assessment" (1996) 45 Int'l & Comp. L. Q. 463, at 467.
[79] Agreement for the implementation of the provisions of the United Nations Convention on the Law of the Sea of 10 December 1982 relating to the Conservation and Management of Straddling Fish Stocks and Highly Migratory Fish Stocks, UNGA Resolution 50/24, December 5, 1995, at para. 4.
[80] Fish Stocks Agreement, Article 2.
[81] Fish Stocks Agreement, Article 4.
[82] Fish Stocks Agreement, Articles 37 and 39.
[83] See A. E. Boyle, "Further development of the 1982 Law of the Sea Convention," in D. Freestone, R. Barnes and D. Ong (eds.), The Law of the Sea – Progress and Prospects (Oxford University Press, 2006) at 42.

treaty despite the fact that they have not consented to be bound by the Convention itself.[84] This is possible because the Fish Stocks Agreement seeks to implement those parts of the Convention that had already been accepted by most states as being part of customary international law.

A second difference in the Fish Stocks Agreement is that it does not go as far as disapplying any provisions of the Convention. Nonetheless, it cannot be doubted that the Agreement does substantially develop the relevant law on the management and conservation of straddling and highly migratory fish stocks. For instance, as Boyle explains, "high seas freedom of fishing under the [Fish Stocks Agreement] is significantly different from the traditional concepts found in Articles 116–117 of the [Convention], most notably in regard to access to high seas stocks and enforcement jurisdiction on the high seas."[85] The Agreement has had the effect of modifying the international law of high seas fisheries in light of subsequent developments in international environmental law. It draws heavily upon those principles of sustainable development expressed in the instruments adopted after the conclusion of UNCLOS III, including the Rio Declaration on Environment and Development, Agenda 21[86] and the Convention on Biological Diversity.[87] For instance, the Fish Stocks Agreement confirms the obligation in the Law of the Sea Convention to take conservation and management measures based on the best scientific evidence available.[88] However, it adds that states, including coastal states acting in areas under their jurisdiction, should apply the precautionary approach as set out in Article 6 and further detailed in Annex II of the Agreement.[89] This requires states

---

[84] For instance, Denmark, Iran and the United States of America have agreed to be bound by the Agreement without, at the time, being a State Party to the Law of the Sea Convention. Since its ratification of the Fish Stocks Agreement on December 19, 2003, Denmark subsequently ratified the Law of the Sea Convention (and by operation of Article 4 of the Part XI Agreement, that Agreement as well) on November 16, 2004.

[85] Boyle, "Further development of the 1982 Convention on the Law of the Sea," at 47.

[86] The preambular language of the Agreement affirms its origins not only in the Law of the Sea Convention, but also in Chapter 17 of Agenda 21.

[87] In regard to the latter, the objective of the Agreement to promote the "long-term conservation and sustainable use" of straddling and highly migratory fish stocks is clearly influenced by the Convention on Biological Diversity which has the objective of "the conservation of biological diversity [and] the sustainable use of its components"; see Convention on Biological Diversity, Article 1.

[88] Fish Stocks Agreement, Article 5(b); Law of the Sea Convention, Article 119(1)(a).

[89] Article 6(2) says that "States shall be more cautious when information is uncertain, unreliable or inadequate. The absence of adequate information shall not be used as a reason for postponing or failing to take conservation measures."

to set precautionary reference points for fish stocks that should not be exceeded. Decisions on catch quotas should be made on the basis of the best scientific evidence available, taking into account uncertainties relating to the size and productivity of the fish stock. Article 6 explicitly says that "states shall be more cautious when information is uncertain, unreliable or inadequate [and] the absence of adequate scientific information shall not be used as a reason for postponing or failing to take conservation and management measures."[90] This provision is clearly inspired by Principle 15 of the 1992 Declaration on Environment and Development, which contains a generally accepted definition of the precautionary approach. In a similar way, the Agreement also promotes the application of the ecosystem approach to straddling and highly migratory fish stocks, obliging states to consider the impact of other factors, human and natural, on the status of target fish stocks and other species and to generally protect the biodiversity of the marine ecosystem.[91] These links to the Rio Principles should not be surprising given that the seeds for the Fish Stocks Agreement are to be found in Agenda 21.

The Agreement also clarifies the duty to cooperate of Articles 63 and 64 of the Law of the Sea Convention. The Agreement reiterates the requirement that:

Coastal States and States fishing on the high seas shall, in accordance with the Convention, pursue cooperation in relation to straddling fish stocks and highly migratory fish stocks either directly or through appropriate subregional or regional fisheries management organizations or arrangements, taking into account the specific characteristics of the subregion or region, to ensure effective conservation and management of such stocks.[92]

Yet the Agreement goes beyond the Convention by explicitly setting out the functions to be exercised by regional fisheries organizations as well as the principles that should guide their operation.[93] Most significantly,

---

[90] Fish Stocks Agreement, Article 6(2).
[91] Fish Stocks Agreement, Article 5(d), (e)(f) and (g). Birnie, Boyle and Redgwell say that the duty to monitor the impact of fishing on the ecosystem as a whole "is very much in keeping with Article 194(5) of the 1982 [LOS Convention] and with the general obligation to protect the marine environment codified in Part XII, but it is the very first time it has been spelt out explicitly in a major fisheries agreement"; P. Birnie, A. E. Boyle and C. Redgwell, *International Law and the Environment* (3rd edn., Oxford University Press, 2009) at 736.
[92] Fish Stocks Agreement, Article 8(1).
[93] Fish Stocks Agreement, Articles 9–12.

the Agreement purports to limit absolute freedom of fishing on the high seas by stating that "only those States which are members of such an organization or participants in such an arrangement, or which agree to apply the conservation and management measures established by such organization or arrangement, shall have access to the fishery resources to which those measures apply."[94] This is perhaps the starkest illustration of how the Fish Stock Agreement modifies the legal framework for fisheries created by the Law of the Sea Convention.

It can be seen from these examples that the Agreement does introduce "significant changes in the international legal regime governing the stocks to which the Agreement applies."[95] Yet, this is achieved without amending or disapplying the provisions of the Convention. This is because the problem with the Convention that needed to be addressed in this context was not objections to the content of the Convention, but the highly ambiguous nature of the fisheries provisions in the Convention. This problem could be solved through further clarification without the need for amendment or disapplication.

3.3 Legal impact of the Fish Stocks Agreement

The Agreement is formally binding only on those states that have become a party under the procedure outlined in Articles 38 and 39 of the Agreement. States may also take the opportunity to provisionally apply the Agreement before it becomes formally binding.[96] Although it started slowly, participation in the Agreement has been gradually increasing. As of January 1, 2010, seventy-seven states were party to the Agreement.[97] Nevertheless, this figure remains well below the number

---

[94] Fish Stocks Agreement, Article 8(4).

[95] W. Edeson, "Towards long-term sustainable use: some recent developments in the legal regime of fisheries," in A. E. Boyle and D. Freestone (eds.), *International Law and Sustainable Development* (Oxford University Press, 1999) at 173. See also M. Hayashi, "The 1995 Agreement on the Conservation and Management of Straddling and Highly Migratory Fish Stocks: significance for the Law of the Sea Convention" (1995) *Ocean and Coastal Management* 51, at 53: "the most significant of them are those relating to the precautionary approach, compatibility of management measures, regional organisations and the freedom of high seas fisheries, duties of the flag state, regional cooperation in enforcement, port state jurisdiction, provisional measures and practical arrangements"; *ibid.*, at 56. See also Birnie, Boyle and Redgwell, *International Law and the Environment*, at 733–4; E. Franckx, "Pacta Tertiis and the Agreement for the Implementation of the Straddling and Highly Migratory Fish Stocks Provisions of the United Nations Convention of the Law of the Sea" (2000) 8 *Tulane J. Int'l & Comp. L.* 49, at 61.

[96] Fish Stocks Agreement, Article 41.

[97] See www.un.org/depts/los/reference_files/status2010.pdf <checked April 9, 2010>.

of states that are party to the Law of the Sea Convention. Indeed, a number of major fishing states stand out as non-parties.[98] In light of this situation, it is important to consider whether the Fish Stocks Agreement has had any normative impact on non-parties?

One argument for the application of the Fish Stocks Agreement to non-parties is that the Agreement functions as an interpretation of the fisheries provisions contained in the Law of the Sea Convention. According to this view, the Agreement may to a certain extent be applied to States Parties to the Law of the Sea Convention, whether or not they have consented to be bound by it. Thus, Freestone and Elferink suggest that "the Agreement and the Convention are fundamentally inter-related in the sense that one can be used to inform the interpretation of the other."[99] This argument is also supported by Anderson, who says that:

in construing the relevant provisions of the Convention, for example, it would probably now be considered appropriate in many, if not all, instances to take into account the terms of the Agreement, as a "subsequent agreement ... regarding the interpretation of [a] treaty or the application of its provisions," within the meaning of Article 31(3)(a) of the Vienna Convention on the Law of Treaties, if only because the interpretation and application of a treaty are inextricably bound up with its implementation.[100]

While it is true that the Fish Stocks Agreement and the Law of the Sea Convention are closely interrelated, the Agreement is not strictly speaking an agreement among the States Parties to the Convention and therefore it can be asked whether it can legitimately be considered as such for the purposes of Article 31(3)(a) of the Vienna Convention on the Law of Treaties. Indeed, it is not obvious that this provision on treaty interpretation was intended to be applied to independent treaties with their own requirements for consent to be bound. The Agreement is probably better qualified as "relevant rule of international law" under Article 31(3)(c) of the Vienna Convention on the Law of Treaties. Yet to

---

[98] See similar comments by Boyle, "Further Development of the 1982 Convention on the Law of the Sea," at 570–1.

[99] See Freestone and Oude Elferink, "Flexibility and innovation in the law of the sea," at 20

[100] Anderson, "The Straddling Stocks Agreement of 1995 – an initial assessment," at 468. See also T. Henriksen, "Revisiting the freedom of fishing and legal obligations of states not party to regional fisheries management organizations" (2009) *Ocean Dev. & Int'l L.* 80, at 81.

be "a relevant rule" under Article 31(3)(c), it is arguable that all parties must also be bound by the relevant rule.[101] This condition would not be satisfied by the Fish Stocks Agreement, which is likely to have fewer parties than the Law of the Sea Convention for the foreseeable future.

Even if the Fish Stocks Agreement is a relevant instrument for the purposes of treaty interpretation, its usefulness for interpretative purposes may in fact be limited. Article 31(3) of the Vienna Convention only requires other instruments to "be taken into account" in the interpretation of treaties. It is important to remember that interpretation is a limited exercise. As Judge Bedjaoui warned in the *Gabcikovo-Nagymaros Case*, there are limits to evolutionary interpretation: "'*interpretation*' is not the same as the '*substitution*' for a negotiated and approved text, of a completely different text, which has neither been negotiated nor agreed."[102] In the context of straddling and highly migratory fish stocks, Henriksen therefore concludes that "the extent to which the norms of the Fish Stocks Agreement may be used in the interpretation of the provisions of the [Convention] depends, inter alia, on the interpretative space provided."[103] On this basis, even if it was accepted that the Agreement could be taken into account in the interpretation the Convention, it would play a very limited part and it would not allow new and novel obligations to be imposed on States Parties to the Convention.

Another way in which the Agreement may be applied to non-parties is if it has influenced the development of customary international law. In this context, as has been argued previously, it is important to note that the Fish Stocks Agreement was negotiated by the international community, including all major fishing and coastal states. It is also significant that the Agreement was ultimately adopted by consensus. Further support for the law-making intention of the participants of the Fish Stocks Conference can be found in the language of the Agreement, much of which is directed at states in general rather than specifically at the States Parties. Thus, one commentator states that

---

[101] See e.g. C. McLachlan, "The principle of systemic integration and Article 31(3)(c) of the Vienna Convention" (2005) 54 *Int'l & Comp. L. Q.* 279, at 313–15; cf. D. French, "Treaty interpretation and the incorporation of extraneous legal rules" (2006) 55 *Int'l & Comp. L. Q.* 281, at 305–6.

[102] *Case Concerning the Gabcikovo-Nagymaros Project* (1997) ICJ Reports 7, Separate Opinion of Judge Bedjaoui, at para. 12.

[103] T. Henriksen, "Revisiting the freedom of fishing and legal obligations of states not party to regional fisheries management organizations," at 81.

"like much of the language in the Law of the Sea Convention, the goal is universal application through direct state usage thus requiring a dissenting state to explain its objections."[104] In fact, if one analyzes the text in detail, it would appear that the language of the instrument has been chosen with care. It is only Article 21 of the Agreement dealing with enforcement and Articles 27–32 on the dispute settlement that are explicitly drafted in terms of "States Parties." It follows that states may have intended at the time of the Fish Stocks Conference that those provisions that are addressed to states generally should have an impact on customary international law for all states.[105] At least in terms of these provisions which are expressed in general terms and which are supported by consensus, the practice of states in negotiating the Agreement may have led to the crystallization of new rules of customary international law. This conclusion would also appear to find some support in subsequent state practice on the management and conservation of straddling and highly migratory fish stocks. Several sources of state practice and *opinio juris* can be considered to support this conclusion.

First, General Assembly resolutions on fisheries adopted following the conclusion of the Fish Stocks Agreement seem to support the view that the Agreement creates obligations for all states. On a number of occasions, the General Assembly has unambiguously called on "all states" to comply with certain provisions of the Agreement, not differentiating between parties and non-parties. For instance, General Assembly Resolution 57/143 calls on "all states to ensure that their vessels comply with the convention and management standards that have been adopted by sub-regional and regional fisheries management organizations and arrangements in accordance with relevant

---

[104] P. Orebech, K. Sigurjonsson, and T. L. McDorman, "The 1995 United Nations Straddling and Highly Migratory Fish Stocks Agreement: management, enforcement and dispute settlement" (1998) 13 *Int'l J. Marine & Coastal L.* 119 at 123. They continue: "such language is designed to create obligation to non-parties to the 1995 Agreement but mere semantics cannot overcome the principle that treaties are only binding upon ratifying states"; *ibid.*, at 124. Indeed, Jackson notes that one of the strengths of the Agreement is its "ready-made language which could be applied in almost any regional fisheries convention"; A. Jackson, "The 2001 Convention on the Conservation and Management of Fishery Resources in the South East Atlantic: an introduction" (2002) 17 *Int'l J. Marine & Coastal L.* 33, at 47.

[105] Cf. Franckx, "Pacta Tertiis and the Agreement for the Implementation of the Straddling and Highly Migratory Fish Stocks Provisions of the United Nations Convention of the Law of the Sea," at 49.

provisions of the Convention and of the Agreement,"[106] echoing Article 18(1) of the Agreement. Similarly, General Assembly Resolution 59/25 urges "all states to apply the precautionary approach and the ecosystem approach widely to the conservation, management and exploitation of fish stocks."[107] It is suggested that these resolutions can be invoked as further evidence of collective state practice and *opinio juris communis* supporting the creation of new norms of customary international law.

It is not only through the General Assembly that states have collectively asserted their support for the rules and principles found in the Fish Stocks Agreement. A variety of other bodies have considered the status of the Agreement.

As the UN specialized agency responsible for fisheries regulation, the Food and Agriculture Organization (FAO) has also been a forum for the development of state practice and *opinio juris* on this subject matter. The role of the FAO itself in developing international fisheries law will be considered in a later chapter. For present purposes, it is worth noting that the Fish Stocks Agreement is referred to in a number of legal instruments adopted by the FAO, including the 1995 Code of Conduct on Responsible Fisheries[108] and the 2009 Agreement on Port State Measures to Prevent, Deter and Eliminate Illegal, Unreported and Unregulated Fishing.[109] To the extent that these instruments reproduce rules and principles found in the Fish Stocks Agreement, they can be considered as evidence that such provisions are accepted by the international community as part of customary international law. A concrete example is found in paragraph 12 of the International Guidelines for the Management of Deep-sea Fisheries in the High Seas, adopted in 2008, which encourages states to inter alia "adopt and implement measures in accordance with the precautionary approach as reflected in Article 6 of the Fish Stocks Agreement."

---

[106] *Agreement for the Implementation of the Provisions of the United Nations Convention on the Law of the Sea of 10 December 1982 relating to the conservation and management of straddling fish stocks and highly migratory fish stocks*, UNGA Resolution 57/143, December 12, 2002, at para. 8; *Sustainable fisheries, including through the 1995 Agreement for the Implementation of the Provisions of the United Nations Convention on the Law of the Sea of 10 December 1982 relating to the Conservation and Management of Straddling Fish Stocks and Highly Migratory Fish Stocks, and related instruments*, UNGA Resolution 59/25, November 17, 2004, at para. 9.

[107] *Ibid.*, at para. 4.

[108] Code of Conduct on Responsible Fisheries, Article 3.2.

[109] 2009 Agreement on Port State Measures to Prevent, Deter and Eliminate Illegal, Unreported and Unregulated Fishing, preamble.

In addition to the practice of states acting through international organizations, individual state practice shows that some states have started to implement the provisions of the new fisheries regime, whether or not they are actually bound by the Agreement. This has been confirmed by many non-parties represented at the 2006 Review Conference on the Fish Stocks Agreement, where it was said that they had "continued their efforts for the conservation and management of fishery resources in accordance with the principles of the Agreement, including within regional fisheries management organizations."[110] In this regard, Jackson notes that the Fish Stocks Agreement formed an essential backdrop to the negotiation of the 2001 Windhoek Convention on the Conservation and Management of Fishery Resources in the South-East Atlantic Ocean, even though the Agreement had not entered into force at that time.[111] In a similar way, the 2000 Honolulu Convention on the Conservation and Management of Highly Migratory Fish Stocks in the Western and Central Pacific Ocean,[112] the 2003 Antigua Convention for the Strengthening of the Inter-American Tropical Tuna Commission[113] and the 2009 Convention on the Conservation and Management of High Seas Fishery Resources in the South Pacific Ocean[114] all recall the relevant provisions of the Law of the Sea Convention *and* the Fish Stocks Agreement. Other regional fisheries management organizations, although continuing to work within their existing legal instruments, have adopted numerous decisions and measures that seek to integrate the provisions of the Agreement into their practice.[115] On this basis, the United Nations Secretary-General

---

[110] *Report of the Review Conference on the Fish Stocks Agreement*, UN Document A/CONF.210/2006/16, at para. 127.

[111] See Jackson, "The 2001 Convention on the Conservation and Management of Fishery Resources in the South East Atlantic: an introduction," at 34. See also C. Hedley, "Entry into force of the United Nations Fish Stocks Agreement: an initial assessment" (2001) 24 *International Fisheries Bulletin* No. 24. The Convention entered into force in April 2003 with three contracting parties: Namibia, Norway and the European Community.

[112] The Convention entered into force on June 19, 2004; see *Oceans and the law of the sea*, UNGA Resolution 59/25, November 17, 2004, at para. 7.

[113] See www.iattc.org/HomeENG.htm <checked July 1, 2010>.

[114] The Convention was concluded in November 2009 and it will enter into force when it has been ratified by eight states, including three coastal states and three fishing states. See www.southpacificrfmo.org/ <checked July 1, 2010>.

[115] *The status and implementation of the Agreement for the Implementation of the Provisions of the United Nations Convention for the Law of the Sea of 10 December 1982 relating to the Conservation and Management of Straddling Fish Stocks and Highly Migratory Fish Stocks (the Fish Stocks Agreement) and its impact on related or proposed instruments throughout*

concludes in his 2003 Report on Sustainable Fisheries that "practice since the adoption of the Agreement demonstrates that even before entry into force, provisions of the Agreement have been widely used as a benchmark for measuring State practice."[116]

Of course, it does not follow that all the provisions of the Agreement are now reflected in rules of customary international law. As noted above, some parts of the Agreement, particularly those parts dealing with enforcement and dispute settlement, are drafted in terms of "States Parties." This deliberate choice of language suggests that these provisions were never intended to crystallize customary international law. Indeed, it is no surprise that the inspection and enforcement regime was one of the most controversial aspects of the Agreement when it was being negotiated and it continues to be subject to further discussion and debate in relevant international institutions.[117] At the 2006 Review Conference on the Fish Stocks Agreement, a number of states indicated that the inspection and enforcement provisions were one of the principal reasons why they had not become a party to the Agreement.[118] The hesitancy of states to accept the enforcement provisions is also confirmed by General Assembly resolutions on fisheries. In contrast to the examples considered above which would seem to confirm the application of many of the rules and principles in the Fish Stocks Agreement to non-parties, those aspects of the General Assembly resolutions on fisheries dealing with the inspection and enforcement provisions of the Agreement are expressly directed only at States Parties to the Agreement. For example, paragraph 10 of General Assembly Resolution 57/143 urges "States parties to the Agreement, in accordance with [Article 21(4)] to inform either directly or through the relevant regional or sub-regional fisheries management organization or arrangement, all States whose vessels fish on the high seas in the same region or sub-region of the form of identification issued by those States parties to officials duly authorized to carry out boarding and inspection functions in accordance with article 21 and 22 of the Agreement." It would appear that this resolution recognizes that the inspection and enforcement provisions of the Agreement remain a matter of treaty

the United Nations system, with special reference to implementation of Part VII of the Fish Stocks Agreement, dealing with the requirements of developing States, Report of the UN Secretary-General, UN Document A/58/215, at para. 46.

[116] Ibid., at para. 7.   [117] Ibid., at para. 57.

[118] Report of the Review Conference on the Fish Stocks Agreement, at paras. 34 and 125.

law. This also explains why the General Assembly continues to call upon all states to ratify or accede to the Fish Stocks Agreement.[119] In order to be fully effective, the Fish Stocks Agreement must be universally accepted as a treaty instrument.

4 Conclusion

The term implementing agreement is not found in the Law of the Sea Convention itself. Rather, the concept of an implementing agreement has arisen from the subsequent practice of states in developing the legal framework for the law of the sea. The negotiation of implementing agreements has been one of the main ways in which states have developed the core principles of the law of the sea regime since the conclusion of the 1982 Convention.

There is no doubt that the two implementing agreements considered in this chapter have had an important impact on the law of the sea by developing the relevant legal regime not only for their parties, but also for other states. It is also clear from the analysis in this chapter that the relationship between the two implementing agreements and the Convention differs in important ways. What they have in common is that they were negotiated in order to solve certain problems that had arisen in the application of the Law of the Sea Convention.

The direct connection between the implementing agreements and the Convention had important implications for the way in which they were negotiated. Given the widespread acceptance of the Convention as creating a legal framework for the oceans, it was also vital that these two instruments would also be generally acceptable to all states. Thus, it was important that as many states as possible were actively involved in the negotiations of the implementing agreements. It is for this reason that the United Nations was an appropriate forum for the conclusion of these instruments. The need for widespread acceptance of the instruments also necessitated the use of consensus decision-making techniques such as those that were first developed at UNCLOS III. Consensus was seen as a vital ingredient for the adoption of these modifications to the law of the sea regime.

---

[119] *Sustainable fisheries, including through the 1995 Agreement for the Implementation of the Provisions of the United Nations Convention on the Law of the Sea of 10 December 1982 relating to the Conservation and Management of Straddling Fish Stocks and Highly Migratory Fish Stocks, and related instruments*, UNGA Resolution 63/112, December 5, 2008, at para. 18.

At the end of the day, it is the political support of the international community for the implementing agreements that distinguishes them from the plethora of other treaties that have been concluded on the law of the sea since 1982. This has been reflected in the regular call by the UN General Assembly for "universal participation" in the implementing agreements.[120] This indicates a clear aspiration on the part of the international community that these instruments should be universally applicable in the same way as the Law of the Sea Convention itself.

In sum, it can be said that implementing agreements have offered an important tool for the development and modification of the law of the sea regime. Unlike the amendment procedures considered in the previous chapter, the negotiation of an implementing agreement is much more likely to preserve the consensus underlying the law of the sea regime and protect the integrity of the Convention. In this context, implementing agreements could remain an important mechanism in the development of the law of the sea in the future as long as the international community continues to value the need for a universal law of the sea that is applicable to all states.[121]

---

[120] See e.g. *Oceans and the law of the sea*, UNGA Resolution 63/111, December 5, 2008, at paras. 3–4. This can be contrasted with the attitude of the General Assembly towards other treaties on the law of the sea. For example, the 2001 General Assembly resolution simply "takes note" of the 2001 Convention on the Protection of Underwater Cultural Heritage; *Oceans and the law of the sea*, UNGA Resolution 56/12, November 28, 2001, at para. 43. See further N. Ferri, "Current legal developments – United Nations General Assembly" (2008) 23 *Int'l J. Marine & Coastal L.* 137.

[121] An implementing agreement is one of the possible outcomes of the current discussions taking place through the United Nations Ad Hoc Open-Ended Informal Working Group on the Conservation and Sustainable Use of Marine Biological Diversity Beyond National Jurisdiction; see *First report of the Working Group*, UN Document A/61/65, at paras. 25, 29, 55, 58, and 61. See also paragraph 11 of the summary of trends prepared by the co-chairs annexed to the Report. See also S. Hart, "Elements of a Possible Implementation Agreement to UNCLOS for the Conservation and Sustainable Use of Marine Biodiversity beyond National Jurisdiction," IUCN Environmental Policy and Law Papers online, Marine Series No. 4, 2008.

5   Developments in the deep seabed mining regime

1 Marine minerals and the International Seabed Area

Although the presence of minerals on the deep seabed was first discovered on the HMS *Challenger* expedition in 1873, it was not until the latter half of the twentieth century that their exploitation became technologically feasible. The regulation of deep seabed mining was addressed for the first time by the UN Seabed Committee and thereafter by delegates gathering at UNCLOS III to negotiate a new convention on the law of the sea. It was the issue that proved to be the most divisive at the Conference and despite protracted negotiations, participants were unable to achieve a compromise.[1] However, further consultations taking place under the auspices of the United Nations Secretary-General succeeded where UNCLOS III had failed. When the Law of the Sea Convention finally entered into force in November 1994, the international regime for the deep seabed found in Part XI of the Convention was substantially modified by the Part XI Agreement that had been adopted by the UN General Assembly in July of that year.[2] It is these two instruments that today provide the framework for the management of the International Seabed Area.[3]

Under Part XI of the Law of the Sea Convention, the Area is designated as the common heritage of mankind and it is managed on behalf of the international community as a whole by an international organization[4] called the International Seabed Authority.[5] Part XI defines the

---

[1] See Chapter 2.   [2] See Chapter 4.
[3] Also referred to as "the Area."
[4] Law of the Sea Convention, Articles 156–157.
[5] Hereinafter, the Authority.

powers of the Authority as well as the rights and duties of states and other actors conducting activities in the Area.

Part XI of the Law of the Sea Convention was never intended to provide a comprehensive legal code covering all aspects of the regulation of the International Seabed Area. Rather, it was intended that the legal regime should develop gradually over time as knowledge of the deep seabed expands. One of the key functions of the Authority is the enunciation of detailed rules and regulations to fill gaps in the framework left by the Law of the Sea Convention.

The purpose of this chapter is to consider the role of the Authority in implementing the Part XI regime. It examines the extent of the law-making powers conferred on the Authority by its constituent instrument as well as how these powers are exercised in practice. It also asks whether there are any limits on the ability of the Authority to modify the regulatory regime in the Convention. The latter question is particularly important given the considerable advances in deep seabed science that have taken place since the conclusion of the Convention in 1982. As our understanding of the oceans continues to improve, the challenge for the Authority is to respond to new discoveries through the progressive development of the legal regime for deep seabed mining.

2 The International Seabed Authority

The Authority came into existence on November 16, 1994, the same day that the Law of the Sea Convention entered into force. The Authority is an intergovernmental organization with international legal personality.[6] It has its headquarters in Jamaica where its organs meet to conduct the business of regulating deep seabed mining.[7] The Authority has its own secretariat that fulfills the administrative functions of the Authority.[8] The secretariat is headed by the Secretary-General,[9] who is assisted by a staff of about thirty individuals.

Cost-effectiveness was one of the principal aims of the Part XI Agreement.[10] As an autonomous international organization, the

---

[6] Law of the Sea Convention, Article 176.
[7] The Authority has on occasion met in New York.
[8] Law of the Sea Convention, Articles 158, 166–168.
[9] The first Secretary-General of the Authority was Satya Nandan of Fiji, who occupied the position for more than ten years. He was replaced by Nii Odunton of Ghana, who will serve as Secretary-General for an initial four-year term from January 1, 2009.
[10] Part XI Agreement, Annex, Section 1, para. 2.

Authority is funded by assessed contributions of its Members.[11] The Authority also receives income from the fees paid by contractors operating in the Area.[12] While the Authority is permitted to borrow funds under Article 174 of the Convention, the exercise of this power is restricted by the Part XI Agreement.[13] This is one of many measures taken through the Part XI Agreement to keep the costs of the organization to a minimum.

States can only become a Member of the Authority by becoming a party to the Law of the Sea Convention and all States Parties to the Convention are *ipso facto* Members of the Authority.[14] Therefore, more than 150 states are Members of the Authority.[15] However, it still falls far short of universal membership. It should be noted that the initial membership of the Authority was broader as any states which had signed the Part XI Agreement or which had consented to its adoption in the General Assembly were eligible for provisional membership of the Authority.[16] It was therefore possible for all interested states to participate in the work of the Authority at the crucial time when it was being set up, without formally becoming a full Member. It is on this basis that the United States was a provisional member of the Authority, including having a seat on the first Council, the first Finance Committee and the first Legal and Technical Commission. All provisional memberships expired on November 16, 1998, although states that are not members may still take part in the work of the Authority as observers.[17]

According to the Law of the Sea Convention, the primary function of the Authority is organizing, carrying out and controlling activities

---

[11] Law of the Sea Convention, Article 171. In the first two years of operation, the Authority was actually financed through the UN budget; see Part XI Agreement, Annex, Section 1, para. 14.

[12] Law of the Sea Convention, Article 171. The remaining balance of the fees paid by pioneer investors was used to establish an endowment fund to assist qualified scientists and technical personnel from developing countries to participate in marine scientific research programmes and activities; see M. Lodge, "Current legal developments – International Seabed Authority" (2009) 24 *Int'l J. Marine & Coastal L.* 185.

[13] Part XI Agreement, Annex, Section 1, para. 14. It does not prohibit all borrowing, only borrowing to cover the administrative costs of the organization.

[14] Law of the Sea Convention, Article 156(2). Note that states do not need to be a party to the Part XI Agreement in order to be a Member of the Authority; see Chapter 4.

[15] There were 160 Members as of December 1, 2009 – see www.isa.org.jm/en/about/members/states <checked May 10, 2010>.

[16] Part XI Agreement, Article 7 and Annex, section 1, para. 12

[17] See below, section 3.3.

in the Area.[18] This role includes both setting the detailed standards that govern the operations of deep seabed mining companies, as well as supervising the implementation of these standards and the general provisions of Part XI.[19] The Authority also has wider responsibilities for the protection of the marine environment in the Area, the promotion of marine scientific research in the Area, and the protection of underwater cultural heritage in the Area.[20] The functions of the Authority are distributed among four main organs: the Assembly, the Council, the Legal and Technical Commission and the Finance Committee.[21]

The Assembly is the plenary organ of the Authority,[22] consisting of all Member States.[23] It has a broad mandate and it is competent to establish general policies on any question or matter within the competence of the Authority.[24] Despite being the most democratic of the organs of the Authority, its powers have been somewhat diminished by the Part XI Agreement, which provides that the Assembly must act in collaboration with the Council on all issues.[25]

The Council is the "executive" organ of the Authority[26] and it consists of thirty-six representatives of the Member States, elected every four years by the Assembly.[27] Which states would have a seat on the Council and how it would make decisions were the subjects of intense discussion during

---

[18] Law of the Sea Convention, Article 153. Article 1(1)(1) of the Convention defines the Area as "the seabed and ocean floor and subsoil thereof, beyond the limits of national jurisdiction."

[19] The Convention also sees a role for the Authority in carrying out deep seabed mining through the so-called Enterprise. However, the operational role of the Enterprise was drastically reduced by the Part XI Agreement, Annex, Section 2.

[20] See e.g. T. Scovazzi, "Mining, protection of the environment, scientific research and bioprospecting: some considerations on the role of the International Seabed Authority" (2004) 19 Int'l J. Marine & Coastal L. 383.

[21] Plans for an Economic Planning Commission were abandoned in the Part XI Agreement; see Part XI Agreement, Annex, Section 1, para. 4.

[22] It is described in Article 160 of the Law of the Sea Convention as the "supreme organ of the Authority."

[23] Law of the Sea Convention, Article 159(1).

[24] Law of the Sea Convention, Article 160(1). Article 160(2) goes on to elaborate a detailed list of powers and functions of the Assembly.

[25] Part XI Agreement, Annex, Section 3, para. 1.

[26] Law of the Sea Convention, Article 162(1). For a full list of the powers and functions of the Council see Article 162(2). To describe it solely as an executive organ is misleading as it also plays an important part in policy-making.

[27] Elections are staggered so that there are in fact elections for half the members every two years; Law of the Sea Convention, Article 161(3). For details of the first election of the Council, see M. Wood, "International Seabed Authority: the first four years" (1999) Max Planck U. N. Ybk 172, at 201–9.

the consultations leading to the conclusion of the Part XI Agreement.[28] The composition of the Council is finely balanced to guarantee that all the major interest groups are represented. This is achieved through the creation of four so-called "chambers" composed as follows:[29]

(a)   Four members from among those States Parties which, during the last five years for which statistics are available, have either consumed more than 2 per cent in value terms of total world consumption or have had net imports of more than 2 per cent in value terms of total world imports of the commodities produced from the categories of minerals to be derived from the Area, provided that the four members shall include one State from the Eastern European region having the largest economy in that region in terms of gross domestic product and the State, on the date of entry into force of the Convention, having the largest economy in terms of gross domestic product, if such States wish to be represented in this group;

(b)   Four members from among the eight States Parties which have made the largest investments in preparation for and in the conduct of activities in the Area, either directly or through their nationals;

(c)   Four members from among States Parties which, on the basis of production in areas under their jurisdiction, are major net exporters of the categories of minerals to be derived from the Area, including at least two developing States whose exports of such minerals have a substantial bearing upon their economies;

(d)   Six members from among developing States Parties, representing special interests. The special interests to be represented shall include those of States with large populations, States which are land-locked or geographically disadvantaged, island States, States which are major importers of the categories of minerals to be derived from the Area, States which are potential producers of such minerals and least developed States.

In addition to the chambers, a further eighteen members shall be elected according to the principle of equitable geographical distribution of seats so that each geographical region (Africa, Asia, Eastern Europe, Latin America and the Caribbean, and Western Europe and Others) shall have at least one seat.[30] In practice, the composition

[28] The Part XI Agreement "disapplies" the original provisions of the Convention, replacing them with an amended text; Part XI Agreement, Annex, section 3, at paras. 15 and 16.

[29] Part XI Agreement, Annex, section 3, paras. 15(a)–(d), replacing Law of the Sea Convention, Article 161(1).

[30] Part XI Agreement, Annex, Section 3, para. 15(e).

of the Council is also subject to a detailed political compromise. On this basis, the agreed allocation of seats in the Council is ten seats to the African Group, nine seats to the Asian Group, eight seats to the Western European Group, seven seats to the Latin American and Caribbean Group, and three seats to the Eastern European Group.[31] As this adds up to thirty-seven and the official total of seats on the Council is thirty-six, it is agreed that each regional group other than the Eastern European Group will relinquish a seat in rotation.[32] The composition of the Council is significant, not only for participation in debates, but also for the voting procedures.[33]

The Legal and Technical Commission is a group of independent experts, specializing in subjects relevant to the exploration for and exploitation and processing of mineral resources, oceanography, protection of the marine environment, or economic or legal matters relating to ocean mining and related fields of expertise.[34] Members of the Commission are elected by the Council.[35] They hold office for five years, although they are eligible for reelection.[36] The Commission fulfills a largely advisory role, ensuring that decisions of the Authority are based upon sound scientific and technical advice and information.[37]

The Finance Committee is created under section 9 of the Part XI Agreement.[38] It is composed of fifteen members with appropriate qualifications relevant to financial matters, serving in an individual capacity. Members are elected by the Assembly.[39] However, the

---

[31] See Wood, "International Seabed Authority: the first four years." at 208.
[32] *Ibid.*   [33] See below, section 3.2.
[34] Law of the Sea Convention, Article 165(1).
[35] See Law of the Sea Convention, Article 163. The Commission is composed of at least fifteen members. In practice, however, the number has been greater as the Council has exercised its powers under Article 163 of the Convention to increase the size of the Commission. As a consequence, the size of the Commission has steadily grown; it was 22 in 1996, 24 in 2001 and 25 in 2006. It is likely that the size of the Commission will stay at 25 in the future; see Press Release, "Seabed Council continues discussion of size and composition of Authority's Expert Body – the Legal and Technical Commission." Document SB/16/10, April 30, 2010.
[36] Law of the Sea Convention, Article 163(6).
[37] Under the Part XI Agreement, the Legal and Technical Commission is also to fulfil the surviving functions of the Economic Planning Commission until the Council decides otherwise or until the approval of the first plan of work for exploitation; Part XI Agreement, Annex, Section 1, para. 4.
[38] Article 162(2)(y) of the Law of the Sea Convention mandated the Council to establish a subsidiary organ to deal with financial matters.
[39] Part XI Agreement, Annex, Section 9, para. 3.

composition of the Committee is designed so that the major con-
tributors to the budget of the Authority are guaranteed a seat and
therefore a greater say over the financial affairs of the organization.[40] In addition, the Committee shall include at least one member
from each of the "chambers" represented on the Council. In electing
other Members of the Finance Committee, the Assembly shall take
into account the need for equitable geographical representation.[41]
While the Finance Committee has no primary decision-making powers under the Convention, the Part XI Agreement makes clear that
decisions having financial or budgetary implications shall be based
on recommendations of the Finance Committee.[42] Therefore, the
Committee wields significant power over certain types of decision
made by the Authority.

The organs of the Authority play a variety of roles within the organization and their responsibility and influence differs depending on
the type of activity concerned. Many of the activities carried out by
the Commission and the Council are of an executive character. For
instance, it is these organs that are responsible for concluding contracts with investors for the exploration for or exploitation of mineral
resources in the Area, as well as supervising the execution of such
contracts.[43] However, it is the powers of the Authority to make rules
and regulations with which we are interested for present purposes.
The following sections will consider the scope of these powers and how
they are exercised in practice.

---

[40] Part XI Agreement, Annex, Section 9, para. 3. This privilege only exists
as long as the administrative costs of the Authority are funded by assessed
contributions.
[41] Part XI Agreement, Annex, Section 9, para. 3.
[42] Part XI Agreement, Annex, Section 3, para. 7. There is a question over the
interpretation of the phrase "based on." Similar language is found in other parts
of the Convention, i.e. Article 76(8), which says that "the limits of the continental
shelf established by a coastal state on the basis of [the recommendations of the
Commission on the Outer Limits of the Continental Shelf] shall be final and
binding." For a discussion of the interpretation of this provision, see T. McDorman,
"The role of the Commission on the limits of the continental shelf: a technical
body in a political world." (2002) 17 *Int'l J. Marine & Coastal L.* 301 at 314; Committee
on Legal Issues of the Outer Limits of the Continental Shelf, in *International Law
Association Report of the Seventy First Conference (Berlin 2004)* (International Law
Association, London, 2004) at 803.
[43] See in particular Law of the Sea Convention, Article 62(2)(g), (i), (j), (k), (l), (p), (w), (x),
(z), as amended by the Part XI Agreement.

3 The adoption of rules and regulations by the International Seabed Authority

3.1 Powers of the International Seabed Authority

The Authority has the power to adopt a variety of rules and regulations. Some of these powers of the Authority are concerned with the internal operation of the organization. For instance, the Authority has the power to adopt rules and regulations for the financial management and internal administration of the organization and on the relationship between the Authority and the Enterprise.[44] The Authority must also adopt criteria for the equitable sharing of financial and other economic benefits derived from activities in the Area.[45] It has a similar power to adopt criteria for the equitable sharing of payments or contributions made under Article 82 of the Convention in relation to the exploitation of nonliving resources of the continental shelf beyond 200 nautical miles.[46] Other powers of the Authority allow it to adopt rules and regulations that are applicable to the conduct of third parties in the Area.[47] These include rules to deal with all aspects of prospecting, exploration and exploitation of polymetallic nodules and other deep sea mineral resources located in the Area, including regulations relating to the prevention and control of pollution, the protection and conservation of natural resources in the Area,[48] the protection of human life,[49] and the erection, emplacement or removal of installations for the purpose of pursuing mining activities in the Area.[50]

These rules and regulations form a core component of the legal regime for deep seabed mining, supplementing the provisions of the Convention. The binding status of rules and regulations adopted by

[44] Law of the Sea Convention, Articles 160(2)(f)(ii) and 162(2)(o)(ii).
[45] Law of the Sea Convention, Articles 160(2)(f)(i) and 162(2)(o)(i).
[46] Law of the Sea Convention, Articles 82(4), 160(2)(f)(i) and 162(2)(o)(i). It has also been suggested that the Authority could develop rules and regulations concerning the methodology for determining the value of payments or contributions under Article 82; M. Lodge, "The International Seabed Authority and Article 82 of the UN Convention on the Law of the Sea" (2006) 21 *Int'l J. Marine & Coastal L.* 323, at 328–9.
[47] Law of the Sea Convention, Articles 160(2)(f)(ii) and 162(2)(o)(ii). See also Annex III, Article 17.
[48] Law of the Sea Convention, Articles 145 and 209. Article 209 requires States to adopt national laws which are at least as effective as the rules adopted by the Authority. See also Article 214.
[49] Law of the Sea Convention, Article 146.
[50] Law of the Sea Convention, Article 147.

the Authority is made clear by Article 137(2) of the Convention, which provides:

The minerals recovered from the Area may ... only be alienated in accordance with this Part and the rules, regulations and procedures of the Authority.

Rules and regulations adopted by the Authority are not only relevant to states but also to investors wishing to operate in the Area. The application of the rules and regulations of the Authority to investors is done by way of contract. All investors must enter into an agreement with the Authority before any prospecting, exploring or exploiting activity is carried out. In the case of prospecting, an investor must provide a written undertaking that it will comply with the Convention and relevant rules, regulations and procedures of the Authority.[51] For exploration and exploitation activities, the investor must enter into a formal contract with the Authority.[52] The standard clauses for contracts to explore the Area for polymetallic nodules are contained in an Annex to the Regulations on Prospecting and Exploration for Polymetallic Nodules in the Area.[53] They stipulate that "the Contractor shall carry out exploration within the terms and conditions of the contract, the Regulations, Part XI of the Convention, the Agreement and other rules of international law not incompatible with the Convention."[54] Thus, the rules and regulations of the Authority become directly binding on investors.

The power to adopt binding rules and regulations differentiates the Authority from many other international organizations whose standard-setting powers usually depend upon the subsequent consent of states.[55] In contrast, rules and regulations validly adopted by the Authority are binding, regardless of individual consent.[56] Under this system there is no room for a state to claim to be a persistent objector.

---

[51] Law of the Sea Convention, Annex III, Article 2. See also *Regulations on Prospecting and Exploration for Polymetallic Nodules in the Area*, Document ISBA/6/A/18, October 4, 2000, Part II.

[52] Law of the Sea Convention, Article 153(3) and Annex III, Article 3(5).

[53] *Regulations on Prospecting and Exploration for Polymetallic Nodules in the Area*, Annex 4.

[54] *Ibid.*, Annex 4, Section 13.1.

[55] See e.g. P. Sands and P. Klein, *Bowett's Law of International Institutions* (6th edn., Sweet & Maxwell, 2009) at 267.

[56] See also Law of the Sea Convention, Articles 208 and 209.

3.2 Decision-making procedures of the International Seabed Authority

The procedures for the adoption of rules and regulations by the Authority are very important given that such rules and regulations are automatically binding without the need for additional approval by states. It is perhaps unsurprising that these procedures were a key point of controversy in negotiating Part XI of the Law of the Sea Convention. According to US policy at the time, it was essential that the decision-making procedure of the proposed institution "fairly reflects and effectively protects the political and economic interests and financial contributions of participating states."[57] To a large extent, any disagreements over the decision-making procedures that prevented a consensus at UNCLOS III were eventually solved through the adoption of the Part XI Agreement.[58] In order to safeguard the interests of all states, the power of the Authority to adopt rules, regulations and procedures are subjected to a complex set of decision-making procedures. This power to adopt rules and regulations is divided between three principal organs of the Authority.

The standard-setting process starts with the Legal and Technical Commission. It is the role of the Commission to consider the technical aspects of the regulations and to draft proposals for further consideration by the Council.[59] Meetings of the Legal and Technical Commission are closed, although discussions on general issues are held in open session which members of the Authority are allowed to attend without participating in the discussions.[60]

Regulations drafted by the Commission are next submitted to the Council. The Council undertakes a detailed scrutiny of the draft regulations and it may make any modifications to the draft regulations it considers appropriate. While a limited number of Member States have seats on the Council, the rules of procedure allow any member of the Authority not represented on the Council to attend. These states are able to participate in discussions but they cannot vote.[61] In any case,

---

[57] United States Department of State, *Law of the Sea Current Policy No. 371*, January–February 1982, cited by D. Larson, "The Reagan rejection of the UN Convention" (1985) 14 *Ocean Dev. & Int'l L.* 337, at footnote 13.

[58] See Chapter 4.

[59] See Law of the Sea Convention, Article 165.

[60] For a summary of the drafting history of the Rules of Procedure of the Commission, see *Report of the Secretary-General of the International Seabed Authority under Article 166, paragraph 4, of the United Nations Convention on the Law of the Sea*, Document ISBA/10/A/3, March 31, 2004, at paras. 31–2.

[61] Rules of Procedure of the Council, Rule 74.

the Council must "seek to promote the interests of all members of the Authority."[62] While this is a reminder to members of the Council that they are acting on behalf of the wider membership, it is doubtful whether this provision creates a legal obligation and even if it did, it is difficult to see how it could be enforced.

Certain other safeguards are built into the decision-making procedure to ensure that the interests of some members cannot override those of others. The decision-making procedures of the Council are designed so that no major interest group can be overruled. In the first place, the Part XI Agreement promotes the adoption of a decision by consensus if possible.[63] In furtherance of this provision, the Council has a power to defer the taking of a decision in order to facilitate further negotiation whenever it appears that all efforts at achieving consensus have not been exhausted.[64] In addition, the Convention sets out a conciliation procedure that can be invoked by the president of the Council in order to try to facilitate a compromise between the differing views of members.[65] According to this procedure, a committee of nine members, with the president as chair, is mandated to produce a proposal that will be acceptable to all members. If it cannot reach agreement, the committee shall report the grounds on which a proposal is being opposed. If consensus ultimately cannot be achieved, ordinarily the adoption of decisions by the Council is subject to a qualified majority vote that requires the approval of a majority of states within each of the "chambers" represented on the Council.[66] This procedure was designed to ensure that decisions of the Council had the support of all of the important interest groups involved in the deep seabed mining regime. While this complex formula goes a long way to promoting a consensus among states, an even stricter decision-making procedure applies to the adoption of rules and regulations by the Council. Under Article 161(8)(d) of the Convention, the Council must adopt any rules or regulations by consensus. Consensus is defined in the Rules of Procedure as "the absence of any formal objection."[67] However, consensus in this context appears to have a different meaning to the use of the word in the other sections of Part XI as there are no alternative rules on voting

---

[62] Part XI Agreement, section 3, at para. 5.
[63] Part XI Agreement, section 3, at para. 2.
[64] Part XI Agreement, section 3, at para. 6.
[65] Law of the Sea Convention, Article 161(8)(e).
[66] Part XI Agreement, section 3, at para. 5.
[67] Rule 59 of the Rules of Procedure of the Council.

which apply in the absence of consensus. Rather, it would appear that the procedure comes closer to unanimity than to consensus as it is understood in other contexts. It follows that any single member of the Council can in practice veto a decision to adopt rules and regulations on deep seabed mining.

Once the proposed regulations are adopted by the Council, they are sent to the Assembly for approval. A two-thirds majority of the Assembly is necessary in order to approve the proposal from the Council, although it will first attempt to achieve consensus on the issue.[68] If the Assembly disagrees with the rules and regulations promulgated by the Council, it must resubmit them to the Council for further consideration. However, the Assembly itself appears to have no power to adopt amendments *proprio motu*.[69]

While the approval of the Assembly is necessary for the final adoption of any regulations, the Convention provides that any rules, regulations or procedures relating to prospecting, exploration, exploitation in the Area and the financial management and internal administration of the Authority which have been adopted by the Council are provisionally valid, pending the approval of the Assembly.[70] Even if the Assembly rejects the recommendations of the Council and the rules and regulations are resubmitted to the Council for further consideration, they will remain provisionally valid. As there is no time limit by which the Council must reevaluate the regulations rejected by the Assembly, rules and regulations adopted by the Council may remain provisionally valid for an indefinite period of time.

These provisions highlight the significance of the Council in the law-making process. In contrast, the role of the Assembly, the most democratic organ of the Authority, is much more limited. It is true that the composition of the Council and its decision-making procedures go a long way to ensuring that the rules and regulations are

---

[68] See Rule 61 of the Rules of Procedure of the Assembly.

[69] It is suggested that the reference to amendments in Article 160(2)(o)(ii) is to amendments to the rules and regulations that have been recommended by the Council. This view is further supported by Article 162(2)(o)(ii) which says that the Council may amend rules and regulations in light of the views expressed by the Assembly.

[70] Law of the Sea Convention, Article 162(2)(o)(ii). Cf. rules and regulations on the equitable sharing of financial and other contributions derived from activities in the Area or made under Article 82. In relation to these types of rules and regulations, the Council has the power only to make recommendations to the Assembly; see Law of the Sea Convention, Article 162(2)(o)(i).

generally acceptable to all the major interest groups, as well as the wider membership of the Authority. Moreover, any member of the Authority not represented on the Council has a right to send a representative to participate in discussions of the Council, albeit without a vote.[71] Nevertheless, it is possible that regulations could be provisionally applied, despite the objections of a number of Members of the Authority. From a practical perspective, a lack of agreement among Member States about the content of any regulations may be a disincentive for potential investors in deep seabed mining activities. Thus, it can be argued that legal certainty and commercial sense require that the regulations be approved by the Assembly before they are applied to mining activities.

Rules and regulations may be amended using the procedures described above. Indeed, the Legal and Technical Commission is mandated to keep all rules and regulations under review and propose changes to the Council.[72] The Assembly or the Council may also request a review of specific rules and regulations. While this incorporates flexibility in the regulatory framework that allows the Authority to respond to scientific or technological developments, it is important to note that the rights of existing contractors are safeguarded because any modifications to the regulations will not be applicable to existing contracts of work. Security of tenure is guaranteed by Article 153(6) of the Convention. Moreover, Article 19(2) of Annex III of the Convention makes clear that "any contract entered into in accordance with [the Convention] may be revised only with the consent of the parties." This provision has been implemented in section 24.2 of the current standard terms of contract, which provides that a contract "may also be revised by agreement between the Contractor and the Authority to facilitate the application of any rules, regulations and procedures adopted by the Authority subsequent to the entry into force of this contract." Thus, it is necessary to negotiate changes to contracts on a case-by-case basis.[73] In these circumstances, the contractor is likely to retain a strong position in negotiations and amendments to regulations cannot be imposed on existing contractors against their will.[74]

---

[71] Law of the Sea Convention, Article 161(9).
[72] Law of the Sea Convention, Article 165(2)(g).
[73] This opinion is supported by the Secretariat; see *Review of outstanding issues with respect to the draft regulations on prospecting and exploration for polymetallic sulphides in the Area*, Document ISBA/14/C/4, April 8, 2008, at para. 32.
[74] It has been suggested that contractors themselves should be permitted to request a review of relevant regulations; see *ibid.*, at para. 33.

3.3 Participation in the decision-making process

It is not only Member States of the Authority who are involved in the law-making process. As noted above, the rules and regulations of the Authority are relevant not only to Member States, but also to other states and non-state actors. There are several categories of other international actors who may have an interest in the development of the regulatory regime for deep seabed mining. First, there are those states that are not yet a Member of the Authority. Secondly, there are other international organizations that may have an overlapping or similar mandate to the Authority. Thirdly, there are nongovernmental organizations (NGOs) with an interest in deep seabed mining, such as mining companies or environmental campaign organizations. The instruments constituting the deep seabed mining regime make various provisions for these actors to participate to some extent in the deliberations of the Authority.

Article 156(3) of the Convention provides that observers at UNCLOS III who have signed the Final Act shall have the right to participate in the Authority as observers in accordance with its rules, regulations and procedures.[75] The internal rules of procedure of the Authority further clarify rights of participation of observers. Rule 82 of the Rules of Procedure of the Assembly permits all states that are not Members of the Authority to take part in the deliberations of the Assembly as observers. Such states have speaking rights but they may not vote. At the time of writing, thirty-five states are registered as observers and many of them actively participate in meetings of the Assembly.[76] Upon invitation, state observers may also participate in meetings of the Council on questions affecting them or within the scope of their activities.[77] For example, the United States, although not a Member of the Authority, has at times taken an active part in discussions of the organization.

Other international organizations and NGOs are more limited in the ways in which they can interact with the Authority. According to Article 169 of the Convention, the Secretary-General of the Authority is empowered to enter into "suitable arrangements" for consultation and cooperation with international organizations and NGOs recognized by

---

[75] It also includes Namibia which was represented at UNCLOS III by the UN Council for Namibia.

[76] See www.isa.org.jm/en/about/members/states/observers <checked March 3, 2010>.

[77] Rules of Procedure of the Council, Rule 75.

the Economic and Social Council of the United Nations (ECOSOC). In pursuance of this provision, the Authority has entered into arrangements with a number of intergovernmental organizations.[78] The Authority concluded a Relationship Agreement with the United Nations in 1997 to promote cooperation between the two organizations.[79] Article 6 of the Relationship Agreement provides for reciprocal representation under which the Authority commits to inviting the United Nations to send representatives to all its meetings and conferences subject to the rules of procedure and practice of the bodies concerned.[80] The Authority has also concluded a Memorandum of Understanding with the International Oceanographic Commission of UNESCO in which the two organizations undertake to "invite each other's representatives to attend and participate in the meetings of their respective governing bodies as observers in accordance with the rules of procedures of such bodies."[81]

It is not necessary to enter into a formal arrangement with the Authority under Article 169 of the Convention in order to qualify for observer status under the rules of procedures of the organs of the Authority, however. Indeed, the ability to request observer status under the rules of procedure of the Authority extends not only to NGOs who are recognized by ECOSOC, but also to "other non-governmental organizations invited by the Assembly which have demonstrated their interest in matters under consideration by the Assembly."[82] In the first four years of operation of the Authority, a number of NGOs were registered as observers, including the Permanent Commission of the South Pacific, Greenpeace International, the International Ocean Institute and the South Pacific Applied Geoscience Commission.[83] Since then, observer status has also been conferred on the International Association of

---

[78] For example, the Secretariat of the Convention on Biological Diversity; see *Statement of the President on the work of the Assembly at the fifth session*, August 27, 1998, Document ISBA/5/A/14, at para. 5.

[79] 1997 Relationship Agreement between the United Nations and the International Seabed Authority, available at www.isa.org.jm/files/documents/EN/Regs/UN-ISA-Agrmnt.pdf <checked March 3, 2010>.

[80] *Ibid.*, Article 6(2).

[81] Memorandum of Understanding between the Intergovernmental Oceanographic Commission of UNESCO and the International Seabed Authority, para. 3, available at www.isa.org.jm/files/documents/EN/Regs/ISA-IOC-MOU.pdf <checked March 3, 2010>.

[82] Rules of Procedure of the Assembly, Rule 82(1)(e).

[83] See Wood, "International Seabed Authority: the first four years." at 222.

Drilling Contractors,[84] the International Conservation Union (IUCN),[85] the World Wildlife Fund and the Commonwealth Secretariat.[86] The Authority has also actively sought the participation of other organizations in its work in order to promote cooperation and coherence in activities impacting upon the Area. In 2009 the Assembly suggested that the Authority should invite the International Cable Protection Committee, an organization composed of government administrations and private companies owning and operating seabed cables, to become an observer given the overlap between its work and that of the Authority.[87]

The rights of participation of observers are governed by the rules of procedure. Such rights will vary depending on the type of actor involved and the organ in which it wishes to participate. For instance, intergovernmental organizations may participate in deliberations of the Assembly upon the invitation of the president.[88] NGOs, on the other hand, may also attend meetings of the Assembly but they are restricted to making oral statements on the invitation of the president.[89] This appears to fall short of full participation in discussions. Similar arrangements apply to meetings of the Council.[90] There is no right for observers to attend meetings of the Legal and Technical Commission. However, the latter may, if it considers it appropriate, consult any intergovernmental organization on matters being discussed by the Commission.[91]

It is not only through observation at formal meetings of the Authority that nonmembers may influence the work of the Authority. The Authority has been proactive in organizing regular workshops on scientific and technical issues, through which experts can participate in discussions over developments and challenges to the deep seabed regime.[92] Participants in workshops include independent academics,

---

[84] *Statement of the President on the work of the Assembly at the fifth session*, Document ISBA/5/A/14, at para. 5.
[85] *Statement of the President on the work of the Assembly at the eleventh session*, Document ISBA/11/A/11, August 25, 2005, at para. 22.
[86] *Statement of the President of the Assembly of the International Seabed Authority on the work of the Assembly at the fifteenth session*, Document ISBA/15/A/9, May 11, 2009, at paras. 5–6.
[87] *Ibid.*, at para. 13.
[88] Rules of Procedure of the Assembly, Rule 82.
[89] Rules of Procedure of the Assembly, Rule 83(3)–(6).
[90] Rules of Procedure of the Council, Rule 75.
[91] Rules of Procedure of the Legal and Technical Commission, Rule 15.
[92] See http://www.isa.org.jm/en/scientific/workshops <checked May 10, 2010>.

scientists and researchers, as well as representatives of contractors and the offshore mining industry. The results of these workshops can have an important influence on the deliberations of the Legal and Technical Commission when preparing recommendations for the Council.[93] Indeed, participants in a workshop on prospects for mining cobalt rich ferromanganese crusts and polymetallic sulphides in the Area held in 2006 were called on to examine the proposals for regulations that had been prepared by the Legal and Technical Commission.[94] While participation in these events is inevitably limited, they represent an important means through which non-state actors can influence the work of the Authority.

In sum, the deliberations of the Assembly involve a broader range of actors that goes beyond those States that are Members of the Authority. The number of observers is currently low, although this could per-haps be attributed to the highly specialized mandate of the Authority. Nevertheless, those NGOs that have been accredited as observers are able to bring pressure to bear on the decision-makers at the Authority. The organization of scientific and technical workshops also provides a mechanism through which the views of independent experts and non-state actors can influence the work of the Authority at a key stage of the drafting process. Ultimately, however, it is the States that are Members of the Authority that control the decision-making process.

4 Formal amendment of the deep seabed mining regime

It was always envisaged that the international regime created under Part XI of the Convention would have to be reviewed in order to ensure that it was operating in such a way that it furthered the aims of the inter-national community. Article 155 of the Convention originally provided for a review conference to take place fifteen years after the commence-ment of commercial mining in the Area. This procedure was additional to a periodic review to be undertaken by the Assembly of the Authority every five years.[95] As originally conceived, the Review Conference was

---

[93] See International Seabed Authority, *Marine Mineral Resources: Scientific Advances and Economic Perspectives* (United Nations, 2004) at 13.

[94] See *Possible adjustments to the draft regulations for prospecting and exploration for cobalt-rich ferromanganese crusts and polymetallic sulphides suggested by the workshop on technical and economic considerations relating to mining polymetallic sulphides and cobalt-rich crusts in the Area with respect to polymetallic sulphides*, Document ISBA/12/C/7, August 8, 2006.

[95] Law of the Sea Convention, Article 154.

controversial because it would have had the power to adopt amendments to the Convention which would have become binding on all States Parties following acceptance by only three fourths of States Parties. In other words, Members could have been bound by amendments without their consent, a feature that was in particular unpopular with those industrialized states who were opposed to the creation of a powerful international organization to oversee the International Seabed Area. As a result of this hostility, the provisions on a review conference were largely disapplied by the 1994 Part XI Agreement.[96]

Any amendments to the treaty provisions of the international regime for deep seabed mining must be achieved through the amendment mechanism found in Part XVII of the Convention.[97] It is the Authority that has the power to adopt amendments to Part XI of the Convention subject to a special amendment procedure contained in Article 314 of the Convention. According to this procedure, any Member of the Authority can propose amendments by submitting a written communication to the Secretary-General of the Authority, who shall in turn circulate the proposal to all other Member States. The proposed amendment is then subject to the approval of the Assembly and the Council, the latter acting by consensus.[98] Consensus in this context has the same meaning as for the adoption of rules and regulations. In other words, any Member of the Council can veto a proposed amendment.[99]

Once amendments have been adopted by the Authority, they must be subsequently accepted by individual States Parties to the Convention. According to Article 316(5) of the Convention, an amendment to Part XI which has been adopted in accordance with Article 314 shall enter into force for all States Parties one year after the deposit of instruments of ratification or accession by three fourths of the States Parties. Acceptance by over three fourths of Member States is a higher threshold than that required for amendments to other parts of the Convention.[100]

---

[96] Part XI Agreement, Annex, Section 4.
[97] See M. Nordquist, *et al.* (eds.), *United Nations Convention on the Law of the Sea 1982 – A Commentary, Vol. 6*, (Martinus Nijhoff, 2002) at para. 155.10.
[98] See Law of the Sea Convention, Article 161(8)(d).
[99] See S. Rosenne *et al.* (eds.), *United Nations Convention on the Law of the Sea – A Commentary, Vol. 6* (Martinus Nijhoff Publishers, 2002) at para. 155.11.
[100] Compare Law of the Sea Convention, Article 316(1), which requires the approval of two thirds of States Parties for an amendment to other parts of the Convention to enter into force.

This provision is notable in that amendments that have been accepted by three fourths of the membership become binding on all the States Parties, whether or not they have individually consented to them. There is no opportunity for an objecting state to prevent the application of the amendment to itself, short of denouncing the Convention.[101] Once again, it is the procedures for adoption of amendments through the Authority that provide a crucial safeguard for the interests of all states.

An apparent limitation on the use of the amendment procedure is found in Article 311(6), which provides:

States Parties agree that there shall be no amendments to the basic principle relating to the common heritage of mankind set forth in Article 136 and that they shall not be party to any agreement in derogation thereof.

The precise effect of this provision has been much debated. It has been suggested that the provision is a declaration of the peremptory status of the principle of the common heritage of mankind. If this were the case, no derogation from the principle is permitted and any agreement in conflict with the principle would be void in accordance with Article 53 of the 1969 Vienna Convention on the Law of Treaties.[102] However, there are problems with this argument. In particular, any mention of *jus cogens* was removed from the text of Article 311(6) in the course of the negotiations.[103] As a result, an intention to confer the status of *jus cogens* on such provisions cannot be easily implied from the text of the Convention. As the International Law Commission says in its commentary to Article 53 of the Vienna Convention on the Law of Treaties, it would not be correct to say that "a provision in a treaty possesses the character of jus cogens merely because the parties have stipulated that no derogation from that provision is to be permitted

---

[101] On denunciation, see Law of the Sea Convention, Article 317. Even then it is arguable that the general principles of Part XI prohibiting exploitation in the national interest are part of customary international law. See Chapter 4.

[102] Article 53 of the Vienna Convention on the Law of Treaties provides that: "A treaty is void if, at the time of its conclusion, it conflicts with a peremptory norm of general international law. For the purposes of the present Convention, a peremptory norm of general international law is a norm accepted and recognized by the international community of States as a whole as a norm from which no derogation is permitted and which can be modified only by a subsequent norm of general international law having the same character."

[103] M. Nordquist *et al.* (eds.), *United Nations Convention on the Law of the Sea – A Commentary*, Vol. 5 (Martinus Nijhoff, 1989) at 241.

so that another treaty which conflicted with that provision would be void."[104]

Even if it is accepted that Article 211(6) confers the status of a peremptory norm on the principle of the common heritage of mankind, it does not follow that no amendments could ever be made to the principle of the common heritage of mankind. As noted by Waldock when he was special rapporteur on the law of treaties, "it would clearly be wrong to consider rules now accepted as rules of jus cogens as immutable of abrogation or amendment in the future."[105] The text of Article 53 of the Vienna Convention on the Law of Treaties itself admits that *jus cogens* norms can be modified by a subsequent norm having the same character. Moreover, a norm cannot maintain the status of *jus cogens* if a substantial majority of the international community no longer consider it as such.[106] In the present context, it would be possible to circumvent the prohibition on amendments to the principle of the common heritage of mankind in Article 211(6) of the Convention by first amending Article 211(6) itself. Thus, the restriction on amendments in Article 211(6) of the Convention cannot be taken as preventing the adoption of amendments to Part XI of the Convention.[107]

The amendment procedures offer one way in which the Authority can alter the provisions of Part XI of the Convention to respond to regulatory challenges posed by new discoveries in relation to the deep seas. However, there are considerable disadvantages to invoking the Part XI amendment procedure. The adoption and approval of amendments to Part XI under this procedure is likely to be a very slow process. The requirement for three fourths of States Parties to accept amendments before they enter into force, while providing an important safeguard to the integrity of the Convention, sets a high threshold. It could take many years for amendments to enter into force. Given these obstacles, it is unsurprising that Members of the Authority have developed the legal regime for seabed mining in other ways that have circumvented the formal amendment procedures.

[104] International Law Commission, "Report of the International Law Commission on the Law of Treaties" (1966-II) *Ybk Int'l L. Commission* 248.
[105] H. Waldock, "Second report on the Law of Treaties" (1963–II) *Ybk Int'l L. Commission* 199. See also "Report of the International Law Commission on the Law of Treaties."
[106] C. L. Rozakis, *The Concept of Jus Cogens in the Law of Treaties* (North-Holland, 1976) at 89–94. Cf. A. Orakhelashvili, *Peremptory Norms in International Law* (Oxford University Press, 2006) at 129–30.
[107] See also Nordquist *et al.* (eds.), *United Nations Convention on the Law of the Sea – A Commentary, Vol. 5*, at 243.

5 The regulatory regime for polymetallic nodules

5.1 *Regulations on prospecting and exploring for polymetallic nodules*

The ability of the Authority to adopt rules and regulations confers on the organization a powerful tool to develop the legal regime for deep seabed mining. It allows the Authority to respond flexibly to issues that may not have been foreseen at the time that the Convention was drafted.

The first set of regulations adopted by the Authority on prospecting and exploring for polymetallic nodules illustrate how the Authority is able to develop the legal regime for the Area.[108] The regulations were drafted by the Legal and Technical Commission between 1997 and 1998 and they were then submitted to the Council for discussion. Amendments and drafting changes were made by the Council before the regulations were provisionally adopted on July 13, 2000.[109] The regulations were authoritatively adopted by the Assembly on the same day following a short debate.[110]

The Polymetallic Nodules Regulations are divided into nine parts covering use of terms; prospecting; applications for the approval of plans of work; contracts for exploration; protection and preservation of the marine environment; confidentiality; general procedures; dispute settlement; and resources other than polymetallic nodules.[111] Many aspects of the Regulations simply reproduce rules that were already contained in the Convention or the Part XI Agreement. For instance, the Regulations implement the so-called parallel system found in Article 8 of Annex III the Convention. Under the parallel system, an application to undertake exploration activities in the Area must cover a total area sufficiently large to sustain two mining operations, one that is to be conducted by the contractor and the other that is to be reserved to the Authority itself.[112] According to the treaties, the applicant is to indicate the coordinates dividing the area into two parts of equal estimated commercial

---

[108] The regulations are limited to prospecting and exploration and a further set of regulations will have to be adopted to apply to exploitation of polymetallic nodules at some stage in the future when exploitation is more likely.

[109] *2001 report of the Secretary-General of the International Seabed Authority*, Document ISBA/7/A/2, May 18, 2001, at paras. 22–3.

[110] See *Decision of the Assembly relating to the Regulations on Prospecting and Exploration for Polymetallic Nodules in the Area*, Document ISBA/6/A/18, July 13, 2000.

[111] *Regulations on Prospecting and Exploration for Polymetallic Nodules in the Area*, Annex.

[112] Law of the Sea Convention, Annex III, Article 8; Part XI Agreement, Annex, Section 1, para. 10.

value and it is up to the Authority, acting through the Council and the Legal and Technical Commission, to designate which of the parts should be reserved to the Authority.[113] It is through the exploration and exploitation of reserved areas that it is envisaged that the international community will participate directly in deep seabed mining.[114]

The Polymetallic Nodules Regulations reproduce many of the rules and procedures concerning the approval of applications as found in the Convention and the Part XI Agreement. They also provide further information on the procedure that applies to the designation of reserved areas and the information that must be provided by an applicant for the purposes of satisfying the treaty requirements.[115] All applications submitted to the Authority must be accompanied by information concerning the financial and technical capabilities of the applicant,[116] as well as an undertaking that the applicant agrees to comply with the applicable obligations created by the Convention and the rules and regulations adopted by the Authority and any contracts entered into between the applicant and the Authority.[117] The application is first considered by the Legal and Technical Commission, which is responsible for considering inter alia whether or not the applicant possesses the necessary financial and technical capability to carry out deep seabed mining operations and whether the proposed plan of exploration will provide effective protection of human health and safety and effective protection of the marine environment.[118] If the conditions specified in the Regulations are met, the Commission must recommend to the Council that the plan of work for exploration should be approved.[119] Plans of work are deemed to be approved by the Council unless it

---

[113] Law of the Sea Convention, Annex III, Article 8; Part XI Agreement, Annex, Section 1, para. 10.
[114] It is the role of the Enterprise, established under Article 170 of the Convention, which was intended to carry out activities in the Area directly. The Part XI Agreement modifies the provisions on mining by limiting the participation of the Enterprise initially to joint ventures. The Part XI Agreement further provides that the contractor that contributed a particular reserved area has the right of first refusal to enter into a joint-venture arrangement with the Enterprise. If the Enterprise does not decide to commence activities in a reserved area within fifteen years of the date on which it is reserved to the Authority, the contractor that contributed the reserved area may submit a plan of work for that reserved area; see Part XI Agreement, Annex, Section 2.
[115] *Regulations on Prospecting and Exploration for Polymetallic Nodules in the Area*, Regulations 15 and 16 and Annex 2, Section 2.
[116] *Ibid.*, Regulation 12.   [117] *Ibid.*, Regulation 14.
[118] *Ibid.*, Regulation 21(3) and (4).   [119] *Ibid.*, Regulation 21(5).

decides to disapprove a plan of work by a decision supported by two thirds of its members present and voting, including a majority of members present and voting in each chamber of the Council.[120] The Council must act within sixty days, otherwise a plan of work is automatically deemed to have been approved.[121]

The Polymetallic Nodules Regulations also introduce some innovations that appear to add to the rights and obligations that are found in the text of Part XI. An excellent example of the way in which the Regulations significantly develop the legal regime for the Area is the section on the protection of the marine environment. The Law of the Sea Convention was concluded at a time when international environmental law was still in its infancy. Although Article 209 of the Convention requires the adoption of measures to prevent, produce and control pollution of the marine environment in the Area, the content of such measures was left to future elaboration by the Authority. Article 145 of the Convention expressly foresees the adoption of regulations for the prevention, reduction and control of pollution from seabed activities, as well as regulations for the protection and conservation of the natural resources of the Area. Furthermore, Annex III specifies that "rules, regulations and procedures shall be drawn up in order to secure effective protection of the marine environment from harmful effects directly resulting from activities in the Area or from shipboard processing immediately above the mine site of minerals derived from that mine site."[122] The precise content of these rules and regulations was left to the discretion of the Authority.

The need for strong protection of seabed ecosystems is strengthened by the recognition that our understanding of the deep seas is still relatively poor.[123] Indeed, the adoption of rules, regulations and procedures for the protection of the marine environment was one of the priority areas for the Authority identified by the Part XI Agreement.[124] It is therefore no surprise that the protection and preservation of the marine environment was a major issue in the drafting of the Polymetallic

[120] Part XI Agreement, Annex, section 2, para. 11. This procedure replaces the procedure contained in Article 162(j) of the Law of the Sea Convention.
[121] *Ibid.*
[122] Law of the Sea Convention, Annex III, Article 17(f).
[123] See *Biodiversity, species range and gene flow in the abyssal Pacific nodule province: predicting and managing the impacts of deep seabed mining*, Document ISBA/14/C/2, February 14, 2008.
[124] Part XI Agreement, Annex, Section 1, para. 5(g).

Nodules Regulations. The protection of the marine environment is an issue that has been integrated into the provisions on prospecting and exploration for the resources covered by the regulations.

Regulation 31 places an overarching obligation on the Authority, states and contractors to take measures to protect and preserve the marine environment in accordance with the precautionary approach as reflected in Principle 15 of the 1992 Rio Declaration on Environment and Development.[125] This provision clearly reflects an evolution in the law since the conclusion of the Convention, as the precautionary approach was not an accepted principle of international law at that time.[126]

While there are no specific environmental requirements imposed on prospectors for polymetallic nodules, the regulations do provide that "prospecting shall not be undertaken if substantial evidence indicates the risk of serious harm to the marine environment." This obligation suggests that prospectors must carry out some form of environmental impact assessment in order to know whether a risk of serious harm might arise.[127] Moreover, prospectors shall notify the Authority if an incident occurs which causes harm to the marine environment.[128]

More detailed obligations with respect to the marine environment are imposed upon entities wishing to conduct exploration activities for polymetallic nodules in the Area. When submitting plans of work for exploration activities, applicants are required to include inter alia a

---

[125] *Regulations on Prospecting and Exploration for Polymetallic Nodules in the Area*, Regulation 31(2). Principle 15 of the Rio Declaration provides that "in order to protect the environment, the precautionary approach shall be widely applied by states according to their capabilities. Where there are threats of serious or irreversible damage, lack of full scientific certainty shall not be used as a reason for postponing cost-effective measures to prevent environmental degradation."

[126] Indeed, the precise status of the precautionary approach remains controversial. See e.g. D. Freestone, "International fisheries law since Rio: the continued rise of the precautionary principle" in A. E. Boyle and D. Freestone (eds.), *International Law and Sustainable Development* (Oxford University Press, 1999); P. Birnie, A. E. Boyle, and C. Redgwell, *International Law and the Environment* (3rd edn., Oxford University Press, 2009) at 159–64.

[127] As has been argued in a different context, "without prior assessment there can be no meaningful notification and consultation in most cases of environmental risk"; Birnie, Boyle and Redgwell, *International Law and the Environment*, at 169.

[128] *Regulations on Prospecting and Exploration for Polymetallic Nodules in the Area*, Regulation 7. The regulations do not specify any particular form that the notification must take, although it can reasonably be argued that it should contain the information required from contractors in similar circumstances; see below.

preliminary assessment of the possible impact of the proposed exploration activities on the marine environment, as well as a description of a program for oceanographic and environmental baseline studies which would allow an assessment of the potential environmental impact of the proposed exploration activities once they have commenced.[129] A contractor is also required to monitor its environmental impacts during exploration and to take "necessary measures to prevent, reduce and control pollution and other hazards to the marine environment arising from its activities in the Area as far as reasonably possible using the best technology available to it."[130] Such measures are vital given that there is still a relative lack of understanding about deep seabed ecosystems and how mining activities may affect them.[131]

Regulation 32 develops rules relating to pollution emergencies that may threaten to significantly harm the marine environment.[132] All contractors must submit a contingency plan to the Secretary-General stating what measures will be taken in the case of an environmental emergency.[133] If a contractor, through its activities in the Area, causes or is likely to cause serious harm to the marine environment, it must immediately warn other contractors and shipping operating in the vicinity.[134] In addition, the contractor must notify the Secretary-General of the incident. The notification must include the coordinates of the area affected, a description of any action being taken by the contractor to prevent, contain or minimize any harm to the marine environment, and any supplementary information reasonably requested by the Secretary-General.[135] In turn, the Secretary-General must notify the Legal and Technical Commission and the Council.[136] The Council may issue emergency orders as may be reasonably necessary to prevent, contain and minimize serious harm to the marine environment.[137] This was foreseen by the Convention, which authorizes the Legal and Technical Commission to "make recommendations to the

---

[129] *Ibid.*, Regulation 18(b) and (c). This requirement was actually imposed by the Part XI Agreement, Annex, Section 1, para. 7.

[130] *Ibid.*, Regulation 31(2) and (4).

[131] See *Biodiversity, species range and gene flow in the abyssal Pacific nodule province: predicting and managing the impacts of deep seabed mining*, Document ISBA/14/C/2, February 14, 2008.

[132] See Law of the Sea Convention, Article 162(w).

[133] *Regulations on Prospecting and Exploration for Polymetallic Nodules in the Area*, Annex 4, section 6.1.

[134] *Ibid.*   [135] *Ibid.*, section 6.2.

[136] *Ibid.*, at Regulation 32(1).   [137] *Ibid.*, Regulation 32(6).

Council to issue emergency orders, which may include orders for the suspension or adjustment of operations, to prevent serious harm to the marine environment arising out of activities in the Area."[138] However, the Regulations also allow the Secretary-General of the Authority to take immediate measures to prevent, contain or minimize the harm.[139] Any measures taken by the Secretary-General are provisional and they will be effective for no longer than ninety days or until the Council has decided what measures it wishes to impose, whichever is shorter. Nevertheless, the provision allows a rapid response to any threat to the marine environment. Permanent measures should be adopted by the Council, taking into account the recommendations of the Legal and Technical Commission.[140] The contractor must reimburse the Authority for any expenses incurred in taking measures to respond to a pollution emergency.[141] These detailed provisions go further than the measures foreseen in the Convention or the Part XI Agreement.

These provisions on protecting the deep seabed environment are important developments in the legal regime relating to the Area. They establish a regime of environmental liability in the Area that confers powers on the Authority to enable it to respond effectively to pollution emergencies, while ensuring that the cost for taking remedial measures is borne by the polluter. Given that scientists are only just beginning to appreciate the complexities of deep seabed ecosystems, it may be that the Authority comes to play a significant role in regulating this aspect of deep seabed activities in the future.[142]

5.2 Recommendations of the Authority

As well as developing the regulatory framework for deep seabed mining through binding rules and regulations, the Authority has also adopted nonbinding instruments relating to the exploration for polymetallic nodules. The use of nonbinding instruments is expressly envisaged by the Polymetallic Regulations as a means of developing the regulatory

---

[138] Law of the Sea Convention, Article 165(2)(k).
[139] *Regulations on Prospecting and Exploration for Polymetallic Nodules in the Area*, at Regulation 32(2).
[140] *Ibid.*, Regulation 32(5). See also Law of the Sea Convention, Article 162(2)(w).
[141] *Regulations on Prospecting and Exploration for Polymetallic Nodules in the Area*, Annex 4, section 6.4.
[142] See Scovazzi, "Mining, protection of the environment, scientific research and bioprospecting." at 383.

framework of deep seabed mining. Regulation 38 confers on the Legal and Technical Commission the general power to adopt "recommendations of a technical or administrative nature for the guidance of contractors to assist them in the implementation of the rules, regulations and procedures of the Authority."

Several of the regulations, especially those dealing with environmental issues, suggest that specific guidelines will be developed in the future.[143] The Commission issued its first set of recommendations relating to environmental baseline studies in 2001,[144] based on the outcomes of a workshop convened by the Authority in June 1998. These recommendations aim to define the biological, chemical, geological and physical components to be measured by the contractors in order to ensure the effective protection of the marine environment. They define the type of data that a contractor should gather in performance of its duties under the regulations. They also specify which activities require prior environmental impact assessment and monitoring programs and specify some of the measurements and observations that the contractor should make both during and after performing a specific activity.[145]

While recommendations are, by their very nature, nonbinding, they represent an important indication of what is expected of contractors by the Authority. The fact that recommendations are drafted and adopted by the same body that initially determines whether contractors are complying with their obligations under the Convention could influence a contractor in deciding whether or not to abide by the recommendations.

---

[143] See *Regulations on Prospecting and Exploration for Polymetallic Nodules in the Area*, Regulations 18(b), 31(2) (4) and (5).

[144] See *Recommendations for the guidance of the contractors for the assessment of the possible environmental impacts arising from exploration for polymetallic nodules in the Area*, Document ISBA/7/LTC/1/Rev.1, February 13, 2002. The Council took note of the recommendations and said that further consideration should be given to them at a future session; see *Statement of the President on the work of the Council at the seventh session*, Document ISBA/7/C/7, July 12, 2001, at para. 9.

[145] It was agreed at the fifteenth session of the Commission in 2009 that a review of the recommendations would be undertaken at the following session; see *Summary report of the Chairman of the Legal and Technical Commission during the fifteenth session*, Document ISBA/15/C/5, May 27, 2009, at para. 14. The Commission was unable to complete its review of the recommendation at the sixteenth session in 2010 and it will continue to examine the recommendations in 2011; see Press Release, "Seabed Council hears LTC report." Document SB/16/B, April 29, 2010, available at www.isa.org.jm/en/sessions/2010/press <checked November 29, 2010>.

What is surprising about the procedure for adopting recommendations under the Polymetallic Regulations is that it does not involve any input from the political organs of the Authority. Recommendations are valid as soon as they are adopted by the Legal and Technical Commission. Paragraph 2 of Regulation 38 provides that the Council may request that the recommendations be withdrawn or modified if it finds that they are inconsistent with the intent and purpose of the Regulations. A strict interpretation of this provision would suggest, however, that the Council cannot force the Commission to alter a recommendation against its wishes. Nor can the Council annul recommendations with which it disagrees. At the same time, regardless of their formal status, recommendations that have been rejected by the Council will lose much of their persuasive authority and there will be less incentive for investors to comply with them. Such a situation could cause legal uncertainty over what is expected from investors, which would be detrimental to the operation of the deep seabed mining regime.

As can be seen from this analysis, the law-making powers of the Authority permit it to substantially develop the regulatory framework for deep seabed mining set out in the Law of the Sea Convention and the Part XI Agreement. These powers allow a degree of flexibility for the regime on deep seabed mining to develop in response to advances in scientific knowledge and understanding of the Area. Such flexibility might be even more important when developing regulations for the mining of recently discovered marine mineral resources in the Area, as will be discussed below.

6 The regulatory regime for polymetallic sulphides and cobalt-rich crusts

The regulatory regime foreseen by Part XI of the Convention is premised upon the mining of polymetallic nodules, which are found partially buried in sediments that cover the abyssal plains of the deep seabed.[146] When UNCLOS III was first convened, polymetallic nodules were the only type of mineral resource known to exist in the deep seas and "the nodules played a significant role in driving the development of the Convention."[147] Thus, many features of Part XI were designed to

---

[146] See *Marine Mineral Resources: Scientific Advancements and Economic Perspectives*, at 58.
[147] *Ibid.*

address the mining of this type of resource. Although the precise density of polymetallic nodules was relatively unknown, it was anticipated
that contractors would need access to large areas of seafloor in order
to make mining ventures economically viable. At the same time, states
were keen to prevent a single operator from developing a monopoly
of deep seabed mining. These considerations led to the inclusion of
detailed conditions in Annex III of the Convention that would apply
to the applications for permission to carry out seabed activities in the
Area. The conditions set out in Annex III include specific requirements
on the size of the area to be exploited, the duration of operations
and other performance requirements. It is these conditions that are
reflected in the Regulations on Polymetallic Nodules discussed above.

We now know that polymetallic nodules are not the only minerals
found on the deep seabed. Since the convening of UNCLOS III, there
have been major breakthroughs in ocean science that have "changed
our view of the ocean basins from big bathtubs that contain materials washed off the land by rivers, to active sources of materials that
form types of mineral deposits different from those derived from the
erosion of land."[148] Polymetallic massive sulphides and cobalt-rich
crusts are two types of mineral resources that have been identified
as a product of chemical and physical processes taking place in the
deep ocean. Cobalt-rich crusts are similar to polymetallic nodules in
that they are formed from the accumulation of metals that have been
dissolved in seawater. They differ from polymetallic nodules, however,
in that the metals "accumulate directly as extensive layers directly on
volcanic rock that forms submerged volcanic seamounts and volcanic
mountain ranges."[149] Polymetallic sulphides, on the other hand, are
formed through chemical reactions between seawater and rocks at
underwater hot springs known as smokers.[150] The different nature of
these resources, in particular their geographical location, means that

---

[148] *Ibid.*, at 27.

[149] *Ibid.*, at 62. The Draft regulations on prospecting and exploration for cobalt-rich
ferromanganese crusts in the Area define "cobalt crusts" as "hydroxide/oxide
deposits of cobalt-rich iron/manganese (ferromanganese) crust formed from direct
precipitation of minerals from seawater onto hard substrates containing minor
but significant concentrations of cobalt, titanium, nickel, platinum, molybdenum,
tellurium, cerium, other metallic and rare earth elements"; see *Regulations on
prospecting and exploration for cobalt-rich ferromanganese crusts in the Area – note by the
Secretariat*, Document ISBA/16/C/WP.2, November 29, 2009.

[150] *Marine Mineral Resources: Scientific Advances and Economic Perspectives*, at 48–9. The
Regulations on prospecting and exploration for polymetallic sulphides in the Area define

designing a regulatory regime for these types of deposits raises very different issues to designing a regime for polymetallic nodules.

Following a request from Russia in August 1998, the Authority is currently working on regulations on prospecting and exploration of polymetallic sulphides and cobalt-rich crusts.[151] The drafting process has prompted difficult questions over the content of the regulations and in particular whether or not the conditions set out in Annex III of the Convention are appropriate for the exploration and exploitation of these types of resources. The issue has been summarized by the former Secretary-General of the Authority as follows:[152]

The basic formal elements of the regulations would be the same as that [sic] for polymetallic nodules. However, because of the localised nature of the deposits there will be differences relating *inter alia* to the size of the area allocated for exploration under the contract, the size of the eventual exploitation area and the system for participation by the Authority either through the application of the parallel system which may not always be practical in this case, or other form of participation, such as equity participation, as well as environmental regulations appropriate to the unique environment in which these deposits are found.

In a paper outlining the considerations to be taken into account when drafting regulations for these minerals, the Secretariat noted that the size of areas to be allocated under the Law of the Sea Convention is not appropriate for polymetallic sulphides and cobalt-rich crusts and that the anti-monopoly provisions contained in Annex III of the Convention also cannot be applied to these types of resources without difficulty.[153] In particular, it would appear that the "parallel system" used for polymetallic nodules is not appropriate for other types of mineral resources.

"polymetallic sulphide" as "hydrothermally formed deposits of sulphides and accompanying mineral resources in the Area, which contain concentrations of metals including, inter alia, copper, lead, zinc, gold and silver"; see *Regulations on prospecting and exploration for polymetallic sulphides in the Area*, Document ISBA/16/C/L.5, May 4, 2010, Regulation 1(3)(d).

[151] It was agreed by the Council that separate regulations would be prepared for polymetallic sulphides and cobalt-rich crusts; see *Review of the outstanding issues with respect to the draft regulations on prospecting and exploration for polymetallic sulphides in the Area*, Document ISBA/14/C/4, April 8, 2008, at para. 5. Priority has been given to developing regulations on polymetallic sulphides.

[152] S. Nandan, "Administering the mineral resources of the deep seabed." in D. Freestone, R. Barnes and D. Ong (eds.), *The Law of the Sea: Progress and Prospects* (Oxford University Press, 2006) at 89.

[153] *Considerations relating to the regulations for prospecting and exploration for hydrothermal polymetallic sulphides and cobalt-rich ferromanganese crusts in the area*, Document ISBA/7/C/2, May 29, 2001, at paras. 19 and 22.

It follows that alternative approaches to fulfilling the objectives of the Convention have been considered.

The Regulations for prospecting and exploration for Polymetallic Sulphides were adopted by the Council and approved by the Assembly in May 2010.[154] Regulation 16 permits applicants wishing to undertake exploration for polymetallic sulphides to choose between either nominating a reserved area or offering an equity interest in the joint venture to the Enterprise.[155] Where a reserve area is nominated, the applicant must identify a site comprising not more than 200 polymetallic sulphide blocks, arranged in two groups of equal estimated commercial value.[156] Where, however, the applicant decides to offer an equity interest in a joint venture, the size of the area to be explored is limited to an area composed of not more than 100 polymetallic sulphide blocks.[157] Thus, under this second option, there is no area that is reserved to the Authority for future exploration and exploitation. Instead, the Enterprise is to obtain, without payment, a minimum of twenty percent of the equity in the joint venture arrangement, although it will only be entitled to profits on half of its equity participation until the applicant has recovered its total equity participation in the joint venture arrangement.[158] The Enterprise will also be entitled to purchase a further thirty percent of the equity participation in the joint venture if it elects to do so.[159] Thus, the Enterprise could in theory obtain up to half of the shares of a company involved in mining for polymetallic sulphides. Shares of the Enterprise will be treated the same as other shares in the joint venture.

This alternative regime for promoting participation of the international community in deep seabed mining is not expressly foreseen in the Convention, which, as explained above, was premised upon the parallel system. Nevertheless, it has been suggested that the alternative system is consistent with the principles contained in Part XI, as modified by the Part XI Agreement.[160] These principles

---

[154] Regulations on prospecting and exploration for polymetallic sulphides in the Area.

[155] See Draft regulations on prospecting and exploration for polymetallic sulphides in the Area, Document ISBA/15/C/WP.1/Rev.1, September 2, 2008, Regulation 16.

[156] Ibid., Regulation 12(4).

[157] Ibid., Regulation 12(2). The blocks must be arranged in at least five clusters and confined within a rectangular area not exceeding 300,000 square kilometres, the longest side not exceeding 1,000 kilometres in length; see Regulations 12(2) and (3).

[158] Ibid., Regulation 19(a).

[159] Ibid., Regulation 19(b).

[160] Analysis of the draft regulations on prospecting and exploration for polymetallic sulphides and cobalt-rich ferromanganese crusts in the Area, Part III: provisions relating to the system

call for "the development of the resources of the Area in accordance with sound commercial principles"[161] and which expressly require the Enterprise to "conduct its initial deep seabed mining operations through joint ventures."[162] While the regulations are based upon those principles that are embodied in Part XI of the Convention, as amended by the Part XI Agreement, they nevertheless develop the Part XI regime in a way that was not envisaged when the regime was first drafted.

Acknowledging the new nature of the challenges posed by these mineral resources, the Regulations themselves call for a review to be carried out five years after they were adopted by the Assembly.[163] In addition, States Parties, the Legal or Technical Commission or contractors through their sponsoring State may request the Council to review the Regulations if it becomes apparent that they are not adequate.[164] The normal amendment procedures will apply to any changes that are deemed necessary to improve the Regulations. Moreover, as noted above, amendments cannot be imposed upon contractors, who will continue to be bound by the contract they entered into with the Authority until they agree to any contractual changes.[165]

This change to the regulatory regime has been achieved without the need to invoke the amendment procedures found in the Convention. There are significant advantages to the approach taken by the Authority in this case. Once adopted, the Regulations are automatically binding and there is no need for individual Member States to formally accept them before they can enter into force. This is not problematic in cases where regulations have been adopted by consensus in both the Council and the Assembly. However, it is possible that there may be disagreements between Members of the Authority on the content of regulations and their compatibility with the Convention and the Part XI Agreement. In this situation, questions may be raised about the validity of the regulations and whether or not they may be challenged through dispute settlement mechanisms.

---

of participation by the International Seabed Authority, Document ISBA/12/C/2/Part III, June 8, 2006, at para. 8.

[161] Part XI Agreement, Annex, Section 6, para. 1.

[162] Part XI Agreement, Annex, Section 3, para. 2.

[163] Regulations on prospecting and exploration for polymetallic sulphides in the Area, Regulation 44(1).

[164] Ibid., Regulation 44(2).   [165] Ibid., Regulation 44(3).

7 Dispute settlement and the deep seabed regime

Alongside the elaborate institutional framework discussed above, Part XI also creates a special dispute settlement mechanism that can be invoked in the case of a dispute arising under Part XI of the Convention. This section considers the judicial organs involved in the settlement of such disputes and what role they may play in developing the deep seabed mining regime, as well as the possibilities for challenging decisions of the Authority through the dispute settlement procedures.

The Seabed Disputes Chamber of the International Tribunal for the Law of the Sea is established in accordance with Part XI and Annex VI of the Convention in order to deal with disputes arising under the deep seabed mining regime.[166] The Chamber is composed of eleven members elected by the judges of the Tribunal from among themselves.[167] Generally speaking, the composition of the Chamber should reflect the principal legal systems of the world.[168] In addition, the Assembly of the Authority may make recommendations as to the general representation and distribution of seats in the Chamber, although it has not done so to date.[169] Although the Chamber is exclusively composed of members of the Tribunal, it operates in practice as an autonomous international tribunal with its own president, its own rules of procedure and its own jurisdictional provisions.[170]

The Chamber is competent to hear disputes arising between states concerning the interpretation and application of Part XI.[171] However, the Chamber differs from other courts and tribunals operating under the Law of the Sea Convention because it is open not only to states, but also to the Authority and private actors involved in deep seabed operations.[172] This is reflected in the broad jurisdiction of the Chamber to deal with a variety of disputes arising under Part XI. The jurisdiction of the Chamber also extends to disputes arising between states and the

---

[166] Law of the Sea Convention, Article 186 and Annex VI, Article 14.

[167] Law of the Sea Convention, Annex VI, Article 35(1). For the current composition of the Chamber, see www.itlos.org/general_information/judges/chambers_en.shtml <checked March 17, 2010>.

[168] Law of the Sea Convention, Annex VI, Article 35(2).

[169] Law of the Sea Convention, Annex VI, Article 35(2).

[170] Tuerk describes it as "a tribunal within a tribunal"; H. Tuerk, "The contribution of the International Tribunal for the Law of the Sea to international law." in E. J. Molenaar and A. G. Oude Elferink (eds.), *The International Legal Regime of Areas beyond National Jurisdiction: Current and Future Developments* (Martinus Nijhoff Publishers, 2010) at 221.

[171] Law of the Sea Convention, Article 187(a).   [172] *Ibid.*, Annex VI, Article 37.

Authority,[173] as well as to disputes between the Authority and contractors or prospective contractors.[174]

At the same time, the jurisdiction of the Chamber over Part XI disputes is not exclusive. In disputes arising between two states concerning the interpretation and application of Part XI of the Convention, the parties to the dispute may agree to submit the dispute to a special chamber of the International Tribunal for the Law of the Sea.[175] Alternatively, one of the parties to such a dispute may insist that the dispute is submitted to an ad hoc chamber of the Chamber itself.[176] Both of these options allow states to have a greater say over the composition of the judicial body that will hear the dispute arising between them.

Another exception to the exclusive jurisdiction of the Seabed Disputes Chamber concerns disputes over the interpretation of contracts concluded between the Authority and investors in the Area. The Convention allows such disputes to be submitted to binding commercial arbitration at the request of either party to the dispute.[177] Such arbitration shall take place according to the UNCITRAL Arbitration Rules unless the contract specifies otherwise or the parties have agreed on some other set of applicable arbitration rules.[178] While this provision reflects the commercial nature of disputes between contractors and the Authority, it also means that the arbitrators selected to decide a dispute in these cases may not have any particular expertise in the law of the sea or indeed in international law at all. To take this into account, an arbitral tribunal constituted to hear such disputes is expressly excluded from interpreting any provisions of the Convention or its Annexes.[179] Rather, such questions must be referred to the Seabed Disputes Chamber for resolution. Once an answer has been given by the Chamber, the arbitral tribunal is required to "render its award in conformity with the ruling of the [Chamber]."[180] Given that the rules and regulations of the Authority are also the product of international negotiation, it is suggested that their interpretation should also be excluded from the jurisdiction of commercial arbitration and that any interpretative issue arising thereunder should also be referred to the Chamber.

---

[173] *Ibid.*, Article 187(b).   [174] *Ibid.*, Article 187(c) and (d).
[175] *Ibid.*, Article 188(1)(a).   [176] *Ibid.*, Article 188(1)(b).
[177] *Ibid.*, Article 188(2)(a).   [178] *Ibid.*, Article 188(2)(c).
[179] *Ibid.*, Article 188(2)(a).   [180] *Ibid.*, Article 188(2)(b).

One function of courts and tribunals is to settle the dispute that has been submitted to them. However, the judicial bodies charged with deciding disputes under Part XI of the Convention may themselves play a role in the development of the Part XI regime. While courts are not law-making bodies in the sense that they cannot create law from scratch, they can nevertheless contribute to the development of law through their role in interpreting the legal texts.[181] These judicial organs may be called on to interpret the wording of Part XI itself, as well as the provisions of the rules and regulations that have been subsequently adopted by the Authority.[182]

When interpreting legal texts, courts are generally constrained by the rules on treaty interpretation that require them to consider the "ordinary meaning to be given to the words of the treaty in their context and in light of their object and purpose."[183] In addition, a court or tribunal may also have reference to the broader context of a treaty, including any subsequent agreements concluded by the parties, as well as the subsequent practice of the parties, which may reveal how they intended the text to be interpreted.[184] The ability of international courts and tribunals to take into account such materials allows the possibility for an evolutionary approach to the interpretation of treaties.[185]

Whereas the Chamber and other judicial bodies constituted under Part XI may have the power to interpret the provisions of Part XI and the regulations, there are also important limits on their jurisdiction. In particular, the text of Part XI suggests that states and contractors are not able to seek judicial review of rules, regulations and procedures adopted by the Authority. In this context, Article 189 of the Convention provides that:

The Seabed Disputes Chamber shall have no jurisdiction with regard to the exercise by the Authority of its discretionary powers in accordance with this Part; in no case shall it substitute its discretion for that of the Authority.

[181] See generally, J. Harrison, "Judicial law-making and the developing order of the oceans" (2007) 22 Int'l J. Marine & Coastal L. 283.
[182] The regulations expressly provide that "Disputes concerning the interpretation or application of these Regulations shall be settled in accordance with Part XI, section 5, of the Convention"; Regulations on Prospecting and Exploration for Polymetallic Nodules in the Area, Regulation 39(1).
[183] Vienna Convention on the Law of Treaties, Article 31(1).
[184] Ibid., Article 31(3).
[185] R. Higgins, "A babel of judicial voices? Ruminations from the bench" (2006) 55 Int'l & Comp. L. Q. 791, at 798; Harrison, "Judicial law-making and the developing order of the oceans." at 295–6.

Without prejudice to article 191, in exercising its jurisdiction pursuant to article 187, the Seabed Disputes Chamber shall not pronounce itself on the question of whether any rules, regulations and procedures of the Authority are in conformity with this Convention, nor declare invalid any such rules, regulations and procedures. Its jurisdiction in this regard shall be confined to deciding claims that the application of any rules, regulations and procedures of the Authority in individual cases would be in conflict with the contractual obligations of the parties to the dispute or their obligations under this Convention, claims concerning excess of jurisdiction or misuse of power, and to claims for damages to be paid or other remedy to be given to the party concerned for the failure of the other party to comply with its contractual obligations or its obligations under this Convention.

The most pertinent effect of the provision is to limit the jurisdiction of the Seabed Disputes Chamber by preventing the Chamber from deciding whether any rules, regulations or procedures adopted by the Authority are in conformity with the Convention and from declaring any such instruments invalid.[186] It would seem from the drafting history that the inclusion of this provision was intended to protect the organs of the Authority from too much interference by the dispute settlement organs.[187] In other words, neither the Chamber nor any other judicial body is able to control the law-making activities of the Authority through judicial review. This leaves any question concerning the compatibility of regulations adopted by the Authority with the Convention to be solved through political organs of the Authority itself. There is no possibility for a judicial organ to quash regulations adopted by the Authority.

In addition to settling disputes concerning the interpretation and application of Part XI in contentious disputes, the Seabed Disputes Chamber also has the power to issue advisory opinions at the request of the Assembly or the Council.[188] Under Article 159(10) of the Convention, the Assembly must request an advisory opinion on the conformity with the Convention of a proposal before the Assembly if the president receives a written request sponsored by at least one fourth of the members of the Authority. The Council may also request an advisory

---

[186] It is limited to deciding whether the application of any rules and regulations in individual cases would be in conflict with the contractual obligations of the parties to the dispute or their obligations under the Convention or claims of damages.

[187] See Rosenne *et al.* (eds.), *United Nations Convention on the Law of the Sea – A Commentary,* Vol. 6, at para. 189.7.

[188] Law of the Sea Convention, Article 191.

opinion on legal issues connected with the exercise of its powers.[189] However, a request cannot come from an individual state or a natural or legal person conducting activities in the Area. Advisory opinions may not be binding in the formal sense, but they can play an important role in clarifying the scope of Part XI or any ambiguities contained in the treaties or the regulations promulgated by the Authority in a similar way to judgments delivered under the contentious jurisdiction of the Chamber.[190]

In contrast to the contentious jurisdiction of the Chamber, it may be possible that questions concerning the compatibility of regulations with the Convention and the Part XI Agreement could be raised as part of a request for an advisory opinion. However, the nonbinding nature of advisory opinions means that the Chamber would not be able to annul any regulations that it thought were incompatible with the Convention and the ultimate decision on what action to take would remain with the political organs of the Authority. This confirms that the dispute settlement procedure in Part XI was not intended to provide a check on the law-making activities of the Authority.

8 Conclusion

The deep seabed mining regime in Part XI of the Law of the Sea Convention has been at the center of developments in the law of the sea over the past quarter of a century. Throughout that time, it has been the subject of division and controversy among states. The entry into force of the Convention following the conclusion of the 1994 Part XI Agreement would seem to signal a new chapter in the history of the deep seabed regime. From that time, development of the regime has taken place through the International Seabed Authority, an international organization specifically designed for that purpose.

To a large extent, the International Seabed Area and the role of the Authority in its regulation is an unprecedented experiment in

---

[189] There is no express provision which specifies how the Council should request an advisory opinion, but see Rosenne *et al.* (eds.), *United Nations Convention on the Law of the Sea – A Commentary, Vol. 6*, at para. 191.1.

[190] The first advisory opinion was requested by the Council on May 6, 2010 in relation to the responsibilities and obligations of sponsoring states under the Convention; see *Decision of the Council of the International Seabed Authority requesting an advisory opinion pursuant to Article 191 of the United Nations Convention on the Law of the Sea*, Document ISBA/16/C/13, May 6, 2010.

international law-making. As noted by one author, "the management of deep sea-bed resources is the first such regime in which the minute details of a 'common heritage' approach to the management of the global common pool resource has been worked out."[191] From the outset, the Authority was designed as a law-making institution and it is equipped with the power to adopt rules and regulations on a variety of topics. Its powers are unlike those of many other international institutions because it can adopt rules and regulations that are binding on states and on non-state actors who are participating in seabed activities.

Given the potential significance of the law-making powers of the Authority to regulate and restrict access to deep seabed minerals, it is perhaps no surprise that their exercise is subject to stringent and complex decision-making procedures. The decision-making procedures of the Authority are designed to ensure that any rules and regulations adopted by the Authority are supported by all of the major interest groups, thus seeking to maintain the consensus over the Part XI regime. The Council is at the center of this process. Any developments in the deep seabed mining regime must be adopted by consensus of the major interest groups sitting on the Council. Without this important safeguard, the broad acceptance of Part XI that took so long to achieve would be placed under threat. Nevertheless, the decision-making procedures do not necessarily ensure complete consensus of all Member States of the Authority. The Assembly, despite the fact that it is the most democratic organ of the Authority, may be sidelined in the law-making process. It follows that a state that is not represented on the Council could become bound by rules and regulations to which it has not consented. The same is true for amendments to the Convention. Once they have been adopted by the Authority and approved by three fourths of the States Parties to the Convention, they are binding on all States Parties.

As has been shown in this chapter, the adoption of regulations by the Authority allows the Authority to progressively develop the deep seabed mining regime. This is particularly true when it comes to developing rules and regulations for new sources of marine minerals in the Area, such as polymetallic massive sulphides and cobalt-rich crusts. These resources require a different regulatory response than polymetallic nodules and the regulations drafted by the Authority have reflected changes to the regime envisaged by the drafters of the Convention. It

---

[191] E. Louka, *International Environmental Law* (Cambridge University Press, 2006) at 83.

is important, therefore, that such changes are supported by a broad consensus of Members representing all interest groups. Indeed, the conditions attached to the adoption of Regulations are more important if one considers the limited options on challenging the validity of Regulations through the dispute settlement procedures created under Part XI.

Amendment procedures are also available to modify and possibly extend the powers of the Authority. This allows the regime to adapt to new challenges unforeseen at the time when the Part XI regime was negotiated. The disadvantage of the amendment procedures is that they are cumbersome and they will cause delays in developing the deep seabed mining regime. Indeed, it is unlikely that the formal amendment procedures would be used by states if the same outcome could be achieved through informal decision-making by the Authority. An example of this are the Polymetallic Sulphide Regulations discussed above. The Regulations would seem to achieve the introduction of a different form of regulation of deep seabed minerals without amending the treaty texts.

It does not follow that the amendment procedures are totally redundant. In the first place, it may be desirable to invoke the formal amendment procedures where a consensus on the adoption of Regulations cannot be achieved. In this scenario, formal amendment may be the only way to achieve complete legal certainty over the status of the deep seabed mining regime. Secondly, the amendment procedures may need to be invoked in the case of substantial changes to the mandate, functions or powers of the Authority. For example, any proposal to enlarge the mandate of the Authority to include the regulation of bio-prospecting in the Area would arguably require an amendment to Part XI as it would entail a thorough revision of the powers of the Authority.[192]

---

[192] See Subsidiary Body on Scientific, Technical and Technological Advice of the Convention on Biological Diversity, Document UNEP/CBD/SBSTTA/8/INF/3/Rev.1, February 22, 2003; Scovazzi, "Mining, protection of the environment, scientific research and bioprospecting." at 408–9.

6   The International Maritime Organization and the international regulation of shipping

1 The international regulation of shipping

By its very nature, shipping is an international business. Around ninety percent of world trade is transported by ships.[1] The global nature of the industry demands global regulation. Indeed, there is a long history of international cooperation in relation to the regulation of shipping. In the early years much of this cooperation took place through ad hoc diplomatic conferences.[2] Following the Second World War, these cooperative efforts were largely placed on an institutional footing through the creation of specialized international organizations. In particular, states established the International Maritime Organization (IMO) as a specialized agency of the United Nations in order to oversee the development of international law concerning maritime transport and related issues.[3]

The IMO had already been in operation for almost thirty-five years by the time that the Law of the Sea Convention was concluded in 1982. The Convention did not seek to interfere with the formal role and functions of preexisting international organizations, which were, in any case, not "subject to the dictats of an intergovernmental conference."[4] Nevertheless, the conclusion of the Law of the Sea Convention has had major consequences for all international organizations involved in maritime affairs. In particular it affected the international regulation

---

[1] See www.marisec.org/shippingfacts/home/ <checked June 14, 2010>.
[2] See G. Breuer, "Maritime safety regulations," in R. Bernhardt (ed.), *Encyclopedia of Public International Law, Vol. 3* (North-Holland, 1997).
[3] Formerly the Intergovernmental Maritime Consultative Organization or IMCO. Its name was changed by amendments adopted in 1975.
[4] J. D. Kingham and D. M. McRae, "Competent international organizations and the law of the sea" (1979) *Marine Policy* 106, at 110.

of shipping by fundamentally revising the legal framework within which the IMO and its Member States must operate.[5] The Convention also explicitly calls on the competent international organizations to progressively develop aspects of the law of the sea relating to maritime safety and the protection of the marine environment. The IMO is one of the principal, and in some cases exclusive, competent international organizations for this purpose.[6]

This chapter will analyze the variety of roles that the IMO plays in relation to the regulation of shipping in order to assess its overall contribution to the evolution of the law in this area. It will analyze the scope of the powers of the IMO to adopt rules and regulations under its constituent instrument, the 1948 Convention on the International Maritime Organization.[7] It will then consider the relevance of the IMO standards for the general framework for the law of the sea. In particular, it analyzes the way in which international standards are incorporated into that legal framework through the so-called "rules of reference" contained in the Law of the Sea Convention. As well as the standard-setting role of the IMO, the chapter takes into account the special role that has been assumed by the IMO under the Law of the Sea Convention as the competent international organization for approving navigational measures proposed by individual states in various maritime zones created by the Convention. Under this function, the IMO acts as a forum for balancing the interests of coastal states and shipping states on a case-by-case basis. Finally, the chapter asks what role, if any, the IMO can play in modifying the jurisdictional framework found in the Law of the Sea Convention. It will be seen that the role of the IMO in developing the law of the sea is much greater than its constituent instrument would suggest.

2 Status and membership of the International Maritime Organization

The IMO was created in 1948 in order to provide a permanent forum for the discussion of shipping issues and the adoption and

---

[5] See e.g. *Impact of the entry into force of the 1982 United Nations Convention on the Law of the Sea on related, existing and proposed instruments and programmes*, report of the Secretary-General, UN Document A/52/491, October 1997.

[6] See section 4.4 below.

[7] Convention on the International Maritime Organization, in International Maritime Organization, *Basic Documents*, Volume One, 2004 edition, at 7.

amendment of shipping standards.[8] It is recognized as a special-ized agency of the United Nations in accordance with Article 57 of the UN Charter.[9] The primary purpose of the IMO, as defined in its constituent instrument, is:

to provide machinery for co-operation among Governments in the field of gov-ernmental regulation and practices relating to technical matters of all kinds affecting shipping engaged in international trade; [and] to encourage and facilitate the general adoption of the highest practicable standards in matters concerning the maritime safety [sic.], efficiency of navigation and prevention and control of marine pollution from ships.[10]

The IMO is composed of a number of organs. The IMO Assembly is the plenary organ that has responsibility for the overall work pro-gramme of the organization, as well as the general policy and budget-ary decisions within the organization.[11] The IMO Assembly only meets once every two years.[12] In between sessions of the Assembly, much of the work of the IMO is conducted through specialist committees and subcommittees. Of particular interest for present purposes are the Maritime Safety Committee and the Marine Environment Protection Committee, both of which are intimately involved in the drafting of new technical standards.[13] Both of these committees and their numer-ous subcommittees are also open to all IMO Members.[14]

The IMO is open to all states.[15] A substantial majority of States Parties to the Law of the Sea Convention are IMO members with only a few exceptions.[16] In any case, meetings of the Organization are open to all

---

[8] For a historical introduction to the IMO, see R. M. M'Gonigle and M. W. Zacher, *Pollution, Politics, and International Law: Tankers at Sea* (University of California Press, 1979) Chapter 3.

[9] Article 1 of the Agreement between the United Nations and the International Maritime Organization, UNTS, Vol. 324, at 274.

[10] IMO Convention, Article 1(a). The original text of Article 1 only referred to the adoption of standards in the field of maritime safety and efficiency of navigation. The text of the IMO Constitution was subsequently amended in 1975 to include the adoption of standards to prevent and control pollution from ships. At the same time, a Marine Environment Protection Committee, with the same status as the Maritime Safety Committee, was created.

[11] IMO Convention, Article 15.   [12] *Ibid.*, Article 14.

[13] *Ibid.*, Articles 29, 39.   [14] *Ibid.*, Articles 27, 37.

[15] *Ibid.*, Article 4. UN members and states attending the 1948 Conference have an automatic right to membership; Articles 5 and 6. Other states may apply subject to approval of two thirds of the Members; Article 7.

[16] For a list of all IMO members, see www.imo.org/About/Membership/Pages/MemberStates.aspx <checked November 29, 2010>. There are fifteen States Parties

UN members, who may participate in proceedings as observers, albeit without a vote.[17] In addition, nonmembers may acquire more formal participation rights if they are party to a treaty falling under the auspices of the IMO. For example, the Convention on the Safety of Life at Sea (SOLAS Convention) provides that "Parties to the Convention, whether or not Members of the Organization, shall be entitled to participate in the proceedings of the Maritime Safety Committee."[18] Similar provisions can be found in most other regulatory treaties.[19]

Non-state actors also play a central role in the work of the IMO. NGOs can apply to the IMO Council for consultative status. In order to acquire consultative status, criteria set by the Organization demand that an NGO must be of a truly international character and that its objectives are in accordance with those of the IMO.[20] In addition, an NGO must be able to demonstrate that it can make a significant contribution to the work of the IMO.[21] The status of NGOs is subject to periodic review by the IMO Council, which may recommend the withdrawal of consultative status if it considers it appropriate.[22] Currently sixty-five NGOs have consultative status at the IMO.[23] The vast majority of these NGOs are industry representatives such as organizations acting on behalf of shipowners and the marine insurance industry.[24] Environmental groups have also started to play a prominent role in discussions of the Organization, in particular the Marine Environmental Protection Committee.[25] This

to the Law of the Sea Convention (Afghanistan*, Andorra*, Armenia*, Belarus*, Botswana*, Burkina Faso*, Chad*, Lao*, Lesotho*, Mali*, Micronesia, Nauru, Niue, Palau, Zambia*) who are not currently IMO members, the majority of which are land-locked countries (marked *).

[17] Rule 4 of the Rules of Procedure of the Assembly provide that the Secretary-General may invite, inter alia, UN members as observers. Similar rules apply to the proceedings of the IMO Council and the IMO Committees.
[18] SOLAS Convention, Article 8(b)(iii).
[19] For instance, Convention on Pollution from Ships, Article 16(2)(c); Anti-Fouling Convention, Article 16(2)(b); Ballast Water Convention, Article 19(2)(b).
[20] Guidelines on the Grant of Consultative Status, in IMO Basic Documents, Vol. 1, 2004 edition, at 129.
[21] Ibid.
[22] Rule 10 of the Rules governing the relationship with nongovernmental organizations, in International Maritime Organization, Basic Texts, Volume One, 2004 edition, at 119.
[23] See www.imo.org/About/Membership/Pages/NGOsInConsultativeStatus.aspx <checked November 29, 2010>.
[24] Prominent organizations are the International Chamber of Shipping, INTERTANKO, INTERCARGO, and the International Council of Classification Societies.
[25] See L. De La Fayette, "The Marine Environment Protection Committee: the conjunction of the law of the sea and international environmental law" (2001)

cross-section of societal interests is important given the fact that the IMO is often called upon to uphold the balance of interests found in the Law of the Sea Convention. Consultative status confers a right to receive the agenda of IMO meetings, the right to submit written statements on items on the agenda, the right to be represented as an observer at IMO meetings, and the right to receive the texts of resolutions adopted by the Organization.[26]

While NGOs do not possess a vote, they can nevertheless have a significant influence on the work of the Organization, and in practice "the IMO's outputs result from a much more complex process than traditional state-to-state multilateralism."[27] This influence is achieved through lobbying of governments before, at and after meetings.[28]

3 Standard-setting by the International Maritime Organization

3.1 Treaty standards

Although the Organization was created primarily as a forum to discuss maritime affairs and to recommend action to its members,[29] it has come to play a central role in preparing technical standards for shipping. Article 2 of the IMO Convention provides that it shall "provide for the drafting of conventions, agreements, or other suitable instruments, and recommend these to Governments and to intergovernmental organizations."[30]

Most technical standards adopted under the auspices of the Organization are found annexed to an international treaty. Such treaties and standards are initially negotiated through the specialized committees and subcommittees of the Organization. However, the IMO does not have the power to adopt treaties itself and it must convene a

---

16 *Int'l J. Marine & Coastal L.* 155; G. Peet, "The role of (environmental) nongovernmental organizations at the Marine Environmental Committee of the International Maritime Organization and at the London Dumping Convention" (1994) 22 *Ocean & Coastal Management* 3.

[26] Rule 6 of the Rules governing the relationship with nongovernmental organizations, in International Maritime Organization, Basic Texts, Volume One, 2004 edition, at 119.

[27] J. Vorbach, "The vital role of non-flag state actors in the pursuit of safer shipping" (2001) *Ocean Dev. & Int'l Law* 27, at 34.

[28] See e.g. Peet, "The role of (environmental) non-governmental organizations at the Marine Environmental Committee of the International Maritime Organization and at the London Dumping Convention," at 9–11.

[29] IMO Convention, Articles 2(a) and (c).   [30] *Ibid.*, Article 2(b).

diplomatic conference for this purpose.[31] Draft treaties are sent by the IMO to a specially convened diplomatic conference for any last-minute negotiations and formal adoption.

Today the IMO is responsible for more than forty international conventions and agreements on a variety of maritime matters and it continues to be an important forum where new regulatory treaties in this field are negotiated and adopted. The regulatory treaties largely fall into two categories: those concerned with maritime safety and those concerned with the protection of the marine environment.

The 1966 Convention on Load Lines, the 1972 Convention on the International Regulations for Preventing Collisions at Sea, the 1974 Convention on Safety of Life at Sea[32] and the 1978/1995 Convention on Standards of Training, Certification and Watchkeeping for Seafarers are the most important treaties containing safety standards. Of these, the Convention on Safety of Life at Sea deals with the widest range of issues. Generally speaking, the treaty deals with the seaworthiness of ships of all types. The first SOLAS Convention was adopted by a diplomatic conference in 1914. One of the first acts of the IMO when it came into existence was to adopt a new SOLAS Convention in 1960. A replacement SOLAS Convention was adopted in 1974 and it is this version, as amended, which regulates safety of shipping at sea today. The technical standards are found in the annex to the treaty, which covers inter alia standards on the construction of ships, life-saving equipment, radio communications, safety of navigation, carriage of cargoes including hazardous cargoes, safety management on ships, and measures to enhance maritime security.

The most important environmental treaty concluded under the auspices of the IMO is the Convention on the Prevention of Marine Pollution from Ships (MARPOL Convention). This treaty originally included five annexes containing technical standards on pollution from oil, noxious liquid substances, packaged substances, sewage and garbage. An additional annex on air pollution from ships was adopted in 1997. In recent years the Organization has also adopted separate treaties regulating the use of anti-fouling systems on ships[33] and regulating the use of ballast water on international voyages.[34]

---

[31] *Ibid.*, Article 2(b).   [32] Hereinafter, SOLAS Convention.
[33] 2001 Convention on Anti-Fouling Systems.
[34] 2004 Convention on Ballast Water.

3.2 Review and amendment of treaties and technical standards

The role of the IMO in standard-setting does not finish when a regulatory treaty is adopted. These treaties, by their very nature, must be adaptable to present-day problems and able to keep up with technological and scientific developments.[35] The majority of the regulatory treaties recognize the IMO as a forum for the drafting and adoption of technical amendments to treaty standards.[36] Modifications to the major regulatory treaties are frequently considered by IMO committees.

The Maritime Safety Committee and the Marine Environment Protection Committee are the two organs that are responsible for the adoption of amendments to most regulatory treaties.[37] Guidelines adopted by the IMO to promote effective and efficient working procedures within the organization specify that new amendments should not be considered until a "compelling need" for the amendment has been demonstrated by the proponents.[38] This requirement places the burden squarely on the proponent of a proposal to show that it is necessary. A proposal may fail at this first hurdle if it does not have sufficient support.[39]

Proposals for amendments may be introduced by any state. While NGOs can only act as observers in IMO organs, in practice they may seek a sponsor state for a particular amendment and they are able to influence the regulatory agenda in this way.

An amendment must pass through several stages before it is finally adopted. Formal procedures for the adoption of amendments

---

[35] Indeed, see Law of the Sea Convention, Article 211(1).

[36] See SOLAS Convention, Article 8. MARPOL Convention, Article 16. Usually as an alternative to an ad hoc diplomatic conference. See also De La Fayette, "The Marine Environment Protection Committee," at 200.

[37] The two lead committees are also assisted by a plethora of specialized subcommittees whose role it is to consider the technical aspects of proposed amendments. These include the Sub-Committee on Dangerous Goods, Solid Cargoes and Containers, the Sub-Committee on Ship Design and Equipment, and the Sub-Committee on Fire Protection. See *Guidelines on the organization and method of work of the Maritime Safety Committee and the Marine Environment Protection Committee and their subsidiary bodies, as amended*, in MSC/Circ.1099/MEPC/Circ.405, Annex, at para. 2.1.

[38] See *ibid.*, Annex, at para. 2.10.2.

[39] For instance, the Legal Committee at its ninety-third session rejected a proposal to place the negotiation of an international instrument to facilitate expeditious investigation of shipboard offences because there was not sufficient evidence of a compelling need.

are specified in the regulatory treaties thereunder. Generally speaking, proposals are initially considered by a technical subcommittee, before the broader policy implications are discussed by the main committee, usually either the Maritime Safety Committee or the Marine Environmental Protection Committee. The main committee will provisionally approve an amendment before it is circulated to states for final adoption at a subsequent meeting.[40] Most of the regulatory treaties specify that an amendment is to be adopted by a two-thirds majority of the parties, present and voting.[41] However, the practice of the two main IMO committees tends to aim towards the adoption of amendments by consensus.[42] Votes are rarely taken in the committees and the participants try to reach a compromise on the proposed changes. Consensus decision-making may prolong the amendment process, although the time in which an amendment is adopted will largely depend on the complexity of the issue and the political will of IMO Members.

Once adopted, amendments are then communicated to the parties for acceptance.[43] At this stage, amendments to technical standards found in the annexes of a treaty are treated differently from amendments to the main body of the treaty. In most cases, technical standards can be amended using tacit amendment procedures. Tacit acceptance procedures were included in most IMO regulatory treaties concluded after 1972 in light of concerns that many amendments that had been adopted by the Organization were not entering into force or were subject to serious delays.[44] The tacit amendment procedures mean that once an amendment to a technical standard has been adopted by the IMO committees, the emphasis is on states to object to the provisions in order to prevent amendments from entering into force. Under both the SOLAS Convention and the MARPOL Convention, amendments to the technical standards are deemed to have been accepted by all contracting parties unless objections are made by more than one third

---

[40] The requirement for circulation of amendments is laid down by the Conventions themselves. See SOLAS Convention, Article 8. MARPOL Convention, Article 16.

[41] SOLAS Convention, Article VIII(b)(iv); MARPOL Convention, Article 16(2)(d); Ballast Water Convention, Article 19(2)(c); Anti-Fouling Convention, Article 16(2)(c).

[42] *Implications of the United Nations Convention on the Law of the Sea for the International Maritime Organization*, IMO Document LEG/MISC/6, September 10, 2008, at 8.

[43] SOLAS Convention, Article 8(b)(v) and (c)(ii).

[44] See "IMO 1948–1998: a process of change," *Focus on the IMO Paper*, 1998, at 9–11. See also M'Gonigle and Zacher, *Pollution, Politics, and International Law*, at 107. Indeed, this was one of the reasons for the adoption of the 1974 SOLAS Convention to replace the 1960 SOLAS Convention.

of contracting states representing at least fifty percent of the world's merchant fleet within a specified period of time.[45] The period during which a state can object varies from treaty to treaty. The MARPOL Convention prescribes a minimum period of ten months for objections to be made.[46] Under the SOLAS Convention, the default period is two years, although this period may be reduced to one year by the agreement of the contracting parties at the time that the amendment is adopted.[47] Indeed, in an attempt to streamline the amendment procedures under the treaty, the Contracting Governments to the SOLAS Convention approved an accelerated amendment procedure in May 1994, which reduces the minimum period from one year to six months where exceptional circumstances prevail.

In practice, it is very rare that states actually rely on their right to object to amendments adopted under the tacit acceptance procedures. Of all the amendments to the SOLAS Convention and the MARPOL Convention that have been adopted to date, only a handful have received objections.[48] In practice, many objections are made simply to allow states additional time to implement the amended regulation in national law and objections are subsequently withdrawn once national legislation has been put in place.[49] The amendment procedures therefore facilitate the swift entry into force of amendments to the technical standards in the treaty. Amendments to the technical standards enter into force for all states that have not objected six months after the date on which the amendments were deemed to have been accepted.[50] Where amendments are perceived as particularly urgent,

[45] SOLAS Convention, Article VIII; MARPOL Convention, Article 16(2)(f)(iii).
[46] MARPOL Convention, Article 16(2)(f)(iii).
[47] SOLAS Convention, Article VIII.
[48] See International Maritime Organization, *Status of Multilateral Conventions and Instruments in respect of which the International Maritime Organization or its Secretary-General performs depositary or other functions, as at 3 June 2010.* A rare example of a substantive objection to an amendment to the SOLAS Convention was made by the United States to an amendment to Chapter XI-1 of the Convention concerning special measures to enhance maritime safety adopted by the Maritime Safety Committee at its eighty-fourth session in May 2008. In its communication to the Secretary-General of the IMO, the United States observed that "The Government of the United States of America objects to the above-described amendment to Chapter XI-1 of the Convention because certain provisions of the Code do not directly promote maritime safety and conflict with important aspects of US domestic law and practice."
[49] For example, see *ibid.*, at 41.
[50] The tacit acceptance procedures under the SOLAS Convention apply to any amendments to the Annexes apart from changes to Chapter I. Chapter I is excluded

the committees may also adopt resolutions encouraging states to give early and effective application to amendments.[51] Such resolutions, while nonbinding, can have the effect of encouraging the rapid implementation of important changes to the regulatory framework.

A significant advantage of the amendment procedures in these regulatory treaties is that it is possible to predict the date on which the amendment will enter into force. When adopting amendments, the committees will indicate the date on which the amendment will be deemed to be accepted and the date on which it will enter into force, subject to the minimum periods provided in the Conventions. This procedure allows the shipping industry to prepare for changes to the regulations. To further protect the interests of shipowners, the SOLAS and MARPOL Conventions specify that amendments that relate to the structure of a ship shall only apply to ships the keels of which have been laid on or after the date on which the amendment enters into force.[52]

Adding new regulations to the SOLAS Convention can be done using the amendment procedures described above. For instance, when a diplomatic conference agreed in December 2002 to add a new chapter on measures to enhance maritime security to the Annex of the SOLAS Convention, the amendment was able to enter into force for all parties within two years.[53] The position is less straightforward under the MARPOL Convention, which has several annexes, each dealing with a different source of marine pollution. While additions to an existing annex will fall within the tacit amendment procedures, the Convention specifies that the adoption of a new annex to the MARPOL Convention is to be treated in the same way as an amendment to the main text of the Convention and requires the express consent of a state before it becomes binding.[54] Thus, the new annex on the prevention of

---

from the tacit amendment procedures because it contains provisions that are not of a technical nature, such as questions of certification, inspection and control of standards which are generally applicable to all of the standards in the Convention. Amendments to these general provisions require the consent of individual states before changes can come into force.

[51] For example, IMO Resolution MEPC.114(50) calling for the early and effective application of regulations 13 G and H of Annex I to the MARPOL Convention.

[52] SOLAS Convention, Article 8(e); MARPOL Convention, Article 16(6).

[53] Chapter XI-2 entered into force on July 1, 2004. One objection was made by the Government of Finland; see *Status of multilateral conventions and instruments in respect of which the International Maritime Organization or its Secretary-General performs depositary functions, as at 31 December 2003*, Document J/86/87, 2004, at p. 36.

[54] MARPOL Convention, Article 16(5).

air pollution from ships adopted by the MARPOL Contracting Parties in 1997 needed to be accepted by two thirds of the parties, the combined merchant fleets of which constitute not less than fifty percent of gross tonnage of the world's merchant fleet, before it could enter into force. As a result, the annex did not enter into force until May 19, 2005 and it is moreover only formally binding on those states that have given their express consent. This significantly slows down the process of adding new areas of regulation to the Convention. De La Fayette suggests that one of the reasons for choosing to frame the regulations on anti-fouling systems as a new convention rather than an additional annex to MARPOL is that "the entry into force provisions for amendments to MARPOL constitute an almost insurmountable barrier to early entry into force."[55]

3.3 Nonbinding instruments

In addition to legally binding standards, IMO committees can also adopt nonbinding instruments. Sometimes, nonbinding instruments are adopted as a prelude to the negotiation of a treaty. For instance, the IMO adopted guidelines on ballast water[56] and anti-fouling systems[57] prior to the negotiations of new treaties on these topics. A similar process can be seen in the case of regulations on ship recycling. At the twenty-third session of the IMO Assembly, Guidelines on Ship Recycling were adopted, along with an instruction to the Marine Environment Protection Committee to keep the matter under review.[58] At the following session the Assembly requested the Committee to start work on developing a legally binding instrument[59] and the International Convention for the Safe and Environmentally Sound Recycling of Ships was adopted in 2009.[60]

---

[55] De La Fayette, "The Marine Environment Protection Committee," at 172.
[56] IMO Resolution A.774(18) on *Guidelines for Preventing the Introduction of Unwanted Pathogens from Ships' Ballast Water and Sediment Discharges.* See A. K.-J. Tan, *Vessel-Source Marine Pollution* (Cambridge University Press, 2006) at 162–74.
[57] MEPC 46(30) on *Measures to Control Potential Adverse Impacts Associated with Use of Tributyl Tin Compounds in Anti-Fouling Paints.*
[58] IMO Resolution A.962(23), subsequently revised by Resolution A.980(24).
[59] IMO Resolution A.981(24) on a *New Legally Binding Instrument on Ship Recycling.* Work on a legally binding instrument commenced at MEPC 54 in March 2006.
[60] See J. Harrison, "Current legal developments – the International Convention for the Safe and Environmentally Sound Recycling of Ships" (2009) 24 *Int'l J. Marine & Coastal L.* 727.

Other IMO resolutions are directly related to the technical standards found in regulatory treaties. Sometimes, the treaty itself may make reference to guidelines or recommendations. For instance, the Ballast Water Convention includes several references to guidelines that the parties must take into account in implementing the Convention. Since the adoption of that treaty, the Marine Environment Protection Committee has been working hard to develop the necessary guidelines.[61] In addition, IMO committees may adopt resolutions that seek to promote a uniform interpretation of a technical regulation.[62] As the contracting parties to a treaty are competent to adopt authoritative interpretations,[63] such interpretative resolutions should not be dismissed as legally irrelevant simply because of their nonbinding status. Thus, it is possible that decisions of IMO organs concerning the interpretation of regulatory treaties could be taken into account by dispute settlement bodies when interpreting and applying the treaties.

4 The incorporation of shipping standards into the Law of the Sea Convention

4.1 Rules of reference

The standards contained in regulatory treaties adopted by the IMO are formally binding only on those states that have accepted them. This is in accordance with the fundamental rule of *pacta tertiis*, according to which treaties are not binding on states that have refrained from being a contracting party. In practice, many of the standards promulgated by the Organization have received widespread acceptance among maritime states. Indeed, most IMO treaties are open to participation by all states, whether or not they are members of the Organization. As a result, some IMO treaties have the benefit of quasi-universal participation, meaning that they apply to most ships around the world. Nevertheless, the IMO does not have the power to adopt standards that are automatically binding on its Member States.[64]

At the same time, shipping standards adopted by the IMO do have a relevance beyond the parties to the regulatory treaties by virtue of

[61] See the reports of MEPC 54 and 55.
[62] Such uniform interpretations are common in relation to the technical annexes to the SOLAS Convention and the MARPOL Convention.
[63] See Vienna Convention on the Law of Treaties, Article 31(3)(a).
[64] Contrast the power of the International Seabed Authority to adopt binding rules and regulations, discussed in Chapter 5.

the provisions on flag state and coastal state jurisdiction over shipping found in the Law of the Sea Convention. The Law of the Sea Convention fundamentally revised the framework for jurisdiction over shipping standards. The Convention qualifies the powers of states to legislate on maritime matters by reference to international standards. These standards are not found in the Convention itself. Rather the Convention refers to standards adopted by other international organizations. In other words, these so-called rules of reference serve to incorporate standards adopted by organizations such as the IMO into the legal framework of the Convention.[65] The effect of a rule of reference varies depending on the precise phrasing of each provision.[66] Some rules of reference simply require states to "take into account" international rules and standards[67] and they do not make compliance with the standards compulsory. In contrast, the effect of other rules of reference is to "impose a legal obligation on a state to respect a standard which it would not otherwise be legally bound to respect."[68]

4.2 Flag state jurisdiction and rules of reference

The jurisdiction of states over ships flying their flag is long-standing and chiefly uncontested.[69] Flag state jurisdiction is universal and the administration of a flag state may enforce rules and regulations against its ships wherever they are in the world. Yet it does not follow that the jurisdiction of flag states is unfettered. Rather, the ability of flag states to regulate ships flying their flags is subject to conditions imposed by the Law of the Sea Convention.

Article 94 of the Law of the Sea Convention requires the flag state to adopt rules and regulations for ships flying its flag regarding "administrative, technical and social matters." Having listed examples of the types of issues that a flag state's regulations must address,[70] Article 94(5) of the Convention continues:

---

[65] See e.g. R. Van Reenen, "Rules of Reference in the new Convention on the Law of the Sea in particular connection with the pollution of the sea by oil from tankers" (1981) *Netherlands Ybk Int'l L.* 3.

[66] On the diversity of language, see e.g. B. Vukas, "Generally accepted international rules and standards," in A. Soons (ed.), *Implementation of the Law of the Sea Convention through International Institutions* (Law of the Sea Institute, 1990) at 406–8.

[67] Law of the Sea Convention, Articles 207 and 212.

[68] B. H. Oxman, "The duty to respect generally accepted international standards" (1991) 24 *New York Uni. J. Int'l L. & Politics* 109, at 144.

[69] See e.g. *The Case of the S. S. Lotus* (1927) PCIJ Reports, No. 10, at 25.

[70] Law of the Sea Convention, Article 94(3).

In taking the measures called for [above] each State is required to conform to generally accepted international standards, procedures and practices and to take any steps which may be necessary to ensure their observance.

This provision makes clear that a flag state does not have total discretion over the standards that it prescribes for ships flying its flag. Any rules or regulations it applies must "conform to" international standards, procedures and practices. This rule of reference therefore incorporates international standards relating to the construction, equipment and seaworthiness of ships, the manning of ships and the training of crews, and the use of signals, the maintenance of communications and the prevention of collisions and it makes them compulsory for all ships.

This provision is based upon the text of Article 10 of the 1958 High Seas Convention and guidance on its interpretation can therefore be found in the drafting history of that instrument.[71] The original draft article prepared by the International Law Commission required the regulations of a flag state to comply with international standards concerning navigational safety and collision avoidance.[72] In other words, the rule of reference seeks to harmonize the regulations adopted by flag states. The inclusion of this rule was dictated by practical necessity. As Hudson stressed to the other members of the International Law Commission during the debate on the subject, "any ship sailing on the high seas was in danger if each ship was free to navigate as it pleased."[73]

Yet it does not necessarily follow that the effect of Article 10 is always to impose a uniform standard for flag states to meet. Article 10 was subsequently amended to include a further reference to regulations relating to safety of life at sea.[74] The addition complicates the interpretation of the Article as the regulation of safety standards raises

---

[71] The International Tribunal for the Law of the Sea has referred to the commentaries of the International Law Commission when interpreting Article 91 of the Law of the Sea Convention; see *The M/V "Saiga" (No. 2) Case (Saint Vincent and the Grenadines v Guinea* (1999) Judgment of the International Tribunal for the Law of the Sea, No. 2, at para. 80. For a historical account of these provisions, see Oxman, "The duty to respect generally accepted international standards."

[72] See International Law Commission, "Commentary to the Articles concerning the law of the sea," (1956 II) *Ybk Int'l L. C.* at 280.

[73] Report of the sixty-fourth meeting of the International Law Commission, 10 July 1950, (1956 I) *Ybk Int'l Law Commission*, at 194.

[74] See International Law Commission, "Commentary to the Articles concerning the law of the sea," at 280.

fundamentally different issues of policy and practice than the regulation of navigation and collision avoidance. In the case of labor conditions of crews, for example, the rule of reference would appear to prescribe an international minimum standard with which states must comply, but which they may exceed if they wish. The latter point is supported by Article 19(8) of the International Labour Organization Constitution which explicitly states that "in no case shall the adoption of any Convention or Recommendation by the Conference, or the ratification of any Convention by any Member, be deemed to affect any law, award, custom or agreement which ensures more favorable conditions to the workers concerned than those provided for in the Convention or Recommendation."[75]

The jurisdiction of flag states over pollution and environmental protection is also linked to international standards by a rule of reference. These obligations were introduced for the first time by the Law of the Sea Convention.[76] Article 211(2) created a new obligation for flag states to adopt regulations that "shall at least have the same effect as that of generally accepted international rules and standards." The meaning of this provision leaves no doubt that it is intended to create an international minimum standard while continuing to permit flag states to adopt stricter pollution measures if they wish.[77] The purpose, as with the provisions on safety and labor standards, is to prevent substandard shipping. As Tan explains, "the lack of any flag state incentives to prescribe and enforce pollution control measures is the very reason why a minimum standard has had to be imposed on the flag states."[78]

4.3 Coastal state jurisdiction and rules of reference

For many years, the doctrine of the freedom of the high seas meant a coastal state's jurisdiction was limited to a relatively narrow ring of waters around its coast. Moreover, the principle of innocent passage

---

[75] Article 19(8) of the ILO Constitution, available at www.ilo.org/ilolex/english/constq. htm <checked June 15, 2010>.

[76] Article 24 of the High Seas Convention simply provides that states shall draw up regulations to prevent pollution by discharge of oil from ships "taking into account existing treaty provisions on the subject."

[77] See for example A. E. Boyle, "Marine pollution under the Law of the Sea Convention" (1985) 79 Am. J. Int'l L. 357, at 353; Oxman, "The duty to respect generally accepted international standards," at 131. Articles 208(3) and 210(6) adopt a comparable approach, requiring coastal states to adopt rules on seabed pollution and dumping which are no less effective than minimum international standards.

[78] Tan, Vessel-Source Marine Pollution, at 179.

sought to restrict the exercise of the enforcement jurisdiction of coastal states over ships simply passing through its territorial sea.[79] Yet, as the incidence of maritime traffic increased, many coastal states started to demand greater rights to regulate shipping passing through their coastal waters.[80] The scope of coastal state jurisdiction over technical shipping standards was the subject of intense discussion during the negotiations at UNCLOS III.

Those IMO regulatory treaties that were negotiated prior to the conclusion of the Law of the Sea Convention largely avoid the question of jurisdiction. For instance, the MARPOL Convention provides that "any violations ... within the jurisdiction of any Party to the Convention shall be prohibited,"[81] while defining jurisdiction in light of international law at the time of application or interpretation.[82] This formulation was designed to ensure consistency with general international law and the outcome of negotiations that were taking place at that time through UNCLOS III.[83] Thus, the technical standards created by the regulatory treaties discussed above are to be applied in the context of the jurisdictional provisions of the Law of the Sea Convention.

In the context of coastal state jurisdiction, the Convention also makes use of rules of reference. It is again necessary to analyze each rule of reference individually according to its wording, its context, and its object and purpose in order to determine its effect.

Article 21 of the Law of the Sea Convention confers a power on coastal states to adopt laws on "the safety of navigation and the regulation of maritime traffic" in its territorial sea. Yet express limits are placed on the power of coastal states to prescribe certain types of

---

[79] See e.g. 1958 Convention on the Territorial Sea and the Contiguous Zone, Articles 14–15 and 19.

[80] See M'Gonigle and Zacher, *Pollution, Politics and International Law*, Chapter 6.

[81] MARPOL Convention, Article 4(2).

[82] MARPOL Convention, Article 9(3). See also the 1972 Dumping Convention, Article 13.

[83] See *Implications of the United Nations Convention on the Law of the Sea for the International Maritime Organization*, at 11; see also A. Blanco-Bazan, "IMO interface with the Law of the Sea Convention," in J. N. Moore and M. Nordquist (eds.), *Current Maritime Issues and the International Maritime Organization* (Martinus Nijhoff Publishers, 1999) at 273; R. Wolfrum, "IMO interface with the Law of the Sea Convention," in J. N. Moore and M. Nordquist (eds.), *Current Maritime Issues and the International Maritime Organization* (Martinus Nijhoff Publishers, 1999) at 231. These sources also note that the IMO Secretariat was actively involved in the negotiations at UNCLOS III in order to ensure consistency in its own work.

standards in this maritime zone. Article 21(2) provides that "[coastal state] laws and regulations shall not apply to the design, construction, manning or equipment of foreign ships unless they are giving effect to generally accepted international rules and standards." The purpose of this provision is to facilitate international trade by preventing the proliferation of technical standards that would stop a ship from freely transiting the world's coastal zones.[84] Thus, the power of the coastal state to legislate on these matters is strictly limited to the prescription of those standards that have been internationally agreed.

Similar limitations are found on the prescriptive jurisdiction of a coastal state in the EEZ. The extension of the jurisdiction of coastal states over environmental issues was one of the innovative features of the Law of the Sea Convention. Yet, from very early in the negotiations, any extension in the exercise of coastal state jurisdiction over environmental matters was linked to the idea of internationally accepted rules and regulations.[85] This link "reflected the crux of a delicately weighed balance of power arrived at between coastal states and shipping nations."[86] Thus, in the EEZ, a coastal state may only adopt regulations "conforming to and giving effect to generally accepted international rules and standards established through the competent international organization or general diplomatic conference."[87] This provision again acts to limit the competence of a coastal state by setting a limit on its prescriptive powers,[88] deterring coastal states from using environmental regulations as a means to restrict the navigational rights of foreign ships.[89]

---

[84] See R. Churchill and V. Lowe, *The Law of the Sea* (3rd edn., Manchester University Press, 1997) at 94; Tan, *Vessel-Source Marine Pollution*, at 180.

[85] See M. Nordquist et al. (eds.), *United Nations Convention on the Law of the Sea 1982 – A Commentary*, Vol. 4 (Martinus Nijhoff Publishers, 1991) at 183 onwards.

[86] International Law Association, "Report of the Committee on Coastal State Jurisdiction relating to Marine Pollution," in *Report of the 69th Conference of the International Law Association*, London, 2000, at 487; see also D. Vignes, "La valeur juridique de certaines regles, normes ou pratiques mentionnees au T.N.C.O. comme generalement acceptees" (1979) 25 *Annuaire Français de Droit International* 712; Boyle, "Marine pollution under the Law of the Sea Convention," at 353.

[87] Law of the Sea Convention, Article 211(5).

[88] See, however, Law of the Sea Convention, Article 211(6), which will be discussed below.

[89] See D. Attard, *The Exclusive Economic Zone in International Law* (Oxford University Press, 1987) at 95; F. Orrego Vicuña, *The Exclusive Economic Zone* (Cambridge University Press, 1989) at 85.

4.4 "Generally accepted international standards"

It can be seen that international standards play a central role in delimiting the scope of flag state and coastal state jurisdiction under the Law of the Sea Convention and it does so by incorporating international standards through rules of reference. There is no particular organization that is competent to adopt these international standards. Standards adopted by a number of institutions, such as the International Labour Organization and the Food and Agriculture Organization, could be relevant for the purposes of the rules of reference. However, the IMO is perhaps the most significant organization in this context in terms of the number of standards adopted under its auspices. Indeed, the IMO claims a special place among these specialized organizations, asserting that "the expression competent international organization, when used in the singular in [the Law of the Sea Convention], applies exclusively to the IMO, bearing in mind the global mandate of the Organization as a specialized agency within the United Nations system."[90]

The most common test for incorporation of standards by the majority of rules of reference relating to shipping is whether or not a standard has been "generally accepted."[91] The advantage of using this term is that it creates a degree of dynamism, as the standards may change over time, without having to amend the Law of the Sea Convention.[92] However, it also raises questions about what is meant by the term "generally accepted."

Some IMO standards clearly qualify as "generally accepted." The SOLAS Convention, for instance, is binding on 99.04 percent of the world merchant fleet in terms of tonnage.[93] There can be no doubt that

---

[90] *Implications of the United Nations Convention on the Law of the Sea for the International Maritime Organization*, Document LEG/MISC/6, September 10, 2008, at 7.

[91] Other qualifications are used in different contexts. Article 210 calls for states to adopt laws that are "no less effective in preventing, reducing, and controlling [pollution from dumping] than the global rules and standards." It is suggested that global rules and standards are equivalent to generally accepted international rules and standards. See Vukas, "Generally accepted international rules and standards," at 406–8; Boyle, "Marine pollution under the Law of the Sea Convention," at 355. Articles 208 and 209 require seabed activities to be no less effective than "international rules, regulations and standards and recommended practices and procedures." The adoption of seabed standards is dealt with in Chapter 5.

[92] L. Sohn, "Implications of the Law of the Sea Convention regarding the protection of the marine environment," in R. B. Krueger and S. A. Riesenfeld (eds.) *The Developing Order of the Oceans* (Law of the Sea Institute, 1985) at 109.

[93] See www.imo.org/About/Conventions/StatusOfConventions/Pages/Default.aspx <checked November 29, 2010). The 1978 Protocol to the SOLAS Convention is

this treaty is generally accepted and it is therefore incorporated through the relevant rules of reference on maritime safety. Comparable figures apply to the 1966 Convention on Load Lines[94] and the 1972 Convention on the International Regulations for Preventing Collisions at Sea.[95] The two compulsory annexes of the MARPOL Convention have also been accepted by a similarly high percentage of the world merchant fleet.[96] Such high levels of participation leave little doubt that the standards contained in these instruments are generally accepted. However, not all IMO regulatory treaties benefit from such high levels of participation. For instance, some of the optional annexes to MARPOL have struggled to attract contracting parties.[97] Moreover, treaties that have been negotiated more recently, such as the 2001 Anti-Fouling Convention[98] and the 2004 Ballast Water Convention,[99] may not attract high levels of participation for many years to come.

It follows from the disparity between levels of acceptance that there is an ambiguity about which standards are generally accepted and therefore which standards are incorporated by the rules of reference. The International Law Association (ILA) Committee on Coastal State Jurisdiction relating to Marine Pollution suggests that the concept of generally accepted standards "was intentionally kept vague in order not to upset the delicate balance which the notion incorporates."[100] Yet uncertainty itself can also seriously undermine the utility of the rules of reference. As Boyle critically notes, "to say

---

ratified by states representing 96.16% of world tonnage and the 1988 Protocol is ratified by states representing 94.40% of world tonnage.

[94] There are 159 states that are party to the Load Lines Convention, representing 99.02% of world tonnage. The 1998 Protocol to the Load Lines Convention has been ratified by states representing 94.60% of world tonnage.

[95] There are 153 states that are party to the Convention on the International Regulations for Preventing Collisions at Sea, representing 98.36% of world tonnage.

[96] There are 150 states that are party to the MARPOL Convention, representing 99.14% of world tonnage.

[97] Annex III has 133 parties representing 95.67% of world tonnage; Annex IV has 125 parties representing 81.98% of world tonnage; Annex V has 140 parties representing 95.23% of world tonnage; and Annex VI has 59 parties representing 84.23% of world tonnage.

[98] The Anti-Fouling Convention entered into force on September 17, 2008 and as at December 31, 2009, it had 45 parties representing 74.23% of world tonnage.

[99] The Bunkers Convention entered into force on November 21, 2008 and as at December 31, 2009, it had 53 parties representing 84.65% of world tonnage.

[100] International Law Association, *Report of the Committee on Coastal State Jurisdiction relating to Marine Pollution*, at 480.

that states have a duty to regulate pollution is to beg the question what regulations they must adopt, a question that the Convention does not satisfactorily answer."[101] Indeed, clarifying the interpretation of which standards are "generally accepted" is vital to delimiting the scope of flag state and coastal state jurisdiction under the Law of the Sea Convention.

One interpretation offered by commentators is that rules and standards are generally accepted if they have satisfied the formal conditions for entry into force.[102] Thus, Valenzuela argues that "the condition ... for the entry into force of IMO conventions – that is the requirement of a substantial number of states parties having among them more than half the tonnage of the world's merchant fleet – seems to have precisely this purpose."[103] It is true that the purpose of the dual condition in the entry into force provisions is intended to prevent treaties entering into force until they are accepted by a significant proportion of maritime states. However, it does not follow that they should be equated with general acceptance. Indeed, there are several problems that arise from this argument. First, the level of acceptance needed for entry into force varies from treaty to treaty: twenty-five states representing fifty percent of world tonnage in the SOLAS Convention;[104] fifteen states representing fifty percent of world tonnage in the MARPOL Convention;[105] thirty states representing thirty-five percent of world tonnage in the Ballast Water Convention;[106] and twenty-five states representing twenty-five percent of world tonnage in the Anti-Fouling Convention.[107] Can it be correct that the threshold for general acceptance can vary so greatly depending on the instrument in which a standard is contained? Secondly, the risk of adopting this interpretation is that, as Timagenis

---

[101] Boyle, "Marine pollution under the Law of the Sea Convention," at 357. See also Churchill and Lowe, *The Law of the Sea*, at 347; P. Birnie, A. E. Boyle and C. Redgwell, *International Law and the Environment* (3rd edn., Oxford University Press, 2009) at 389–90.

[102] For instance, M. Valenzuela, "IMO: public international law and regulation," in D. M. Johnston and N. G. Letalik (eds.), *The Law of the Sea and Ocean Industry: New Opportunities and Restraints* (Law of the Sea Institute, 1984) at 145. For a similar approach, see Boyle, "Marine pollution under the Law of the Sea Convention," at 356.

[103] Valenzuela, "IMO: public international law and regulation," at 145.

[104] SOLAS Convention, Article 10(1).

[105] MARPOL Convention, Article 15(1).

[106] Ballast Water Convention, Article 18(1).

[107] Anti-Fouling Convention, Article 18(1).

puts it, "small minorities could impose their wishes on other states."[108] Thirdly, the outcome of this approach to interpretation is that all treaties containing international standards that have entered into force will qualify as generally accepted under the rules of reference. Yet, the Law of the Sea Convention makes a distinction between generally accepted international standards and "applicable international standards."[109] The latter concept implies that a treaty may be legally binding for some states without being generally accepted.[110] This distinction would be lost if all standards that had entered into force were also considered to be generally accepted. A final reason why this argument should be rejected is that it assumes that an international standard will be found in a treaty instrument. However, this may not always be the case. It was certainly envisaged by the International Law Commission when drafting Article 10 of the High Seas Convention that it covered "regulations which are a product of international cooperation, without necessarily having been confirmed by formal treaties."[111] As noted above, the IMO occasionally adopts standards in the form of nonbinding instruments. Provided these standards meet the requirement of general acceptance, there is no reason why they should not fall within the scope of the rules of reference in the Law of the Sea Convention.

An alternative argument suggests that the concept of "general acceptance" concentrates not on formal acceptance of a standard under the terms of a treaty but on whether or not a standard has been accepted in state practice. Thus, Van Reenan argues that "the meaning of 'generally accepted international rules' can be found in the criteria for determining whether certain ... rules have become world-wide rules of customary law."[112] On this view, standards become generally accepted

---

[108] G. J. Timagenis, *International Control of Marine Pollution* (Oceana Publications, 1980) at 606.

[109] The term applicable international regulations is found in Articles 42, 60, 94, 213, 214, 216, 217, 218, 219, 220, 226, 228 and 230.

[110] However, it is logical that applicable standards encompass generally accepted standards, as the latter are by definition "applicable" to all states; see Van Reenen, "Rules of Reference in the new Convention on the Law of the Sea in particular connection with the pollution of the sea by oil from tankers," at 12–13; International Law Association, *Report of the Committee on Coastal State Jurisdiction relating to Marine Pollution*, at 481–2.

[111] International Law Commission, "Commentary to the Articles concerning the Law of the Sea," at 281. It would seem that the Commission had in mind the International Regulations on Signals, which, until 1972, were contained in a nonbinding instrument.

[112] Van Reenen, "Rules of Reference in the new Convention on the Law of the Sea," at 11. Others have argued that the strict threshold for the creation of customary law is too high and that a lower level of acceptance is appropriate; Timagenis,

when they have achieved the status of customary international law. This allows standards contained in treaties, as well as in nonbinding instruments, to fall within the scope of a rule of reference.

This latter interpretation is consistent with the position prior to the conclusion of the Law of the Sea Convention, where many technical standards relating to navigation and maritime safety were accepted as rules of customary international law. Indeed, the language of "general acceptance" is strikingly similar to that employed by the United States Supreme Court in the case of *The Scotia*, which concerned the status of merchant shipping regulations first promulgated by the United Kingdom but later applied to vessels from other states. In that case, the Court held that "many of the usages which prevail, and which have the force of law, doubtless originated in the positive prescriptions of a single state, which were first of limited effect, but which, when generally accepted, became universal obligations."[113] It is precisely this effect of extending the application of standards to all states that the rules of reference are intended to achieve. Thus, there would seem to be a strong parallel between the rules of reference and the process of creating customary international law.

The customary international law interpretation of the general acceptance test is often criticized because it is said that "there would be no use for having [the] rule of reference in the 1982 Convention since states would be bound by customary international law anyway."[114] Yet many of the rules in the Law of the Sea Convention serve to codify or crystallize customary international law.[115] The rules of reference are nevertheless useful because they clarify the process through which international standards can become binding on all states.

Arguably, the way in which a standard is adopted by the IMO is an important way in which to identify whether or not it has become generally accepted. Certainly, if a standard has been opposed by a number of states at the adoption stage, this will hinder its ultimate prospects for becoming a generally accepted international standard. In contrast, the existence of consensus among members of the IMO may make it

---

International Control of Marine Pollution, at 605. See also K. Hakapää, *Marine Pollution in International Law* (Suomlainen Tiedeakatemia, 1981) at 121; International Law Association, *Report of the Committee on Coastal State Jurisdiction relating to Marine Pollution*, at 478.

[113] *The Scotia* (1871) 81 US Report 170, at 187.
[114] See the criticism in International Law Association, *Report of the Committee on Coastal State Jurisdiction relating to Marine Pollution*, at 478.
[115] See Chapter 2.

more likely that a standard will be generally accepted. It is in this sense that the consensus decision-making procedures employed by the IMO are highly significant in facilitating the creation of generally accepted international shipping standards that can be incorporated into the Law of the Sea Convention through rules of reference.

It should be noted that this interpretation of "generally accepted" falls far short of conferring a legislative competence on international organizations charged with the elaboration of international standards.[116] The mere adoption or approval of an international standard by an international organization is not sufficient to establish general acceptance. Whereas the discussions and deliberations leading to the adoption of an international instrument may sometimes contribute to the crystallization of customary international law,[117] particularly when they are supported by consensus, the nature of technical standards means that it would be difficult to conclude that the standards had been generally accepted as legally binding if there were no additional evidence that states had actually implemented them in practice.[118] Thus, some of the most convincing evidence of state practice and *opinio juris* for the creation of customary international law in this context will be the subsequent implementation and enforcement of international standards by states. This may be demonstrated partly through the actual transposition of shipping standards into domestic law.

It is not only the actions of individual states that count as evidence of subsequent state practice and *opinio juris* for these purposes. Monitoring of compliance may also take place formally or informally at the international level and the action of states taken through international organizations may therefore also constitute evidence of state practice concerning the general acceptance of international standards. States increasingly pursue issues of compliance with international standards through diplomatic institutions, such as the IMO[119] or other organizations such as the General Assembly.

---

[116] Cf. Oxman, "The duty to respect generally accepted international standards," at 149–50.

[117] See Chapter 1.

[118] See Oxman, "The duty to respect generally accepted international standards," at 152.

[119] The Sub-Committee on Flag State Implementation was created in 1992 to assess the implementation of mandatory IMO conventions and to identify the difficulties which flag states face in fully implementing IMO instruments. See also *Resolution on*

Examples of such evidence can be found in General Assembly resolutions on the law of the sea. These resolutions regularly deal with maritime safety and the protection of the marine environment, reviewing developments in regulatory activity. A careful reading of these resolutions reveals that the General Assembly sometimes calls upon states to comply with certain instruments adopted by the IMO, whether or not they are a party thereto. For instance, in its 2005 resolution, the General Assembly "calls upon states to effectively implement the International Ship and Port Facility Security Code and related amendments to the International Convention for the Safety of Life at Sea."[120] This appeal was repeated in its 2006 resolution.[121] Another paragraph of the 2005 resolution

urges states to take all necessary measures to ensure the effective implementation of the amendments to the International Convention on Maritime Search and Rescue and to the International Convention for the Safety of Life at Sea relating to the delivery of persons rescued from sea to a place of safety upon their entry into force as well as the associated Guidelines on the Treatment of Rescued Persons at Sea.[122]

In 2006 states were similarly required to "ensure that masters on ships flying their flag take the steps required by relevant instruments to provide assistance to persons in distress at sea."[123] A footnote to this resolution refers to the SOLAS Convention and the Search and Rescue Convention as the relevant instruments. These resolutions go beyond simply bringing instruments to the attention of states or encouraging states to ratify or accede to international standards, as is often the case with General Assembly resolutions. The text of this resolution is unambiguously addressed to all states, urging them to ensure effective implementation of certain standards, whether or not they are a party. It is submitted that these resolutions themselves provide evidence that the instruments that they address are generally accepted for the purposes of the rules of reference in the Law of the Sea Convention.

the self-assessment of flag state performance, Resolution A.881(21); Voluntary audit scheme adopted at IMO's 24th Assembly, IMO Briefing 51/2005, December 7, 2005.

[120] Oceans and the law of the sea, UNGA Resolution 60/30, November 29, 2005, at para. 53. See an almost identical call in Oceans and law of the sea, UNGA Resolution 64/71, December 4, 2009, at para. 85.

[121] Oceans and the law of the sea, UNGA Resolution 61/222, December 20, 2006, at para. 60.

[122] UNGA Resolution 60/30, at para. 59.

[123] UNGA Resolution 61/222, at para. 70.

The language in the example above can be contrasted with softer language used in the context of other international standards. For instance, in Resolution 61/222 adopted in 2006 the General Assembly simply

> encourages states that have not done so to become parties to the Protocol of 1997 (Annex VI – Regulations for the Prevention of Air Pollution from Ships) to the International Convention for the Prevention of Pollution from Ships, 1973 as amended by the Protocol of 1978 relating thereto, and furthermore to ratify or accede to the International Convention on the Control of Harmful Anti-Fouling Systems of Ships 2001, as well as the International Convention for the Control and Management of Ships' Ballast Water and Sediments 2004, thereby facilitating their early entry into force.[124]

This statement falls short of calling on states to comply with these instruments, suggesting that they are not yet generally accepted and therefore they do not fall within the scope of the rules of reference on environmental protection. It can also be contrasted with assertions of the General Assembly that are aimed at particular states. For example, in 2009 the General Assembly called on "States that have accepted the amendments to regulation cl-1/6 of the International Convention for the Safety of Life at Sea, 1974, to implement the Code of International Standards and Recommended Practices for a Safety Investigation into a Marine Casualty or Marine Incident, which will take effect on 1 January 2010."[125] This latter statement is directed solely at those states that have formally accepted the regulation, rather than to states generally. The choice of language in these resolutions would suggest that they have been carefully drafted by states and they cannot therefore be relied upon as evidence of state practice and *opinio juris* that a standard is generally accepted.

If the concept of generally accepted standards is interpreted to mean those standards that have gained the status of rules of customary international law, it does not necessarily follow that all states will always be bound to implement those standards through the rules of reference. While a single state might not be able to block the creation of a rule of customary international law, according to the persistent objector principle, a state will not be bound by a rule of customary international

---

[124] UNGA Resolution 61/30, at para. 81. See a similar call in relation to the 1996 Protocol to the Convention on the Prevention of Dumping of Wastes and Other Matter 1972 in UNGA Resolution 60/30, at para. 63.
[125] UNGA Resolution 64/71, at para. 95.

law to which it has promptly and consistently objected.[126] Can a state be a persistent objector to a generally accepted international standard that has been incorporated in the Law of the Sea Convention by a rule of reference?

On the one hand, it could be argued that the concept of a persistent objector is not expressly mentioned in the rules of the reference in the Law of the Sea Convention and therefore it is not possible for a state to object to a rule once it has become generally accepted. However, one objection to this approach is that it would override the express right of a state to object to an amendment to a technical annex of an IMO regulatory treaty as established by those treaties themselves.[127] If this right of objection is to be maintained, the principle of the persistent objector must be read into the rules of reference. Thus, a state may prevent the application of an international standard to itself if it objects to that standard from the outset.

In practice, however, this caveat may have little actual application. The use of consensus decision-making procedures by the IMO when adopting technical standards and amendments thereto will by and large avoid persistent objectors. Indeed, very few objections are actually made to amendments under the tacit amendment procedures in IMO treaties.[128] It follows that standards adopted at the IMO may, through the operation of the rules of reference in the Law of the Sea Convention, become almost universally binding.

5 Traffic measures and the role of the International Maritime Organization

5.1 The approval role of the International Maritime Organization

In addition to the adoption of technical standards regulating the design, construction and operation of ships, another way of improving safety at sea is the adoption of measures to control the navigation of ships in particular areas of sea. There are various types of traffic measures which can be used for this purpose, including traffic separation schemes, separation zones, traffic lanes, roundabouts, inshore traffic

---

[126] See *Anglo-Norwegian Fisheries Case* (1951) ICJ Reports 116.
[127] See above.
[128] See International Maritime Organization, *Status of Multilateral Conventions and Instruments in respect of which the International Maritime Organization or its Secretary-General performs depositary or other functions, as at 3 June 2010.*

zones, two-way routes, recommended routes, deep water routes and areas to be avoided.[129]

Coastal states have always had the ability to propose and adopt traffic measures in the territorial sea in order to improve safety of navigation.[130] This is confirmed by Article 22(1) of the Law of the Sea Convention which says that "coastal states may, where necessary having regard to safety of navigation, require foreign ships exercising the right of innocent passage through its territorial sea to use such sealanes and traffic separation schemes as it may designate or prescribe for the regulation of the passage of ships." Such schemes are mandatory and they must be complied with by ships.[131] When adopting such traffic measures, the coastal state must take into account the recommendations of the competent international organization, in this case, the IMO.[132] However, the language of this provision makes it clear that the role of the IMO in this situation is purely recommendatory. Arguably, the purpose of this provision is to require the coastal state to consult with affected states through the relevant international organization. Indeed, the view of other states is only one factor to be taken into account alongside other factors including the existence of any channels customarily used for international navigation, the special characteristics of channels and other maritime features in the area, the special characteristics of any ships navigating in the area and the density of traffic.

The situation differs in other maritime zones in which the coastal state has acquired powers to regulate shipping. It was considered by the drafters of the Convention that the jurisdiction of coastal states to adopt navigation measures in these other maritime zones should be balanced against the interests of other members of the international community. In order to maintain this balance, states are often obliged to seek the approval of the IMO, as the "competent international organization," before they impose compulsory navigational measures in these maritime zones.[133] Oxman calls this the "approval role" of the IMO.[134]

---

[129] *General provisions on ships' routeing*, Resolution A.572(14), as amended, at para. 2.1.

[130] 1958 Convention on the Territorial Sea and Contiguous Zone, Article 17.

[131] Law of the Sea Convention, Article 21(4).

[132] Law of the Sea Convention, Article 22(3).

[133] It is the Maritime Safety Committee which fulfills this role; see Resolution A.858(20) on the procedure for the adoption and amendment of traffic separation schemes, routeing measures other than traffic separation schemes including the designation and substitution of archipelagic sea lanes and ship-reporting systems.

[134] B. H. Oxman, "Environmental protection in archipelagic waters and international straits – the role of the International Maritime Organization" (1995) 10 *Int'l J. Marine & Coastal L.* 467, at 468.

5.2 Navigational measures in international straits

One area where the IMO has an approval role is in relation to measures to promote safety of navigation in international straits. The purpose of the regime on international straits found in Part III of the Convention is to limit the interference of coastal states with ships passing through important maritime traffic routes that would otherwise fall within the territorial sea of the coastal state and thus within their "sovereign" jurisdiction.[135] Ships navigating through international straits are duly given a right of transit passage that is subject to fewer limitations than the traditional right of innocent passage in the territorial sea.

The power for strait states to adopt legislative measures is provided in Article 42 of the Convention subject to specific limitations including a general prohibition that states bordering straits shall not hamper transit passage and that transit passage shall not be suspended.[136] Article 42(1)(a) provides that "states bordering straits may adopt laws and regulations relating to transit passage through straits in respect of ... the safety of navigation and the regulation of maritime traffic, as provided in article 41."

As well as specifying the types of measures that a littoral state may take in international straits, navigational measures adopted under Article 41 are also subject to a special adoption procedure. Central to this process is the approval role of the IMO. Article 41(4) requires strait states to submit proposals to designate, prescribe or substitute sea lanes and traffic separation schemes to the IMO "with a view to adoption." The procedure strictly circumscribes the powers of both strait states and the IMO.

First, a strait state may only designate, prescribe or substitute the applicable measures once it has been "adopted" at the international level. This is confirmed by Article 41(7), which provides that "ships in transit passage shall respect applicable sea lanes and traffic separation schemes established in accordance with this article." As one commentary suggests, "by implication, there is no obligation under

---

[135] See generally J. Moore, "The Regime of Straits and the Third United Nations Conference on the Law of the Sea" (1980) 74 *Am. J. Int'l L.* 77.

[136] Law of the Sea Convention, Articles 41(2) and 44. In addition, the competence of the strait state to regulate pollution from ships is limited to "giving effect to applicable international rules and regulations regarding the discharge of oil, oily waste and other noxious substances in the strait"; Article 42(1)(b); see M. Nordquist *et al.* (eds.), *United Nations Convention on the Law of the Sea 1982 – A Commentary, Vol. 2* (Martinus Nijhoff Publishers, 1993) at 375–6.

this Convention to respect sea lanes or traffic separation schemes unless they have been established in accordance with the conditions [in Article 41]."[137] In other words, adoption by the IMO would appear to be a prerequisite to the validity of traffic measures applied to international straits.

The role of the IMO is to scrutinize measures formulated by the strait state in order to decide whether such measures are "necessary" to promote safety of navigation. In doing so, it must also ensure that the proposal complies with "generally accepted international regulations."[138] For these purposes, the IMO General Provisions on Ships' Routeing are relevant.[139] The General Provisions serve to clarify the role of the IMO in the decision-making process and what factors should be taken into account when determining whether a particular traffic measure is necessary.[140] However, the factors in the General Provisions are not exhaustive and the IMO may take into account other considerations on a case-by-case basis.

While the powers of the littoral state are limited by the IMO, the powers of the IMO are also limited. For instance, the IMO may only approve measures that have the support of the littoral state. Where there is more than one state bordering the strait concerned, they must all consent to the traffic measures.[141]

It follows that IMO Members and the strait state must negotiate a mutually acceptable solution.[142] In light of these considerations, the IMO acts as an important forum in which the interests of all states, including strait states and user states, can be taken into account and balanced in deciding whether to adopt proposed traffic measures.

---

[137] Nordquist et al. (eds.), *United Nations Convention on the Law of the Sea 1982 – A Commentary*, Vol. 2, at 365.
[138] Law of the Sea Convention, Article 41(3).
[139] *General provisions on ships' routeing as amended*, Resolution A.572(14).
[140] See *ibid.*, paras. 3.2 and 3.3.
[141] Law of the Sea Convention, Article 41(5). See S. B. Kempton, "Ship routeing measures in international straits," in E. Mann Borgese et al. (eds.), *Ocean Yearbook 14* (International Ocean Institute, 2000) at 243.
[142] See Nordquist et al. (eds.), *United Nations Convention on the Law of the Sea 1982 – A Commentary*, Vol. 2, at 363. Where the strait passes through the territorial sea of two or more states, those states must cooperate in formulating proposals before submitting them to the IMO for consideration; Law of the Sea Convention, Article 41(5).

5.3 The adoption of sea lanes in archipelagic waters

The IMO also plays an approval role in relation to sea lanes through archipelagic waters. The concept of archipelagic waters and archipelagic sea lanes was introduced by Part IV of the Law of the Sea Convention, which seeks to reconcile the political and security interests of archipelagic states with the interests of shipping states.[143] The Convention provides that archipelagic states can exercise sovereignty over waters enclosed by archipelagic baselines,[144] but that this sovereignty is subject to the right of vessels to continuous, expeditious and unobstructed transit passage through archipelagic sea lanes between one part of the high seas or EEZ and another part of the high seas or EEZ.[145] Article 53(4) provides that "sea lanes and air routes shall traverse the archipelagic waters and the adjacent territorial sea and shall include all normal passage routes used as routes for international navigation or overflight." Archipelagic states are under a duty to prescribe such sea lanes in accordance with the conditions and procedures set out in the Convention. Failure to prescribe sea lanes or air routes does not mean that ships will not be able to pass through archipelagic waters. Article 53(12) confirms that "if an archipelagic state does not designate sea lanes or air routes, the right of archipelagic sea lanes passage may be exercised through the routes normally used for international navigation."

In order to ensure that these conditions are met, the Convention provides for international scrutiny and the approval of archipelagic sea lane proposals by the IMO. Under Article 53 of the Law of the Sea Convention, the archipelagic state is under an obligation to refer any proposals for an archipelagic sea lane to the IMO "with a view to their adoption."[146] As with the case for navigational measures in international straits, the IMO provides a forum in which competing interests can be reconciled. The approval procedure foresees a dialogue between the archipelagic state and other IMO members.[147]

---

[143] In general, see M. Munavvar, *Ocean States – Archipelagic Regimes in the Law of the Sea* (Martinus Nijhoff Publishers, 1995); Office for Ocean Affairs and the Law of the Sea, *Archipelagic States – Legislative History of Part IV of the United Nations Convention on the Law of the Sea* (United Nations, 1990).

[144] Law of the Sea Convention, Article 49.

[145] Law of the Sea Convention, Article 53(3).

[146] Law of the Sea Convention, Article 53(9).

[147] See Munavvar, *Ocean States – Archipelagic Regimes in the Law of the Sea*, at 169.

Any proposals for archipelagic sea lanes must also comply with generally accepted international regulations.[148] The IMO is once again the source of such regulations. As the concept of archipelagic sea lanes was an innovation, the IMO has had to develop a new set of regulations on this topic. The General Provisions on the Adoption, Designation and Substitution of Archipelagic Sea Lanes were first adopted by the Maritime Safety Committee in May 1998.[149] These provisions purport to "provide guidance for the preparation, consideration and adoption of proposals for the adoption, designation and substitution of archipelagic sea lanes."[150] They complement the provisions found in the Convention by specifying the procedure that will be followed by the Organization in considering proposals for archipelagic sea lanes, as well as the criteria that will be taken into account in the designation process. The General Provisions on Archipelagic Sea Lanes thus fill in the gaps that are left by the Convention.

In the first instance, the General Provisions on Archipelagic Sea Lanes confirm that the IMO is the competent organization for adopting archipelagic sea lanes in accordance with the relevant provisions of the Law of the Sea Convention.[151] They then go on to explain the responsibilities of governments submitting proposals for archipelagic sea lanes. They provide that the government of an archipelagic state should consult at an early stage with other user governments and the IMO.[152] This provision implies that governments shall start consultations when first drawing up proposals, prior to their submission to the IMO. The General Provisions also stipulate the type of information that governments should include in a proposal.[153] It has been suggested that the requirement for archipelagic states to consult and to take into account the opinions of other states "seem to lessen the practical effect of any pre-existing power of veto held by the archipelagic states" and "in this way, the General Provisions reinforce the ascendancy of user interests in the archipelagic sea lanes passage regime."[154] Yet, the General Provisions on Archipelagic Sea Lanes would seem to do no more than promote the maximum possible cooperation between

---

[148] Law of the Sea Convention, Article 53(8).
[149] *General provisions on archipelagic sea lanes*, IMO Resolution MSC.71(69) as amended by Resolution MSC.165(78).
[150] *Ibid.*, at para. 1.1.   [151] *Ibid.*, at para. 3.1.
[152] *Ibid.*, at para. 3.6.   [153] *Ibid.*, at para. 3.10.
[154] C. Johnson, "A rite of passage: the I.M.O. consideration of the Indonesian archipelagic sea lanes submission" (2000) 15 *Int'l J. Marine & Coastal L.* 317, at 324.

the archipelagic state and user states at all stages of the process which furthers the underlying object and purpose of the Convention regime on archipelagic waters.

Another aspect of the General Provisions on Archipelagic Sea Lanes that has been the subject of criticism is the concept of a "partial archipelagic sea lanes proposal." This term derives from the General Provisions, which define the concept as one "which does not meet the requirement to include all normal passage routes and navigational channels as required by [the Convention]."[155] If a state is submitting a partial archipelagic sea lanes proposal, the General Provisions require that the state must also provide periodic reports to the IMO of its plans for conducting further surveys and studies towards the proposal of additional archipelagic sea lanes.[156] Throughout this process, the IMO will retain "continuing jurisdiction" over the process of adopting archipelagic sea lanes until the requirements of the Law of the Sea Convention are met.[157] In the meantime, the right of archipelagic passage may continue to be exercised through all normal passage routes used for international navigation or overflight in other parts of archipelagic waters where sea lanes have not been designated.[158] One author argues that "the concept of a partial proposal or designation was not envisaged in the Law of the Sea Convention" and it has the effect of undermining the provisions on archipelagic sea lanes.[159] He concludes that the concept converts much of Article 53 into "excessive verbiage" as "if a complete [archipelagic sea lanes] designation must at all times include 'all routes,' then there is no situation in which substitution can be called for, nor is there any opportunity to eliminate redundant routes."[160] Yet, this criticism would appear to be unfair. Arguably, the concept of a partial sea lane proposal is no more than a procedural device that aims to satisfy the condition in Article 53(4) that archipelagic sea lanes must include all normal passage routes used as routes for international navigation or overflight. It serves to emphasize that the final designation

---

[155] *General Provisions for the Adoption, Designation and Substitution of Archipelagic Sea Lanes*, IMO Resolution MSC.165(78), adopted on May 17, 2004, at para. 2.2.2.

[156] *General Provisions on archipelagic sea lanes*, at para. 3.12.

[157] IMO Resolution MSC.71(69), at para. 3.5.

[158] *General provisions on archipelagic sea lanes*, at para. 6.7.

[159] J. L. Batongbacal, "Barely skimming the surface: archipelagic sea lanes navigation and the IMO," in A. Oude Elferink and D. Rothwell (eds.), *Oceans Management in the 21st Century: Institutional Frameworks and Responses* (Koninklikje Brill NV, 2004) at 55–6.

[160] *Ibid.*, at 56.

of archipelagic sea lanes rests with the IMO in cooperation with the archipelagic state, and any impasse over the status of sea lanes must be solved through continuing negotiations.

One area in which the General Provisions on Archipelagic Sea Lanes do not provide further guidance is the question of what is meant by "routes normally used for international navigation." The General Provisions simply reproduce the definition found in the Convention. It may have been thought that this was an area in which the IMO, as the competent international organization in this field, could have usefully clarified the content of the regime on archipelagic sea lanes. Instead, the IMO has opted to deal with this question on a case-by-case basis through negotiations in the Maritime Safety Committee.[161] Through discussing specific proposals for archipelagic sea lanes, states may be able to reach compromises on an acceptable solution to a particular application. The difficulty with such an approach is that it may not promote consistency between particular cases. It would be preferable for the Organization, through its discussions on particular proposals, to develop more objective criteria that can guide states that may wish to designate archipelagic sea lanes in the future.

5.4 Mandatory navigational measures in the Exclusive Economic Zone

A third area where the IMO has powers of approval under the Law of the Sea Convention relates to the adoption of certain navigational measures by coastal states in the EEZ.[162] In terms of navigation, the EEZ is largely analogous to the high seas. The Convention expressly saves the right of freedom of navigation and overflight of all states in the EEZ.[163] It follows that it is not normally appropriate to apply mandatory navigational measures in that area.[164] There is no general provision in the Convention that allows coastal states to adopt mandatory navigational

---

[161] Batongbacal also brings attention to the important role played by informal negotiations between interested actors outside of the formal IMO framework; ibid., at 54. Indeed, he argues that the IMO is not the appropriate forum to resolve conflicts over the designation of archipelagic sea lanes as its competence is limited to commercial vessels, whereas the key issues in this context are concerned with state and military vessels; ibid., at 66.

[162] Law of the Sea Convention, Article 211(6).

[163] Law of the Sea Convention, Article 58(1).

[164] G. Plant, "International traffic separation schemes in the new law of the sea" (1985) Marine Policy 134, at 145–6.

measures in the EEZ, although there are exceptional circumstances in which such measures may be prescribed.

One exception is the power to establish safety zones around any artificial islands, installations or structures that are established by the coastal state in the EEZ or in the continental shelf. According to Article 60(5), such zones shall not exceed 500 meters in width, unless they are authorized by generally accepted international standards or as recommended by the competent international organization. The IMO claims to be the competent international organization for the purposes of this Article. In the first place, the Convention foresees the role of the Organization as setting standards that will determine the scope of a coastal state's discretion on this matter. The IMO adopted Resolution A.671(16) on Safety Zones and Safety of Navigation Around Offshore Installations and Structures, which includes recommendations for governments to take into account when establishing safety zones around offshore installations. However, Article 60(5) could also be interpreted as permitting the Organization to make specific recommendations in individual cases that are submitted to it. In other words, the IMO has also a role in relation to the approval of safety zones around offshore installations in excess of 500 meters.

A second exception is found in Article 211(6) of the Convention, which says that a state may propose special mandatory measures to protect a particular, clearly defined area of its EEZ from pollution from ships if generally accepted international standards are inadequate to meet special circumstances of a technical nature. This is a complex provision that requires careful analysis.

Article 211(6) only becomes applicable where special mandatory measures are required for recognized technical reasons in relation to oceanographical and ecological conditions or for reasons relating to the utilization of an area, the protection of its resources or the particular character of its traffic. The coastal state must produce scientific and technical evidence in support of its claims. Once this threshold has been met, it would appear that two categories of measures are anticipated under Article 211(6).

First, paragraph (a) allows coastal states to adopt "laws and regulations for the prevention, reduction, and control of pollution from vessels implementing such international rules and standards or navigational practices as are made applicable, through the organization, for special areas." The reference to special areas brings to mind the concept of special areas in Annexes I, II, V and VI of the MARPOL

Convention. A special area under the MARPOL Convention is defined as "a sea area where for recognized technical reasons in relation to its oceanographical and ecological condition and to the particular character of its traffic the adoption of special mandatory measures ... is required."[165] If a special area is designated under MARPOL, then special protective measures apply.[166] For example, the Baltic Sea and the North Sea have been designated as special areas under Annex VI of the MARPOL Convention so that more restrictive limits on sulfur content of fuel oil apply to ships navigating in these areas.

The similarities in language used in MARPOL and Article 211(6) of the Law of the Sea Convention are striking. The link is further supported by the fact that the coastal state must provide information on the "necessary reception facilities," a requirement of some of the special areas under the MARPOL Convention. Indeed, Timagenis makes the point that a "special area was mainly understood during the negotiations to refer to the special areas established by the [MARPOL] Convention."[167] In this respect, Article 211(6) seems to simply confirm the ability of coastal states to adopt and enforce higher standards that are associated with Special Areas approved by the IMO.[168]

The types of measures foreseen by Article 211(6) are not limited to the types of special measures applied to special areas under the MARPOL Convention, however.[169] Under paragraph (c) of Article 211(6), a coastal state may adopt "additional laws and regulations for the same area for the prevention, reduction and control of pollution from vessels." These additional laws and regulations are not required to implement generally accepted international rules and standards and they may impose stricter standards. The types of measures that could be proposed under this provision are therefore potentially powerful tools for coastal states to protect the marine environment in their adjacent waters. Nevertheless, there are important restrictions on the use of this power.

---

[165] MARPOL Convention, Annex I, Regulation 1(10). Provisions on special areas are also found in Annexes II and V.

[166] See e.g. MARPOL Annex I, Regulation 10(2) and (3).

[167] He calls for the concept of special areas to be further clarified; Timagenis, *International Control of Marine Pollution*, at 612–13 in footnote 73.

[168] See also *Guidelines for the Designation of Special Areas under MARPOL 73/78*, IMO Resolution A.972(22), adopted November 29, 2001.

[169] *Ibid.* See also Nordquist *et al.* (eds.), *United Nations Convention on the Law of the Sea 1982 – A Commentary*, Vol. 4, at 181.

First, any measures adopted may not "require foreign vessels to observe design, construction, manning or equipment standards other than generally accepted international rules and standards."[170] As with the restriction of a coastal state's legislative powers in the territorial sea, the purpose of this provision is to prevent the proliferation of technical standards that would stop a ship from freely transiting the world's oceans.[171]

Secondly, in order to prevent the imposition of unilateral impediments to freedom of navigation, Article 211(6) requires the coastal state to consult other interested states through the competent international organization. The exceptional nature of the provision is stressed by the fact that technical and scientific evidence must be submitted by the coastal state in support of the proposal. Under the procedure, the competent organization has twelve months to consider the proposal and if it agrees that the conditions are met, the coastal state may adopt the proposed laws and regulations.[172] As the competent organization under this provision, the role of the IMO is to ensure that the interests of coastal states and shipping states are balanced so that protective measures proposed by the coastal state do not unduly infringe on freedom of navigation in this zone. Thus, it would seem that the possibilities for adopting measures under this potentially broad provision ultimately depend on the ability of states to reach a mutually satisfactory solution through negotiations at the IMO.

5.5 Decision-making under the approval procedures

What is common to all of the provisions discussed above is the need for the IMO to approve the proposed arrangements. However, none of these provisions specify precisely what is meant by approval.

If approval is to take place according to the ordinary decision-making procedures of the main IMO committees that are responsible for making such decisions, it would appear that a majority of those Members present and voting would be sufficient.[173] Yet there are a number of problems with this approach. First and foremost, this approach means that a decision could be taken that overrides the concerns of a state or group of states with a major interest in the issue. In the context

---

[170] *Ibid.*   [171] See above.

[172] For further comment, see Nordquist *et al.* (eds.), *United Nations Convention on the Law of the Sea 1982 – A Commentary, Vol. 4*, at 205.

[173] See Rules of Procedure of the Marine Environment Protection Committee, Rule 27; Rules of Procedure of the Maritime Safety Committee, Rule 26(1).

of the delicate balance of rights and obligations under the law of the sea framework, it is highly questionable whether such an approach is appropriate. Many of the decisions made by the IMO in this context go to the heart of the navigational regime agreed at UNCLOS III. Thus, majority voting is unlikely to be accepted by states.

It is more likely that the approval of special navigational measures must be taken by consensus. Indeed, it is the type of decision-making that is reflected in the practice of the IMO, despite its formal rules of procedure. Consensus ensures that the interests of all states are taken into account in the decision-making process. It means that the IMO can act as a forum in which measures can be adopted that take into account the views of all interested parties.

5.6 Innovative navigational measures and the law-making role of the International Maritime Organization

The navigational regimes for international straits, archipelagic waters and the EEZ have been carefully crafted in order to balance the ability of coastal states to promote maritime safety and environmental protection in their adjacent waters against the navigational rights and freedoms of foreign shipping. The IMO plays a crucial role in maintaining this balance. As the competent international organization in this field, the IMO is able to approve a number of navigational measures proposed by coastal states. However, it must be asked whether the IMO is limited to approving those navigational measures expressly mentioned in the Convention or whether it is possible for the IMO to approve the adoption of new and innovative navigational measures? This issue has been raised on a number of occasions in the IMO.

One example is the role that the IMO has played in the approval of ship-reporting systems. Developments in satellite and computer technology have greatly expanded the tools available for coastal states to manage shipping passing through their adjacent waters. Modern technology allows coastal states to actively manage and control maritime traffic.[174] A ship-reporting system requires a ship to report its name, position and related information to the coastal state when it enters

---

[174] Active Marine Traffic Control is defined by Corbet as "any pragmatic involvement in the navigation of a ship by a person or persons not on board the ship." It is to be contrasted with Passive Marine Traffic Control, which is largely based upon predetermined codes, rules and regulations. See A. Corbet, "Navigation management: post-Donaldson" (1995) 19 *Marine Policy* 477.

a certain maritime area.[175] Moreover, ship-reporting systems can be interactive so that the coastal state authorities can also offer information and navigational advice to shipping.[176] A ship-reporting system can also form a component of a vessel traffic service scheme that allows the coastal state to issue mandatory directions to maritime traffic. These tools permit a coastal state more opportunity to monitor and control the passage of ships through its waters in order to promote safety and efficiency of navigation and the protection of the marine environment.[177]

The application of these navigational measures to maritime zones such as international straits and archipelagic waters may affect the balance of interests achieved in the Convention. As noted by Plant, "it is ... difficult to envisage any IMO authorization of ... [ship-reporting systems] extending beyond territorial waters that would not involve some effect upon the navigation/environmental protection balance in those waters affected in the Convention."[178] Yet there is no mention of ship-reporting systems in the Law of the Sea Convention. Nevertheless, the practice of the IMO appears to confirm that ship-reporting systems may be applied to a range of maritime zones. Indeed, one of the first ship-reporting systems to be approved by the IMO was applied to the Torres Strait and Great Barrier Reef area.[179] This system required all ships of more than fifty meters and all ships carrying bulk hazardous or potentially polluting cargoes to report to the coastal authorities when entering and leaving the strait, as well as at strategic points throughout their passage. Other systems were subsequently adopted for the Straits of Malacca and Singapore and the Straits of Bonifacio in May 1998,[180] and for the Dover Strait in December 1998.[181] As ship-reporting systems are not among those navigational measures expressly mentioned in the provisions of the Convention governing navigation in

---

175 SOLAS Convention, Regulation V/11(1).
176 Sometimes called Vessel Traffic Services.
177 SOLAS Convention, Regulation V/11(1).
178 G. Plant, "The relationship between international navigation rights and environmental protection" in H. Ringbom (ed.), *Competing Norms in the Law of Marine Environmental Protection* (Kluwer Law, 1997) at 26.
179 *Mandatory ship reporting systems*, IMO Resolution MSC.52(66), adopted May 30, 1996. It has been subsequently amended by *Amendments to the existing mandatory ship reporting system in the Torres Strait and Inner Route of the Great Barrier Reef*, IMO Resolution MSC.161(78), adopted May 17, 2004.
180 *Mandatory ship reporting systems*, IMO Resolution MSC.73(69), adopted May 19, 1998.
181 *Mandatory ship reporting systems*, IMO Resolution MSC.85(70), adopted December 7, 1998.

international straits, this practice of the IMO should be interpreted as a modification of the navigational regime in Part III of the Convention.[182] Mandatory ship-reporting systems have also been approved in the EEZ on the grounds of environmental protection[183] and maritime safety,[184] despite the fact that they are not expressly mentioned among those measures that may be applied by coastal states to the EEZ.

The practice of the IMO would suggest that the use of ship-reporting systems in international waters is subject to important limitations. First, it appears that such measures must be approved by the IMO before they can be applied by coastal states in zones of maritime jurisdiction other than the territorial sea. This is because the coastal states have limited powers in such zones and therefore the IMO plays an important role in ensuring that the coastal state does not encroach on the navigational rights of shipping. Without the approval of the IMO, the coastal state cannot presume that it is competent to impose such measures in international straits, in archipelagic sea lanes or in the EEZ. Secondly, it would appear that the power of coastal states does not extend to enforcing compliance with ship-reporting systems. While not all resolutions approving ship-reporting systems deal with enforcement measures, debates at the IMO Legal Committee have suggested that the powers of coastal states in this regard are limited.[185] Indeed, more recent ship-reporting systems, such as that for the Dover Straits, first adopted in December 1998, confirm that the application of a ship-reporting system does not allow the coastal state to hamper the passage of ships that fail to comply with reporting requirements. Rather, the description of the scheme provides that "if reports are not submitted and the offending ship can be positively identified, then information will be passed to the relevant Flag State Authorities for investigation and possible prosecution in accordance with national legislation. Information will also be made available to Port State Control inspectors."[186] A similar position is taken in other resolutions

---

[182] See Plant, "The relationship between international navigation rights and environmental protection," at 25.

[183] *Mandatory ship reporting system in the western European particularly sensitive sea area*, IMO Resolution MSC.190(79), adopted December 6, 2004.

[184] *Mandatory ship reporting system in Greenland waters*, IMO Resolution MSC.126(75), adopted May 20, 2002.

[185] See *Report of the Legal Committee on the work of its eighty-seventh session*, IMO Document LEG 87/17, October 23, 2003, at para. 200.

[186] IMO Resolution MSC.85(70), Annex 2, at para. 9.

on ship-reporting systems, and the first ship-reporting system applicable to the Torres Strait and the Great Barrier Reef area was amended in 2004 in a way that made these limitations clear.[187]

Another prominent example of extending the scope of navigational measures available under the Convention is the proposal for compulsory pilotage in the Torres Strait made by Australia and Papua New Guinea in 2003. These states made this proposal as part of their application to extend the preexisting Great Barrier Reef Particularly Sensitive Sea Area (PSSA), which had been approved in 1990, to include the Torres Strait.[188] The Torres Strait is an important shipping lane that provides access from Northern Australia to the East and South Coast of Australia, as well as New Zealand and the South Pacific islands. Navigation through the strait is rendered particularly difficult due to its unusual shallowness, often measuring no more than thirteen meters deep. This can make transit precarious for large, laden vessels.[189] Anxiety over passage through the strait is increased by its close proximity to the Great Barrier Reef, which is located at the eastern end of the strait. It was therefore considered suitable for designation as a PSSA.

The purpose of a PSSA is to offer special protection to an area because of its significance for recognized ecological, socio-economic or scientific attributes where such attributes may be vulnerable to damage by international shipping activities.[190] Yet, PSSA designation by itself does not involve any restrictions on shipping. Rather, the proposing state must propose additional "associated protective measures."[191]

In order to protect the vulnerable marine ecosystem in the vicinity of the Torres Strait, Australia and Papua New Guinea proposed a recommended two-way shipping route through the strait and a compulsory pilotage system similar to that already operated by Australia in the section of the Great Barrier Reef falling within its internal waters.

---

[187] See IMO Resolution MSC.161(78), adopted May 17, 2004, Annex, at para. 9.1.

[188] See *Identification and protection of special areas and particularly sensitive sea areas, extension of existing Great Barrier Reef PSSA to include Torres Strait Region*, submitted by Australia and Papua New Guinea, IMO Document MEPC 49/8, April 10, 2003.

[189] See S. Kaye, *The Torres Strait* (Martinus Nijhoff Publishers, 1997) at 14. See also S. Bateman and M. White, "Compulsory pilotage in the Torres Strait: overcoming unacceptable risks to a sensitive marine environment" (2009) 40 *Ocean Dev. & Int'l L.* 184.

[190] *Revised guidelines for the identification and designation of particularly sensitive sea areas*, IMO Resolution A.982(24) at Annex, para 1.2. Hereinafter, the Revised Guidelines.

[191] Revised Guidelines, at para. 1.2 and para. 8.3.4.

Pilotage involves the taking onboard of an experienced mariner who is able to guide the ship through navigationally challenging waters. The two states argued that a system of compulsory pilotage was necessary because of the low levels of compliance of shipping with the system of recommended pilotage that had already been approved by the IMO for the Torres Strait.[192] It was alleged that compliance with the recommended pilotage scheme had fallen from 70 percent to 32 percent for eastbound voyages, and from 55 percent to 38.5 percent for westbound voyages.

The proposal for a two-way recommended route was uncontroversial as it fell squarely within the ambit of Articles 41 and 42 of the Convention, which allow strait states to apply sea lanes and traffic separation schemes in international straits once they have been approved by the IMO.[193] However, compulsory pilotage does not feature in these articles and the legal basis for such a measure was questioned by several states.[194]

On the one hand, Australia and Papua New Guinea argued that the Law of the Sea Convention did not prohibit the establishment of compulsory pilotage schemes in such areas.[195] According to this argument, pilotage is sufficiently similar to the measures that are anticipated in Article 41 and they are impliedly allowed under the Convention.[196] However, such an argument is not necessarily supported by the text of the provision or by its drafting history. Article 42 provides that "states bordering straits may adopt laws and regulations relating to transit passage through straits in respect of … the safety of navigation and the regulation of maritime traffic, as provided for in Article 41." Yet sea lanes and traffic separation schemes are the only two types of measures mentioned in Article 41. The ordinary meaning of this provision seems to suggest that these are the only measures that may be adopted by a strait state in order to regulate maritime traffic in transit passage. This

---

[192] Under *Use of pilotage services in the Torres Strait and the Great North East Channel*, IMO Resolution A.710(17), adopted November 6, 1991. See *Torres Strait PSSA Associated Protective Measures – Compulsory Pilotage, submitted by Australia and Papua New Guinea*, IMO document LEG 89/15, August 24, 2004.

[193] See above.

[194] See *Report of the Legal Committee on the work of its eighty-ninth session*, IMO Document LEG/89/16, November 4, 2004, at para. 224.

[195] See IMO Document LEG/89/15, in particular at paras. 11 and 23.

[196] See R. Beckman, "PSSAs and transit passage – Australia's pilotage system in the Torres Strait challenges the IMO and UNCLOS" (2007) 38 *Ocean Development & Int'l L.* 325, at 330.

restrictive interpretation of the Convention is, moreover, consistent with both the legislative history and the policy underlying the scheme in Part III of the Convention, which seeks to strictly regulate the powers of a littoral state in international straits.[197] Opponents of the proposal accordingly stressed that the right of unimpeded transit passage was one of the most critical freedoms in the Law of the Sea Convention and they feared that failure to comply with the scheme might lead to the strait states imposing sanctions on transiting vessels.[198] Other states thought that the introduction of compulsory pilotage per se was an impediment of the right to transit passage and therefore incompatible with the Convention.[199] Certainly, the need for a ship to stop and take on a pilot could hinder, although not prevent, passage through the strait.

The polarization of views prevented the IMO Legal Committee from reaching a conclusion on the legality of compulsory pilotage in straits used for international navigation.[200] When the Maritime Safety Committee and the Marine Environmental Protection Committee came to consider the application, they were able to agree on language that left the precise legal implications of the measures ambiguous. It was agreed to extend the existing system of pilotage within the Great Barrier Reef to the Torres Strait without specifying that it is compulsory.[201] At the same time, the United States and others stressed that they only supported the measure if it was interpreted as a recommendation.[202] The operative paragraph of the resolution "recommends that Governments recognize the need for effective protection of the Great Barrier Reef and Torres Strait region and inform ships flying their flag that they should act in accordance with Australia's system of pilotage."[203] The chair of the Marine Environment Protection Committee confirmed in 2006 that the use of the word recommends

---

[197] See *ibid.*, at 344. T. Koh, "A Passage to Maritime Safety," 7th Cedric Barclay Memorial Lecture, February 27, 2007, available at www.siac.org.sg/cms/pdf/20070226-TK.pdf <checked June 15, 2010>.

[198] See IMO Document LEG 89/16, at para. 232.

[199] *Ibid.*, at para. 233.   [200] *Ibid.*, at para. 241.

[201] As Roberts notes, "no where [sic.] in the relevant IMO resolution does it explicitly refer to compulsory pilotage"; J. Roberts, "Compulsory pilotage in international straits: the Torres Strait PSSA proposal" (2006) 37 *Ocean & Coastal Management* 93, at 101–2.

[202] See *Report of the Marine Environment Protection Committee on its fifty-third session*, IMO Document MEPC 53/24, July 25, 2005, at para. 8.6.

[203] *Designation of the Torres Strait as an extension of the Great Barrier Reef Particularly Sensitive Sea Area*, IMO Resolution, MEPC.133(53), adopted on July 22, 2005, at para. 3.

in resolutions adopted by the Committee indicates that the content of the resolution is of a recommendatory nature.[204]

Australia adopted a compulsory pilotage scheme in 2006. The scheme requires vessels over seventy meters and all vessels carrying oil, chemical and liquefied gas to use a pilot through the Torres Strait.[205] A ship that fails to comply with the compulsory pilotage scheme may be arrested and the master may be prosecuted when the ship next enters an Australian port, although Australia made clear that it was not intending to arrest ships while in transit passage. However, the difference of views over the permissibility of compulsory pilotage in international straits, as well as the disagreements about the meaning of the IMO relevant resolution, means that the Australian compulsory pilotage scheme is vulnerable to challenge by other states that are affected by it.[206]

The situation would arguably have been different if the IMO had approved the proposal by Australia and Papua New Guinea by consensus, which would indicate that the international community as a whole approved of the development. This example shows that while the IMO can play a role in the informal modification of the Convention regime, it is limited by the need to foster consensus before it can be successful. In the absence of a clear consensus, a state arguably cannot implement innovative navigational measures without risking legal challenge in international courts and tribunals.

6 Conclusion

This chapter has analyzed several functions undertaken by the IMO in order to assess the organization's contribution to the evolution of the law of the sea.

One of the functions of a specialized international organization, such as the IMO, is to negotiate and adopt international standards in its particular field of competence. However, the IMO was not originally conceived as a law-making institution and it has no powers under its constituent instrument to adopt generally applicable international rules and regulations. Strictly speaking, the results of the IMO's

[204] MEPC 53/24, at para. 8.1.
[205] See AMSA Marine Order No. 54 and Australian Marine Notices 8/2006 and 16/2006.
[206] See e.g. the comments of the Ambassador of Singapore to the UN General Assembly in December 2007, available at http://app.mfa.gov.sg/pr/read_content.asp?View,9047, <checked November 29, 2010>.

standard-setting activities are only binding on those states that accept them by becoming party to the treaties in which they are contained. Yet an analysis of the formal powers of the Organization only reveals part of the picture. As this chapter has illustrated, the operation of the rules of reference in the Law of the Sea Convention also means that the activities of the IMO, as one of the competent organizations in the law of the sea, have a much wider significance. These rules of reference have the effect of incorporating generally accepted international standards into the global framework for the law of the sea. Moreover, they are crucial to the overall balance between coastal state and flag state powers under the Convention.

It does not follow that the IMO has attained legislative powers. The transformation of IMO rules and regulations into generally accepted international standards must be assessed on a case-by-case basis and it will depend on the content of the standards, as well as the practice of relevant states. Thus, the importance of the IMO is as a forum in which to bring together states in order to achieve general acceptance. At the same time, the broad membership of the IMO and its technical expertise make it a prime institution to develop such generally accepted international rules and regulations. Not only does the IMO bring together all interested states, but it also permits the participation of important non-state actors such as the representatives of shipowners and environmental organizations. Moreover, the analysis in this chapter has also demonstrated that the IMO has adapted its decision-making procedures in order to facilitate such general acceptance. Whereas the formal rules of procedure of the Organization allow for majority voting for the adoption of standards, in practice the Organization pursues consensus decision-making as far as possible. This institutional practice arguably goes a long way to facilitating the transformation of IMO standards into universal international law. In this sense, it can be considered a law-making institution to the extent that it can promulgate and promote generally accepted international shipping standards.

The IMO also has another key role to play in several of the navigational regimes under the Law of the Sea Convention where the consent of the IMO is needed before states can adopt and apply navigational measures. In such instances, the IMO provides a forum in which states can seek to balance the interests of coastal states against the interests of the wider international community.

The powers of the IMO to adopt and approve navigational measures are not necessarily limited to those situations foreseen in the

Convention. As an organization that includes the majority of flag states and coastal states, as well as representatives from key civil society groups, it has been suggested that the IMO may also provide a forum in which modifications to the navigational regimes in the Law of the Sea Convention can be agreed. In this regard, the Organization has increasingly been faced with difficult legal and political questions over the interpretation and development of the law of the sea framework within which it must operate. It should be remembered that the IMO has tackled such issues even before the conclusion of the Law of the Sea Convention. The IMO Legal Committee was first created to deal with the complex legal issues that arose following the sinking of the *Torrey Canyon* off the coast of the United Kingdom in March 1967[207] and the adoption of the 1969 Intervention Convention in response to that incident provides an early precedent of the IMO dealing with important questions of maritime jurisdiction.[208] It continues this role today by discussing key issues in the implementation of the framework for the law of the sea in relation to navigation, maritime safety and the protection of the marine environment from shipping pollution. One of the advantages of the IMO as a forum for such discussions is that it focuses exclusively on maritime issues. Moreover, it offers an expertise in maritime and shipping matters that ensure that the outcome of any negotiations takes into account the technical aspects of the problem.

It appears from this analysis that the IMO plays a fundamental role in upholding the balance of rights and interests between coastal states and shipping states that underlies the whole of the international law of the sea, both through its standard-setting role and through its approval role. This is the case despite the fact that the IMO has no formal mention in the Law of the Sea Convention apart from as a body to nominate experts for the purposes of special arbitration under Annex VIII.[209] In conclusion, the IMO offers another example of informal mechanisms for change being used by states in preference to the formal amendment procedures found in the Convention. Yet it should also be noted that such informal modifications of the legal framework will only be effective if they are supported by a consensus of the international

---

[207] See R. Balkin, "The establishment and work of the IMO Legal Committee," in M. Nordquist and J. N. Moore (eds.), *Current Maritime Issues and the International Maritime Organization* (Martinus Nijhoff Publishers, 1999) at 291–308.

[208] See Blanco-Bazan, "IMO interface with the Law of the Sea Convention," at 270.

[209] Law of the Sea Convention, Annex VIII, Article 2(2).

community. In this regard, it is significant that the IMO provides a standing forum dedicated to the discussion and resolution of maritime issues. Moreover, the widespread participation of states and non-state actors in the work of the IMO, as well as the decision-making procedures it employs, both contribute to its success as a key institution in the evolution of the law of the sea.

7   The contribution of the Food and Agriculture Organization to international fisheries law

1 Introduction

Fishing has traditionally been one of the most important uses of the oceans and is an important source of food for many communities. In 2008 81.9 million tonnes of fish were landed from vessels fishing at sea.[1] Unsurprisingly, many states have a keen interest in fishing and fishing rights have been at the root of several major international disputes concerning the law of the sea in the past.[2]

The regulation of fisheries is only dealt with in the general terms by the Law of the Sea Convention. The approach of the Convention on this topic is "primarily based upon the nationality orientated approach."[3] Under the Convention it is for flag states and coastal states to take measures relating to fisheries falling under their jurisdiction.[4] At the same time, the Convention stresses that, wherever fish stocks are located, states should cooperate as may be necessary for their management and conservation.[5] Cooperation is also central to the Fish Stocks Agreement that was adopted in 1995 in order to strengthen the regulatory framework applicable to highly migratory and straddling fish stocks.[6]

---

[1] *State of the World Fisheries and Aquaculture 2008* (Food and Agriculture Organization, 2009) at 3.
[2] See e.g. *Anglo-Norwegian Fisheries Case* (1951) ICJ Reports 116; *Fisheries Jurisdiction Cases* (1974) ICJ Reports 3 and 175; *Fisheries Jurisdiction Case (Spain v Canada)* (1998) ICJ Reports 432; *Southern Bluefin Tuna Arbitration (Australia & New Zealand)* (2000) Int'l Leg. Materials 1359.
[3] R. Wolfrum, "Fishery Commissions," in R. Bernhardt (ed.), *Encyclopedia of Public International Law, Vol. 2* (North-Holland, 1989) at 117.
[4] Law of the Sea Convention, Articles 61–62, 118–119.
[5] Law of the Sea Convention, Articles 61(2), 63, 64, 117, 118.
[6] Fish Stocks Agreement, Article 8. See also Chapter 4.

There is no single international institution with responsibility for the development of international fisheries law. Much cooperation takes place at the regional or sub-regional level through regional fisheries bodies that are responsible for setting quotas, gear regulations and other specific fisheries measures. However, the mandates of regional fisheries bodies are necessarily limited by the area for which they are responsible and they tend to also be restricted to regulating fishing for certain fish stocks.[7]

Several global institutions are also involved in the development of fisheries law and policy, including the UN General Assembly and the Food and Agriculture Organization. The role of these organizations in fisheries law and policy will be considered in this chapter. The focus is on law-making activity at the international level and it will concentrate on the role of these institutions in promoting the progressive development of international law in order to meet the multifaceted challenges posed by fisheries conservation and management in the twenty-first century. Because of its specialist nature, particular attention will be paid to the work of the Food and Agriculture Organization FAO, which has adopted a number of instruments dealing with fisheries regulation. The chapter will analyze these instruments and ask what impact they have had on international fisheries law. Given the multifaceted nature of fisheries regulation, the chapter will also consider the relationship between the FAO and regional fisheries bodies.

2 The United Nations General Assembly and fisheries

Fisheries issues are regularly on the agenda of the UN General Assembly. While fisheries are debated by the General Assembly as part of its annual debate on the law of the sea,[8] the General Assembly has had a practice of adopting a separate resolution on fisheries since 1989.

One of the first resolutions dedicated to fisheries that was adopted by the General Assembly was the 1989 resolution on large-scale pelagic driftnet fishing and its impact on the living and marine resources

---

[7] This is particularly the case for highly migratory fish stocks such as tuna; e.g. the Commission for the Conservation of Southern Bluefin Tuna, the Inter-American Tropical Tuna Commission, the International Commission for the Conservation of Atlantic Tunas and the Indian Ocean Tuna Commission. One of the few general regional fisheries bodies with a responsibility to manage tuna stocks is the Western and Central Pacific Fisheries Commission.

[8] See Chapter 8.

of the world's oceans and seas.[9] This resolution was adopted in response to the particular concerns raised by a group of South Pacific states about the use of large-scale pelagic drift nets, some over 30 miles in length, on the high seas and their impact on fish stocks and other marine species.[10] The resolution proposes a moratorium on all large-scale pelagic driftnet fishing by June 30, 1992 in the absence of conservation and management measures based upon sound scientific evidence.[11] The resolution was adopted by consensus of the General Assembly.

In order to assess the normative impact of the resolution, one must consider the language used. Whereas it would seem to codify some existing international obligations, the wording of the resolution would seem to suggest that it did not intend to place new obligations upon fishing states. The preamble to the resolution affirms that "all members of the international community have a duty to cooperate globally and regionally in the conservation and management of living resources on the high seas, and a duty to take, or to cooperate with others in taking, such measures for their nationals as may be necessary for the conservation of those resources." Moreover, the operative provisions of the resolution call on members of the international community to strengthen their cooperation in this regard. These provisions would seem to reflect pre-existing commitments of states under the Law of the Sea and customary international law. When it comes to the establishment of a moratorium, however, it is notable that the resolution only "recommends" that all members of the international community "agree to" the measures outlined in the resolution. This use of hortatory language would suggest that the members of the General Assembly did not intend to create legal obligation. In other words, the resolution does not purport to establish a binding moratorium on states or other fishing entities.[12] At most, it can be seen as an

---

[9] *Large-scale pelagic driftnet fishing and its impact on the living and marine resources of the world's oceans and seas*, UNGA Resolution 44/225, December 22, 1989.

[10] See Tarawa Declaration on Driftnet Fishing, adopted by the South Pacific Forum on July 10 and 11, 1989.

[11] UNGA Resolution 44/225, at para. 4(a). The resolution also recommends that immediate action be taken to progressively reduce large-scale pelagic driftnet fishing in the South Pacific region with a view to cessation of such activities by July 1, 1991. In other areas the resolution recommends an immediate ban on the expansion of large-scale pelagic driftnet fishing on the high seas pending the start of the moratorium.

[12] See W. T. Burke, "Regulation of driftnet fishing on the high seas and the new international law of the sea" (1991) 3 *Geo. Int'l Env. L. Rev.* 265, at 277–8.

agreement to agree in the future. It would seem to be best interpreted as a call to states to consider what action they can take to implement a moratorium. This interpretation is supported by paragraph 6 of the resolution, which calls upon the organization and programs of the United Nations, as well as regional and subregional fisheries organizations, to urgently study large-scale pelagic driftnet fishing and to report to the Secretary-General on the issue.[13] The resolution adopted a year later by the General Assembly outlined the actions that had been taken by the international community through such organizations, including the South Pacific Conference, the Organization of Eastern Caribbean States, the Meeting of the Nine Western Mediterranean Countries on Dialogue and Cooperation in the Western Mediterranean, the North Pacific Fisheries Commission and the International Whaling Commission.[14] Thus, it can be said that the General Assembly saw itself as a catalyst for international action rather than a law-maker. Even though the resolution itself did not create legally binding obligations, it nevertheless spurred legal action on the part of the international community.

The General Assembly has adopted a number of other resolutions dealing with specific fisheries issues, such as fisheries bycatch and discards[15] and unauthorized fishing in zones of national jurisdiction.[16] As with the resolutions on driftnet fishing, the General Assembly has limited itself to restating existing rules and principles of international law and calling for particular action to be taken by other international institutions with a competence in the area concerned.

Since 2003 the General Assembly has had a practice of adopting a single resolution dealing with all fisheries-related issues.[17] In this resolution, the General Assembly regularly reaffirms its commitment "to the long-term conservation, management and sustainable use of

[13] UNGA Resolution 44/225, at para. 6.

[14] *Large-scale pelagic driftnet fishing and its impact on the living and marine resources of the world's oceans and seas*, UNGA Resolution 45/197, December 21, 1990. See also *Large-scale pelagic driftnet fishing and its impact on the living and marine resources of the world's oceans and seas*, UNGA Resolution 46/215, December 20, 1991.

[15] *Fisheries by-catch and discards and their impact on the sustainable use of the world's living marine resources*, UNGA Resolution 49/118, December 19, 1994.

[16] *Unauthorized fishing in zones of national jurisdiction and its impact on the living marine resources of the world's oceans and seas*, UNGA Resolution 49/116, December 19, 1994.

[17] *Sustainable fisheries, including through the 1995 Agreement for the Implementation of the Provisions of the United Nations Convention on the Law of the Sea of 10 December 1982 relating to the Conservation and Management of Straddling Fish Stocks and Highly Migratory Fish Stocks, and related instruments*, UNGA Resolution 58/14, November 24, 2003.

the marine living resources of the world's oceans and seas and the obligations of States to cooperate to this end."[18] At the center of this resolution is consideration of the implementation of the Fish Stocks Agreement, which has been designated as an implementing agreement by the General Assembly.[19] The resolution also surveys all other recent developments in fisheries law and policy.

It can be seen from this short survey that, by and large, General Assembly resolutions on fisheries are not used as law-making instruments. Rather, they are a means of drawing attention to the current threats to fish stocks and encouraging international efforts taking place in other institutions to address them. This is perhaps unsurprising given the lack of time that the General Assembly can dedicate to fisheries and law of the sea issues each year.

3 The Food and Agriculture Organization and fisheries

A much more significant institution in terms of developing international fisheries law is the Food and Agriculture Organization. The FAO was founded in 1945 as an intergovernmental organization with a mandate to "collect, analyse, interpret and disseminate information relating to nutrition, food and agriculture."[20] The term "agriculture" in the FAO constitution is defined to include fishing and aquaculture.[21] Today, fisheries constitute one of the core activities of the FAO's work program.[22] The work of the FAO on fisheries comprises the collection and dissemination of information, the provision of technical advice and support to states and regional fisheries bodies, as well as the development of international instruments relating to fishing.

The FAO has a number of characteristics that make it an important forum for the discussion and development of international fisheries law. First, it is a United Nations specialized agency.[23] In this capacity, the FAO is regularly called upon by the UN General Assembly to

---

[18] *Sustainable fisheries, including through the 1995 Agreement for the Implementation of the Provisions of the United Nations Convention on the Law of the Sea of 10 December 1982 relating to the Conservation and Management of Straddling Fish Stocks and Highly Migratory Fish Stocks, and related instruments*, UNGA Resolution 64/72, December 4, 2009, at para. 1.

[19] See Chapter 4.   [20] FAO Constitution, Article I(1).   [21] *Ibid.*

[22] For an overview of the work of the FAO on fisheries, see www.fao.org/fishery/en <checked June 9, 2010>.

[23] Agreement between the United Nations and the Food and Agriculture Organization of the United Nations, June 10, 1946, Article I.

undertake studies and other activities in relation to the international framework for the conservation and management of fisheries[24] and the General Assembly has recognized "the critical role played by the Food and Agriculture Organization of the United Nations in providing expert technical advice, in assisting with international fisheries policy development and management standards, and in collection and dissemination of information on fisheries-related issues."[25] Indeed, the General Assembly often calls upon the FAO to undertake specific activities in relation to developments in fisheries law and policy.[26] In other words, the FAO is one of the most prominent institutions in which fisheries issues are considered in detail at the international level. The importance of the FAO is further underlined by its global membership. With 191 Member Nations, the FAO is one of the largest UN specialized agencies.[27] Alongside states, the FAO permits the participation of representatives from other intergovernmental and nongovernmental organizations in its proceedings as observers.[28] This broad membership means that all interested states are able to participate in discussions on fishing that take place within the FAO.

Most fisheries issues are dealt with in the first instance by the Fisheries Committee, which was created as a permanent standing body of the Organization in 1965.[29] Initially, the Committee was composed

---

[24] E.g. *Sustainable fisheries, including through the 1995 Agreement for the Implementation of the Provisions of the United Nations Convention on the Law of the Sea of 10 December 1982 relating to the Conservation and Management of Straddling Fish Stocks and Highly Migratory Fish Stocks, and related instruments*, UNGA Resolution 63/112, December 5, 2008, at paras. 15, 35, 36, 46, 71, 122; *Sustainable fisheries, including through the 1995 Agreement for the Implementation of the Provisions of the United Nations Convention on the Law of the Sea of 10 December 1982 relating to the Conservation and Management of Straddling Fish Stocks and Highly Migratory Fish Stocks, and related instruments*, UNGA Resolution 58/14, November 24, 2003, at para. 28; *Agreement for the Implementation of the Provisions of the United Nations Convention on the Law of the Sea of 10 December 1982 relating to the Conservation and Management of Straddling Fish Stocks and Highly Migratory Fish Stocks*, UNGA Resolution 54/32, November 24, 1999, at paras. 9, 10.

[25] *Sustainable fisheries, including through the 1995 Agreement for the Implementation of the Provisions of the United Nations Convention on the Law of the Sea of 10 December 1982 relating to the Conservation and Management of Straddling Fish Stocks and Highly Migratory Fish Stocks, and related instruments*, UNGA Resolution 61/105, December 8, 2006, at para. 88.

[26] See e.g. UNGA Resolution 64/72, at paras. 16, 37, 38, 49, 63, 75, 111, 127 and 145.

[27] See www.fao.org/Legal/member-e.htm (checked June 9, 2010). In addition, the European Union is a Member alongside its Member States. The Faroe Islands is an Associate Member.

[28] General Rules of the Organization, Rule XVII.

[29] See *Amendment to Article V-6 of the Constitution (Committee on Fisheries)*, FAO Conference Resolution 13/65, December 1965. See generally, J. Swan and B. P. Sastia,

of 30 FAO Member States representative of those countries with interests in fish stocks and the fishing industry. Since 1972, however, the Committee has been open to all FAO Members[30] and it also permits representatives of the United Nations and other specialized agencies, regional fishery bodies and nongovernmental organizations to take part in its proceedings.[31] Generally the Committee meets biennially.[32] It has subcommittees on aquaculture[33] and trade[34] and it has the power to establish any additional subsidiary bodies that it deems necessary.[35]

The mandate of the Committee is to:[36]

(a)   review the programs of work of the Organization in the field of fisheries and their implementation;

(b)   conduct periodic general reviews of fishery problems of an international character and appraise such problems and their possible solutions with a view to concerted action by nations, by FAO and by other intergovernmental bodies;

(c)   similarly review specific matters relating to fisheries referred to the Committee by the Council or the Director General, or placed by the Committee on its agenda at the request of a Member Nation in accordance with the Rules of Procedure of the Committee, and make recommendations as may be appropriate;

(d)   consider the desirability of preparing and submitting to Member Nations an international convention under Article XIV of the Constitution to ensure effective international cooperation and consultation in fisheries on a world scale;

(e)   report to the Council or tender advice to the Director General, as appropriate, on matters considered by the Committee.

It can be seen from this list that the Committee has a broad remit and it effectively provides a global, intergovernmental forum to assess all problems relating to fisheries and aquaculture.[37] Yet, as a subsidiary organ of

---

"Contribution of the Committee on Fisheries to global fisheries governance 1977–1997," *FAO Fisheries Circular C938*, 1999.

[30] *Ibid*. See also *Amendment to Article V of the Constitution and Rules XXIX, XXX, XXXII, XXXIV and XXV*, FAO Conference Resolution 24/75, November 1975 which formalized the open membership of the Committee.

[31] See www.fao.org/fishery/about/cofi/en <checked November 4, 2009>.

[32] *Ibid.*

[33] See www.fao.org/fishery/about/cofi/aquaculture/en <checked November 12, 2009>.

[34] See www.fao.org/fishery/about/cofi/trade/en <checked November 12, 2009>.

[35] Rules of Procedure of the Fisheries Committee, Rule VII.

[36] General Rules of the Organization, Rule XXX.

[37] For further information on the work of the Committee on Fisheries, see www.fao.org/fishery/about/cofi/en <checked June 9, 2010>.

the FAO, the Committee does not have any of formal decision-making powers of its own. Where action is deemed necessary, the Fisheries Committee must report to either the FAO Council or to the FAO Conference and it is up to these organs to take the appropriate action.

The organs of the FAO are capable of adopting decisions and resolutions on particular subjects. However, like most international organizations, the FAO is not a legislative body and it cannot adopt decisions that are *ipso facto* binding on FAO Members. The decision-making powers of the FAO are expressly limited to making "recommendations to Member Nations and Associate Members concerning questions relating to food and agriculture, for consideration by them with a view to implementation by national action."[38] Such recommendations are not formally binding, although, as will be seen below, this does not necessarily mean that they will be without legal effects.

The FAO also has a role in treaty-making.[39] Article XIV of the FAO Constitution permits the FAO to submit conventions concerning food and agriculture to its Member Nations for approval. Conventions may be adopted by a two-thirds majority of the FAO Conference that is composed of all FAO Members.[40] The FAO Council, made up of forty-nine Members elected by the Conference, is also competent to adopt conventions and agreements relating to specific geographical areas or supplementary treaties intended to implement conventions adopted by the Conference.[41] This power has been used to adopt some treaties establishing regional fisheries bodies, such as the Agreement for the Establishment of the Indian Ocean Tuna Commission, which was approved by the FAO Council in November 1993.[42]

Prior to adoption, the proposed text of conventions and agreements are usually the subject of technical consultation among FAO Members, as well as scrutiny by independent experts.[43] This mechanism ensures that the provisions of the treaty are sufficiently informed by specialist opinion, although at the end of the day it is open for states to make any changes to the text that may have been proposed by the experts. Any

---

[38] FAO Constitution, Article 4(3).
[39] See generally J. P. Dobbert, "Food and agriculture," in O. Schachter and C. Joyner (eds.), *United Nations Legal Order, Vol. 2* (Cambridge University Press, 1995) at 922–3.
[40] FAO Constitution, Article XIV(1).
[41] FAO Constitution, Article XIV(2).
[42] See *Agreement for the Establishment of the Indian Ocean Tuna Commission*, FAO Council Resolution 1/105, November 1993.
[43] Article XIV(1) of the FAO Constitution requires that "a technical meeting or conference ... has assisted in drafting the convention or agreement."

conventions or agreements adopted by the FAO Conference are open to all members of the United Nations or its specialized agencies[44] provided that they do not entail any financial obligations for the FAO or Member Nations that decide not to become a party to them.[45]

Both treaties and nonbinding instruments have been used by the FAO in the field of fisheries in order to promote the progressive development of international law on the subject. Some examples will be considered in the following section along with an analysis of their contribution to the international law of fisheries.

4 Fisheries instruments adopted by the Food and Agriculture Organization

4.1 1993 Agreement to Promote Compliance with International Conservation and Management Measures by Fishing Vessels on the High Seas

Perhaps the most important fisheries treaty concluded under the auspices of the FAO is the 1993 Agreement to Promote Compliance with International Conservation and Management Measures by Fishing Vessels on the High Seas.[46] The purpose of this treaty is to address the problems caused by fishing vessels that attempt to avoid the application of internationally agreed conservation and management measures applicable to the high seas through reflagging to the registries of states which are not bound by such measures.[47] Reflagging has been identified as one of the serious threats to high seas fisheries and various international conferences recognized that governmental action needed to be taken to combat this practice. In 1992 the UN Conference on Environment and Development called on states to "take effective action, consistent with international law, to deter reflagging of vessels by their nationals as a means of avoiding compliance with applicable conservation and management rules for fishing activities on the high seas."[48]

---

[44] FAO Constitution, Article XV(3)(b).
[45] FAO Constitution, Article XV(3)(c).
[46] 1993 Agreement to Promote Compliance with International Conservation and Management Measures by Vessels on the High Seas (1994) 33 *Int'l Leg. Materials* 969. Hereinafter, Compliance Agreement.
[47] See D. Balton, "The Compliance Agreement," in E. Hey (ed.), *Developments in International Fisheries Law* (Kluwer Law International, 1999) at 37–8.
[48] Agenda 21, at para. 17.53. See also Declaration of Cancún, at para. 13: "States should take effective action, consistent with international law, to deter reflagging

This issue was already on the agenda of the FAO, which convened a technical consultation in September 1992, the results of which were reported to the FAO Council at its 102nd session in November 1992. The FAO Council agreed that there was a need for an international agreement and it decided a treaty should be urgently negotiated.[49]

It took a little over a year for the Compliance Agreement to be negotiated. An Informal Group of Experts was convened in February 1993 to draw up an initial draft of the agreement, which was submitted to the twentieth session of the Fisheries Committee the following month. The draft and the comments of the Committee were further considered by the FAO Council in June 1993. Those issues that could not be resolved by the Council were discussed through informal consultations that took place on the fringes of the United Nations Fish Stocks Conference, which happened to be taking place at that time. The text was reconsidered by the FAO Council at its meeting in November 1993 before being submitted to the FAO Conference for formal adoption later the same month.[50] The Agreement certainly goes to show that, where sufficient political will exists, states can rapidly agree the content of new international treaties.

As noted above, the primary purpose of the Compliance Agreement is to combat the problem of flags of convenience being used by fishing vessels. The Compliance Agreement does not seek to alter the jurisdictional framework for fisheries that is found in the Law of the Sea Convention. Rather, the Agreement is premised upon the exclusive jurisdiction of the flag state for high seas fisheries, as reflected in Article 92 of the Convention, according to which "ships shall sail under the flag of one State only and, save in exceptional circumstances cases expressly provided for in international treaties or in this Convention, shall be subject to its exclusive jurisdiction on the high seas." The Compliance Agreement purports to prescribe how flag states should effectively exercise jurisdiction over ships flying their flag. To this end, the preamble to the Compliance Agreement explicitly provides that "the objective of this Agreement can be achieved through specifying

of vessels as a means of avoiding compliance with applicable conservation and management rules for fishing activities on the high seas."

[49] See *Report of the FAO Council, hundred and second session, 9–20 November 1992*, Document CL 102/REP, at para. 58.

[50] *Agreement to Promote Compliance with International Conservation and Management Measures by Fishing Vessels on the High Seas*, FAO Conference Resolution 15/93, November 1993.

flag States' responsibility in respect of fishing vessels entitled to fly their flag and operating on the high seas."[51]

The overarching responsibility of flag states under the Agreement is found in Article 3.1, which provides that "each party shall take such measures as may be necessary to ensure that fishing vessels entitled to fly its flag do not engage in any activity that undermines the effectiveness of international conservation and management measures." The Agreement continues to specify a number of particular measures that parties must take in order to fulfill this general responsibility.

First and foremost, the Compliance Agreement obliges a party to prevent vessels flying its flag to be used for fishing on the high seas unless they have been authorized to do so.[52] The Agreement specifies that a party shall not authorize fishing vessels to fish on the high seas unless it is able to exercise effective responsibility in respect of that vessel, "taking into account the links that exist between it and the fishing vessel concerned."[53]

At the center of the Agreement is the requirement for contracting parties to refuse to authorize "any fishing vessel previously registered in the territory of another Party that has undermined the effectiveness of international conservation and management measures to be used for fishing on the high seas"[54] unless the state is satisfied that "to grant an authorisation ... would not undermine the object and purpose of the Agreement."[55] It is this provision that aims to prevent the reflagging of vessels that are seeking to avoid the application of international conservation and management standards. This obligation applies regardless of whether or not the fishing vessel was previously registered in a party or a nonparty to the Agreement, although the Agreement does acknowledge that a state may not have sufficient information to judge whether a vessel previously flagged to a nonparty has undermined international conservation and management measures.[56]

Another key obligation under the Agreement is the requirement that parties exchange information about fishing vessels authorized to fish on the high seas.[57] This obligation is central to the treaty as the exchange of information is vital to allow flag states to know when it is appropriate to authorize, or indeed withdraw authorization from,

---

[51] Compliance Agreement, preamble.
[52] *Ibid.*, Article 3.   [53] *Ibid.*, Article 3(3).
[54] *Ibid.*, Article 5(3).   [55] *Ibid.*, Article 3(5)(d).
[56] *Ibid.*, Article 5(b).   [57] *Ibid.*, Article 5(1).

individual fishing vessels. In furtherance of this general duty to exchange information, certain obligations are placed on the flag state to obtain information about fishing vessels flying their flag. First, if a vessel is authorized to fish on the high seas, parties to the Agreement are obliged to enter its details onto a record.[58] Fishing vessels entered on the record shall be marked in such a way that they are readily identifiable in accordance with generally accepted standards, such as the FAO's own standard specifications for the marking and identification of fishing vessels.[59] In addition, Article 6 creates an obligation to make readily available to the FAO basic information about fishing vessels flying their flag that are authorized to fish on the high seas. On the basis of this information, the FAO shall maintain a register of fishing vessels and it shall circulate such information to the parties.[60]

The Compliance Agreement entered into force on April 24, 2003, but to date it has attracted only thirty-nine parties, including the European Union.[61] In other words, it is far from a universal treaty, even though many of the major fishing states have become a party to the Agreement. This demonstrates that the speedy conclusion of a treaty does not necessarily mean it will be successful.

It can also be asked whether the Compliance Agreement has had any broader normative impact. Some parts of the Compliance Agreement would appear to reassert preexisting rules of customary international law. For instance, the general principle of flag state control over fishing vessels is arguably a codification of customary international law. The preamble to the Compliance Agreement itself refers to the fact that "under international law as reflected in the United Nations Convention on the Law of the Sea, all States have the duty to take, or to cooperate with other States in taking, such measures for their respective nationals as may be necessary for the conservation of the living resources of the high seas." The preamble also asserts the existence of the "duties of every State to exercise effectively its jurisdiction and control over vessels flying its flag, including fishing vessels and vessels engaged in the

---

[58] Ibid., Article 4. The Agreement recognizes the required record may constitute a separate record of fishing vessels or form part of a general record of vessels maintained by the flag state; see Article 1(d).

[59] Ibid., Article 3(6).

[60] Ibid., Article 6. In furtherance of Article 6, the FAO has developed the High Seas Vessels Authorization Record (HSVAR) database; see www.fao.org/fishery/collection/compliance-agreement/en <checked June 9, 2010>.

[61] See www.fao.org/Legal/treaties/012s-e.htm <checked June 8, 2010>.

transhipment of fish." The existence of such a duty is also supported by subsequent General Assembly resolutions that have called upon states "not to permit vessels flying their flag to engage in fishing on the high seas without having effective control over their activities and to take specific measures to control fishing operations by vessels flying their flag."[62] In this context, the Compliance Agreement represents further evidence that these principles are part of customary international law.

On the other hand, the evidence would not seem to support the argument that the Compliance Agreement has made a broader impact on customary international law by crystallizing or creating new rules. First and foremost, the Compliance Agreement is clearly directed at parties, rather than at states generally. In this way, it can be contrasted with other instruments such as the Fish Stocks Agreement,[63] suggesting that the drafters of the Compliance Agreement did not have a clear intention to influence customary international law. Rather, the specific obligations were intended only to bind those states that became a party to the treaty. Indeed, many of these obligations are of an institutional nature, requiring specific cooperation with the FAO.[64] As such, they do not translate easily into customary international law and they can only really create obligations for those states that explicitly consent to be bound. This conclusion would appear to be supported by considering fisheries resolutions adopted by the UN General Assembly that do not call on states to take the precise measures that are outlined in the Compliance Agreement, such as maintaining a record and transmitting the relevant information to the FAO. Rather, the General Assembly has merely encouraged states and other fishing entities to accept the Compliance Agreement.[65] This clearly falls short of calling for "universal participation" as the General Assembly has done in the case of the Fish Stocks Agreement. In this sense, the Compliance Agreement probably cannot be classified as an implementing agreement.[66] Rather than being seen as a central pillar of the modern international law of the sea, it is perhaps more realistic to consider it as a technical solution to tackle a narrow problem arising in the management of high seas fish stocks.

---

[62] UNGA Resolution 54/32, at para. 7. See also UNGA Resolution 63/112, at para. 45.
[63] See Chapter 4.
[64] See in particular Article 6.
[65] UNGA Resolution 54/32, at para. 5. UNGA resolution 63/112, at paras. 37–8.
[66] Cf. A. E. Boyle, "Further development of the 1982 the Law of the Sea Convention," in D. Freestone, R. Barnes and D. Ong (eds.), *The Law of the Sea – Progress and Prospects* (Oxford University Press, 2006) at 42, footnote 13.

4.2 Code of Conduct on Responsible Fisheries

Perhaps the most important FAO instrument in the field of fisheries is the Code of Conduct on Responsible Fisheries, which was adopted at the twenty-eighth session of the FAO Conference in 1995 following several years of discussion in the Committee on Fisheries and a variety of expert and technical consultations.[67] The Code has a very broad scope, covering the capture, processing and trade of all types of fish, wherever they are found, including marine fisheries, inland fisheries and aquaculture.[68] It is aimed not only at states, but also at all other actors with an interest in fisheries activities, including relevant international organizations, such as regional fisheries bodies and private companies involved in the capture and processing of fish.[69]

The Code is intended to establish principles and criteria for the elaboration of national and international policies for responsible fisheries.[70] Responsible fishing was defined in the Declaration of Cancún, adopted at the 1992 International Conference on Responsible Fishing, as encompassing "the sustainable utilization of fisheries resources in harmony with the environment; the use of capture and aquaculture practices which are not harmful to ecosystems, resources or their quality; the incorporation of added value to such products through transformation processes meeting the required sanitary standards; the conduct of commercial practices so as to provide consumers access to good quality products."[71]

In furtherance of its goal of promoting responsible fishing, the Code sets out the principles and international standards of conduct for those involved in the fishing sector. The Code is divided into twelve articles. The general principles of responsible fishing are found in Article 6 of the Code. The overarching principle in Article 6.1 provides that "States and users of living aquatic resources should conserve aquatic ecosystems. The right to fish carries with it the obligation to do so in

---

[67] The Code of Conduct is available at www.fao.org/fishery/ccrf/en <checked July 12, 2010>. The resolution adopting the Code of Conduct is contained in Annex 2 to the Code. A more detailed drafting history of the Code of Conduct is contained in Annex 1 to the Code.

[68] Code of Conduct on Responsible Fisheries, Article 1.3.

[69] Ibid., Article 1.2.

[70] Ibid., Article 2.2.

[71] Declaration of the International Conference on Responsible Fishing, held in Cancún, Mexico from May 6–8, 1992, available at http://legal.icsf.net/icsflegal/uploads/pdf/instruments/res0201.pdf <checked November 19, 2009>.

a responsible manner so as to ensure effective conservation and management of the living aquatic resources." Other important concepts and principles found in Article 6 include the ecosystem approach, the precautionary approach, integrated coastal area management, and transparency in decision-making. Many of these principles are further elaborated in the subsequent articles of the Code, which include more detailed guidance on fisheries management,[72] fishing operations,[73] aquaculture development,[74] coastal area management,[75] postharvest practices and trade,[76] and fisheries research.[77]

The Code was never intended to be a stand-alone instrument and many of its principles have also been further developed through the negotiation of additional nonbinding instruments. These include international plans of action on sharks, seabirds and fishing capacity, which were adopted by the Fisheries Committee in February 1998,[78] and an international plan of action on illegal, unreported and unregulated (IUU) fishing, which was adopted by the Fisheries Committee in March 2001.[79] Further plans of action have also been suggested, such as an international plan of action to reduce or eliminate bycatch and discards.[80] In general, the international plans of action build upon the provisions of the Code of Conduct and provide more detail on the sort of measures that states are expected to take in order to meet the objectives of the Code. For example, the International Plan of Action for Reducing Incidental Catch of Seabirds in Longline Fisheries expressly elaborates the need identified in Article 7.6.9 of the Code to take appropriate measures to minimize, inter alia, catch of nontarget species including non-fish species.[81]

---

[72] Code of Conduct on Responsible Fisheries, Article 7.
[73] *Ibid.*, Article 8.   [74] *Ibid.*, Article 9.
[75] *Ibid.*, Article 10.   [76] *Ibid.*, Article 11.   [77] *Ibid.*, Article 12.
[78] Available at ftp://ftp.fao.org/docrep/fao/006/x3170e/X3170E00.pdf <checked November 10, 2009>.
[79] Available at www.fao.org/DOCREP/003/y1224E/Y1224E00.HTM <checked November 10, 2009>. For an overview, see W. Edeson, "The International Plan of Action on Illegal Unreported and Unregulated Fishing: the legal context of a non-legally binding instrument" (2001) 16 *Int'l J. Marine & Coastal L.* 603.
[80] UNGA Resolution 63/112, at para. 76. The Committee on Fisheries agreed at its twenty-eighth session in March 2009 to convene an expert consultation followed by a technical consultation in order to promulgate international guidelines on bycatch management and the reduction of discards; see *Report of the twenty-eighth session of the Committee on Fisheries*, 2–6 March 2009, FAO Fisheries and Aquaculture Report R902, at para. 72.
[81] See also Article 8.5 of the Code of Conduct.

Another related instrument takes the form of the International Guidelines for the Management of Deep Sea Fisheries in the High Seas, which were adopted by states at an FAO Technical Consultation held in August 2008. Until recently, deep sea fish stocks have not been subject to widespread commercial fishing, but advances in technology, as well as reduced opportunities to catch other fish species, mean that an increasing number of deep sea fish species are being targeted by the fishing industry.[82] Yet these species have characteristics that make them particularly susceptible to overexploitation. They also tend to be found in vulnerable marine ecosystems that can be damaged by destructive fishing practices. Thus, the FAO responded to calls from the international community to address the problems posed by so-called "bottom" fishing.[83] The issue was taken up by the Committee on Fisheries in 2005, where the deficiencies of the legal and policy framework were discussed by FAO Members. The Committee recognized that existing instruments should be applied to deep sea fisheries, while at the same time acknowledging that new approaches to fisheries management may be appropriate for deep sea stocks.[84] The Committee therefore agreed to develop a code of practice or technical guidelines in order to address these issues.[85]

The purpose of the Guidelines is to "provide tools to ... facilitate and encourage the efforts of states and [regional fisheries bodies] towards sustainable use of marine living resources exploited by deep sea fisheries, the prevention of significant adverse impacts on deep sea [vulnerable marine ecosystems] and the protection of marine biodiversity that these ecosystems contain."[86] Although the Guidelines are not expressed to be part of the Code in the same way as the International Plans of Action,[87] the different title given to the instrument should not be given too much weight. The Guidelines clearly make a link with preexisting instruments by calling on states and regional fisheries bodies to

---

[82] See www.fao.org/fishery/topic/12356/en <checked January 5, 2010>.
[83] UNGA Resolution 59/25, at paras. 66–9. See also UNGA Resolution 61/105, at paras. 81–7.
[84] *Report of the twenty-sixth session of the Committee on Fisheries*, 7–11 March 2005, FAO Fisheries Report R780, at paras. 86–7.
[85] *Ibid.*, at para. 89. See also *Report of the twenty-seventh session of the Committee on Fisheries*, 5–9 March 2007, FAO Fisheries Report R830, at para. 77.
[86] International Guidelines for the Management of Deep-Sea Fisheries in the High Seas, at para. 6.
[87] The UN General Assembly had suggested that the FAO develop an international plan of action under the Code; see UNGA Resolution 61/105, at para. 89.

recognize the need to manage deep sea fisheries in accordance with the Code and the general principles set out in the Fish Stocks Agreement.[88] Moreover, the Guidelines build upon many preexisting principles already set out in the Code and related instruments. For instance, the Guidelines reiterate the importance of the ecosystem approach and the precautionary approach to fisheries management,[89] and they set out a series of measures to achieve the responsible management of deep sea fisheries, many of which overlap with measures proposed under preexisting instruments. There is a particular emphasis on the protection of rare and fragile ecosystems found in the deep sea. Owing to the poor scientific understanding of deep sea ecosystems, attention is given to habitat protection. Under the Guidelines, states and regional fisheries bodies are encouraged to identify areas or features where vulnerable marine ecosystems are known or likely to occur.[90] Guidelines are provided on what should be taken into account when identifying vulnerability[91] and flag states and regional fisheries bodies are encouraged to conduct assessments to establish if deep sea fishing activities are likely to produce significant adverse impacts thereon.[92] Where vulnerable marine ecosystems have been identified, states and regional fisheries bodies are encouraged to close such areas until appropriate conservation and management measures have been established.[93] States and regional fisheries bodies are also encouraged to design an appropriate protocol for how fishing vessels should respond if they come into contact with a vulnerable marine ecosystem.[94]

The development of the International Plans of Action and the International Guidelines on Deep Sea Fisheries recognizes that particular species of fish may need special attention and the application of more specific rules. Yet these instruments are still drafted as general principles and they require further implementation by states and regional fisheries bodies before they can be applied in practice.

The FAO Department of Fisheries has also issued technical guidelines on the implementation of the Code of Conduct.[95] These technical guidelines provide further details on how the Code should be implemented. However, the technical guidelines have not been approved by any intergovernmental organ and they cannot therefore be considered

---

[88] International Guidelines for the Management of Deep-Sea Fisheries in the High Seas, at para. 21.
[89] Ibid., at para. 12.   [90] Ibid., at para. 12(ii).   [91] Ibid., at para. 42.
[92] Ibid., at para. 47.   [93] Ibid., at para. 66.   [94] Ibid., at para. 67.
[95] www.fao.org/fishery/ccrf/publications/guidelines/en <checked July 12, 2010>.

an integral part of the Code in the same way as the International Plans of Action.[96]

As noted by Moore, one of the most important aspects of the Code and the accompanying instruments is their "all-encompassing scope" and the fact that they take a "systematic approach ... to cover all aspects of fisheries management and development."[97] Within the FAO, the Code provides the overarching framework within which the majority of the work of the FAO on fisheries is now conducted.[98] Meetings of the Committee on Fisheries regularly consider progress in implementing the Code of Conduct for Responsible Fisheries and responses to a biennial questionnaire on this issue circulated by the FAO Secretariat to all FAO Member States.[99]

However, the Code is not a treaty and, therefore, it is not formally binding on states or any other entity. Indeed, the Code reiterates in the very first article that it is voluntary.[100] In a similar way, the International Plans of Action also clearly affirm their voluntary status.[101]

On the other hand, the Code of Conduct cannot be completely dismissed in terms of its effect on international law. The Code itself notes that "certain parts of it are based on relevant rules of international law."[102] There is clearly an overlap between the Code of Conduct and the Law of the Sea Convention. The Code declares that it is "to be interpreted and applied in conformity with the relevant rules of international law, as reflected in the United Nations Convention on the Law of the Sea, 1982. Nothing in this Code prejudices the rights, jurisdiction and duties of States under international law as reflected in the Convention."[103] Many of the provisions of the Code confirm the

---

[96] G. Moore, "The Code of Conduct on Responsible Fisheries," in E. Hey (ed.), *Developments in International Fisheries Law* (Kluwer Law International, 1999) at 89.

[97] *Ibid.*, at 94.

[98] *Progress in the implementation of the Code of Conduct on Responsible Fisheries and related international plans of action*, December 2004, Document COFI/2005/2, at para. 3.

[99] In 2007 it was agreed that the Sub-Committees on Aquaculture and on Fish Trade would take responsibility for monitoring the implementation of Articles 9 and 11 of the Code respectively; *Report of the twenty-seventh session of the Committee on Fisheries*, March 5–9, 2007, at para. 21.

[100] Code of Conduct, Article 1.1.

[101] IPOA-Seabirds, para. 8; IPOA-Sharks, para. 10; IPOA-Capacity, para. 4; IPOA-IUU, para. 4. See also the comments made by states on the adoption of the IPOA-IUU, as reported in Edeson, "The International Plan of Action on Illegal Unreported and Unregulated Fishing," at 608–9.

[102] Code of Conduct on Responsible Fisheries, Article 1.1.

[103] *Ibid.*, Article 3.1.

application of rules of international law found in the Law of the Sea Convention and the Fish Stocks Agreement. The Code also overlaps with other existing international agreements relating to fisheries. For example, the Code of Conduct reiterates the general principles found in the preamble to the Compliance Agreement requiring states to exercise effective jurisdiction over vessels flying their flag as well as the need for flag states to maintain records of all fishing vessels that have been authorized to be used for fishing.[104] This overlap is not surprising as the Compliance Agreement asserts that it will "form an integral part of the International Code of Conduct for Responsible Fishing."[105] Thus, the Code often serves to complement existing instruments. In this way one source describes all of these instruments as a package of measures that together "confront fisheries problems at different levels and on different fronts."[106]

On the other hand, it is doubtful whether the Code has had the effect of crystallizing new rules of customary international law. Almost all of the provisions of the Code are stated in terms of what states "should" do. Moreover, it is clear from the drafting history that states negotiating the Code carefully chose this language. As Edeson suggests, "most of the [International Plans of Action] and the Code of Conduct have many clauses that would not have had a chance of surviving were it not for the fact they were placed in the context of voluntary or non-binding instruments."[107] The drafting history and the choice of hortatory language means that not much of the Code could be described as being of a "potentially norm-creating character" so as to make it possible to influence the crystallization of rules of customary international law requiring specific conduct from states or other actors.[108]

Aside from the creation of customary international law, there may be other ways in which the Code has influenced the development of

---

[104] See *ibid.*, Article 8.2. The Code of Conduct is of course broader than the Compliance Agreement as it deals with all types of fishing activities and not just fishing on the high seas.

[105] Compliance Agreement, preamble. For comments on the interrelationship between the Compliance Agreement and the Code of Conduct, see Moore, "The Code of Conduct on Responsible Fisheries," at 90. See also Edeson, "The International Plan of Action on Illegal Unreported and Unregulated Fishing," at 169.

[106] *Report of the Second Informal Meeting of Parties to the Fish Stocks Agreement*, at para. 30; see also Moore, "The Code of Conduct on Responsible Fisheries," at 92.

[107] W. Edeson, "Closing the gap: the role of 'soft' international instruments to control fishing" (1999) 20 *Australian Ybk Int'l L.* 83, at 103.

[108] *North Sea Continental Shelf Cases* (1969) ICJ Reports 3, at para. 72.

international fisheries law. Although its provisions may not be sufficiently clear and precise to create *rules* of customary international law,
much of the Code can be seen as laying down *general principles* on the
conservation and management of fish stocks. General principles are of
a different character to rules of customary international law. As Boyle
and Chinkin explain, "mediating norms or principles need not impose
obligations or regulate conduct, they do not depend on state practice
and they do not need the same clarity or precision as rules."[109] Yet they
can influence the future development of international law in a number
of ways.

First, the general principles can be used in the elaboration of future
binding instruments. Indeed, this role is expressly recognized in the
objectives of the Code of Conduct, which state it is to "provide guidance which may be used where appropriate in the formulation and
implementation of international agreements and other legal instruments, both binding and non-binding."[110] Thus, the Code can be used
as a frame of reference for the international community, as well as
individual states, in drawing up legal instruments aimed at addressing
all manner of fisheries issues. This can be seen in the drafting of the
several fisheries instruments, both by the FAO and by other relevant
international organizations such as regional fisheries bodies.[111]

The general principles in the Code of Conduct may also have an influence on the development of international law through the role that
they may play in litigation. General principles are one of the sources of
international law to be applied by international courts and tribunals, as
identified in Article 38(1) of the ICJ Statute. While this instrument only
refers to "general principles of law recognized by civilized nations" as
deduced from national legal systems, it is also widely accepted that
it encapsulates general principles derived from international law.[112]
Although such general principles will neither dictate the outcome of a
dispute nor can they override explicit treaty or customary rules, they
can nevertheless affect the way in which international courts and tribunals decide cases. This process is illustrated by the role played by the
concept of sustainable development in the *Case Concerning the Gabcikovo-
Nagymaros*.[113] Lowe describes how, in this case, sustainable development

---

[109] A. E. Boyle and C. Chinkin, *The Making of International Law* (Oxford University Press,
2007) at 224.
[110] Code of Conduct, Article 2(d).   [111] See below.
[112] Boyle and Chinkin, *The Making of International Law*, at 223.
[113] *Case Concerning the Gabcikovo-Nagymaros Project* (1997) ICJ Reports 7, at para. 140.

acts as "a legal concept exercising a kind of interstitial normativity, pushing and pulling the boundaries of true primary rules when they threaten to overlap or conflict with each other."[114] It is suggested that the concept of responsible fishing and the general principles found in the Code of Conduct and associated instruments could play a similar role in influencing the development and application of other primary rules of international law related to fisheries in international dispute settlement.

Of course, the Code can only successfully play these roles if it is widely supported by states. Boyle and Chinkin argue that "what gives general principles of this kind their authority and legitimacy is ... the endorsement of states."[115] It would seem that the Code has achieved such a status.[116] In 1999 an FAO Ministerial Meeting on Fisheries adopted a Declaration on the Implementation of the Code of Conduct in which they committed themselves to implement the Code and the International Plans of Action as a matter of priority, as well as calling upon "all users of fisheries resources to apply the Code of Conduct for Responsible Fisheries."[117] A few years later, the Reykjavik Conference on Responsible Fisheries in the Marine Ecosystem held in 2001 reaffirmed the principles of the Code of Conduct and the four international plans of action.[118] Support for the general application of the Code of Conduct is also found outside of the framework of the FAO. For instance, the UN General Assembly has recognized that "the Code of Conduct for Responsible Fisheries of the Food and Agriculture Organization of the United Nations and its associated international plans of action set out principles and global standards of behavior for responsible practices for conservation of fisheries resources and the management and development of fisheries"[119] and it has urged states and subregional and regional fisheries management organizations and arrangements to implement and promote the application of the Code within their areas

---

[114] V. Lowe, "Sustainable development and unsustainable arguments," in A. E. Boyle and D. Freestone (eds.), *International Law and Sustainable Development* (Oxford University Press, 1999) at 33.

[115] Boyle and Chinkin, *The Making of International Law*, at 224.

[116] See M. Gavouneli, *Functional Jurisdiction in the Law of the Sea* (Martinus Nijhoff Publishers, 2007) at 108.

[117] Rome Declaration, available at www.fao.org/DOCREP/005/X2220e/X2220e00.HTM <checked November 10, 2009>.

[118] See *Report of the Reykjavik Conference on Responsible Fisheries in the Marine Ecosystem*, FAO Fisheries Report No. 658, Document FIID/R658(Tri), Annex I.

[119] UNGA Resolution 63/112, preamble.

of competence[120] and to develop as a matter of priority national plans of action to put into effect the FAO International Plans of Action.[121]

It follows from this analysis that the Code of Conduct is an important international instrument that cannot be ignored by states. Even though the Code is not legally binding on states, it provides an important framework for the future development of international fisheries law.

4.3 2009 Agreement on Port State Measures to Prevent, Deter and Eliminate Illegal, Unreported and Unregulated Fishing

One of the most recent fisheries instruments to be negotiated by the FAO is the Agreement on Port State Measures to Prevent, Deter and Eliminate Illegal, Unreported and Unregulated Fishing,[122] which was adopted by the FAO Conference in November 2009. The genesis of the Agreement on Port State Measures is the International Plan of Action on IUU Fishing, which calls on states to "use measures, in accordance with international law, for port State control of fishing vessels in order to prevent, deter and eliminate IUU fishing."[123] Further to this instrument, a Model Scheme on port state control was developed under the auspices of the Committee on Fisheries.[124] The Model Scheme encouraged FAO Members to "maintain an effective system of port state control for foreign fishing vessels calling at [their] ports, with a view to promoting the effectiveness of relevant conservation and management measures,"[125] including denying the use of port facilities to those vessels that were suspected of conducting or supporting IUU fishing.[126] At its twenty-seventh session in 2007, the Committee on Fisheries decided to pursue the drafting of a new legally binding instrument based on the Model Scheme.[127] As with many FAO instruments, the text was initially prepared by the secretariat and it was first submitted to an

---

[120] E.g. *Sustainable fisheries, including through the 1995 Agreement for the Implementation of the Provisions of the United Nations Convention on the Law of the Sea of 10 December 1982 relating to the Conservation and Management of Straddling Fish Stocks and Highly Migratory Fish Stocks, and related instruments*, UNGA Resolution 60/31, November 29, 2005, at para. 30; UNGA Resolution 63/112, at para. 39.
[121] E.g. UNGA Resolution 60/31, at para. 31; UNGA Resolution 63/112, at paras. 13, 42, 70.
[122] Hereinafter, Agreement on Port State Measures.
[123] IPOA – IUU Fishing, at para. 52; available at www.fao.org/DOCREP/003/y1224e/y1224e00.htm <checked July 12, 2010>.
[124] See the Model Scheme on Port State Measures to Combat IUU Fishing (Model Scheme).
[125] *Ibid.*, at para. 2.1.   [126] *Ibid.*, at paras. 2.5–2.7.
[127] *Report of the Twenty-seventh meeting of the Committee on Fisheries*, Rome, March 5–9, 2007, at para. 68.

expert consultation composed of ten experts acting in their individual capacity.[128] The draft agreement produced by the expert consultation was subsequently submitted to a Technical Consultation attended by ninety-two FAO Members, one FAO Associate Member, representatives from three specialized agencies of the United Nations and observers from twenty other intergovernmental organizations and international NGOs.[129] The Technical Consultation conducted a thorough review of the draft text, which was then submitted to the FAO Conference for adoption in November 2009.[130]

The central aim of the Agreement on Port State Measures is to promote inspection of fishing vessels entering the ports of parties to the Agreement in order to verify whether or not they have been engaged in IUU fishing. As with the Compliance Agreement, the Agreement on Port State Measures does not alter the jurisdictional framework of the law of the sea and the Agreement is very clear that it is not intended to "prejudice the rights, jurisdiction and duties of parties under international law."[131] Indeed, the Agreement only purports to set minimum standards of port state control and states may take more stringent port state measures as permitted by international law.[132]

The Agreement requires parties to take a number of specific measures to combat IUU fishing.[133] In relation to port states, the Agreement requires parties to designate particular ports to which fishing vessels

[128] *Report of the expert consultation to draft a legally-binding instrument on port state measures*, Washington DC, United States of America, September 4–8, 2007, FAO Fisheries Report No. 846, Document FIEL/R846(En).

[129] *Report of the technical consultation to draft a legally-binding instrument on port state measures*, Rome, June 23–27, 2008, January 26–30, 2009, May 4–8, 2009 and August 24–28, 2009, FAO Fisheries and Aquaculture Report No. 914, Document FIEL/R914(En).

[130] See J. Swan, "Port state measures to combat IUU fishing: international and regional developments" (2006–2007) 7 *Sus. Dev. L. and Pol'y* 38.

[131] Agreement on Port State Measures, Article 4(1).

[132] *Ibid.*, preamble and Article 4(1)(b). Explicit references are made to a "minimum standard" in Articles 8, 12, 13, 14 of the Agreement. See also the views of the European Communities and Chile in the Technical Consultation; *Report of the Technical Consultation to Draft a Legally-Binding Instrument on Port State Measures*, at paras. 14 and 20.

[133] Article 1(e) of the Agreement defines IUU fishing by reference to the International Plan of Action on IUU Fishing. Many states were unhappy with this definition due its inherent ambiguity, but the perceived urgency of adopting the instrument led states to accept the definition for the present time; see *Report of the Technical Consultation to Draft a Legally-Binding Instrument on Port State Measures*, at paras. 21–6.

may request entry[134] and to require certain information to be submitted by the fishing vessel before it is permitted to enter the port.[135] If a party suspects a vessel has engaged in IUU fishing, in particular where a vessel has been included on a blacklist compiled by regional fisheries bodies, it is required to refuse entry to any of its ports.[136] In addition, the Agreement requires parties to undertake an inspections regime in respect of fishing vessels[137] and to report to the flag state on the results of the inspection.[138] Where there are clear grounds for believing that a vessel has engaged in IUU fishing, the port state shall deny the use of its port for landing, transhipment, packaging or processing of fish or any other port services such as refueling and resupplying.[139] Where infractions are reported to the flag state, the flag state is required to take appropriate enforcement action.[140] The agreement does not permit port states to take enforcement action themselves, however, thus confirming rules on exclusive flag state jurisdiction on the high seas.[141]

As with the FAO Compliance Agreement, there is a strong emphasis in the FAO Agreement on Port State Measures on information exchange. Article 14 of the Agreement requires parties to establish a mechanism for the direct exchange of electronic information, preferably through the FAO. Such information exchange is vital if the Agreement is going to achieve its objectives, as port states need to have access to information on which to base their decisions not to allow vessels into port.

The Agreement also promotes the provision of financial and technical assistance to developing countries to assist them in the implementation of the Agreement.[142] To this end, an ad hoc working group is created "to periodically report and make recommendations to the Parties on the establishment of funding mechanisms including a scheme for contributions, identification and mobilization of funds, the development of criteria and procedures to guide implementation, and progress in the implementation of the funding mechanisms."[143]

As a treaty, the Agreement is open to participation by states and regional economic integration organizations[144] and it shall enter into

---

[134] Agreement on Port State Measures, Article 7.
[135] *Ibid.*, Article 8.   [136] *Ibid.*, Article 8bis(3).
[137] *Ibid.*, Article 11.   [138] *Ibid.*, Article 14.
[139] *Ibid.*, Article 17(1)(b).   [140] *Ibid.*, Article 21(3bis).
[141] Law of the Sea Convention, Article 92(1).
[142] Agreement on Port State Measures, Article 21.   [143] *Ibid.*, Article 21(6).
[144] *Ibid.*, Articles 25–27. See, however, Article 3(5), which provides: "As this Agreement is global in scope and applies to all ports, the Parties shall encourage all other

force once twenty-five instruments of ratification or accession have been submitted.[145] Yet, in a similar way to the Compliance Agreement, the Agreement on Port State Measures is specifically drafted in terms of contracting parties and many of the obligations are of such specific nature that they are unsuitable for translation into customary international law.

That is not to say that the Agreement is not significant for nonparties. The measures taken by those port states that are party to the Agreement will be applicable to all fishing vessels. Indeed, the Agreement expressly calls for its "fair, transparent and non-discriminatory" application.[146] The fishing vessels of nonparties will therefore be just as affected by the application of the Agreement, even though it is not legally binding on them. A system of port state measures against vessels suspected of engaging in IUU fishing may be an effective way of combating this practice. Like the other FAO instruments, however, whether it works will depend on how states and regional fisheries bodies implement the measures in the Agreement in practice.

5 Fisheries instruments and rules of reference in the Law of the Sea Convention and the Fish Stocks Agreement

As noted at the outset, the Law of the Sea Convention itself contains few specific rules on fishing and it merely requires coastal states and flag states to take measures to ensure the conservation and management of fish stocks falling under their jurisdiction. States have a large amount of discretion in how they do this. One of the few prescriptions is the duty to "take into account any generally recommended international minimum standards, whether sub-regional, regional, or global."[147] Original proposals for this text by six Eastern European states would have required measures to be "in accordance with the

---

entities to apply measures consistent with its provisions. Those that may not otherwise become Parties to this Agreement may express their commitment to act consistently with its provisions." See comments of states on participation made in the context of the Technical Consultation; *Report of the Technical Consultation to Draft a Legally-Binding Instrument on Port State Measures*, at paras. 30–3.

[145] Agreement on Port State Measures, Article 29.
[146] *Ibid.*, Article 3(4). See also Article 23.
[147] Law of the Sea Convention, Article 119(1)(a). Article 61(3) of the Convention also requires a coastal state to "take into account [of] … any generally recommended international minimum standards" when taking conservation and management measures in their exclusive economic zone.

recommendations of the competent fishery organization consisting of representatives of interested States in the region concerned and other States engaged in fishing in the region."[148] This approach would have arguably given a much stronger role to regional fisheries bodies, while making no mention of rules or standards adopted at the global level. Other states preferred a less central role for international institutions in the adoption of fisheries conservation and management measures. The United States suggested that states should establish allowable catch and other conservation measures, "taking into account any generally agreed global and regional minimum standards."[149] The Evensen Group of Legal Experts proposed similar language, albeit making reference to "generally recommended regional or global minimum standards."[150] It is this language that was incorporated into the informal single negotiating text and that survived in the final Convention, albeit with minor drafting changes.

The language of generally recommended international minimum standards is arguably broad enough to incorporate most fisheries standards adopted by the FAO, whether or not they are contained in treaties or nonbinding instruments. However, this provision does not require states to comply with generally recommended international minimum standards. Rather it is a relatively weak requirement to "take into account" such standards, which does not necessarily necessitate fishing states following what the standards say. This is in stark contrast to the role of rules of reference in relation to shipping standards adopted by the International Maritime Organization that were considered in a previous chapter.[151]

The weaknesses with the rules of reference in the fisheries provisions of the Law of the Sea Convention were well known when it came to negotiating the new generation of fisheries instruments and consequently a stricter approach to the incorporation of technical standards was taken. In contrast to the weaker wording of the Law of the Sea Convention, Article 10 of the Fish Stocks Agreement requires states to "adopt and apply generally recommended international minimum standards for the responsible conduct of fisheries operations." This provision is arguably a stronger provision, as it requires states not merely to take into account generally recommended international minimum

---

[148] See M. Nordquist *et al.* (eds.), *United Nations Convention on the Law of the Sea 1982 – A Commentary, Vol. 2* (Martinus Nijhoff Publishers, 1993) at 600.
[149] *Ibid.*, at 602.   [150] *Ibid.*, at 604.   [151] See Chapter 6.

standards but to adopt and apply them. In particular, it would seem to be directed at the Code of Conduct on Responsible Fishing, which was adopted in October 1995, just two months prior to the adoption of the Fish Stocks Agreement itself. Arguably, the effect of this provision is to make the Code and other relevant FAO instruments binding on States Parties to the Fish Stocks Agreement.[152] Yet, as noted above, the contents of the Code of Conduct are rarely normative in the sense that they require specific action to be taken by states or other international actors. Rather, the Code of Conduct and related instruments set forth general principles that should inform states when they create their own national fisheries policies. Thus, States Parties to the Agreement are required to take into account these principles, but they still retain a degree of discretion when designing their own management and conservation measures.[153]

6 Cooperation between the FAO and regional fisheries bodies

The FAO is not the only international institution with responsibility for regulating fisheries. Indeed, the FAO has no direct involvement in the adoption of conservation and management measures for particular fish stocks. As a former senior legal advisor to the FAO has noted, the effectiveness of the Code and the Compliance Agreement will depend on the introduction of subordinate measures to give effect to them.[154] The implementation of conservation and management measures will fall to a variety of other international institutions.

Regional fisheries bodies are at the forefront of international efforts to achieve the conservation and sustainable utilization of fish stocks.[155] The Law of the Sea Convention demands that fishing states cooperate with regional fisheries bodies when setting management and conservation measures.[156] Furthermore, Article 8 of the Fish Stocks Agreement emphasizes the centrality of regional fisheries bodies in fisheries management by providing that "where a subregional or

---

[152] See Moore, "The Code of Conduct on Responsible Fisheries," at 92.
[153] Cf. P. Birnie, A. E. Boyle and C. Redgwell, *International Law and the Environment* (3rd edn., Oxford University Press, 2009) at 729–30.
[154] W. Edeson, "Towards long-term sustainable use: some recent developments in the legal regime of fisheries," in A. E Boyle and D. Freestone (eds.), *International Law and Sustainable Development* (Oxford University Press, 1999) at 165.
[155] For a brief history of fisheries commissions, see Wolfrum, "Fishery Commissions."
[156] Law of the Sea Convention, Articles 61(2), 63, 64, 118.

regional fisheries management organization or arrangement has the competence to establish conservation and management measures for particular straddling fish stocks or highly migratory fish stocks, states fishing for the stocks on the high seas and relevant coastal states shall give effect to their duty to cooperate by becoming members of such organization or participants in such arrangements, or by agreeing to apply the conservation and management measures established by such organization or arrangement."[157] Where there is no existing regional fisheries body, states are exhorted to cooperate in the establishment of one.[158] In other words, one of the primary mechanisms for carrying out the duty of cooperation in fisheries matters under the Law of the Sea Convention is participation in the work of regional fisheries bodies.

There are currently about forty-four regional fisheries bodies,[159] all of which have different forms and functions. The powers of regional fisheries bodies can include "the collection, analysis and dissemination of information and data, to the coordination of fisheries management through joint schemes and mechanisms, to decision-making related to the conservation, management, development and responsible use of resources."[160] The precise powers possessed by a particular institution will depend on its constituent instrument. However, a general distinction can be drawn between those organizations that are advisory in nature and those that have a power to adopt binding regulatory measures.[161]

If the principles developed under the auspices of the FAO are to be effective, it is vital that they are taken into account and implemented by regional fisheries bodies. None of the instruments adopted by the FAO are strictly speaking binding on regional fisheries bodies. Nevertheless, the FAO has recognized the importance of working closely with regional fisheries bodies in order to promote the application of the globally agreed fisheries instruments. To some extent,

---

[157] Fish Stocks Agreement, Article 8(3).
[158] Ibid., Article 8(5).
[159] See www.fao.org/fishery/topic/16800/en <checked July 14, 2010>.
[160] Ibid. See also Fish Stocks Agreement, Article 10.
[161] One recent study suggests that the current trend is to establish bodies with regulatory functions and able to take binding decisions; see J. Swan, "Decision-making in Regional Fishery Bodies or arrangements: the evolving role of RFBs and international agreement on decision-making processes," FAO Fisheries Circular No. 995, 2004, at 10.

the ability of the FAO to achieve this aim depends on the status of the regional fisheries bodies and their relationship with the FAO.[162]

Although the FAO does not itself directly regulate the conservation and management of particular fish stocks, it has been involved in setting up international institutions in order to carry out this role. Several regional fisheries bodies have been established under Article VI of the FAO Constitution, which allows the FAO to create commissions or committees to advise on the formulation and implementation of policy and to study and report on matters pertaining to the objectives of the organization. Regional fisheries bodies established under Article VI of the FAO Constitution include the Fishery Committee for the Eastern Central Atlantic (CECAF)[163] and the Western Central Atlantic Fishery Commission (WECAFC).[164] Both of these are advisory in nature and they do not have the power to set conservation and management measures for the fish stocks for which they are responsible. Indeed, Article VI of the FAO Constitution would not seem to permit the creation of bodies with binding decision-making powers.

Regional fisheries bodies established under Article VI of the FAO Constitution are classified as subsidiary organs of the FAO and they are therefore subject to the supervision and control of superior FAO organs, such as the Committee on Fisheries and the FAO Council. It follows that regional fisheries bodies in this category have limited autonomy as their terms of reference and reporting procedures are initially approved by and may subsequently be amended by the FAO.[165] Thus, the FAO has the most influence over these types of regional fisheries bodies and it can directly seek to ensure that the principles developed through the FAO are taken into account by these institutions. This is illustrated by the decision in 2006 to revise the statute of the Western Central Atlantic Fishery Commission, which was amended inter alia to require the Committee to "have due regard for and promote the application of the provisions of the FAO Code of Conduct on Responsible Fisheries and its related instruments, including the precautionary approach and the ecosystem approach to fisheries management."[166] On the other hand, institutions within this category are also financed from the regular

---

[162] Developed from www.fao.org/fishery/topic/16918/en <checked July 14, 2010>.
[163] See www.fao.org/fishery/rfb/cecaf/en <checked July 14, 2010>.
[164] See www.fao.org/fishery/rfb/wecafc/en <checked July 14, 2010>.
[165] FAO Constitution, Article VI.3.
[166] *Revised statute of the Western Central Atlantic Fishery Commission*, FAO Council Resolution 1/131, at para. 2(a).

FAO budget or from voluntary contributions channeled through the FAO. This factor may hinder their ability to build capacity or to achieve certain aims set by the FAO fishery instruments.[167]

Another way in which the FAO can create regional fisheries bodies is through the negotiation and adoption of a treaty under Article XIV of the FAO Constitution. The Regional Committee for Fisheries (RECOFI),[168] the General Fisheries Commission for the Mediterranean (GFCM),[169] the Indian Ocean Tuna Commission (IOTC)[170] and the Asia-Pacific Fisheries Commission (APFC)[171] were all established in this way. For this category of regional fisheries bodies, the FAO can also exercise significant influence on the mandate and powers of the institution during the negotiations of the constituent instrument. Moreover, the involvement of the FAO in the drafting of these instruments also allows the inclusion of provisions that will promote cooperation between the institution and the FAO once it has been established. For example, the Indian Ocean Tuna Commission is required by its constituent instrument to cooperate with the FAO by providing information on their activities and programs[172] and allowing representatives of the FAO to participate in meetings.[173] However, as regional fisheries bodies in this category are constituted by a separate treaty, they are formally autonomous bodies and, once created, they are independent from direct FAO supervision and control. Thus, they are not obliged to follow recommendations or advice from the FAO if they decide otherwise.

Some regional fisheries bodies are created completely independently from the FAO. The North West Atlantic Fisheries Organization (NAFO), North East Atlantic Fisheries Commission (NEAFC), Western and Central Pacific Fisheries Commission (WCPFC), Inter-American Tropical Tuna Commission (IATTC) and the Commission on the Conservation of Antarctic Marine Living Resources (CCAMLR) are all examples of important regional fisheries bodies that fall into this category. Some of

[167] See *Meeting of FAO and non-FAO Regional Fishery Bodies or Arrangements*, FAO Fisheries Report No. 597, Document FIPL/R597(En), at para. 29.
[168] See www.fao.org/fishery/rfb/recofi/en <checked July 14, 2010>.
[169] See www.fao.org/fishery/org/gfcm_inst/en <checked July 14, 2010>.
[170] See www.fao.org/fishery/org/iotc_inst/en <checked July 14, 2010>.
[171] See www.fao.org/fishery/rfb/apfic/en <checked July 14, 2010>.
[172] Agreement for the Establishment of the Indian Ocean Tuna Commission, Article 5(2)(f).
[173] For example, the Agreement for the Establishment of the Indian Ocean Tuna Commission, Article 6(8).

these regional fisheries have a minor link with the FAO as the depositary functions under the constituent instrument are imposed upon the
FAO Director General.[174] However, many others have no formal connection with the FAO at all. These institutions have the greatest degree of
autonomy from the FAO.

Even in the case of regional fisheries bodies with no formal link
to the FAO, it does not follow that they have not been influenced by
fisheries instruments adopted by the FAO. For example, the constituent instrument of the Northwest Atlantic Fisheries Organization,
originally adopted in November 1978, was recently amended to take
into account recent developments in international fisheries law. The
amended preamble to the Convention on Co-operation in Northwest
Atlantic Fisheries explicitly refers to both the 1993 FAO Compliance
Agreement and the 1995 FAO Code of Conduct on Responsible Fisheries
and the new text seeks to implement many of the principles found in
these other instruments.[175]

Indeed, there are a number of strategies that have been pursued
by the FAO in order to promote the development of international
fisheries law through regional fisheries bodies. In its role as over-
seer of the Code of Conduct[176] and related instruments, the Fisheries
Committee attempts to monitor the work of all types of regional
fisheries bodies, whether or not they have a formal relationship with
the FAO. Regional fisheries bodies are regularly invited to take part
in the work of the Fisheries Committee as observers. The Committee
requests and collates information on measures taken by both states
and regional fisheries bodies to implement the Code of Conduct. This
is done through the distribution of a questionnaire. However, the
process of collecting information has not been straightforward and
in its 2005 Report on the Implementation of the Code of Conduct,
the FAO Secretariat noted that reporting from states had declined
by over fifty percent and only half of the regional fisheries bodies
had responded to the questionnaire.[177] By 2009 response rates had

---

[174] For example, the International Commission for the Conservation of Atlantic Tunas
(ICCAT) and the South East Atlantic Fisheries Organization (SEAFO).
[175] For the text of the amendment, see www.nafo.int/publications/frames/general-a17.
html <checked July 12, 2010>.
[176] See Code of Conduct on Responsible Fisheries, Article 4.2.
[177] *Progress in the implementation of the Code of Conduct on Responsible Fisheries and Related
International Plans of Action*, December 2004, Document COFI/2005/2, at para. 2.
It was suggested that the implementation of the Code should be monitored less
frequently in order to achieve a higher response rate; at para. 63.

further declined.[178] This highlights the difficulties faced by the FAO in trying to coordinate fisheries policy and promote best practice among fishing states and regional fisheries bodies.

The FAO has also sought to coordinate developments in international fisheries management through the convening of joint meetings of regional fisheries bodies. The first such meeting took place in 1999 and it was attended by eighteen regional fisheries bodies, encompassing both FAO and non-FAO institutions.[179] The focus of the meeting was on identifying the common challenges faced by regional fisheries bodies and how they could promote the implementation of international fisheries instruments, such as the Fish Stocks Agreement and the Code of Conduct on Responsible Fisheries.[180] Such joint meetings have taken place at regular intervals since 1999, alongside the meeting of the Committee on Fisheries.

It has been stressed that the role of the FAO in such meetings is informal and it acts as a facilitator only.[181] The purpose of the meetings is to promote discussion and information-sharing among relevant fisheries bodies, in particular on the implementation of the principles found in fisheries instruments adopted by the FAO. For instance, action against IUU fishing and the implementation of the ecosystems-based approach was the focus of discussion at the fourth meeting in 2005.

Although the first meeting was attended by a wide range of actors including states and nongovernmental organizations, participation in the meeting has gradually become narrower over time. At the second meeting, it was agreed that the meeting was primarily for the secretariats of regional fisheries bodies and participation should be thus limited.[182] In line with this decision, the third meeting refused to allow a number of interested NGOs to participate.[183] It has been stressed that "the general scope of the Meeting, being informal, would be information exchange and administration, as well as enhancing cooperation

---

[178] *Progress in the Implementation of the Code of Conduct on Responsible Fisheries, Related International Plans of Action and Strategy,* Document COFI/2009/2, at para. 2.

[179] See *Report of Meeting of FAO and non-FAO Regional Fishery Bodies or Arrangements,* at para. 1.

[180] See *ibid.,* at para. 6.

[181] See FAO website www.fao.org/fishery/rsn/en <checked July 12, 2010>.

[182] *Report of the second meeting of FAO and non-FAO Regional Fishery Bodies or Arrangements,* February 20–21, 2001, FAO Fisheries Report No. 645, Document FIPL/R645(En), at para. 69.

[183] *Report of the third meeting of Regional Fisheries Bodies,* March 3–4, 2003, FAO Fisheries Report No. 703, Document FIPL/R703(En), at para. 6.

among regional fisheries bodies ... there would be no decision making implications involved and policy may be a background but not a
directive."[184] The title of this initiative was changed in 2005 to the
Regional Fisheries Body Secretariat Network to underline both the
informal nature of the meeting, but also the fact that participants in
the forum continued to cooperate through intersessional dialogue.[185]

Although the FAO has acted in order to facilitate cooperation and
coordination between regional fisheries bodies, there are limits
to the influence that it can bring to bear. This is vividly illustrated
by the debate over the review of regional fisheries bodies and how
they have implemented international fisheries law, including generally recommended international minimum standards on responsible
fisheries. This debate has arisen in the context of the duty on states
under Article 13 of the Fish Stocks Agreement to "strengthen existing subregional and regional fisheries management organizations and
arrangements in order to improve their effectiveness in establishing
and implementing conservation and management measures for straddling and highly migratory fish stocks."[186] The UN General Assembly
has also urged regional fisheries bodies to "strengthen and modernize
their mandates and the measures adopted by such organizations or
arrangements, and to implement modern approaches to fisheries management, as reflected in the [Fish Stocks Agreement] and other relevant international instruments."[187] The Committee on Fisheries agreed
at its twenty-sixth session in 2005 that regional fisheries bodies should
be invited to undertake performance reviews.[188] In discussions on how
this can be achieved, it was noted that the FAO has no authority in this
area over regional fisheries bodies created outside of the FAO institutional structure and any review scheme of regional fisheries bodies'
practices would require the consent of the governing council of each
body.[189] The FAO itself acknowledged that it had no inherent authority to lead this process, but it nonetheless noted that there is a need
to develop common criteria for the evaluation of regional fisheries

---

[184] *Report of the fourth meeting of Regional Fisheries Bodies*, March 14–15, 2005, FAO
Fisheries Report No. 778, Document FIPL/R778(En), at para. 5.
[185] *Ibid.*, at para. 7.
[186] See also 2004 Rome Declaration on IUU Fishing, at para. 5.
[187] UNGA Resolution 63/112, at para. 89.
[188] *Report of the twenty-sixth session of the Committee on Fisheries*, March 7–11, 2005, at
paras. 111–112.
[189] *Report of the Fourth Meeting of Regional Fisheries Bodies*, Rome, March 14–15, 2005, at
para. 11.

bodies.[190] Further debate on the subject took place at the Fish Stocks Agreement Review Conference in May 2006. On this occasion, delegates were again split over whether regional fisheries bodies should be responsible for conducting a review of their performance themselves or whether they should be subject to some independent scrutiny on the basis of a uniform set of criteria.[191] The final text adopted by the 2006 Review Conference urged regional fisheries bodies to conduct performance reviews, including some element of independent evaluation, with a view to publishing the results.[192] This compromise text does not specify precisely what form the independent evaluation should take and regional fisheries bodies have interpreted this element in different ways. For example, the Commission for the Conservation of Southern Bluefin Tuna was reviewed internally by its members with the final report being subject to an external review by an independent expert,[193] whereas the International Commission for the Conservation of Atlantic Tuna appointed an external panel of three independent members to conduct the review from the outset.[194] Whether or not the FAO is involved in the process, however, compliance with instruments adopted by the FAO is likely to be a major part of the criteria against which regional fisheries bodies are reviewed.

It can be seen from this summary of the relationship between the FAO and regional fisheries bodies that the FAO exercises little formal authority over many of these institutions. Nevertheless, the FAO plays an important catalytic and coordinating role by bringing together these institutions to discuss common challenges and what can be done to address them. In doing so, it is able to promote the adoption and application of the principles and concepts agreed by the FAO in the context of the fisheries conservation and management schemes designed by regional fisheries bodies.

---

[190] *Report of the twenty-seventh session of the Committee on Fisheries*, March 5–9, 2007, at para. 86.

[191] See *Summary of the UN Fish Stocks Agreement Review Conference: 22–26 May 2006*, Earth Negotiations Bulletin, Vol. 7, no. 61, May 29, 2006, at p. 4.

[192] *Ibid.*, at p. 5. See also *Report of the twenty-eighth session of the Committee on Fisheries*, March 2–6, 2009, at para. 15.

[193] Commission for the Conservation of Southern Bluefin Tuna, *Part One, Self Assessment*, July 2008; Commission for the Conservation of Southern Bluefin Tuna, *Part Two, Report of the Independent Expert*, September 2008.

[194] International Commission for the Conservation of Atlantic Tunas, *Report of the Independent Review*, Document PLE-106/2008, September 2008, at 5.

7 Conclusion

The regulation of fisheries is a complex field of international law that involves a variety of international institutions at the global and regional levels. The importance of conserving and managing fish stocks in a sustainable and responsible manner is regularly emphasized by the UN General Assembly, but measures to achieve these objectives are largely left to other institutions. Among these, the FAO stands out as a specialist forum that is capable of significantly influencing the development of international fisheries law. The advantage of the FAO is that it brings together all states, whether or not they are party to the Fish Stocks Agreement or a member of regional fisheries bodies. As such, it is able to address the challenges of modern fisheries management from a holistic perspective with the involvement of all relevant actors.

In 1997 one study concluded that the Committee on Fisheries of the FAO had "contributed to the shaping the management and utilization of world fisheries and has demonstrated strong leadership in global fisheries governance."[195] Since that time, the FAO has undoubtedly continued to play a pivotal role in this respect. In particular, the FAO has adopted a number of instruments that have sought to develop international fisheries law. Some of these have taken the form of international treaties, such as the 1993 Compliance Agreement and the 2009 Agreement on Port State Measures. These treaties require parties to take specific measures to promote the conservation and sustainable use of fish stocks and to combat practices such as IUU fishing. The relevance of these treaties for nonparties is limited, however, and they cannot be considered as law-making instruments. On the other hand, the FAO can be said to have actively developed international fisheries law through the use of nonbinding instruments that have served to crystallize international support for new principles that can be applied to the conservation and management of fisheries. In particular, the Code of Conduct on Responsible Fisheries is a valuable instrument. The principles in the Code of Conduct and related instruments are not directly binding on states and other international actors in the sense that they demand particular measures to be taken. Rather their importance lies in their ability to provide a framework for the development of fisheries conservation and management measures and policies by other actors such as fishing states, other fishing entities and regional

---

[195] Swan and Sastia, "Contribution of the Committee on Fisheries to global fisheries governance 1977–1997."

fisheries bodies. The procedures used for the adoption of these instruments has also ensured that a wide range of actors has participated in their negotiation and conclusion and the instruments reflect the interests and needs of the international community.

Clearly the FAO is not the only institution working in this field. It operates alongside a number of other international institutions that coexist at the global and regional levels. The Committee on Fisheries has itself expressed some concern about the proliferation of institutions that address fisheries-related issues.[196] It is clear that if the FAO is to continue its successful role in influencing the development of international fisheries law, it must work closely with those other institutions with an interest in fisheries law and policy.

There is already a long tradition of cooperation between the FAO and the UN General Assembly, which is facilitated by the existence of a relationship agreement concluded between the two organizations.[197] This agreement provides for reciprocal representation and the exchange of information and documents between the UN and the FAO. This is one example of interinstitutional cooperation and coordination, a topic which will be considered in more detail in Chapter 8.

The FAO also actively cooperates on fisheries issues with a range of other international institutions, albeit on a more informal basis. This includes not only regional fisheries bodies, which play a vital role in international fisheries conservation and management, but also a number of international organizations concerned with the conservation of natural resources. Where their interests overlap, the FAO seeks to ensure that such institutions take into account the principles relating to fisheries developed at the global level. One example is the evolving relationship between the FAO and the Conference of the Parties to the Convention on International Trade in Endangered Species (CITES). The growing activity of CITES in relation to endangered fish species has required the FAO to increase its interaction with this body. Following a number of years of informal collaboration, particularly in relation to the provision of scientific and technical expertise concerning the listing of fish species as endangered species under the CITES regime, the FAO entered into a Memorandum of Understanding (MOU) with CITES

---

[196] *Report of the twenty-sixth session of the Committee on Fisheries*, March 7–11, 2005, at para. 33.

[197] Agreement between the United Nations and the Food and Agriculture Organization of the United Nations, signed June 10, 1946, available in (1947) 1 *Int'l Organization* 239.

in 2006 to further strengthen cooperation between the two organizations.[198] The MOU provides for regular exchange of information and observers, although the two institutions remain independent in terms of the policies that they may adopt.

This chapter has also considered the types of measures taken by the FAO to cooperate with regional fisheries bodies in order to ensure the coherent development of this field of international law. It has been seen how the FAO has promoted information exchange and dialogue between regional fisheries bodies in order to promote best practices in fishing conservation and management.

Ultimately, the FAO has little direct influence over these other institutions with an interest in fisheries and there is no guarantee that international fisheries law will develop in a coherent and coordinated manner. This is one of the potential problems of fragmentation of international law-making, an issue that will be explored in more detail in the final chapter of this book.

[198] The text of the Memorandum of Understanding is available at www.cites.org/eng/disc/sec/FAO-CITES-e.pdf <checked June 10, 2010>.

8 Cooperation, coordination and conflict between international institutions

1 The problem of fragmentation in international law-making

Previous chapters have demonstrated the range and variety of international organizations and institutions that are involved in developing the law of the sea regime at the global level. Each institution has a distinct membership, as well as a specific mandate defining the range of issues that fall within its sphere of competence. This has been called the principle of speciality by the International Court of Justice:[1]

> The Court need hardly point out that international organizations are subjects of international law which do not, unlike States, possess a general competence. International organizations are governed by the "principle of speciality," that is to say, they are invested by the States which create them with powers, the limits of which are a function of the common interests whose promotion those States entrust to them.

The specialization of international organizations brings with it certain benefits. For instance, Hafner explains that "specialization accommodates various needs and concerns of the states engaged in international law-making, and states perceive that their individual positions are better respected in these special regimes than in a global one."[2] Moreover, specialized organizations can offer expertise in a specific area, which can be important when dealing with technical issues.

Yet the creation of specialized international organizations, institutions and regimes may also lead to the potential fragmentation of

---

[1] *Advisory Opinion on the Legality of the Use by a State of Nuclear Weapons in Armed Conflict* (1996) ICJ Reports 66, at para. 25.

[2] G. Hafner, "Pros and cons ensuing from fragmentation of international law" (2004) 25 *Mich. J. Int'l L.* 849, at 858–9.

international law. Fragmentation is not a new phenomenon. Writing in 1953, Wilfred Jenks observed that:[3]

law-making treaties are tending to develop in a number of historical, functional and regional groups which are separate from each other and whose mutual relationships are in some respects analogous to those of separate systems of municipal law.

While decentralization has always been a feature of the international legal system, it is widely appreciated that this phenomenon is increasing.[4] The proliferation of law-making activity is partly a result of the gradual expansion of the international legal sphere and the creation of more and more specialized international organizations to deal with new areas of activity.[5] These international institutions operate autonomously and there is no formal hierarchy between them. As a consequence, there is a concern in certain quarters that the increasing fragmentation of the law-making process can pose a threat to the coherent development of international law. As noted by the International Law Commission (ILC) in its study on the fragmentation of international law, "the problem, as lawyers have seen it, is that such specialized law-making and institution-building tends to take place with relative ignorance of legislative and institutional activities in the adjoining fields and of the general principles and practices of international law."[6]

The ILC study also noted that there are different types of fragmentation.[7] First, fragmentation may occur when different interpretations are made of the general law. For example, two tribunals may take differing views on the meaning or scope of a rule of customary international law.[8] Secondly, fragmentation may occur when a specialist

---

[3] W. Jenks, "The conflict of law-making treaties" (1953) 30 *Brit. Ybk Int'l L.* 401, at 403.

[4] *Fragmentation of international law: difficulties arising from the diversification and expansion of international law*, Report of the Study Group of the International Law Commission, Document A/CN.4/L.682, April 13, 2006, at para. 8.

[5] See Hafner, "Pros and cons ensuing from fragmentation of international law," at 856.

[6] *Fragmentation of international law: difficulties arising from the diversification and expansion of international law*, at para. 8.

[7] *Ibid.*, at para. 47.

[8] Many commentators doubt the seriousness of this problem; see R. Higgins, "A babel of judicial voices? Ruminations from the bench" (2006) 55 *Int'l & Comp. L. Q.* 791; B. Simma, "Universality of international law from the perspective of a practitioner" (2009) 20 *European J. Int'l L.* 265, at 279. A prominent example of such a conflict exists in the field of international investment law where different arbitral awards were

regime diverges from general international law. Finally, fragmentation may arise when overlapping rules are developed by states within separate, specialist regimes. It is primarily the latter variant of fragmentation that we are concerned with in the present context. How can one avoid the fragmentation of the law of the sea that may arise as a result of the range and diversity of institutions that operate in this field of law?

Views as to the seriousness of institutional fragmentation differ. For instance, the threat of fragmentation caused by the proliferation of international organizations is downplayed by Prost and Clark, who argue that because international organizations are designed to deal with a specific class of issues, conflicts of competence are unlikely to occur.[9] Yet, this view may underestimate the potential for overlap and competition between international organizations. Although the mandates of international organizations are defined to deal with specific subject matters, the possibility for competition arises because many issues cannot be authoritatively classified as belonging to one area of international law or another.[10] Characterizations such as "trade law," "environmental law," "human rights law" or indeed "law of the sea" can only be "informal labels that describe the instruments from the perspective of different interests or different policy objectives" and "most international instruments may be described from various perspectives."[11] In this context, it doesn't matter how clearly and precisely the competence of an international organization is drafted, overlaps cannot be completely avoided. It follows that many international problems could fall within the mandate of more than one institution

---

delivered in two cases brought on the same facts; see *CME v Czech Republic*, Final UNCITRAL Award dated March 14, 2003 and *Ronald Lauder v Czech Republic*, UNCITRAL Award dated September 3, 2001. See C. Brower and J. Sharpe, "Multiple and conflicting international arbitral awards" (2003) 4 *J. World Investment* 211.

[9] M. Prost and P. Kingsley Clark, "Unity, diversity and fragmentation of international law: how much does the multiplication of international organizations really matter?" (2006) 5 *Chinese J. Int'l L.* 341, at 343–4. They continue: "even where overlapping activities tend to develop into rivalry or competition, such competition will not automatically have consequences in terms of international law's unity ... Only if [international organizations] act as some sort of autonomous law makers will their multiplication be a potential source of disorder and fragmentation."

[10] See H. G. Schermers and N. Blokker, *International Institutional Law* (4th edn., Martinus Nijhoff Publishers, 2003) at para. 1703.

[11] *Fragmentation of international law: difficulties arising from the diversification and expansion of international law*, at para. 21.

and there is the potential for divergent regulatory approaches to be taken.

The risk of fragmentation is further increased because international institutions tend to approach problems from the particular perspective dictated by the aims and objectives that are set out in their constituent instrument. In an enlightening article on regime theory, Haas describes how the creation of specialist international institutions tends to foster the establishment of so-called "epistemic communities," composed of international civil servants and scientists, as well as representatives of interested nongovernmental organizations and the relevant governmental departments of states with a primary interest in that area.[12] The emergence of such interest groups tends to emphasize the promotion of particular values and priorities within that regime.[13] As stated by the ILC report on the fragmentation of international law, "each rule-complex or 'regime' comes with its own principles, its own form of expertise and its own 'ethos', not necessarily identical to the ethos of neighbouring specialization."[14] Thus, although international institutions may formally be composed of a similar set of states, they develop their own institutional culture that can influence their regulatory response to a particular problem.

The competing activities of international institutions are by no means accidental. Often it is a result of states attempting to exploit the overlap between the mandates of international institutions in an attempt to influence the content of the proposed rules or standards. This phenomenon of so-called "regime-shifting" is another side effect of the proliferation of international organizations.[15] In accordance with this practice, a state may attempt to introduce an issue into a forum in which it knows that its particular values and interests will be promoted. Gillespie gives the example of whaling states

---

[12] P. M. Haas, "Do regimes matter? Epistemic communities and Mediterranean pollution" (1989) 43 *Int'l Org.* 377.

[13] See similar observations by M. Koskeniemmi and P. Leino, "Fragmentation of international law? Postmodern anxieties" (2002) 15 *Leiden J. Int'l L.* 553, at 578.

[14] *Fragmentation of international law: difficulties arising from the diversification and expansion of international law*, at para. 15.

[15] L. Helfer, "Regime shifting: the TRIPs Agreement and new dynamics of international intellectual property lawmaking" (2004) 29 *Yale J. Int'l L.* 1; see also E. Benvenisti and G. W. Downs, "The empire's new clothes: political economy and the fragmentation of international law" (2007–2008) 60 *Stan. L. Rev.* 595; M. Koskenniemi, "The politics of international law – 20 years on" (2009) *European J. Int'l L.* 7, at 9.

seeking to promote the liberalization of cetacean regulation through the Conference of the Parties to the Convention on International Trade in Endangered Species[16] in order to avoid a stricter approach to the regulation of whaling that is prevalent with the International Whaling Commission.[17] CITES places a greater emphasis on sustainable use of species and it is therefore aligned with the interests of the whaling states. In contrast, the predominant philosophy of the International Whaling Commission has been concerned with conservation of cetaceans. Since 1985 the International Whaling Commission has pursued a strategy of prohibiting commercial whaling. If anything, the exploitation of the differences in the mandates of various international organizations is likely to increase the prospects of fragmentation and normative conflict.

The risk of fragmentation is particularly acute in an area such as the law of the sea where a large number of organizations and institutions are working on overlapping issues. Such overlaps arise in relation to many different maritime issues. A clear example is the issue of qualifications and training of ships crew. This topic falls squarely within the responsibility of both the International Labour Organization (ILO)[18] and the International Maritime Organization (IMO).[19] Both organizations have adopted instruments that purport to deal with the training of seafarers. The ILO is the UN specialized agency with responsibility for labor rights and it is from this perspective that the organizations have approached the topic of training. Since its inception in 1918, the ILO has adopted a number of labor conventions on seafarers' rights, including most recently the 2006 Maritime Labour Convention, a comprehensive treaty on seafarers' rights which covers inter alia training for seafarers.[20] As the UN specialized agency with responsibility for a wide range of shipping matters, the IMO has also been active in regulating safe working practices on board ships. In 1995 it adopted an updated Convention on Standards of Training, Certification and Watchkeeping

---

[16] Hereinafter, CITES.

[17] A. Gillespie, "Forum shopping in international environmental law: the IWC, CITES, and the management of cetaceans" (2002) 33 *Ocean Dev. & Int'l L.* 17.

[18] ILO Constitution, Preamble. See also the 1970 Vocational Training (Seafarers) Recommendation (R137); 1978 Merchant Shipping (Minimum Standards) Convention (C147); 2006 Maritime Labour Convention.

[19] See IMO Convention, Article I(a).

[20] 2006 Maritime Labour Convention, Annex, Regulation 1.3. For an overview, see J. Harrison, "Current legal developments – International Labour Organization" (2008) *Int'l J. Marine & Coastal L.* 125.

for Seafarers. While the objectives of these two organizations are not diametrically opposed, the potential for conflict nevertheless arises because they may approach these issues from different perspectives and without knowledge of what the other organization has done.[21]

In light of the contemporary concerns about fragmentation of international law, questions arise about what measures can be taken in order to avoid conflicts in law arising in the first place. Cooperation between institutions in their law-making activities could offer an important way in which to avoid fragmentation and normative conflict. Two perspectives on this question will be considered in this chapter. In the first place, it will consider vertical approaches to the promotion of coordination among different international institutions. In doing so, it will ask what role the United Nations, as an institution with general competence over all aspects of the law of the sea, can play in promoting coherent law-making. Secondly, the chapter will consider horizontal approaches to coordination and cooperation. This section will focus on arrangements between international institutions through which they seek to work more closely together on issues in which they both have an interest. It will ask how international institutions can avoid conflict by pursuing cooperation and coordination strategies at the stage when new international rules are still being developed.[22]

Of course, there is no guarantee that efforts at coordination will be successful. If we take the risk of fragmentation from the proliferation of international organizations seriously, important questions are also raised about how rules produced within special regimes interact with each other and how they interact with general rules and principles of international law.[23] The final section of this chapter will therefore ask whether there are clear and appropriate rules for dealing with conflicts of norms at the international level.

---

[21] See F. Morgenstern, *Legal Problems of International Organizations* (Grotius Publications, 1986) at 26–7. The relationship between these two organizations will be considered in more detail below.

[22] This aspect of fragmentation was not dealt with by the ILC; *Fragmentation of international law: difficulties arising from the diversification and expansion of international law*, at para. 13. See C. Leathley, "An institutional hierarchy to combat fragmentation of international law: has the ILC missed an opportunity?" (2007) *J. Int'l L. & Politics* 259.

[23] As noted by Hafner, conflicts can also arise between different sets of secondary rules, e.g. dispute settlement regimes; Hafner, "Pros and cons ensuing from fragmentation of international law," at 857.

2 Vertical coordination of international law-making activities

2.1 Coordination through the United Nations

As noted above, the problem of fragmentation arises because all international organizations and institutions operate independently and autonomously. The international legal system has no central institutional framework. Yet there is one international organization that occupies a particularly prominent place in the international legal order and which may be able to influence the activities of other international institutions. Among the dozens of institutions that have been created since the Second World War, the United Nations stands out because of its broad mandate, as well as its quasi-universal membership.

The United Nations was created in 1945 in order to maintain international peace and security, to develop friendly relations among states and to achieve international cooperation in solving international problems of an economic, social, cultural or humanitarian character.[24] Despite its broad mandate, the United Nations was never intended to deal with all international issues. Rather, there was a desire among the drafters of the UN Charter to isolate those technical issues that required international cooperation from the inherently political aspects of international relations. The latter would fall within the work of the United Nations itself, whereas specialized agencies would be created to foster cooperation in technical and specialized fields of international cooperation.[25] The so-called specialized agencies of the United Nations system have their own constituent instruments. More importantly, they have separate legal personality and they control their own agendas and their own budgets.

There was also an awareness among the architects of the UN system of the need to coordinate the activities of the various international institutions that were created at this time. As a result, the United Nations system was based upon a network of cooperative arrangements between the United Nations and the specialized agencies.[26] While the United Nations itself is not hierarchically superior to the specialized agencies, it does possess some powers through which it can seek to

---

[24] UN Charter, Article 1.
[25] See Schermers and Blokker, *International Institutional Law*, at para. 1693.
[26] See B. Simma *et al.* (eds.), *The Charter of the United Nations – A Commentary* (2nd edn., Oxford University Press, 2002) at 952–3; J. P. Cot and A. Pellet (eds.), *La Charte des Nations Unies* (Economica-Bruylant, 1985) at 892; Schermers and Blokker, *International Institutional Law*, at para. 1692.

influence the agenda of these institutions. The UN Charter expressly foresees that the United Nations shall, through the General Assembly and the Economic and Social Council (ECOSOC), coordinate the policies and activities of the specialized agencies. The following sections will consider the general powers of coordination possessed by the United Nations under the UN Charter as well as the more specific mechanisms and processes which have been designed to increase cooperation and coordination in relation to the law of the sea in particular.

2.2 Powers under the United Nations Charter and relationship agreements

Article 57 of the UN Charter requires that "the various specialized agencies, established by inter-governmental agreement and having wide international responsibilities, as defined in their basic instruments, in economic, social, cultural, educational, health, and related fields, shall be brought into relationship with the United Nations."[27] The means by which this was done was through the conclusion of treaties, known as relationship agreements, between the United Nations and the specialized agencies.[28] The relationship agreements are designed to improve cooperation between the specialized agencies and the United Nations. A number of provisions found in the relationship agreements are dictated by the UN Charter itself, whereas other provisions have been developed through practice of the institutions. Common features of most relationship agreements are provisions for information exchange,[29] reporting on relevant activities,[30] reciprocal exchange of representatives and powers to propose agenda items.[31]

Central to the relationship between the United Nations and the specialized agencies is the power of the United Nations under Article 58 of

---

[27] The power to enter into agreements with such agencies is conferred on ECOSOC by Article 63(1), albeit subject to the approval of the General Assembly.

[28] E.g. Agreement concerning the Relationship between the International Labour Organization and the United Nations [UN–ILO Relationship Agreement]; Agreement concerning the Relationship between the Food and Agriculture Organization of the United Nations and the United Nations [UN–FAO Relationship Agreement]; Agreement concerning the Relationship between the International Maritime Organization and the United Nations [UN–IMO Relationship Agreement].

[29] UN–ILO Relationship Agreement, Article V; UN–FAO Relationship Agreement, Article V; UN–IMO Relationship Agreement, Article V.

[30] UN–ILO Relationship Agreement, Article V; UN–FAO Relationship Agreement, Article V; UN–IMO Relationship Agreement, Article V.

[31] UN–ILO Relationship Agreement, Article III; UN–FAO Relationship Agreement, Article III; UN–IMO Relationship Agreement, Article III.

the UN Charter to "make recommendations for the coordination of the policies and activities of the specialized agencies." Yet, such recommendations, as their name suggests, are not legally binding and the specialized agencies are under no obligation to follow them. In other words, the relationship between the United Nations and other international institutions is one of relative equality between partners, rather than a hierarchy.[32] Nevertheless, Article 64 of the UN Charter also calls for ECOSOC to make arrangements with specialized agencies to obtain reports on the steps taken to give effect to its recommendations, in particular those concerning the coordination of international policy-making discussed above. This provision is partly operationalized by the relationship agreements themselves, which often place an obligation on the specialized agencies to arrange for the submission, as soon as possible, to their competent organs of all formal recommendations that are made to them by the General Assembly or ECOSOC.[33] Many relationship agreements also call on specialized agencies to report back to the United Nations on "the action taken ... to give effect to such recommendations, or on the other results of their consideration."[34] While this may be thought of as a way in which the United Nations organs can influence the actions of specialized agencies, the phrasing of this obligation underlines the noncompulsory nature of the duty to cooperate, as it leaves open the possibility that the specialized agencies will not follow a recommendation of the United Nations. Rather they may report back that, after consideration, it was decided not to follow the recommendation. In other words, the UN organs lack any formal powers to compel coordination of law-making by other international organizations under these provisions.

The UN Charter only makes provision for the negotiation of relationship agreements between the United Nations and the specialized agencies. In practice, however, the United Nations has also concluded similar agreements with other international organizations that have not been formally designated as specialized agencies.

The most prominent example in the context of the law of the sea is the relationship agreement between the United Nations and the

---

[32] Simma *et al.* (eds.), *The Charter of the United Nations – A Commentary*, at 1002.
[33] UN–ILO Relationship Agreement, Article IV, UN–FAO Relationship Agreement, Article IV, UN–IMO Relationship Agreement, Article IV.
[34] Identical text in UN–ILO Relationship Agreement, Article IV, UN–FAO Relationship Agreement, Article IV, UN–IMO Relationship Agreement, Article IV.

International Seabed Authority.[35] In the agreement between these two institutions, the United Nations recognizes the International Seabed Authority as "the organization through which States Parties to the Convention shall, in accordance with Part XI of the Convention and the Agreement, organize and control activities in the seabed and ocean floor and subsoil thereof, beyond the limits of national jurisdiction ... particularly with a view to administering the resources of the Area."[36] The Agreement also recalls that the Authority is an "autonomous international organization"[37] while recognizing that the Authority undertakes "to conduct its activities in accordance with the purposes and principles of the [United Nations] Charter."[38] Many of the provisions of this relationship agreement are similar to the provisions found in the relationship agreements concluded with the specialized agencies. For example, the agreement contains a provision on the exchange of representatives between the two institutions. Prior to the conclusion of the relationship agreement in 1997, the Authority had already been granted observer status at the General Assembly.[39] The relationship agreement notes this decision and it extends the invitation to other UN bodies and conferences, "subject to such decisions as may be taken concerning the attendance of their meetings by observers" and "subject to the rules of procedure and practice of the bodies concerned."[40] The agreement also includes a provision calling for the exchange of information, publications and reports of mutual interest.[41]

There are other areas where the agreement between the United Nations and the International Seabed Authority subtly differs from other relationship agreements that have been concluded with specialized agencies. For example, unlike many of the specialized agencies, the Authority is not under an express duty to respond to recommendations made by the organs of the United Nations. Nevertheless, the relationship agreement does contain a general duty to "cooperate closely with each other and consult each other on matters of mutual

---

[35] Agreement concerning the relationship between the United Nations and the International Seabed Authority (UN–ISA Relationship Agreement), UNTS, Vol. 1967, II-1165.

[36] *Ibid.*, Article 2(1).   [37] *Ibid.*, Article 2(2).   [38] *Ibid.*, Article 2(4).

[39] *Observer status for the International Seabed Authority in the General Assembly*, UNGA Resolution 51/6, October 24, 1996.

[40] UN–ISA Relationship Agreement, Article 6.

[41] *Ibid.*, Article 8(1). As with the specialized agencies, special provisions are made for cooperation and provision of information to the Security Council and the International Court of Justice; Articles 4, 5.

interest,"[42] as well as an obligation to "furnish special studies or information requested by the United Nations."[43] These obligations could arguably be interpreted as being wide enough to require the Authority to respond to any recommendations from the General Assembly or other UN organs, although, as with the other specialized agencies, the Authority would not be obliged to follow any recommendation directed towards it.

The formal relationship agreements provide the legal framework in which the United Nations cooperates with other, more specialized international institutions. Yet, as has been seen, they rarely require specific action to be taken. Ultimately, cooperation between institutions rests not on legal obligation but on diplomacy and the development of good relations. This is perhaps underlined by the fact that none of the relationship agreements include dispute settlement provisions, which indicates that they were not intended to create judicially enforceable rights per se.[44] Nevertheless, the relationship agreements do provide a basis for creating legitimate expectations about the types of actions that organizations should take in order to cooperate. Moreover, they have formed the basis for the development of more specific mechanisms to promote cooperation in areas such as the law of the sea.

As recognized by the United Nations Commission on Sustainable Development, "because of the complex and interrelated nature of the oceans, oceans and seas present a special case as regards the need for international coordination and cooperation."[45] The General Assembly has also regularly called for improved cooperation and coordination between international institutions involved in developing the law of the sea.[46] Building on the network of relationship agreements discussed in this section, the United Nations, led by the General Assembly, has taken a number of steps to improve cooperation and coordination in the law of the sea.

2.3 Coordination by the United Nations in the law of the sea

2.3.1 Report of the Secretary-General on Oceans and the Law of the Sea

A centerpiece of the law of the sea activities undertaken by the United Nations is the annual report prepared by the Division for Ocean Affairs

---

[42] *Ibid.*, Article 3(2).   [43] *Ibid.*, Article 8(5).

[44] See A. E. Boyle, "Some reflections on the relationship between treaties and soft law" (1999) 48 *Int'l & Comp L. Q.* 901, at 909.

[45] Decision 7/1, para. 40.

[46] E.g. *Oceans and the law of the sea*, UNGA Resolution 63/111, December 5, 2008, at para. 166; *Oceans and law of the sea*, UNGA Resolution 64/71, December 4, 2009, at para. 194.

and the Law of the Sea on behalf of the UN Secretary-General. Reporting on developments in the law of the sea is expressly called for by the Law of the Sea Convention itself. As depositary to the Law of the Sea Convention, the UN Secretary-General is required to produce a report on "issues of a general nature that have arisen with respect to [the] Convention," which is to be provided to "all States Parties, the Authority and competent international organizations."[47] Indeed, even before the Convention entered into force, the Secretary-General had already been requested to report to the General Assembly on developments in the law of the sea. The practice began in 1982 when the General Assembly requested the Secretary-General to report on developments in relation to the work on preparing for the implementation of the Convention and its own resolutions on the law of the sea.[48] When the Convention did ultimately enter into force, the General Assembly decided it was to "undertake an annual review and evaluation of the implementation of the Convention and other developments relating to ocean affairs and the law of the sea"[49] and the Secretary-General was mandated to prepare an annual "comprehensive report, for the consideration of the Assembly, on developments relating to the law of the sea, taking in account relevant scientific and technological developments."[50] While this report of the Secretary-General is also intended to serve as the report required by Article 319 of the Convention,[51] it goes beyond matters concerning the developments with respect to the Convention and it includes information on all aspects of the oceans and law of the sea. In practice, the report covers all possible areas of maritime policy, including sections dealing with maritime safety and security, marine science and technology, conservation and management of marine fishery resources, marine biological diversity, protection and preservation of the marine environment, sustainable development and climate change.[52]

The report is compiled from information requested from international institutions by the General Assembly. In this regard, the

---

[47] Law of the Sea Convention, Article 319(2)(a).
[48] See *Third United Nations Conference on the Law of the Sea*, UNGA Resolution 37/66, December 3, 1982, at para. 10; see also *Third United Nations Conference on the Law of the Sea*, UNGA Resolution 38/59, December 14, 1983, at para. 8.
[49] *Oceans and the law of the sea*, UNGA Resolution 49/28, December 6, 1994, at para. 12.
[50] *Ibid.*, at para. 15(a).
[51] *Ibid.*; see also UNGA Resolution 64/71, at para. 204.
[52] This list of topics is taken from *Oceans and the law of the sea, report of the Secretary-General*, UN Document A/63/63, March 10, 2008.

General Assembly regularly calls on "the competent international organizations, as well as funding institutions ... to contribute to the preparation of the comprehensive report of the Secretary-General on oceans and the law of the sea."[53] It follows that it is not only specialized agencies and other UN organs and bodies that are asked to report on their activities but all relevant institutions, regardless of their formal status or relationship with the United Nations. In regard to those institutions with which it has concluded a relationship agreement, the United Nations can rely on the rights contained in those agreements in order to obtain information for its annual law of the sea report. Otherwise, it must depend on the goodwill of the organizations concerned.

The General Assembly has noted "the critical role of the annual comprehensive report of the Secretary-General, which integrates information on developments relating to the implementation of the Convention and the work of the Organization, its specialized agencies and other institutions in the field of ocean affairs and the law of the sea at the global and regional levels."[54] The report serves to facilitate cooperation and coordination of maritime policy in a number of ways.

First, it can be argued that the report is in itself a means of achieving better policy coordination.[55] The collection and dissemination of information concerning the activities of a variety of institutions involved in the law of the sea is one way in which to avoid duplication of work. This is, however, a limited form of "negative coordination"[56] that can only indirectly contribute to avoiding conflicts.

Another important function of the Secretary-General's report is to feed into discussion at the General Assembly towards the adoption of the annual resolution on oceans and the law of the sea. This process has the potential to actively facilitate cooperation and coordination between international institutions through making particular recommendations for future activity based upon the information contained in the Secretary-General's report on the law of the sea. Indeed, this is one of the most important mechanisms through which the UN General Assembly seeks to promote cooperation and coordination in this field.

---

[53] E.g. *Oceans and the law of the sea*, UNGA Resolution 59/24, November 17, 2004, at para. 96.

[54] UNGA Resolution 63/111, at para. 174.

[55] Making this point, see *ibid.*, at para. 174.

[56] Schermers and Blokker, *International Institutional Law*, at para. 1705.

2.3.2 General Assembly resolutions on oceans and the law of the sea

The annual resolution of the General Assembly on the law of the sea is a lengthy document which often runs to more than 150 paragraphs and which covers a wide range of law of the sea matters. The resolution is usually adopted by the plenary of the UN General Assembly in late November or early December each year. However, as Treves explains, "the [law of the sea] debate [in the General Assembly is] just the tip of the iceberg. Negotiations for the preparation of the resolution [start] weeks and sometimes months in advance."[57] The formal General Assembly debate on the resolution is usually preceded by a series of informal and formal consultations on a draft resolution. De La Fayette observes that resolutions on the law of the sea "are negotiated as seriously as international agreements."[58]

A major function of the resolution is to promote the coordination of oceans policy and law-making activities in this field. Most resolutions contain a general encouragement to states to "work closely with and through international organizations, funds and programs, as well as the specialized agencies of the United Nations system and relevant international conventions, to identify emerging areas of focus for improved coordination and cooperation and how best to address these issues."[59] In addition, resolutions are often targeted directly at international organizations, promoting cooperation or recommending certain action. In general, the General Assembly does not identify a particular institution, preferring to address the "competent international organization" or simply "global and regional bodies," thus following the practice of the Convention itself.[60] For example, General Assembly resolution 59/24 noted the need for "States and competent international organizations to urgently consider ways to integrate and improve, on a scientific basis and in accordance with the Convention and related agreements and instruments, the management of risks to

---

[57] T. Treves, "The General Assembly and the Meeting of States Parties in the implementation of the LOS Convention," in A. G. Oude Elferink (ed.), *Stability and Change in the Law of the Sea: The Role of the LOS Convention* (Martinus Nijhoff Publishers, 2005) at 60.

[58] L. De La Fayette, "The role of the UN in international oceans governance," in D. Freestone, R. Barnes and D. Ong (eds.), *The Law of the Sea: Progress and Prospects* (Oxford University Press, 2006) at 69.

[59] UNGA Resolution 63/111, at para. 166. Identical text is found in resolutions adopted in 2007, 2006, 2005 and 2004.

[60] See e.g. Law of the Sea Convention, Article 197.

the marine biodiversity of seamounts, cold water corals, hydrother-mal vents and certain other underwater features."[61] Failure to specify particular institutions has both advantages and disadvantages. On the one hand, it means that no organizations working on a particular issue will be excluded from the call for cooperation, simply because they are not expressly named. On the other hand, the resolutions tend to be indefinite and as a result they may have less impact than if they were directed at particular institutions.

Occasionally, a resolution will designate or invite a specific organiza-tion to undertake an activity. For example, the 2004 General Assembly Resolution invites the International Hydrographic Organization and the International Maritime Organization to continue their coordi-nated efforts to jointly adopt measures for the transition to electronic nautical charts.[62] In most instances where a particular organization is named, it is in relation to an activity that is already underway. In other words, the General Assembly does not seek to identify which institutions it considers to be the appropriate organization to take up a particular issue. Rather, the resolutions act as a legitimizing tool for activities already taking place through international institutions.

As was noted above, those institutions that have a relationship agreement with the United Nations may be under an obligation to consider recommendations for cooperation and coordination made by the General Assembly in its annual resolution on the law of the sea. Ultimately, however, the resolutions are not binding on other institutions. This may explain why the recommendations made by the General Assembly are rather vague. Indeed, instances where the United Nations has sought to be more proactive in coordinating inter-national organizations illustrate that it may actually meet resistance. An example is the attempt by the UN Secretary-General in 2003 to convene a meeting of interested international organizations to discuss problems with flag state implementation of international standards.[63] Several UN agencies were invited to attend the meeting, including the IMO, the ILO, the FAO, the Organization for Economic Cooperation and Development, the United Nations Environment Programme and the

---

[61] UNGA Resolution 59/24, at para. 68. See also paras. 66, 70, 77.
[62] *Ibid*, at para. 36.
[63] See *Consultative Group on flag state implementation – report of the Secretary-General*, Document A/59/63, March 5, 2004, at para. 5. The letter from Greenpeace, the International Transport Workers' Federation and WWF, calling for "a concerted multi-agency approach" to substandard shipping, is contained in Annex I.

United Nations Conference on Trade and Development. At the meeting the IMO was highly critical of the initiative, arguing that it would be best left to organizations themselves to pursue a sectorial approach to the problem. Following the meeting, the IMO Secretary-General wrote to the UN Secretary-General, stressing that, in the view of the former, "policy issues concerning the role, responsibilities and actions of member States which derive from their obligations as IMO member States and from their adherence to IMO Conventions and regulations are not subjects which need additional coordination at inter-agency meetings."[64] Although such resistance to cooperation is rare, it highlights the limitations of a decentralized system that relies on goodwill for its successful operation. In situations of divergent interests or political differences between organizations, the procedure for cooperation and coordination through the United Nations Charter is extremely weak.[65] As concluded by one study on the role of the United Nations in coordinating international policy, "the UN can only rely on effective coordination if there has been sufficient consultation in advance and if the result has been accepted in substance by all the parties."[66]

2.3.3 Open-Ended Informal Consultative Process on the Law of the Sea

One way in which states have tried to improve the process of coordinating oceans policy at the United Nations is through the establishment of the Open-Ended Informal Consultative Process on the Law of the Sea.[67] The genesis for the ICP is a decision of the Commission on Sustainable Development in April 1999 which recognized that the General Assembly was the appropriate body to provide coordination on oceans issues, but at the same time noted that there were weaknesses in its working methods. The Commission on Sustainable Development therefore recommended that "the General Assembly ... give more time for the consideration and the discussion of the Secretary-General's report on oceans and the law of the sea and for the preparation for the debate on this item in the plenary."[68] The Commission suggested that this could be achieved through the creation of an informal process that would feed into the deliberations of the General Assembly.[69] Following this recommendation, the ICP was

---

[64] *Ibid.*, at Annex III.
[65] Simma *et al.* (eds.), *The Charter of the United Nations – A Commentary*, at 996.
[66] *Ibid.*, at 967.   [67] Hereinafter, ICP.   [68] See Decision 7/1, para. 40(3).
[69] The Commission stressed that the creation of a new institution should be avoided if possible; Decision 7/1, at para. 40(4).

established by General Assembly Resolution 54/33 of November 24, 1999. The ICP was initially established for a three-year period,[70] but its mandate has subsequently been renewed a number of times.[71]

The purpose of the ICP is to aid the effective and constructive consideration of developments in the law of the sea by the General Assembly, concentrating on areas that call for a strengthening of coordination and cooperation between states and international organizations.[72] In particular, the origins of the ICP in the work of the Commission on Sustainable Development suggests that the process should focus on issues related to the sustainable development of the oceans, although in practice there have been no explicit links to this theme.[73] The main subject matter for each meeting of the ICP is usually set by the General Assembly,[74] although the detailed agenda is worked out by the cochairs (who are nominated by the president of the General Assembly) in cooperation with interested delegations.[75] In addition to the main themes set by the General Assembly, the ICP is also able to consider additional matters through plenary discussions, although the limited time frame for the meeting inevitably restricts this possibility.[76]

Not only does the ICP allow more time for states to engage in debates on developments in the law of the sea, but it also introduces a number of improvements to the way in which these issues are considered.

One innovative feature of the ICP is the use of discussion panels in which experts are invited to make presentations on the topics under consideration. The use of experts has been warmly welcomed as

---

[70] *Sectoral theme: oceans and seas*, UNGA Resolution 54/33, November 24, 1999, at para. 4.

[71] *Oceans and the law of the sea*, UNGA Resolution 57/141, December 12, 2002, at para. 60; *Oceans and the law of the sea*, UNGA Resolution 60/30, November 29, 2005, at para. 99; UNGA Resolution 63/111, at para. 160.

[72] See UNGA Resolution 54/33, at para. 2.

[73] See the criticism made at the 2009 meeting of the ICP; *Report of the work of the United Nations Open-Ended Informal Consultative Process on Oceans and the Law of the Sea at its tenth meeting*, Document A/64/131, July 13, 2009, at para. 26. In its 2009 resolution the General Assembly noted that "the perspective of the three pillars of sustainable development should be further enhanced in the examination of the selected topics"; UNGA Resolution 64/71, at para. 186.

[74] An exception was the first meeting of the ICP whose subject matter was selected at an informal meeting convened by the cochairs; see *Oceans and the law of the sea – report of the Secretary-General*, UN Document A/64/66, March 13, 2009, at para. 22.

[75] General Assembly Resolution 54/33, at para. 3(f). See also UN Document A/64/66, at para. 15.

[76] As noted by the Secretary-General, "At the first few meetings, a range of subjects was addressed in the plenary sessions ... but in recent years, interventions have concentrated predominantly on the topic of focus, as reflected in the agreed elements"; UN Document A/64/66, at para. 24.

Topics of the meetings of the Informal Consultative Process

Year	Topic
2000	(i) Responsible fisheries and illegal, unreported and unregulated fisheries (ii) Economic and social impacts of marine pollution and degradation, especially in coastal areas
2001	(i) Marine science and the development and transfer of marine technology, as mutually agreed, including capacity-building in this regard (ii) Coordination and cooperation in combating piracy and armed robbery at sea
2002	(i) Protection and preservation of the marine environment (ii) Capacity-building, regional cooperation and coordination and integrated ocean management
2003	(i) Safety of navigation, for example, capacity-building for the production of nautical charts (ii) Protecting vulnerable marine ecosystems
2004	New sustainable uses of the oceans, including the conservation and management of the biological diversity of the seabed in areas beyond national jurisdiction
2005	(i) Fisheries and their contribution to sustainable development (ii) Marine debris
2006	Ecosystem approaches and oceans
2007	Marine genetic resources
2008	Maritime security and safety
2009	Implementation of the outcomes of the Consultative Process, including a review of its achievements and shortcomings in the first nine meetings
2010	Capacity-building in ocean affairs and the law of the sea, including marine science

improving the information available to delegates when discussing law of the sea issues, although the need for greater representation of developing countries on panels has also been stressed.[77]

The ICP also differs from meetings of the General Assembly because it is open to greater participation by observers, both from other international institutions as well as from relevant NGOs. Resolution 54/33 establishing the ICP extends an invitation to "all States Members of the

---

[77] *Report of the work of the United Nations Open-Ended Informal Consultative Process on Oceans and the Law of the Sea at its tenth meeting*, at para. 56.

United Nations, States members of the specialized agencies, all parties to the [1982 Law of the Sea] Convention, entities that have received a standing invitation to participate as observers in the work of the General Assembly pursuant to its relevant resolutions, and intergovernmental organizations with competence in ocean affairs."[78] It is the widespread participation of a range of actors in the ICP that is generally considered to be one of its main advantages.[79]

Not only do these aspects of the process ensure that the oceans policy is fully informed by expert opinion and a wide range of views representing the international community as a whole, it also considerably increases the transparency of the process. This can be contrasted with the process of negotiating the General Assembly resolution on the law of the sea. Many of the debates concerning the content of the resolution take place by way of informal consultations outside of the main General Assembly debate, often behind closed doors. While this allows frank discussion and difficult political trade-offs to be made between interested states, it significantly detracts from the transparency of the process. The time-consuming nature of the process also means that many smaller states, particularly those with small delegations at the United Nations and limited resources, may struggle to participate effectively in the negotiation of the resolutions at the formative stage. In addition, non-state actors with an interest in the law of the sea, including international organizations and NGOs, may be excluded from the talks.

There is some recognition by the international community of the problems inherent in the process of negotiating the annual law of the sea resolution. In 2006 the General Assembly noted its desire to "improve the efficiency of, and effective participation of delegations in, the informal consultations concerning the annual General Assembly resolution on oceans and the law of the sea" and it thereby decided to limit the period of the consultations to four weeks and to timetable them in such a way that they do not clash with meetings of the Sixth Committee of the General Assembly.[80] These measures may go some

---

[78] UNGA Resolution 54/33, at para. 3(a).
[79] In its submission to the review of the ICP, Canada states that "the informal nature of the exchanges that take place among States and stakeholders is ICP's paramount strength"; Canadian submission on Informal Consultative Process, available at www.un.org/Depts/los/general_assembly/contributions64.htm <checked July 13, 2010>. See also *Report of the work of the United Nations Open-Ended Informal Consultative Process on Oceans and the Law of the Sea at its tenth meeting*, at para. 62.
[80] *Oceans and law of the sea*, UNGA Resolution 61/222, December 20, 2006, at para. 133.

way to addressing the ability of smaller states, and in particular developing countries, to participate in the informal consultations. However, they do not address other aspects of transparency such as the involvement of non-state actors and intergovernmental organizations in the process.

Despite broad agreement on the benefits of the ICP, among both developed and developing countries,[81] there is still some disagreement about the precise purpose of the ICP. The resolution establishing the ICP makes clear that it is expressly prohibited from pursuing on its own initiative legal or juridical coordination among legal instruments or institutions.[82] However, there are differing views on whether the ICP should simply be a forum for discussion on new and innovative issues that have arisen in the law of the sea and ocean affairs, or whether it should be a forum for attempting to negotiate text to be included in the General Assembly resolution on the law of the sea. Although it is not expressly called on to do so in its mandate, the ICP has in practice attempted to negotiate so-called "agreed elements," which are forwarded to the General Assembly for possible inclusion in its annual resolution.[83] Indeed, quite often the suggestions made by the ICP have been incorporated into the subsequent General Assembly resolution on the law of the sea.[84] Yet in the 2009 review of the ICP, several states were critical of this practice, arguing that the ICP had not been created as a decision-making body and its informal and consultative nature did not lend itself to the negotiation of text.[85] There was also a divergence of views as to whether this role of the ICP was a duplication of the work of the General Assembly or whether it served to facilitate the negotiations that take place at the General Assembly by reducing the necessary time frame.[86]

[81] For example, submissions of states on the Informal Consultative Process, available at www.un.org/Depts/los/general_assembly/contributions64.htm <checked July 13, 2010>; see also Contribution of the G77 and China to the Tenth Session of the Informal Consultative Process, Document A/AC.259/19, May 14, 2009, available at www.un.org/Depts/los/consultative_process/consultative_process.htm <checked July 13, 2010>.
[82] See UNGA Resolution 54/33, at para. 3(d).
[83] UNGA Resolution 54/33, at para. 3(h).
[84] See UN Document A/64/66, Annex.
[85] *Report of the work of the United Nations Open-Ended Informal Consultative Process on Oceans and the Law of the Sea at its tenth meeting*, at para. 67.
[86] *Ibid.*, at paras. 68 and 70.

Given the emphasis on cooperation and coordination in the resolution establishing the ICP, it is suggested that attempting to agree on common approaches to new and emerging problems in the law of the sea is an inevitable task for the ICP. Often such problems will fall within the mandate of one or more international institutions and it is therefore highly desirable for those institutions to be involved in the development of any recommendation on the future action. Indeed, as noted above, this may facilitate compliance by these bodies with the recommendations emanating from the United Nations. It is of course always open to the General Assembly to reconsider any suggestions made by the ICP. However, it should be careful in making changes to the "agreed elements" proposed by the ICP as any alternative formula may not gain the support of the relevant international actors and they may therefore not be an effective in practice.

One of the biggest drawbacks of the ICP is the limited scope of topics that it can feasibly discuss within the short time frame in which it meets. The fact that the ICP can only consider a handful of topics each year means that many other issues that are dealt with in the negotiations on the annual General Assembly resolution on the law of the sea do not benefit from the multidisciplinary and integrative approach that is fostered by the ICP. The only way to do this would be to increase the time and resources available to the ICP so that it was able to consider more subjects. In theory, the ICP could act as a substitute for the negotiations within the General Assembly on all oceans issues. However, such a reform would weaken the control of states over the negotiation process and they are unlikely to accept this in practice.

3 Horizontal cooperation and coordination between international institutions

3.1 Introduction

It has been seen that there are obvious limits to the ability of vertical coordination to achieve coherence in international law-making activities. In recognition of this, institutions have also sought to pursue horizontal coordination between themselves. In other words, institutions have directly cooperated with one other and promoted closer ties when undertaking the development of new or existing instruments.

The constituent instruments of most international organizations contain a provision which calls on them to cooperate with other international organizations "in matters which may be of common concern"[87] or with other organizations which have "specialized responsibilities in related fields."[88] Many international institutions have sought to formalize their cooperation through the conclusion of relationship agreements. In common with the relationship agreements concluded between the United Nations and specialized agencies, these relationship agreements specify precisely what steps international institutions should take in order to cooperate with one another. The following section will consider a case study of the relationship between the International Maritime Organization and the International Labour Organization to demonstrate how this may work in practice.

3.2 Overlap between the activities of the International Maritime Organization and the International Labour Organization

As noted above, the ILO and the IMO are both specialized agencies of the United Nations with specialist mandates relating to working conditions and shipping respectively. While one might think that the activities of these institutions were fairly discrete, there is nevertheless a potential overlap in their activities.

A key area of overlap concerns the regulation of working standards at sea and the treatment of seafarers. On the one hand, this issue is regulated by the International Maritime Organization, whose mandate covers all issues relating to shipping.[89] However, working standards on ships is also a subject that falls within the scope of the International Labour Organization, which was set up in 1919 to promote improvements in conditions of labor around the world.[90] Since its inception, the ILO has been active in promoting the safe working standards for seafarers and fish-workers. In total the ILO has hosted ten special sessions devoted to maritime labor standards and it has adopted numerous instruments, binding and nonbinding, on this topic. Given the overlapping nature of their mandates, there is clearly the potential for the work of these two organizations to come into conflict. Not only do the organizations have different perspectives from which they approach

---

[87] IMO Convention, Article 60. See also Article 61.
[88] ILO Constitution, Article 12.   [89] See Chapter 6.
[90] ILO Constitution, preamble, available at www.ilo.org/ilolex/english/constq.htm <checked July 14, 2010>.

the issues within their mandate, in this particular case they also have different compositions.

The IMO is a traditional intergovernmental organization composed solely of states. Non-state actors only participate in the IMO as observers.[91] In contrast, the ILO is unique as an international organization in that it includes representatives of workers and employers on its main organs.[92] Article 3(1) of the ILO Constitution provides that the International Labour Conference, the plenary organ of the ILO, shall be composed of "four representatives of each of the Members, of whom two shall be Government delegates and the two others shall be delegates representing respectively the employers and the workpeople of each of the Members." This tripartism is at the heart of the work of the ILO and the nongovernmental representatives are involved in all ILO activities, including decision-making on the creation of new norms. In other words, the outcome of the decision-making process is not only influenced by states, but also by non-state actors. It follows that there may be differences between the way that the two organizations approach the same problem. How, then, in practice do they seek to minimize the risk of producing regulations or standards that may conflict?

3.3 Relationship Agreement between the International Maritime Organization and the International Labour Organization

The principal instrument regulating the interaction of these two institutions is the Relationship Agreement between the International Maritime Organization and the International Labour Organization.[93] This instrument gives positive application to the general obligations to consult found in their respective constituent instruments.[94] The Relationship Agreement provides in Article I that the two institutions will "act in close cooperation with each other and will consult each other regularly in regard to matters of common interest." This principle is given effect through a number of specific obligations.

First, the Agreement provides for reciprocal representation between the two organizations.[95] The ILO is entitled to attend meetings of the

---

[91] See Chapter 6.   [92] ILO Constitution, Article 3(1).
[93] Agreement between the International Labour Organization and the Intergovernmental Maritime Consultative Organization (IMO–ILO Relationship Agreement), available at www.ilo.org/public/english/bureau/leg/agreements/imo. htm <checked April 10, 2009>.
[94] IMO Convention, Articles 60–61; ILO Constitution, Article 12.
[95] IMO–ILO Relationship Agreement, Article II.

IMO Assembly, the IMO Council and the Maritime Safety Committee in relation to those agenda items in which the ILO has an interest. In turn, the IMO is invited to attend meetings of the International Labour Conference, the ILO Governing Body and the Joint Maritime Commission. The organizations attend as observers and they may participate in deliberations, albeit without a vote. The provision on reciprocal representation is flexible in that it allows further arrangements to be made in relation to other meetings that consider matters in which both institutions have an interest.

Secondly, the relationship agreement calls for the "fullest and promptest exchange of information and documents" between the two institutions.[96] This provision applies to all materials produced by the two organizations subject to a safeguard for confidential material. Furthermore, the two organizations agree to "combine their efforts to secure the greatest possible usefulness and utilization of statistical information" in order to avoid duplication in the collection of such information and thereby minimizing the burden placed upon states in providing such information.[97]

Perhaps one of the most interesting provisions in the relationship agreement between the IMO and the ILO relates to the creation of joint committees.[98] The International Labour Organization and the International Maritime Organization may refer to a joint committee any question of common interest if it appears desirable to them to do so.

A joint committee constituted under the relationship agreement between the IMO and the ILO is to be composed of representatives appointed by each organization.[99] It is important to note that the joint committee is not concerned with cooperation between secretariats. Rather, it is composed of representatives of member states of each organization. A joint committee therefore brings together a cross-section of the membership of the two institutions into a single forum. As well as representatives of the two organizations, representatives of the United Nations and other institutions may also be invited to participate in meetings of the joint committee.[100] This procedure has been used on a number of occasions to consider issues that are of common interest to both institutions. Two examples will be considered below in order to illustrate how the joint committees operate in practice.

---

[96] *Ibid.*, Article IV.   [97] *Ibid.*, Article VI.
[98] *Ibid.*, Article III.1.   [99] *Ibid.*, Article III.2.
[100] *Ibid.*, Article III.3.

3.4 Joint Working Group on Liability and Compensation Regarding Claims for Death, Personal Injury and Abandonment of Seafarers

A good example of the important role that joint committees can play in interinstitutional cooperation is the international response to the question of liability and compensation regarding claims for death, personal injury and abandonment of seafarers. This issue was first raised at a meeting of the IMO Legal Committee in April 1998. While the issue was one that fell within the mandate of the IMO, which has traditionally adopted instruments concerning financial liability arising from maritime activities, it was also clear that the issue was of interest to the ILO as the specialized agency concerned with the rights of workers.

The establishment of a joint IMO/ILO Ad Hoc Expert Working Group was approved by the ILO Governing Body in November 1998 and by the IMO Legal Committee in April 1999. The working group was to be composed of eight ILO participants (four seafarers and four shipowner representatives) and eight representatives of the IMO, although other delegations were able to attend meetings of the working group as observers.[101] The working group was mandated to "examine the issue of financial security for crew members and their dependants with regard to the payment of compensation in cases of death and personal injury and abandonment," taking into account the existing IMO and ILO instruments.[102] At its first meeting the working group confirmed that liability and compensation regarding claims for death, personal injury and abandonment of seafarers was a problem that required an international solution. Noting the complementary character of the mandates of the two organizations, the working group recommended to its parent institutions that "a joint IMO/ILO approach was the best way to examine the problems and to make appropriate recommendations to their respective parent bodies."[103] Following two further sessions, the working group adopted two resolutions and accompanying guidelines in 2001, the first on financial security in the case of abandonment of

---

[101] See Terms of Reference, Note by the IMO/ILO Secretariats, Document IMO/ILO/WGLCCS 1/5, at para. 4.

[102] See Terms of Reference, Note by the IMO/ILO Secretariats, Document IMO/ILO/WGLCCS 1/5, at para. 5.

[103] *Report of the Joint IMO/ILO Ad Hoc Expert Working Group on Liability and Compensation Regarding Claim for Death, Personal Injury and Abandonment of Seafarers*, Document IMO/ILO/WGLCCS 1/11, at para. 11.1.

seafarers and the second on liability and compensation for injury to and death of seafarers. These instruments were subsequently adopted by both the ILO Governing Body[104] and by the IMO Assembly in November 2001.[105] As the name of these instruments suggests, the Guidelines are not binding. Rather, their purpose is to assist states in identifying the crucial issues relating to liability and financial security when adopting national schemes on abandonment and contractual claims arising from the injury or death of seafarers.[106] Nevertheless, they provide an example of an international instrument that has been drafted through a cooperative process that takes into account the values and objectives of both international organizations with an interest in the subject matter.

The adoption of the Guidelines in 2001 was not the end of the cooperative process, however. Both organizations agreed that the joint working group should continue monitoring the implementation of the Guidelines and consider whether a longer-term solution was required.[107] Indeed, at a special maritime session of the International Labour Conference in 2006, it was agreed that "the way forward would be for the Joint Ad Hoc Working Group to develop a standard accompanied by guidelines, which could be included in the Maritime Labour Convention or another existing instrument, at a later date."[108] At its seventh session in February 2008, the working group agreed that a mandatory long-term solution to abandonment was necessary and it commenced negotiations on the content of such an instrument.[109]

Although some progress was made on the substance of a legally binding instrument, it was more difficult to reach agreement on what form the instrument should take. Some states were of the view that the text should be drafted as an amendment to the 2006 Maritime Labour

---

[104] See *Report of the Committee on Sectoral and Technical Meetings and Related Issues*, ILO Document 282/10, November 2001, at para. 72.

[105] *Guidelines on Financial Security in Case of Abandonment of Seafarers*, IMO Assembly Resolution A.930(22); *Guidelines on Shipowners' Responsibilities in Respect of Contractual Claims for Personal Injury to or Death of Seafarers*, IMO Assembly Resolution A.931(22).

[106] *Ibid.*, at para. 1.1.

[107] See *Report of the third session of the Joint IMO/ILO Ad Hoc Expert Working Group on Liability and Compensation Regarding Claims for Death, Personal Injury and Abandonment of Seafarers (30 April–4 May 2001)*, ILO Document GB.282/STM/5.

[108] *Resolution concerning the joint IMO/ILO Ad Hoc Expert Working Group on Liability and Compensation Regarding Claim for Death, Personal Injury and Abandonment of Seafarers.*

[109] *Report of the seventh session of the Joint IMO/ILO Ad Hoc Expert Working Group on Liability and Compensation Regarding Claim for Death, Personal Injury and Abandonment of Seafarers*, Document ILO/IMO/CDWG/2008/3, at para. 105.

Convention.[110] In contrast, others argued for the adoption of a new, self-standing instrument. Even then, there was disagreement whether a self-standing instrument should be adopted under the auspices of the IMO or the ILO.[111]

Ultimately, it was agreed that the instrument should take the form of an amendment to the 2006 Maritime Labour Convention. This means that the proposal must be adopted according to the procedure set out in that treaty. It was therefore anticipated by the working group that the proposal would be submitted to a special tripartite commission in accordance with Article XV of that Convention, once the Convention had entered into force.[112] In practice, however, the amendment has been adopted through a joint process, which has involved representatives of the IMO and the ILO, as well as regular input from the permanent organs of these institutions. The use of a joint committee in this context means that the proposed solution to the problem of abandonment has benefited from the combined expertise of the two organizations.[113] Moreover, the use of the joint committee prevented both institutions addressing the problem independently, thus avoiding a potential conflict of norms.

3.5 Joint Working Group on Ship Scrapping

The second example of the role that a joint committee can play in promoting cooperation and coordination between international organizations is the Joint Working Group on Ship Scrapping constituted in February 2005. What differentiates this working group from the previous example is the involvement of a third institution: the Conference of the Parties to the Basel Convention on the Control of Transboundary Movements of Hazardous Wastes and their Disposal. Article III.3 of the Relationship Agreement between the IMO and the ILO does allow a joint committee to invite other specialized agencies to be represented

---

[110] See e.g. Government of Norway, *Report of the Seventh Session of the Joint IMO/ILO Ad Hoc Expert Working Group on Liability and Compensation Regarding Claim for Death, Personal Injury and Abandonment of Seafarers*, at para. 33; Shipowners representative, *ibid.*, at para. 111.

[111] See e.g. Government of the Philippines, *ibid.*, at para. 32; cf. Government of the United States, *ibid.*, at para. 109.

[112] See *Report of the ninth session of the Joint IMO/ILO Ad Hoc Expert Working Group on Liability and Compensation regarding Claims for Death, Personal Injury and Abandonment of Seafarers (2–6 March 2009)*, IMO Document LEG/95/4/1, at para. 5.

[113] See the express comments to this end in the *Report of the eight session of the Joint IMO/ILO Ad Hoc Expert Working Group*, Document ILO/IMO/WGPS/8/2008/5, at para. 9.

at its meetings.[114] Despite the fact that the Conference of the Parties to the Basel Convention is not a specialized agency and it had not previously entered into any formal relationship agreement with either the IMO or the ILO, it was still able to participate in the joint committee. Thus, the joint committee on ship scrapping demonstrates the flexible nature of many cooperative arrangements.[115]

The Joint Working Group on Ship Scrapping was established by a decision of the fifty-first session of the IMO Marine Environment Protection Committee, the Seventh Conference of the Parties (COP) to the Basel Convention and the 291st session of the ILO Governing Body. It was constituted of delegates from each institution, namely five government representatives from the Basel COP, five government representatives from the IMO, five worker representatives nominated by the ILO and five employer representatives nominated by the ILO. As is standard practice with joint committees, it was also open to observers from other governments, intergovernmental organizations and NGOs.

The Joint Committee on Ship Scrapping also differs from the previous example in terms of the task with which it was allocated. Unlike the issue of liability and compensation regarding claims for death, personal injury and abandonment of seafarers where there was a legal void to be filled by the organizations concerned, the subject of ship scrapping was an issue that had previously been dealt with on a number of occasions by all three institutions. Thus there were three sets of instruments already covering the issue of ship scrapping. The first institution to specifically deal with this topic was the Conference of the Parties to the Basel Convention, which adopted Technical Guidelines for the Environmentally Sound Management of the Full and Partial Dismantling of Ships in December 2002.[116] At about the same time, the IMO had been working on Guidelines on Ship Recycling, which were adopted by the IMO Assembly in 2003 and subsequently amended in 2005.[117] Finally, Guidelines on Safety and Health in Shipbreaking

---

[114] Tripartite collaboration is not uncommon. For instance, in 2005 a joint committee was formed by the IMO, the ILO and the FAO in order to develop a Code of Safety for Fishermen and Fishing Vessels and Voluntary Guidelines for the Design, Construction and Equipment of Small Fishing Vessels; see IMO News, No. 1, 2008, at 10.

[115] On this point, see Schermers and Blokker, *International Institutional Law*, at para. 1706.

[116] Decision VI/24 of the Basel Convention COP.

[117] IMO Assembly Resolution A.962(23), later amended by IMO Assembly Resolution A.980(24).

were adopted by the ILO Governing Body in March 2004.[118] Each of the instruments approached the issue of ship scrapping from the particular perspective of the organization concerned. There were several concerns over this fragmented approach to the topic. First, there was a question of whether all aspects of ship scrapping were dealt with or whether there were gaps in the regulatory framework. Secondly, there was a question whether the approaches of the different organizations were compatible. Indeed, it was argued by the Basel Action Network and Greenpeace International in a submission to the first meeting of the Working Group on Ship Scrapping that the IMO Guidelines were in conflict with the requirements of the Basel Convention and the principles and guidelines subsequently developed pursuant to that treaty.[119]

It was the fragmentation of international law on this particular topic that was the concern of the Joint Working Group on Ship Scrapping. The mandate of the Joint Working Group was to undertake a comparative analysis of the instruments and work programs of the three organizations with the aim of identifying any overlaps, ambiguities or conflicts between them and to make appropriate recommendations to tackle any problems identified. This task was concluded at the second session of the working group in December 2005 when the working group concluded that there were "no significant conflicts between the three sets of guidelines and cross references are made with frequency between the guidelines."[120] Nevertheless, the Joint Working Group did note that there were some significant differences between the relevant instruments[121] and it was also suggested that terminology and concepts relating to certain issues could be harmonized to make the instruments more coherent.[122]

Another important outcome of the Joint Working Group was the endorsement of the plans of the secretariats of the three institutions to collaborate on joint technical assistance programs. In pursuit

---

[118] 289th Session of the ILO Governing Body.

[119] See *Report of the first session of the Joint Working Group on Ship Scrapping*, Document ILO/IMO/BC WG 1/8, at para. 3.8. The two NGOs argued there were three main areas where the instruments were inconsistent: prior-decontamination, ships as waste, and the obligations of exporting states; see *The IMO Guidelines on ship recycling (Annotated)*, Submitted by Greenpeace International and the Basel Action Network (BAN), Document ILO/IMO/BC WG1/7/3, February 7, 2005, at para. 1.10.

[120] *Report of the second session of the Joint Working Group on Ship Scrapping*, Document ILO/IMO/BC WG 2/11, Annex 2, at para. 1.

[121] *Ibid.*, Annex 2, at paras. 31, 55, 79, 83.

[122] *Ibid.*, Annex 2, at paras. 28, 35, 45, 74.

thereof, the three secretariats proposed the development of a Global Programme for Sustainable Ship Recycling.[123] Such initiatives are not only important to ensure that a coherent approach is taken towards technical assistance, but they are also vital if any of the instruments adopted by the three institutions are going to be effective.

Independently of the Joint Working Group, the three institutions continued to cooperate on the issue of ship recycling throughout the process of drafting a new treaty under the auspices of the IMO. Although the Joint Working Group was not directly involved in the negotiation of a new treaty, it undoubtedly had some influence on the negotiations that were already underway in the IMO towards a Convention on Ship Recycling.[124] Indeed, members of the Joint Working Group were expressly asked to comment on an early draft of a possible treaty prepared by Norway[125] and the Joint Working Group made certain recommendations on aspects which should be included in the treaty. In addition, representatives of the ILO and the Basel Convention secretariat (UNEP) attended the negotiations both in the Marine Environment Protection Committee and at the Hong Kong diplomatic conference that was held in May 2009.[126] The results of this cooperation can be seen in the final text of the Convention for the Safe and Environmentally Sound Recycling of Ships, which integrates many of the principles found in the instruments prepared by the three institutions. The preamble to the Convention expressly notes the role of the ILO and the Basel Convention in relation to ship recycling and it cites the three instruments that had already been adopted on this topic. Article 15 of the Convention provides that it shall not prejudice the rights and obligations of parties under other international agreements, which would include the Basel Convention. More specifically, the Annex to the Convention, which contains the regulations applicable to ships owners and the operators of recycling facilities, says that:

---

[123] *Global Programme for Sustainable Ship Recycling*, Document ILO/IMO/BC WG 3/3/1.
[124] IMO Assembly Resolution A.981(24) called on the Marine Environment Protection Committee to develop a new legally binding instrument on ship recycling which should regulate ship recycling, including ship construction, operation and preparation, so as to facilitate safe and environmentally sound recycling, the operation of ship recycling facilities in a safe and environmentally sound manner and the establishment of an appropriate enforcement mechanism.
[125] *Report of the Second Session of the Joint Working Group on Ship Scrapping*, at paras. 4.10–4.12.
[126] See the *Final Act of the International Conference on the Safe and Environmentally Sound Recycling of Ships*, Document SR/CONF/46, May 19, 2009, at para. 5.

Parties shall take measures to implement the requirements of the regulations of this Annex taking into account relevant and applicable international rules and standards, recommendations and guidance developed by the International Labour Organization and the relevant and applicable technical standards, recommendations and guidance developed under the Basel Convention.[127]

This provision is an illustration of the awareness of states for the need to avoid conflict when interpreting and applying instruments dealing with the same subject matter.

Nor will the adoption of the 2009 Convention on Ship Recycling be the end of the cooperation between the three institutions on this issue. It was pointed out at the third meeting of the Joint Working Group, which was convened in October 2008 following the adoption of a draft Convention on Ship Recycling, that there was still a need to coordinate the activity of the organizations after the entry into force of the Convention as the standards and guidelines adopted by the Basel COP and the ILO would remain applicable.[128] Indeed, the two organizations will continue to be involved in the process of drafting guidelines under the new Convention as observers at the IMO.[129] The Convention itself makes express provision for the involvement of other institutions in the adoption of amendments to the appendices that contain lists of hazardous substances. Regulation 6(2) provides that when the IMO receives a proposed amendment, it shall bring the proposal to the attention of the United Nations and its specialized agencies, intergovernmental organizations having agreements with the IMO and NGOs in consultative status with the IMO.[130] Any proposal must also, prior to adoption by the IMO, be considered by a technical group, which may include, inter alia, representatives of the United Nations and its specialized agencies and other intergovernmental organizations with expertise in the risks posed by such substances to the environment or to human life and health.[131] The ILO and the Basel Convention Secretariat are

---

[127] Ship Recycling Convention, Annex, Regulation 3.
[128] *Report of the third session of the Joint Working Group on Ship Scrapping*, Document ILO/IMO/BC WG 3/6, at para. 117.
[129] See "ILO welcomes new regulations on ship breaking as crisis boosts the industry," Press Release, May 29, 2009.
[130] Technically, the Conference of the Parties to the Basel Convention does not fall into any of these categories, but it is likely that this institution would be consulted on any proposed amendment given its strong interest in this area of regulation.
[131] Ship Recycling Convention, Annex, Regulation 7(1). Note, however, that only representatives of the Parties may participate in formulating any recommendations to the committee; see regulation 7(3).

clearly appropriate institutions to participate in these mechanisms. In this way, even though the IMO is clearly the lead institution in relation to the subject matter of the Convention, provision is made for the involvement of other international institutions in its continuing implementation.

The purpose of this case study has been to demonstrate the range and flexibility of activities that international institutions can undertake when cooperating with one another. These activities can be highly effective in ensuring the coherent development of international law. If they are to be successful, however, they first require institutions to recognize that there is an overlap and the institutions must be willing to engage in cooperative endeavors. There is no mechanism in which to force international institutions into cooperating with one another. Inevitably, there will be occasions where these conditions will not be met. In this situation, difficult questions arise about how to manage conflict between international rules originating in different regimes.

4 Solving conflicts in the applicable law

While there are various ways in which international institutions can seek to harmonize their work programs, success is not guaranteed. It is still the case that new rules and standards may be developed in separate regimes and there may ultimately be a conflict between the resulting rules. The question that arises is, how do treaties produced in different regimes interact? If there is a conflict in the applicable law, which instrument takes priority?

From the outset, it must be recognized that although instruments may be developed in different organizations, they all belong to a single system of international law.[132] It follows that "no treaty, however special its subject-matter or limited the number of parties, applies in a normative vacuum but refers back to a number of general, often unwritten principles of customary international law concerning its entry into force, and its interpretation and application."[133] It is to these

[132] J. Pauwelyn, *Conflict of Norms in Public International Law* (Cambridge University Press, 2003) at 37; *Fragmentation of international law: difficulties arising from the diversification and expansion of international law*, at para. 33. Cf. G. Hafner, "Risks ensuing from the fragmentation of international law," in *International Law Commission, Report on the work of its fifty-second session (1 May-9 June and 10 July-18 August 2000), Official Records of the General Assembly, Fifty-fifth session, Supplement No. 10* (A/55/10), annex.
[133] See M. Koskenniemi, "Fragmentation of international law: the function and scope of the lex specialis rule and the question of self-contained regimes," paper

rules of international law that we must look in order to deduce how different instruments interact.

Before considering how to solve treaty conflicts, it is first necessary to say what we mean by this term. Various authors have put forward different definitions of conflict. For example, Jenks says that "a conflict in the strict sense of direct incompatibility arises only where a party to the two treaties cannot simultaneously comply with its obligations under both treaties."[134] As Pauwelyn also points out, a conflict may also emerge if an obligation in one treaty prevents a state from exercising a right contained in another treaty, and he concludes that "two norms are in a relationship of conflict if one constitutes, has led to, or may lead to, a breach of the other."[135] On the other hand, the concept of conflict is arguably not broad enough to encapsulate "a situation where two rules or principles suggest different ways of dealing with a problem"[136] and it is likely that such situations will be able to be resolved through interpretation rather than through the application of conflict rules.[137]

Normative conflict is one of the most difficult issues faced by an international lawyer. Legal certainty and the ability to identify which rule applies in a specific situation is a value that is highly desirable in any legal system. Yet international law, as a predominantly horizontal legal system, has no hierarchy in the sources of law.[138] Indeed, it will be seen that although some guidance can be found in the law of treaties,

prepared for the International Law Commission, 2004, at 7; paper available at untreaty.un.org/ilc/sessions/55/fragmentation_outline.pdf <checked July 14, 2010>.

[134] Jenks, "The conflict of law-making treaties," at 426.
[135] Pauwelyn, *Conflict of Norms in Public International Law*, at 175.
[136] *Fragmentation of international law: difficulties arising from the diversification and expansion of international law*, at para. 25.
[137] As several authors have noted there is a general presumption against conflict in international law and "when faced with two possible interpretations, one of which harmonizes the meaning of the two norms in question, the meaning that allows for harmonization of the two norms – and hence avoids conflict – ought to be preferred"; Pauwelyn, *Conflict of Norms in Public International Law*, at 230–41. The principle of systemic integration is reflected in Article 31(3)(c) of the Vienna Convention on the Law of Treaties, which provides that in the process of treaty interpretation, "there shall be taken into account, together with the context, ... any relevant rules of international law applicable in the relations between the parties." See C. McLachlan, "The principle of systemic integration and Article 31(3)(c) of the Vienna Convention on the Law of Treaties" (2005) 54 *Int'l & Comp. L. Q.* 279; D. French, "Treaty interpretation and the incorporation of extraneous legal rules" (2006) 55 *Int'l & Comp. L. Q.* 281.
[138] See M. Akehurst, "The hierarchy of the sources of international law" (1974–75) *Brit. Ybk Int'l L.* 273, at 273.

which contains basic priority rules to determine which treaty is applicable in the case of a particular conflict, these rules fail to provide much predictability as to the likely outcome of a treaty conflict.[139]

Today the most prominent conflict rule is Article 30 of the 1969 Vienna Convention on the Law of Treaties. It is important to note that Article 30 does not address the validity of conflicting treaties and there is no suggestion that a treaty can invalidate another treaty with which it conflicts.[140] Rather, priority rules are intended to determine which of the competing provisions should prevail in the legal relations between two states. In the words of one commentator, "the purpose of Article 30 is to determine, in the event of competing treaties, which one governs the mutual relationship between the contracting parties."[141]

It is perfectly possible that a treaty may specify in its own provisions its relationship with other treaties on a similar subject matter. This is recognized by Article 30(2) of the Vienna Convention, which allows the drafters of a treaty some leeway to specify its relationship with other treaties if they wish to confirm the priority of another treaty, whether it is earlier or later. To this end, the general conflict rules found in Article 30 are merely intended to be residual in character and apply in the absence of any specific conflict rules.[142] The inclusion of specific conflict rules may assist in identifying the applicable law in a particular situation. An example is Article 311(1) of the Law of the Sea Convention, which states that "this Convention shall prevail, as between States Parties, over the Geneva Conventions on the Law of the Sea of 29 April 1958." This leaves no doubt that the 1982 Convention takes priority over the earlier treaties on the law of the sea, although

---

[139] C. J. Borgen, "Resolving treaty conflicts" (2005) 37 *George Washington Int'l L. Rev.* 573, at 619.

[140] An exception is the position of peremptory norms; see Vienna Convention on the Law of Treaties, Articles 53 and 64.

[141] A. Sadat-Akhavi, *Methods of Resolving Conflicts between Treaties* (Martinus Nijhoff Publishers, 2003) at 72.

[142] I. Sinclair, *The Vienna Convention on the Law of Treaties* (Manchester University Press, 1984) at 97. See also A. Aust, *Modern Treaty Law and Practice* (2nd edn., Cambridge University Press, 2007) at 227; Pauwelyn, *Conflicts of Norms in Public International Law*, at 263; A. E. Boyle and C. Chinkin, *The Making of International Law* (Oxford University Press, 2007) at 252. The residual character of the rules of priority in Article 30 has most recently been supported by the International Law Commission Study Group on the Fragmentation of International Law: "ultimately, it was left for the will of States to establish priority among successive treaties in accordance with their interests"; *Fragmentation of international law: difficulties arising from the diversification and expansion of international law*, at para. 38.

these earlier treaties presumably remain in force for those contracting parties who do not become a party to the 1982 Convention.[143] In contrast, a specific conflict clause in a treaty may confer priority on other treaties concluded before or after that treaty. An example is Article 22 of the Convention on Biological Diversity, which provides that "the provisions of the Convention shall not affect the rights and obligations of any Contracting Party deriving from existing international agreement, except where the exercise of those rights and obligations would cause a serious damage or threat to biological diversity." This provision suggests that the previous treaties continue to govern the activities of states regardless of the conclusion of the Convention on Biological Diversity, unless the application of the prior treaty is likely to lead to serious damage or threat to biological diversity. In such a case, "the Convention trumps the other agreement."[144]

It has been suggested by several commentators that states should consider including such provisions in treaties to try to clarify their interaction with other instruments, thus avoiding having to rely on the more general rules of conflict considered below. Thus, Borgen suggests that "thoughtful drafting of treaty provisions is the most effective way to avoid or resolve potential treaty conflicts"[145] and he explicitly calls for the insertion of clauses to "enumerate related prior treaties and explicitly state that the current treaty is hierarchically superior or inferior to each prior treaty."[146] However, it is an arduous task to predict every possible treaty conflict and it is likely that some potential conflicts may not be foreseen. In such situations, recourse must still be had to the general conflict rules in Article 30.

The central priority rule in Article 30 is the *lex posterior* principle.[147] According to this principle, the later treaty should prevail over the earlier treaty. It should again be stressed that the conclusion of a later conflicting treaty does not affect the validity of the prior treaty, which

---

[143] It is possible that the 1958 treaties may also be displaced in part by customary international law; see *Delimitation of the Maritime Boundary in the Gulf of Maine Area* (1984) ICJ Reports 246 at para. 124; see also *United Kingdom–French Continental Shelf Case* (1977) 54 International Law Reports at 47.

[144] L. Glowka *et al.*, *A Guide to the Convention on Biological Diversity* (IUCN – The World Conservation Union, 1996) at 109.

[145] Borgen, "Resolving treaty conflicts," at 584.

[146] *Ibid.*, at 638. See also Jenks, "The conflict of law-making treaties," at 452.

[147] International Law Commission, "Draft articles on the law of treaties: report of the Commission to the General Assembly" (1966 II) *Ybk Int'l L. Commission* at 217.

continues to be in force in accordance with the principle of *pacta sund servanda*.[148]

The principle of *lex posterior* is firmly based in a contractual notion of treaties and it reflects the idea that states can change their minds about the content of the law and that the later expression of this intent should prevail.[149] However, there are several drawbacks with the application of this general principle to treaties.

A fundamental problem with the application of the *lex posterior* principle is determining which treaty is later in time.[150] Some authors argue that the date of adoption is most pertinent.[151] Conceptually this is the simplest approach to resolving conflicts, as there will be a single relevant date for all states. However, it has also been argued that the date of entry into force is more important for the purposes of determining the later treaty.[152] This attaches more importance to the intention of individual states when they decide to become a party, but it has the disadvantage that the relevant time will differ from state to state. Pauwelyn criticizes the process of dating treaties altogether, arguing that "the fiction of later legislative intent overruling earlier legislative intent loses its attraction as soon as the same context – same constellation changes."[153] Indeed, the rarity of such constellations casts doubt on reliance on the later intention of the parties. This view would appear to be supported by the International Law Commission in its recent report on the fragmentation of international law, where it says that "the straightforward priority of one treaty over another ... cannot be reasonably assumed on a merely chronological basis" and it has called for "a more nuanced approach" to resolving treaty conflicts.[154]

---

[148] An exception is the position of peremptory norms; see Vienna Convention on the Law of Treaties, Articles 53 and 64.

[149] International Law Commission, "Draft articles on the law of treaties: report of the Commission to the General Assembly," at 217.

[150] See E. W. Vierdag, "The time of the conclusion of a multilateral treaty: Article 30 of the Vienna Convention on the Law of Treaties and Related Provisions" (1988) *British Ybk Int'l L.* 75.

[151] I. Sinclair, *The Vienna Convention on the Law of Treaties* (Manchester University Press, 1984) at 98; Aust, *Modern Treaty Law and Practice*, at 229; Borgen, "Resolving treaty conflicts," at 602.

[152] W. Czaplinski and G. Danilenko, "Conflicts of norms in international law" (1990) *Netherlands Ybk Int'l L.* 1, at 19.

[153] Pauwelyn, *Conflict of Norms in Public International Law*, at 368–9.

[154] *Fragmentation of international law: difficulties arising from the diversification and expansion of international law*, at para. 272, and paras. 225–6. See also Pauwelyn, *Conflict of Norms in Public International Law*, at 370; Boyle and Chinkin, *The Making of International Law*, at 248.

The report of the Commission continues: "it may often be more useful to refer directly to the will of the parties than to the lex posterior principle for which, as also noted above, it may simply give expression."[155] How one identifies the will of the parties, however, is not clear. In many cases conflicts will not necessarily have been foreseen, so it is unlikely to be any relevant indication of how a conflict should be resolved in the preparatory materials. Alternatively, states negotiating a treaty may differ on what its relationship with other treaties should be.

A conflict rule that has been suggested as an alternative to the *lex posterior* principle is the *lex specialis* principle, according to which the more specific treaty provision should apply. Indeed it has been argued that the *lex specialis* principle is inherent in Article 30, which in its title refers to the application of "successive treaties relating to the same subject-matter." Some have argued that this should be construed strictly so that Article 30 only applies to those treaties that impinge directly on another treaty.[156] This approach limits the scope of Article 30, so that "[it] is not applicable to the thornier issues of what happens when treaties have different foci but overlapping issue areas."[157] It is suggested that this approach is perhaps too narrow and treaties should be considered as having the same subject matter if they are indeed capable of coming into conflict or being incompatible. Pauwelyn puts it succinctly when he says, "if there is a genuine conflict between two treaty norms, the two treaty norms must necessarily deal with the same subject matter."[158]

In any case, taking the *lex specialis* principle as an alternative conflict rule comes with its own difficulties.[159] The concept of speciality is almost as ambiguous as the concept of a later treaty. Several indicators have been suggested, such as the subject matter and the number of contracting parties,[160] although none are completely satisfactory. In the words of one commentator, "at times, specificity is in the eye of

---

[155] *Fragmentation of international law: difficulties arising from the diversification and expansion of international law*, at para. 243. See also para. 252.

[156] Aust, *Modern Treaty Law and Practice*, at 229.

[157] Borgen, "Resolving treaty conflicts," at 603.

[158] Pauwelyn, *Conflict of Norms in Public International Law*, at 364. See also *Fragmentation of international law: difficulties arising from the diversification and expansion of international law*, at paras. 21–2.

[159] P. Reuter, *Introduction au Droit des Traites* (Kegan Paul International, 1995) at 130. See also *Fragmentation of international law: difficulties arising from the diversification and expansion of international law*, at para. 64, and footnote 74.

[160] Pauwelyn, *Conflict of Norms in Public International Law*, at 389.

the beholder."[161] Ultimately the principle of *lex specialis* simply acts as another Latin label for the intention of the parties, without necessarily shedding much light on how to identify such an intention.

Further problems arise as to how these two conflict rules may relate to one another. Sometimes the two principles will lead to the same conclusion. This was the case in the *Mavromattis Palestine Concessions Case* where the Permanent Court of International Justice considered the relationship between the Mandate for Palestine conferred on the United Kingdom in 1922 and Protocol XII to the 1923 Lausanne Peace Treaty. The Court concluded that "in cases of doubt, the Protocol, being a special and more recent agreement, should prevail."[162] Yet, in other situations, the principles may suggest contradictory outcomes, in which case the fiction of intention is fully revealed. The International Law Commission has concluded that "the question boils down to an assessment of which aspect – 'speciality' or 'temporality' – seems more important in this connection."[163] What is more important would appear to depend on the particular context of a conflict. While providing flexibility in the priority rules, this conclusion also leads to a lack of certainty in the way in which normative conflict will be solved.

It is clear from this analysis that problems of conflicts of treaties cannot be easily solved. As the International Law Commission itself admitted, there is no single set of rules that govern how to deal with conflicts of international law.[164] In the view of the Commission:

interpretative maxims and conflict-solution techniques such as the lex specialis, lex posterior or lex superior ... enable seeing a systemic relationship between two or more rules, and may thus justify a particular choice of the applicable standards, and a particular conclusion. They do not do this mechanically, however, but rather as "guidelines," suggesting a pertinent relationship between the relevant rules in view of the need for consistency of the conclusion with the perceived purposes or functions of the legal system as a whole.[165]

This is a highly unsatisfactory conclusion from the perspective of legal certainty, although perhaps inevitable in a legal system that lacks any central institutional structures. It may be, however, that law cannot

---

[161] Borgen, "Resolving treaty conflicts," at 613.
[162] *The Mavromattis Palestine Concessions Case* (1924) PCIJ Reports, Series A, No. 2, at 31.
[163] *Fragmentation of international law: difficulties arising from the diversification and expansion of international law*, at para. 233.
[164] *Ibid.*, at para. 36.   [165] *Ibid.*

provide a solution to questions of interactions between different legal instruments and legal regimes. In reality, these are questions of policy and, as such, they can only be tackled by political fora. This truth about the nature of treaty conflict would appear to be reflected in the conclusion of the International Law Commission on the subject when it says, "conflicts between specialized regimes may be overcome by law, even [if] the law may not go much further than require a willingness to listen to others, take their points of view into account and to find a reasoned resolution at the end."[166] This may be why states have been reluctant to send questions concerning conflicts of treaties to international court or tribunals.

It may be that, at the end of the day, solutions to complex treaty conflicts may have to be remitted to the international institutions that originally negotiated them. In this context, the cooperative mechanisms discussed earlier in this chapter take on an even more important character, as they are not only the way in which treaty conflicts can be avoided at the time of negotiation, but they also become a potential means through which treaty conflicts can be resolved once they have arisen. For example, the mechanism of a joint committee could be used by international institutions that have promulgated the two conflicting treaties in order to decide what the relationship between them is. Such clarification can take two forms. First, it may simply confirm that one treaty takes priority over the other. However, the situation may not always be so simple. In cases of complex treaty interaction, it is likely that states may want both treaties to apply simultaneously and a solution of declaring the priority of one treaty over the other is too simplistic. What may be necessary is a process of renegotiation in order to ensure the compatibility of two treaties. It is only in this way that the objectives and values of both treaty regimes can be safeguarded.

5 Conclusion

The decentralized nature of the international legal system means that law-making takes place in a variety of institutional fora. This chapter has analyzed the consequences of this eclectic approach to law-making and it has considered what mechanisms are available to alleviate the perceived problems that might arise as a result of fragmentation. The conclusion is that there are limits to the legal responses to the issue.

---

[166] *Ibid.*, at para. 487.

There is no institutional hierarchy between different organizations and so no institution can claim to have an exclusive role in any particular area of regulation. Moreover, when a conflict of norms does arise, international law cannot provide a clear solution. Whereas various legal principles, such as *lex posterior* and *lex specialis*, can be invoked, there is little clarity or certainty in their application to particular cases of conflict.

One should perhaps not be too surprised about this conclusion. It is a direct outcome of the nature of international law based upon the fundamental principle of state sovereignty. Where law cannot provide answers, one must instead look to political cooperation to try to bridge the gap between different functional regimes.

The need for and importance of institutional cooperation and coordination in ocean affairs has been identified at the international level by a variety of actors, including the Commission on Sustainable Development and the UN General Assembly. It could even be said that this need is underpinned by a legal duty for states and international institutions to cooperate. Cooperation underpins much of the law of the sea and the duty for international institutions to cooperate with one another can often be found in their constituent instruments. Yet, as recognized by the Permanent Court of International Justice in its Advisory Opinion on Railway Traffic between Lithuania and Poland, "an obligation to negotiate does not imply an obligation to reach an agreement."[167] Rather, all the law can say is that negotiation or cooperation must be "meaningful."[168] In other words, this is an obligation of conduct, rather than of result. In the context of interinstitutional cooperation, this may mean an exchange of views between the two institutions, or at least an offer to exchange views. It may also require institutions to share information in relation to their planned lawmaking activities.

There is no single way in which the duty to cooperate can be fulfilled. What the law can usefully provide, however, is procedures and

---

[167] *Advisory Opinion on Railway Traffic between Lithuania and Poland* (1931) PCIJ Rep., Series A/B, No. 42, 108, at 116.

[168] *North Sea Continental Shelf Cases* (1969) ICJ Reports 3, at para. 85. An interesting analysis of the duty to negotiate in good faith can be found in the *Arbitration between Guyana and Suriname, Award of 17 September 2009*, at paras. 461 onwards, available at www.pca-cpa.org/upload/files/Guyana-Suriname%20Award.pdf <checked June 1, 2010>. See also *Case Concerning Pulp Mills on the River Uruguay* (2010) ICJ Reports at para. 147.

mechanisms through which interinstitutional cooperation can take place. In this context, the relationship agreement between the IMO and the ILO has been put forward as a good model for the way in which institutions can work together to avoid normative conflict in the first place, as well as to reconcile potentially conflicting instruments if that is necessary. Specifying what procedures must be followed is a helpful way to give meaning to the otherwise ambiguous duty of cooperation. While law can assist in this way, it is also important to note the ongoing contact between institutions and the development of mutual trust and respect is also important. Without this vital ingredient of political will, no attempts to improve cooperation and coordination will be successful. As noted by Mosoti in a different context, "none of these instruments of collaboration can achieve their purpose if there is no willingness to collaborate on the part of the institutions themselves."[169]

---

[169] V. Mosoti, "Institutional cooperation and norm creation in international organizations," in T. Cottier, J. Pauwelyn and E. Bürgi Bonanomi (eds.), *Human Rights and International Trade* (Oxford University Press, 2005) at 172.

9   Conclusion

1 Developing the law of the sea regime through institutions

The law of the sea is a broad area of international law that covers topics
as varied as navigation, environmental protection, fishing, deep seabed mining and scientific research, among others. Today, it is generally accepted that the 1982 United Nations Convention on the Law of
the Sea is a "constitution for the oceans,"[1] providing "the legal framework within which all activities in the oceans and seas must be carried
out."[2] The Convention covers almost all conceivable ocean activities.
Yet the law of the sea has not stood still since the conclusion of the
1982 Convention. In some cases the Convention only provides a broad
framework and states have had to develop detailed rules and standards
to regulate a particular activity. In other cases the Convention regime
has had to be adapted in order to take into account technological and
scientific developments in relation to the oceans, as well as changes
in the political values of the international community. Many of the
developments in the law of the sea regime have taken place through
international institutions.

It is the law-making activities of a variety of international institutions that has been the focus of this study. The purpose of this book has
been to analyze which institutions have been involved in the ongoing
development of the law of the sea and what role they have played. It
is hoped that this case study of international law-making can contribute to improving the way we understand the role of international

---

[1] "A constitution for the oceans," Remarks by Tommy T. B. Koh, of Singapore, President
of the Third United Nations Conference on the Law of the Sea, available at www.
un.org/depts/los/convention_agreements/texts/koh_english.pdf <checked August 10,
2010>.
[2] *Oceans and the law of the sea*, UNGA Resolution 64/71, December 4, 2009, preamble.

institutions in the development of the international legal order by identifying some of the factors that can assist them in fulfilling this function, as well as highlighting some of the potential problems that can arise. This conclusion will provide an overview of the findings of the study and it will attempt to identify some of the key lessons to be learned.

In the absence of an international legislative process, a universal legal order of the oceans can only come about if it is supported by all states. The principal value of international institutions in this context is that they can provide a venue in which all relevant actors can discuss legal and policy developments in an attempt to reach a solution that is generally acceptable. In an area of international law such as the law of the sea, which affects the interests of all states, such a process is indispensible.

The ways in which institutions can facilitate the creation of universal international law were outlined in Chapter 1. It was seen that international institutions are not limited to validating existing trends of individual state practice or proposing possible rules for future adoption by individual states. In many cases, international institutions have actively set out to modify existing international law and it is the deliberations within institutions that have led to the emergence of a new legal regime.

The negotiation of the Law of the Sea Convention itself is a key illustration of this law-making process in operation. From the outset, the goal of UNCLOS III was the creation of a legal regime that was as acceptable to as many states as possible. Although the Convention has not been formally accepted by all states, it was argued in Chapter 2 that many of the rules and principles in the Convention are binding on all states as a matter of customary international law. Thus it has largely succeeded in creating a universal legal order of the oceans applicable to all maritime activities. It was suggested that this transformation of many of the Convention rules into universal law can be attributed largely to the way in which they were negotiated.

Many of the international institutions considered in this book have sought to further develop the law of the sea regime found in the Convention, while also trying to preserve its integrity. If international institutions are to successfully contribute to the development of international law in this way, however, there are several conditions that must be met. The following sections will consider some of the most important factors that can influence the creation of universal law.

2 Participation and inclusivity in law-making

If they are to facilitate the creation of universal international law, it is vital that international institutions are able to bring together all of the relevant actors in a single forum. It is arguably because of its broad membership that the United Nations has been at the forefront of developments in the law of the sea over the past half-century. It is one of the few international organizations with a quasi-universal membership and a broad mandate that can consider all aspects of the law of the sea. It is for this reason that discussions and debates within UN organs and conferences have on many occasions been able to foster sufficient state practice and *opinio juris* to crystallize and generate customary international law applicable to all states. Not only was the UN the forum which convened UNCLOS III, it has also been the catalyst for other major developments in the law of the sea since the conclusion of the Law of the Sea Convention, including the negotiation of the Part XI Agreement and the Fish Stocks Agreement.

In contrast, a lack of widespread participation in a particular institution may mean that its law-making potential is reduced. This is illustrated by the limited role played by the Meeting of the States Parties in developing the law of the sea. The Meeting of the States Parties brings together more than 150 states in a forum that is solely concerned with law of the sea matters. However, the absence of some important states as full participants in this forum has meant that its contribution to developing the law of the sea regime has been restricted to fulfilling those limited functions that are expressly conferred on it by the Convention.[3] Most of these functions concern the implementation of provisions and procedures that are only relevant to the States Parties. States have resisted using the Meeting of the States Parties as a forum for the discussion of general developments in the law of the sea regime. That may of course change if the Convention achieves its target of universal participation. Until that time, states are likely to continue to want substantive issues concerning the law of the sea to be discussed in other fora where all states can be represented on an equal basis.

This explains why the UN General Assembly has continued to play a key role in the development of the law of the sea since the conclusion of the Convention. Adoption of the annual General Assembly resolution on oceans and law of the sea offers an opportunity for all states to discuss the most important developments in this area of law. The

---

[3] See Chapter 3.

2004 decision of the General Assembly to establish an Ad Hoc Open-ended Informal Working Group to examine the legal issues involved in the protection of biodiversity in areas beyond national jurisdiction would seem to confirm that states consider the United Nations to be the most appropriate forum in which the development of the law of the sea regime should be discussed.[4] Although this topic already falls within the mandates of a number of other international organizations and treaty bodies, it was argued that a sectoral approach to this issue was inadequate.[5] To this end, at the first meeting of the Working Group it was noted by several delegates that "the General Assembly was gen-erally considered to be the appropriate forum for addressing marine biological diversity beyond areas of national jurisdiction, owing to its role as the global forum with competence to deal comprehensively with complex, multidisciplinary issues."[6] Not only was the General Assembly inclusive in its membership, it also had a broad mandate which covered all aspects of the problem.

While composition can be a key factor in determining which institu-tions are most appropriate for developing international law, it does not mean that those institutions which lack broad membership are unim-portant and they can be safely ignored. Treves has pointed out that the Meeting of the States Parties can potentially act as "a forum that can be used in order to exercise pressure on non-parties, in which action can be undertaken that might create political difficulty or embarrass-ment for such non-parties, that might make them regret not being in a position to orient, or hamper, such action."[7] Thus, even those states that have not become a party to the Law of the Sea Convention have found it necessary to participate as observers in the institutions cre-ated by the Convention in order to ensure that their interests are pro-tected. This is illustrated by the fact that the United States has been a vocal observer in both the Meeting of the States Parties, as well as the International Seabed Authority. The United States has also made

---

[4] *Oceans and the law of the sea*, UNGA Resolution 59/24, November 17, 2004, at para. 73.

[5] See generally L. De La Fayette, "A new regime for the conservation and sustainable use of marine biodiversity and genetic resources beyond the limits of national jurisdiction" (2009) 24 *Int'l J. Marine & Coastal L.* 221.

[6] *Report of the Ad Hoc Open-Ended Informal Working Group to study issues relating to the conservation and sustainable use of marine biological diversity beyond areas of national jurisdiction*, Document A/61/65, March 20, 2006, at para. 7.

[7] T. Treves, "The General Assembly and the Meeting of States Parties in the implementation of the LOS Convention," in A. Oude Elferink (ed.), *Stability and Change in the Law of the Sea: The Role of the LOS Convention* (Martinus Nijhoff Publishers, 2005) at 62.

regular observations and comments on the submissions of other states to the Commission on the Outer Limits of the Continental Shelf. These activities can be interpreted as recognition by a powerful state that its sovereign interests may still be affected by a regime to which it is not a full participant.[8]

It is also clear from this study that it is not only states that are involved in the law-making process. Intergovernmental organizations and NGOs are also prominent actors in their own right in international affairs.

The decision of the General Assembly to establish the Informal Consultative Process testifies to the importance of inclusivity and transparency in modern international law-making. The Informal Consultative Process opens up discussions on key issues concerning ocean affairs to a broader range of actors than would otherwise be involved in discussions at the General Assembly. The General Assembly resolution establishing the Informal Consultative Process recognizes both "the important role that international organizations have in relation to ocean affairs and in promoting sustainable development of the oceans and seas and their resources," as well as "the significant contribution that major [social] groups, as identified in Agenda 21,[9] can make to this goal."[10] A key feature of the process is the involvement of independent experts in discussion panels that are designed to inform the debate on oceans policy.[11] A variety of intergovernmental organizations

---

[8] In this vein, Senator Lugar noted at the 2007 Senate Foreign Relations Committee hearing on the Law of the Sea Convention that "Opponents seem to think that if the U.S. declines to ratify the Law of the Sea, the United States can avoid any multilateral responsibilities or entanglements related to the oceans. But unlike some treaties, such as the Kyoto Agreement and the Comprehensive Test Ban Treaty, where U.S. non-participation renders the treaty virtually inoperable, the Law of the Sea will continue to form the basis of maritime law *regardless of whether the U.S. is a party.* Consequently, the United States cannot insulate itself from the Convention merely by declining to ratify." See http://lugar.senate.gov/news/record. cfm?id=284885&& <checked August 11, 2010>.

[9] The major social groups are women; youth and children; indigenous people; nongovernmental organizations; local authorities; workers and trade unions; business and industry; scientific and technical community; and farmers.

[10] *Results of the review by the Commission on Sustainable Development of the sectoral theme of "oceans and seas": international coordination and cooperation,* UNGA Resolution 54/33, November 24, 1999, preamble.

[11] The importance of the experts was stressed by many delegations at the tenth session of the Informal Consultative Process in 2009. The need for a wide representation of panellists from developing countries was emphasized by many delegations and the setting-up of a database of experts was suggested; see *Report of*

and NGOs also take part in the discussions and they are able to contribute to the outcomes of the process.

Most other international institutions considered in this book also involve non-state actors in the law-making process in some capacity. The International Seabed Authority regularly hosts workshops and seminars involving scientific and other experts. These workshops have had a significant influence on the content of the rules and regulations adopted by the Authority to manage seabed mineral resources. In the FAO, regional fisheries bodies and other intergovernmental organizations are key participants in the discussions and debates on fisheries law and policy. Similarly, nongovernmental representatives from the shipping industry and environmental groups are actively engaged with the work of the IMO.

Despite the increasing involvement of non-state actors in these international institutions, it is clear that states retain a tight grip on international law-making activities.[12] In most cases representatives of intergovernmental and nongovernmental organizations are only able to participate as observers.[13] As such they are limited in the extent to which they can participate in formal decision-making. Charnowitz observes that "whatever influence [NGOs] have is achieved through the attractiveness of their ideas and values. No NGO is guaranteed influence … Influence must be constantly earned."[14] An extreme illustration of this fact is that states often police which NGOs are permitted to qualify as observers[15] and states can also decide to completely exclude non-state actors from negotiations if they wish.

Even in the case of the Informal Consultative Process, the limited role of non-state actors is starkly apparent. The Informal Consultative Process is limited to making recommendations to the General Assembly on a select few topics. Moreover, these recommendations are in no way binding on the General Assembly and the key discussions on the annual General Assembly resolution on the law of the sea continue to take

the work of the United Nations Open-Ended Process on Oceans and Law of the Sea at its tenth meeting, Document A/64/131, July 13, 2009, at para. 56.

[12] See A. E. Boyle and C. Chinkin, The Making of International Law (Oxford University Press, 2007) Chapter 2.

[13] One exception to this rule is the International Labour Organization, which includes representatives of employers and workers on national delegations.

[14] S. Charnowitz, "Nongovernmental organizations and international law" (2006) 100 Am. J. Int'l L. 348, at 348.

[15] See e.g. Guidelines on the Grant of Consultative Status, in IMO Basic Documents, 2004 edition, Vol. I, at 129.

place in private through informal consultations between states. This state of affairs means that it is difficult to know precisely what policy considerations underlie the final resolution of the General Assembly.

This lack of transparency is to be lamented and it is at variance with key international declarations such as Agenda 21, which stresses the importance of "genuine involvement of all social groups" in policy-making and implementation.[16] Fulfilling this aspiration, however, would require a fundamental reform of the way in which international institutions currently operate in order to give more control to non-state actors to set the agenda and to influence the final decision-making process.

3 The importance of consensus

While participation is an important factor in the ability of international institutions to develop international law, it is also vital to consider how decisions are made. Given the central role that consent continues to play in international law, international institutions will only be able to generate a universal legal framework for the law of the sea if they are able to foster agreement between all the relevant actors.

The importance of consensus in the law of the sea can be traced back to the convening of UNCLOS III. Widespread dissatisfaction, particularly among developing countries, with the existing 1958 conventions on the law of the sea was one of the principal reasons why states committed themselves to reforming this area of international law. It was realized at an early stage by states attending UNCLOS III that their efforts would only be successful if the negotiations took into account the interests of all categories of states. Consensus was central to the decision-making procedures of the conference. Several procedural innovations were employed in order to bring together different interest groups that had formed at the conference.[17] In particular, the extensive use of informal consultations and the delegation of responsibility for producing a compromise text to the chairs of the negotiating committees were key mechanisms designed to promote consensus. Without these techniques, forging a consensus of more than 150 states with very different interests would have been a significant, if not insurmountable, challenge.

---

[16] Agenda 21, at para. 23.1.   [17] See Chapter 2.

Despite differences in their mandates and powers, what all the institutions considered in this study have in common is that they have sought to preserve the consensus which prevails over the law of the sea. It is notable that many of the techniques utilized at UNCLOS III are now employed by other international organizations when dealing with law of the sea issues.

For instance, consensus decision-making procedures were central to the negotiation of the two implementing agreements considered in Chapter 4. Indeed, the need for these instruments arose because consensus could not be achieved during the initial negotiation of the Law of the Sea Convention. Thus, without consensus, these instruments would not have resolved the problems that they were intended to address. In both cases states were able to reach a compromise on outstanding issues on the law of the sea agenda through the use of decision-making techniques that had first been developed at UNCLOS III. As a result, both of these instruments can be said to have legal implications beyond those states that have formally consented to be bound by them.[18]

In some cases consensus is built into the decision-making procedures of an institution. The Rules of the Procedure of the Meeting of the States Parties require the institution to "conduct its work on the basis of general agreement."[19] It is only when all efforts at achieving general agreement have been exhausted that the Meeting of the States Parties may proceed to a vote.[20] In some cases it is clear that states have foregone the opportunity to use the available voting procedures in order to make one final attempt at reaching a compromise. For instance, at the seventeenth Meeting of the States Parties in 2007, the representatives of the African and Asian Groups introduced a proposal to change the allocation of seats on the Tribunal and the Commission in order to reflect the growth of States Parties from those two regions.[21] It was proposed that these two groupings should be allocated an additional seat, which would rotate between them.[22] However, this proposal

---

[18] See Chapter 4.
[19] *Rules of procedure for meetings of the States Parties*, Document SPLOS/2/Rev.4, January 24, 2005, Rule 54.
[20] *Ibid.*
[21] *Report of the seventeenth meeting of States Parties (14 to 23 June 2007)*, Document SPLOS/164, at para. 94.
[22] See *Decision on the allocation of seats on the Commission on the Limits of the Continental Shelf and the International Tribunal for the Law of the Sea*, Document SPLOS/163, Annexes I and II.

was not acceptable to some states, particularly the developed countries that would have lost a seat on the Tribunal if the proposal were accepted. In order to try and reach a compromise, it was agreed to defer any decision to a later meeting. Further discussions were held prior to the eighteenth Meeting of the States Parties in 2008, but still no generally acceptable solution was forthcoming. Nevertheless, delegates emphasized that all efforts should be made to resolve the issue through consensus. At the same time, some states were of the opinion that the objective of reaching consensus could not stand in the way of making a decision.[23] To this end, a decision was adopted by the eighteenth Meeting of the States Parties in which it was agreed that "[the Meeting] will have exhausted all efforts to reach a general agreement, by the nineteenth meeting of the States Parties, on the allocation of seats for the Commission on the Limits of the Continental Shelf and the International Tribunal for the Law of the Sea."[24] Ultimately it was not necessary to have recourse to a vote as delegates settled upon a so-called "Arrangement for the allocation of seats on the International Tribunal for the Law of the Sea and the Commission on the Limits of the Continental Shelf." According to this arrangement, five members of the Tribunal would be elected by the Group of African States, five by the Group of Asian States, three by the Group of Eastern European States, four by the Group of Latin American States and three by the Group of Western European and Other States. The remaining seat was to be elected from among the Group of African States, the Group of Asian States and the Group of Western European and Other States.[25] Although the States Parties from the African and Asian Groups could have pushed through their proposal by insisting upon a vote, they agreed to the compromise "in a spirit of cooperation and consensus."[26] Underlying this decision is undoubtedly the fact that the legitimacy of the Tribunal and the Commission could be negatively affected if they did not have the support of all relevant states. This example also shows

---

[23] *Report of the eighteenth meeting of States Parties (13–20 June 2008)*, Document SPLOS/184, at para. 103.

[24] *Decision on the allocation of seats on the Commission on the Limits of the Continental Shelf and the International Tribunal for the Law of the Sea*, Document SPLOS/182, at para. 1.

[25] *Arrangement for the allocation of seats on the International Tribunal for the Law of the Sea and the Commission on the Limits of the Continental Shelf*, Document SPLOS/201, at paras. 1 and 2.

[26] See the comments by the delegations of the Asian and African Groups; *Report of the nineteenth meeting of States Parties (22–26 June 2009)*, Document SPLOS/203, para. 102.

how consensus decision-making can be assisted by the threat of a vote in some circumstances.

Consensus is also built into the decision-making procedures of the International Seabed Authority, which is established under Part XI of the Law of the Sea Convention. According to its constituent instrument, the Authority is required to attempt to achieve consensus before proceeding to formal voting.[27] Moreover, a special decision-making procedure applies to the adoption of rules and regulations for the conduct of activities in the Area. This is important given that the Authority is one of the few institutions with a power to adopt rules and regulations that are automatically binding on states whether or not they have individually consented to them. Rules and regulations can only be adopted if they are supported by a consensus of those major interest groups represented on the Council. Seats are specifically allocated to states representing importers and exporters of minerals, states which have made the largest investments in deep seabed mining, and developing states whose interests may be most affected by the deep seabed mining regime. In this way, the decision-making procedures of the Authority are explicitly designed so that no relevant interests can be ignored in the drafting of rules and regulations. Moreover, once adopted by the Council, rules and regulations cannot be overturned either by the Assembly or through the dispute settlement procedures in Part XI of the Convention.[28]

In other cases consensus has developed as an informal practice of international institutions. This preference for consensus means that formal decision-making procedures are often set aside in favor of trying to foster an acceptable compromise among all participants in the decision-making process.

In the case of the IMO, consensus decision-making procedures are used in order to promote the general application of shipping standards adopted by that organization. Most IMO standards are included in the annex to an international treaty. Despite the existence of majoritarian decision-making procedures that are applicable to the amendment of the relevant regulatory treaties, the IMO tends to adopt amendments to technical standards by consensus.[29] This practice has potentially important implications for the status of shipping standards. As explained in Chapter 6, the Law of the Sea Convention makes "generally

---

[27] Part XI Agreement, Annex, Section 3, at paras. 2 and 3.
[28] See Chapter 5.   [29] See Chapter 6.

accepted" international rules and standards applicable to all states through the use of rules of reference, whether or not those states are formally bound by the standards in their original form. While there is no clear definition of what is generally accepted, it can be argued that those rules adopted by consensus at the IMO are more likely to qualify as such, as there is a greater chance they will be implemented by states in practice.

The recognition of the need to protect and preserve the integrity of the law of the sea regime is another reason that the formal decision-making procedures of an institution may be set aside in favor of consensus decision-making. The use of informal decision-making mechanisms is perhaps most starkly illustrated by the modification of certain provisions of the Law of the Sea Convention by the Meeting of the States Parties. The Meeting of the States Parties has modified several aspects of the Convention regime relating to the International Tribunal for the Law of the Sea and the Commission on the Outer Limits of the Continental Shelf through the adoption of an ordinary decision, instead of invoking the formal amendment procedures found in the Convention. Yet the decisions of the Meeting of the States Parties surveyed in Chapter 3 have only been successful in modifying the law of the sea regime in the Convention because they have been supported by consensus.

It was also seen in Chapter 6 that informal decision-making has also been used by the IMO to approve traffic measures that are not explicitly foreseen in the Convention's navigation regime. For instance, the IMO has approved the use of compulsory ship reporting systems in international straits. The existence of consensus among IMO Members means that these measures are unlikely to be challenged, despite the fact that they do not have an express basis in the Law of the Sea Convention.

On the other hand, the controversy over the use of compulsory pilotage schemes in international straits demonstrates the limits of informal decision-making.[30] The proposal for compulsory pilotage in the Torres Strait has no explicit basis in the Law of the Sea Convention, which strictly limits the types of navigational measures that may be taken by states bordering an international strait. In this case IMO Member States were unable to reach a satisfactory compromise. In the absence of consensus, one is left with uncertainty over the legal status

[30] See Chapter 6.

of the measures adopted by Australia and the possibility of legal challenge by affected states.[31]

This last example also demonstrates that the existence of international institutions to oversee the implementation of the law of the sea regime may reduce the opportunities for successful unilateral action by states. The availability of a standing institution to oversee the implementation of an international regime means that states can collectively scrutinize the actions of individual states and they can condemn any action that they consider to be incompatible with existing international rules. Such international pressure may persuade a state to refrain from taking its proposed unilateral action. At the same time, the existence of a multilateral forum allows an opportunity for all of the affected actors to discuss the situation and it may be possible for them to accommodate their different interests. This is illustrated by the aftermath of the *Prestige* oil spill. Following the sinking of the *Prestige*, a single-hulled tanker flying the flag of the Bahamas, in Spanish waters in November 2002, several European states responded with controversial proposals to ban single-hulled tankers from transiting European waters. Such proposals were clearly incompatible with the freedom of navigation enshrined in the Law of the Sea Convention and protests were made by maritime states. However, negotiations at the IMO led to a compromise between the EU and maritime states that included an agreement on the accelerated phasing-out of single-hulled tankers through an amendment to the relevant MARPOL regulations.[32] This compromise avoided unilateral and arguably illegal action being taken by European states and it demonstrates the mediatory role that can be played by international institutions.

4 Promoting coherence in the law of the sea

It can be seen that many institutions are involved in the ongoing development of the law of the sea. These institutions have diverse memberships, mandates and powers. Arguably the eclectic nature of law-making

---

[31] As noted by Boyle, "unsuccessful unilateralism is far more likely today to result not merely in protest, but in litigation, and probable defeat"; A. E. Boyle, "EU unilateralism and the law of the sea" (2006) 21 *Int'l J. Marine & Coastal L.* 15, at 20.

[32] See A. K.-J. Tan, *Vessel-Source Marine Pollution* (Cambridge University Press, 2006) at 147–55. The European Community did restrict single-hulled tankers from using European ports, although such action is arguably compatible with the Law of the Sea Convention; see Boyle, "EU unilateralism and the law of the sea."

in such a regime as the law of the sea is inevitable. The option of creating a single organization responsible for all aspects of the law of the sea was briefly mooted by the International Law Commission in its codification of the law of the sea in the 1950s, but the idea was firmly rejected by the special rapporteur who considered that it was neither feasible nor necessary.[33]

At the same time there are significant challenges posed by the decentralized nature of international law-making. Inevitably, there are overlaps in the competence of institutions, no matter how specialized their mandate. Indeed, overlaps will occur not only between institutions involved in maritime affairs. The law of the sea may also overlap with other areas of international law. This possibility is illustrated by the *Swordfish* dispute between the European Community and Chile. In that case Chile had denied European fishing vessels access to its ports because it argued that the European Community had failed in its duty to conserve high seas stocks of swordfish, as outlined inter alia in Articles 116–119 of the Law of the Sea Convention. The case was brought before a special chamber of the International Tribunal for the Law of the Sea by Chile.[34] In turn, the European Community argued that Chile was obliged under Article V of the General Agreement on Trade and Tariffs to grant freedom of transit to European goods and it initiated parallel dispute settlement proceedings under the Dispute Settlement Understanding of the World Trade Organization.[35] Although the dispute was settled before a decision was reached on the merits in either forum,[36] the case demonstrates the dangers of institutional fragmentation, as well as the interrelationship between treaties dealing with what at first sight appear to be distinct aspects of international law. Thus, even the creation of a single international organization with full competence over all aspects of the law of the sea would not eradicate the threat of fragmentation, as the law of the sea itself is not a self-contained regime and it overlaps with other fields of international law. Ultimately, there is a need to manage the tensions

---

[33] International Law Commission, "Regime of the High Seas and Regime of the Territorial Sea" (1956-II) *Ybk Int'l L. Commission* 1, at paras. 9–18.

[34] By agreement of the parties, a special chamber of five members was constituted to hear the dispute; see *Case Concerning the Conservation and Sustainable Exploitation of Swordfish Stocks in the South-Eastern Pacific Ocean*, Order of December 20, 2000.

[35] See *Chile – Measures affecting the transit and importation of swordfish, Request for Consultations by the European Communities*, WT/DS193/1, April 26, 2000.

[36] See *Case Concerning the Conservation and Sustainable Exploitation of Swordfish Stocks in the South-Eastern Pacific Ocean*, Order of December 16, 2009.

between international rules emerging from different institutional frameworks.

The potential for conflicts of norms arising from different institutional frameworks was considered in Chapter 8, which also looked at possible mechanisms to deal with this threat. It concluded that there are no clear-cut legal solutions to a conflict of norms. Rather, it is preferable to manage conflicts on a case-by-case basis. Once again, institutions can perform a leading role in this process.

In the context of the law of the sea, it is again the United Nations that has been at the forefront of promoting cooperation between different institutions. In particular, the annual report of the Secretary-General provides a useful overview of almost all developments in the law of the sea, including those taking place through intergovernmental organizations and conferences, treaty bodies and other informal arrangements. The General Assembly reviews these activities and it often makes recommendations for cooperation between institutions. Yet it was also seen in Chapter 8 that the General Assembly is limited in the actions that it can take in order to ensure that different international institutions coordinate their activities. Rather, coordination must be pursued between individual institutions themselves. It was suggested that the conclusion of relationship agreements can assist in promoting cooperation and coordination between international institutions by defining the normative framework in which institutions are expected to interact. Moreover, relationship agreements can specify particular procedural mechanisms through which institutions can coordinate and even harmonize their law-making activities. The use of joint committees or working groups was particularly highlighted as a means of ensuring that conflicts of norms do not arise in the first place. Joint committees or working groups may also provide a possible mechanism for solving conflicts in a way that is acceptable to both institutions, as is illustrated by the example of the Joint Working Group established between the IMO, the ILO and the Basel Convention COP to coordinate their efforts on ship scrapping and recycling.

It appears from this study that states are all too aware of the importance of maintaining consensus in order to promote a stable yet flexible framework for the law of the sea. Institutions have been central to this process. Institutions may not possess legislative powers but they are able to provide a forum for cooperation between all states, as well as other relevant actors. Debates and discussions within international institutions contribute to a continuing crystallization of the law of the sea, maintaining the consensus on the applicable legal framework and ultimately developing the universal law of the sea. This is an ongoing process. The law of sea is not immune to change and new challenges will constantly arise which will put pressure on the prevailing legal framework. Therefore, states must continue to employ the law-making techniques and the conflict avoidance mechanisms discussed in this book if the universal legal order of the oceans is to survive.

Bibliography

BOOKS

Alvarez, J. E. *International Organizations as Law-Makers* (Oxford University Press, 2005)

Amerasinghe, C. F. *Principles of the Institutional Law of International Organizations* (2nd edn., Cambridge University Press, 2005)

Attard, D. *The Exclusive Economic Zone in International Law* (Oxford University Press, 1987)

Aust, A. *Modern Treaty Law and Practice* (2nd edn., Cambridge University Press, 2007)

Birnie, P., A. E. Boyle and C. Redgwell, *International Law and the Environment* (3rd edn., Oxford University Press, 2009)

Boyle, A. E. and C. Chinkin, *The Making of International Law* (Oxford University Press, 2007)

Brierly, J., *The Law of Nations* (Oxford University Press, 1963)

Brown, E. *The International Law of the Sea* (Dartmouth Publishing Company, 1994)

Brownlie, I. *Principles of Public International Law* (6th edn., Oxford University Press, 2003)

Chinkin, C. *Third Parties in International Law* (Clarendon Press, 1993)

Churchill, R. and V. Lowe, *The Law of the Sea* (3rd edn., Manchester University Press, 1997)

Cot, J. P. and A. Pellet (eds.), *La Charte des Nations Unies* (Economica-Bruylant, 1985)

Danilenko, G. M. *Law-making in the International Community* (Martinus Nijhoff Publishers, 1993)

Gavouneli, M. *Functional Jurisdiction in the Law of the Sea* (Martinus Nijhoff Publishers, 2007)

Glowka, L. *et al.*, *A Guide to the Convention on Biological Diversity* (IUCN – The World Conservation Union, 1996)

Hakapää, K. *Marine Pollution in International Law* (Suomlainen Tiedeakatemia, 1981)

Higgins, R. *The Development of International Law through the Political Organs of the United Nations* (Oxford University Press, 1963)
  Problems and Process – International Law and How We Use It (Oxford University Press, 1994)
International Seabed Authority, *Marine Mineral Resources: Scientific Advances and Economic Perspectives* (United Nations, 2004)
Jennings, R. and A. Watts (eds.), *Oppenheim's International Law, Vol. 1, Peace* (9th edn., Longman, 1992)
Kaye, S. *The Torres Strait* (Martinus Nijhoff Publishers, 1997)
Klein, N. *Dispute Settlement in the UN Convention on the Law of the Sea* (Cambridge University Press, 2005)
Louka, E. *International Environmental Law* (Cambridge University Press, 2006)
Mann Borgese, E. *The Oceanic Circle: Governing the Seas as a Global Resource* (United Nations University Press, 1998)
McDougal, M. S. and W. T. Burke, *Public Order of the Oceans* (Yale University Press, 1962)
McNair, A. D. *The Law of Treaties*, (Oxford University Press, 1961)
Merrills, J. *International Dispute Settlement* (4th edn., Cambridge University Press, 2005)
M'Gonigle, R. M. and M. W. Zacher, *Pollution, Politics, and International Law: Tankers at Sea* (University of California Press, 1979)
Morgenstern, F. *Legal Problems of International Organizations* (Grotius Publications, 1986)
Munavvar, M. *Ocean States – Archipelagic Regimes in the Law of the Sea* (Martin Nijhoff Publishers, 1995)
Nordquist, M. *et al.* (eds.), *United Nations Convention on the Law of the Sea 1982 – A Commentary, Vol.1* (Martin Nijhoff Publishers, 1985)
  United Nations Convention on the Law of the Sea 1982 – A Commentary, Vol. 2 (Martinus Nijhoff Publishers, 1993)
  1982 United Nations Convention on the Law of the Sea – A Commentary, Vol. 3 (Martinus Nijhoff Publishers, 1995)
  United Nations Convention on the Law of the Sea 1982 – A Commentary, Vol. 4 (Martinus Nijhoff Publishers, 1991)
  United Nations Convention on the Law of the Sea – A Commentary, Vol. 5 (Martinus Nijhoff Publishers, 1989)
  United Nations Convention on the Law of the Sea 1982 – A Commentary, Vol. 6, (Martinus Nijhoff, 2002)
O'Connell, D. P. *The International Law of the Sea* (Oxford University Press, 1982)
Oda, S. *The Law of the Sea in our Time: The United Nations Seabed Committee 1968–1973* (Sijthoff, 1977)
Office for Ocean Affairs and the Law of the Sea, *Archipelagic States – Legislative History of Part IV of the United Nations Convention on the Law of the Sea* (United Nations, 1990)
Orakhelashvili, A. *Peremptory Norms in International Law* (Oxford University Press, 2006)

Orrego Vicuña, F. *The Exclusive Economic Zone* (Cambridge University Press, 1989)

Pauwelyn, J. *Conflict of Norms in Public International Law* (Cambridge University Press, 2003)

Ragazzi, M. *The Concept of International Obligations Erga Omnes* (Clarendon Press, 1997)

Reuter, P. *Introduction au Droit des Traites* (Kegan Paul International, 1995)

Rosenne, S. *Committee of Experts for the Progressive Codification of International Law (1925–1928)* (Oceana Publications, 1972)

Rosenne, S. et al. (eds.), *United Nations Convention on the Law of the Sea – A Commentary, Vol. 6* (Martinus Nijhoff Publishers, 2002)

Rozakis, C. L. *The Concept of Jus Cogens in the Law of Treaties* (North-Holland, 1976)

Sadat-Akhavi, A. *Methods of Resolving Conflicts between Treaties* (Martinus Nijhoff Publishers, 2003)

Sands, P. and P. Klein, *Bowett's Law of International Institutions* (6th edn., Sweet & Maxwell, 2009)

Sanger, C. *Ordering the Oceans* (Zed Books, 1986)

Schachter, O. *International Law in Theory and Practice* (Martinus Nijhoff Publishers, 1991)

Schermers, H. G. and N. Blokker, *International Institutional Law* (4th edn., Martinus Nijhoff Publishers, 2003)

Shaw, M. *International Law* (5th edn., Cambridge University Press, 2003)
International Law (6th edn., Cambridge University Press, 2008)

Simma, B. et al. (eds.), *The Charter of the United Nations – A Commentary* (2nd edn., Oxford University Press, 2002)

Sinclair, I. *The Vienna Convention on the Law of Treaties* (Manchester University Press, 1984)
The International Law Commission (Grotius Publications, 1987)

Tan, A. K.-J. *Vessel-Source Marine Pollution* (Cambridge University Press, 2006)

Timagenis, G. J. *International Control of Marine Pollution* (Oceana Publications, 1980)

United Nations, *The Work of the International Law Commission* (United Nations, 1988)

World Commission on Environment and Development, *Our Common Future* (Oxford University Press, 1987)

BOOK CHAPTERS AND JOURNAL ARTICLES

Akehurst, M. "Custom as a source of international law" (1974–75) *Brit. Ybk Int'l L.* 1.
"The hierarchy of sources of international law" (1974–75) *Brit. Ybk Int'l L.* 273

Anderson, D. "Efforts to ensure universal participation in the United Nations Convention on the Law of the Sea," (1993) 42 *Int'l & Comp. L. Q.* 654

"Further efforts to ensure universal participation in the United Nations Convention on the Law of the Sea" (1994) 43 *Int'l & Comp. L. Q.* 886

"The Straddling Stocks Agreement of 1995 – an initial assessment" (1996) 45 *Int'l & Comp. L. Q.* 463

Arrow, D. W. "Seabeds, sovereignty and objective regimes" (1983–84) 7 *Fordham Int'l L. J.* 169

Balkin, R. "The establishment and work of the IMO Legal Committee," in M. Nordquist and J. N. Moore (eds.), *Current Maritime Issues and the International Maritime Organization* (Martinus Nijhoff Publishers, 1999) 291

Balton, D. "The Compliance Agreement," in E. Hey (ed.), *Developments in International Fisheries Law* (Kluwer Law International, 1999) 31

Bateman, S. and M. White, "Compulsory pilotage in the Torres Strait: overcoming unacceptable risks to a sensitive marine environment" (2009) 40 *Ocean Dev. & Int'l L.* 184

Batongbacal, J. L. "Barely skimming the surface: archipelagic sea lanes navigation and the IMO," in A. Oude Elferink and D. Rothwell (eds.), *Oceans Management in the 21st Century: Institutional Frameworks and Responses* (Koninklikje Brill NV, 2004) 49

Baxter, R. "Custom and treaty" (1970) 129 *Recueil des Cours* 27

"Multilateral treaties as evidence of customary international law" (1967) *Brit. Ybk Int'l L.* 275

Beckman, R. "PSSAs and transit passage – Australia's pilotage system in the Torres Strait challenges the IMO and UNCLOS" (2007) 38 *Ocean Development & Int'l L.* 325

Benvenisti, E. and G. W. Downs, "The empire's new clothes: political economy and the fragmentation of international law" (2007–2008) 60 *Stan. L. Rev.* 595

Blanco-Bazan, A. "IMO interface with the Law of the Sea Convention," in J. N. Moore and M. Nordquist (eds.), *Current Maritime Issues and the International Maritime Organization* (Martinus Nijhoff Publishers, 1999) 269

Borgen, C. J. "Resolving treaty conflicts" (2005) 37 *George Washington Int'l L. Rev.* 573

Boyle, A. E. "Marine pollution under the Law of the Sea Convention" (1985) 79 *Am. J. Int'l L.* 357

"Dispute settlement and the Law of the Sea Convention: problems of fragmentation and jurisdiction" (1997) 46 *Int'l & Comp. L. Q.* 37

"Some reflections on the relationship between treaties and soft law" (1999) 48 *Int'l & Comp L. Q.* 901

"EU unilateralism and the law of the sea" (2006) 21 *Int'l J. Marine & Coastal L.* 15

"Further development of the 1982 Law of the Sea Convention," in D. Freestone, R. Barnes and D. Ong (eds.), *The Law of the Sea – Progress and Prospects* (Oxford University Press, 2006) 40

Breuer, G. "Maritime safety regulations," in R. Bernhardt (ed.), *Encyclopedia of Public International Law, Vol. 3* (North-Holland, 1997) 318.

Brower, C. and J. Sharpe, "Multiple and conflicting international arbitral awards" (2003) 4 *J. World Investment* 211

Brunee, J. "Coping with consent: law-making under multilateral environmental agreements" (2002) 15 *Leiden J. Int'l L.* 1

Burke, W. T. "Regulation of driftnet fishing on the high seas and the new international law of the sea" (1991) 3 *Geo. Int'l Env. L. Rev.* 265

Buzan, B. "'United we stand...' – informal negotiating groups at UNCLOS III" (1980) 4 *Marine Policy* 183

   "Negotiating by consensus: developments in technique at the United Nations Conference on the Law of the Sea" (1981) 75 *Am. J. Int'l L.* 324

Caminos, H. and M. R. Molitor, "Progressive development of international law and the Package Deal" (1985) 79 *Am. J. Int'l L.* 871

Charney, J. "Universal international law" (1993) 87 *Am. J. Int'l L.* 529

Charnowitz, S. "Nongovernmental organizations and international law" (2006) 100 *Am. J. Int'l L.* 348

Cheng, B. "United Nations resolutions on outer space: instant customary international law?" in B. Cheng (ed.), *International Law: Teaching and Practice* (Stevens, 1982)

Chodosh, H. "Neither treaty nor custom: the emergence of declarative international law" (1991) 26 *Texas J. Int'l L.* 87

Churchill, R. "The impact of State Practice on the jurisdictional framework contained in the United Nations Convention on the Law of the Sea," in A. Oude Elferink (ed.) *Stability and Change in the Law of the Sea: The Role of the LOS Convention* (Martinus Nijhoff Publishers, 2005) 91

Corbet, A. "Navigation management: post-Donaldson" (1995) 19 *Marine Policy* 477

Czaplinski, W. and G. Danilenko, "Conflicts of norms in international law" (1990) *Netherlands Ybk Int'l L.* 1

D'Amato, A. "Trashing customary international law" (1987) 91 *Am. J. Int'l L.* 657

De La Fayette, L. "The Marine Environment Protection Committee: the conjunction of the law of the sea and international environmental law" (2001) 16 *Int'l J. Marine & Coastal L.* 155

   "The role of the UN in international oceans governance," in D. Freestone, R. Barnes and D. Ong (eds.), *The Law of the Sea: Progress and Prospects* (Oxford University Press, 2006) 63

   "A new regime for the conservation and sustainable use of marine biodiversity and genetic resources beyond the limits of national jurisdiction" (2009) 24 *Int'l J. Marine & Coastal L.* 221

Dobbert, J. P. "Food and agriculture," in O. Schachter and C. Joyner (eds.), *United Nations Legal Order, Vol. 2* (Cambridge University Press, 1995) 907

Doulman, D. J. "Structure and process of the 1993–1995 United Nations Conference on Straddling Fish Stocks and Highly Migratory Fish Stocks," *FAO Fisheries Circular No. 898 FID/C898*

Edeson, W. "Closing the gap: the role of 'soft' international instruments to control fishing" (1999) 20 *Australian Ybk Int'l L.* 83

"Towards long-term sustainable use: some recent developments in the legal regime of fisheries," in A. E Boyle and D. Freestone (eds.), *International Law and Sustainable Development* (Oxford University Press, 1999) 165

"The International Plan of Action on Illegal Unreported and Unregulated Fishing: the legal context of a non-legally binding instrument" (2001) 16 *Int'l J. Marine & Coastal L.* 603

Engo, P. "Issues of the First Committee," in B. H. Oxman and A. W. Koers (eds.), *The 1982 Convention on the Law of the Sea* (Law of the Sea Institute, 1983) 33.

Evensen, J. "Keynote address," in B. H. Oxman and A. W. Koers (eds.), *The 1982 Convention on the Law of the Sea* (Law of the Sea Institute, 1983) xxi

"Working methods and procedures in the Third United Nations Conference on the Law of the Sea" (1986) 199 *Recueil des Cours* 414

Fauteux, P. "The Canadian Legal Initiative on High Seas Fishing" (1993) 4 *Ybk Int'l Env'l L.* 51

Ferri, N. "Current legal developments – United Nations General Assembly" (2008) 23 *Int'l J. Marine & Coastal L.* 137

Franckx, E. "Pacta Tertiis and the Agreement for the Implementation of the Straddling and Highly Migratory Fish Stocks Provisions of the United Nations Convention of the Law of the Sea" (2000) 8 *Tulane J. Int'l & Comp. L.* 49

Freestone, D. "International fisheries law since Rio: the continued rise of the precautionary principle" in A. E. Boyle and D. Freestone (eds.), *International Law and Sustainable Development* (Oxford University Press, 1999) 135

Freestone, D. and A. Oude Elferink, "Flexibility and innovation in the law of the sea – will the LOS Convention amendment procedures ever be used?" in A. Oude Elferink (ed.), *Stability and Change in the Law of the Sea: The Role of the LOS Convention* (Martinus Nijhoff Publishers, 2005) 169

French, D. "Treaty interpretation and the incorporation of extraneous legal rules" (2006) 55 *Int'l & Comp. L. Q.* 281

Gillespie, A. "Forum shopping in international environmental law: the IWC, CITES, and the management of cetaceans" (2002) 33 *Ocean Dev. & Int'l L.* 17

Haas, P. M. "Do regimes matter? Epistemic communities and Mediterranean pollution" (1989) 43 *Int'l Org.* 377

Hafner, G. "Risks ensuing from the fragmentation of international law," in *International Law Commission, Report on the work of its fifty-second session (1 May-9 June and 10 July-18 August 2000), Official Records of the General Assembly, Fifty-fifth session, Supplement No. 10 (A/55/10)*

"Pros and cons ensuing from fragmentation of international law" (2004) 25 *Mich. J. Int'l L.* 849

Harrison, J. "Judicial law-making and the developing order of the oceans" (2007) 22 *Int'l J. Marine & Coastal L.* 283

"Current legal developments – international labour organization" (2008) *Int'l J. Marine & Coastal L.* 125

"Current legal developments – the International Convention for the Safe and Environmentally Sound Recycling of Ships" (2009) 24 *Int'l J. Marine & Coastal L.* 727

Hart, S. "Elements of a Possible Implementation Agreement to UNCLOS for the Conservation and Sustainable Use of Marine Biodiversity beyond National Jurisdiction," *IUCN Environmental Policy and Law Papers online*, Marine Series No. 4, 2008

Hayashi, M. "The 1995 Agreement on the Conservation and Management of Straddling and Highly Migratory Fish Stocks: significance for the Law of the Sea Convention" (1995) *Ocean and Coastal Management* 51

Helfer, L. "Regime shifting: the TRIPs Agreement and new dynamics of international intellectual property lawmaking" (2004) 29 *Yale J. Int'l L.* 1

Henriksen, T. "Revisiting the freedom of fishing and legal obligations of states not party to regional fisheries management organizations" (2009) *Ocean Dev. & Int'l L.* 80

Higgins, R. "A babel of judicial voices? Ruminations from the bench" (2006) 55 *Int'l & Comp. L. Q.* 791

Jackson, A. "The 2001 Convention on the Conservation and Management of Fishery Resources in the South East Atlantic: an introduction" (2002) 17 *Int'l J. Marine & Coastal L.* 33

Jenks, W. "The conflict of law-making treaties" (1953) 30 *Brit. Ybk Int'l L.* 401

Jennings, R. Y. "The discipline of international law," in *Report of the 57th Conference of the International Law Association* (Madrid, 1976) 620

"The identification of international law," in B. Cheng (ed.), *International Law: Teaching and Practice* (Stevens, 1982) 3

Jiminez de Arechaga A., "Custom," in A. Cassese and J. J. Weiler (eds.), *Change and Stability in International Law-Making* (Walter de Gruyter, 1988) at 2–4.

Johnson, C. "A rite of passage: the I.M.O. consideration of the Indonesian archipelagic sea-lanes submission" (2000) 15 *Int'l J. Marine & Coastal L.* 317

Kempton, S. B. "Ship routeing measures in international straits," in E. Mann Borgese *et al.* (eds.), *Ocean Yearbook 14* (International Ocean Institute, 2000) 232

Kingham J. D. and D. M. McRae, "Competent international organizations and the law of the sea" (1979) *Marine Policy* 106

Koh, T. and S. Jayakumar, "An overview of the negotiating process of UNCLOS III," in M. Nordquist *et al.* (eds.), *United Nations Convention on the Law of the Sea 1982 – A Commentary, Vol. 1* (Martinus Nijhoff Publishers, 1985) 29

Kokott, J. "States, sovereign equality," in R. Wolfrum *et al.* (eds.), *Max Planck Encyclopedia of Public International Law* (Oxford University Press, online edition updated August 2007) available at www.mpepil.com/

Koskenniemi, M. "The politics of international law – 20 years on" (2009) *European J. Int'l L.* 7

Koskeniemmi, M. and P. Leino, "Fragmentation of international law? Postmodern anxieties" (2002) 15 *Leiden J. Int'l L.* 553

Kwiatkowska, B. "The High Seas Fisheries Regime: at a point of no return?" (1993) 8 *Int'l J. Marine & Coastal L.* 327

Larson, D. "The Reagan rejection of the UN Convention" (1985) 14 *Ocean Dev. & Int'l L.* 337

Leathley, C. "An institutional hierarchy to combat fragmentation of international law: has the ILC missed an opportunity?" (2007) *J. Int'l L. & Politics* 259

Lee, L. T. "The Law of the Sea Convention and third states" (1983) 77 *Am. J. Int'l L.* 541

Lodge, M. "The International Seabed Authority and Article 82 of the UN Convention on the Law of the Sea" (2006) 21 *Int'l J. Marine & Coastal L.* 323

"Current legal developments – International Seabed Authority" (2009) 24 *Int'l J. Marine & Coastal L.* 185

Lowe, V. "The United Kingdom and the Law of the Sea," in T. Treves (ed.), *The Law of the Sea: The European Union and its Member States* (Martinus Nijhoff Publishers, 1997)

"Sustainable development and unsustainable arguments," in A. E. Boyle and D. Freestone (eds.), *International Law and Sustainable Development* (Oxford University Press, 1999) 19

McDorman, T. "The role of the Commission on the limits of the continental shelf: a technical body in a political world," (2002) 17 *Int'l J. Marine & Coastal L.* 301

McLachlan, C. "The principle of systemic integration and Article 31(3)(c) of the Vienna Convention" (2005) 54 *Int'l & Comp. L. Q.* 279

McNair, A. D. "The functions and differing legal character of treaties" (1930) *Brit. Ybk Int'l L.* 100

Moore, G. "The Code of Conduct on Responsible Fisheries," in E. Hey (ed.), *Developments in International Fisheries Law* (Kluwer Law International, 1999) 85.

Moore, J. "The Regime of Straits and the Third United Nations Conference on the Law of the Sea" (1980) 74 *Am. J. Int'l L.* 77

"Customary international law after the Convention," in R. B. Krueger and S. A. Riesenfeld (eds.), *The Developing Order of the Oceans* (Law of the Sea Institute, 1984) 41

Mosoti, V. "Institutional cooperation and norm creation in international organizations," in T. Cottier, J. Pauwelyn and E. Bürgi Bonanomi (eds.), *Human Rights and International Trade* (Oxford University Press, 2005) 165

Nandan, S. "The efforts undertaken by the United Nations to ensure universality of the Convention," in E. L. Miles and T. Treves (eds.), *Law of the Sea: New Worlds, New Discoveries* (Law of the Sea Institute, 1992) 349

"Administering the mineral resources of the deep seabed," in D. Freestone, R. Barnes and D. Ong (eds.), *The Law of the Sea: Progress and Prospects* (Oxford University Press, 2006) 75

Nelson, D. "The new deep sea-bed mining regime" (1995) 10 *Int'l J. Marine & Coastal L.* 189

"The development of the Legal Regime of High Seas Fisheries," in A. E. Boyle and D. Freestone (eds.), *International Law and Sustainable Development* (Oxford University Press, 1999) 121

Orebech, P., K. Sigurjonsson, and T. L. McDorman, "The 1995 United Nations Straddling and Highly Migratory Fish Stocks Agreement: management, enforcement and dispute settlement" (1998) 13 *Int'l J. Marine & Coastal L.* 119

Orrego Vicuña, F. "The Law of the Sea experience and the corpus of international law: effects and interrelationships," in R. B. Krueger and S. A. Riesenfeld (eds.), *The Developing Order of the Oceans* (The Law of the Sea Institute, 1984) 5

Osieke, E. "The legal validity of ultra vires decisions of international organizations" (1983) 77 *Am. J. Int'l L.* 239

Oxman, B. H. "The Third United Nations Conference on the Law of the Sea: The Seventh Session (1978)" (1979) 73 *Am. J. Int'l L.* 1

"The duty to respect generally accepted international standards" (1991) 24 *New York Uni. J. Int'l L. & Politics* 109

"Environmental protection in archipelagic waters and international straits – the role of the International Maritime Organization" (1995) 10 *Int'l J. Marine & Coastal L.* 467

Oxman, B. H. and J. R. Stevenson, "The preparations for the Law of the Sea Conference" (1974) 68 *Am. J. Int'l L.* 1

Peet, G. "The role of (environmental) non-governmental organizations at the Marine Environmental Committee of the International Maritime Organization and at the London Dumping Convention" (1994) 22 *Ocean & Coastal Management* 3

Plant, G. "International traffic separation schemes in the new law of the sea" (1985) *Marine Policy* 134

"The Third United Nations Conference on the Law of the Sea and the Preparatory Commission: models for United Nations law-making?" (1987) 36 *Int'l & Comp. L. Q.* 525

"The relationship between international navigation rights and environmental protection," in H. Ringbom (ed.), *Competing Norms in the Law of Marine Environmental Protection* (Kluwer Law, 1997) 11

Pronto, A. N. "Some thoughts on the making of international law" (2008) 19 *Euro. J. Int'l L.* 601

Prost M. and P. Kingsley Clark, "Unity, diversity and fragmentation of international law: how much does the multiplication of international organizations really matter?" (2006) 5 *Chinese J. Int'l L.* 341

Roberts, J. "Compulsory pilotage in international straits: the Torres Strait PSSA proposal" (2006) 37 *Ocean & Coastal Management* 93

Rosand, E. "The Security Council as global legislature: ultra-vires or ultra-innovator?" (2005) 28 *Fordham Int'l L. J.* 10

Rothwell, D. "Oceans management and the law of the sea in the twenty-first century," in A. Oude Elferink and D. Rothwell (eds.), *Oceans Management in the 21st Century: Institutional Frameworks and Responses* (Koninklijke Brill NV, 2004) 329

Scott, S. V. "The LOS Convention as a constitutional regime for the oceans," in A. G. Oude Elferink (ed.), *Stability and Change in the Law of the Sea: The Role of the LOS Convention* (2006, Martinus Nijhoff Publications) 9

Scovazzi, T. "Evolution of international law of the sea" (2000) 286 *Recueil des Cours* 39

"Mining, protection of the environment, scientific research and bioprospecting: some considerations on the role of the International Seabed Authority" (2004) 19 *Int'l J. Marine & Coastal L.* 383

Simma, B. "From bilateralism to community interest in international law" (1994) 250 *Recueil des Cours* 221

"Universality of international law from the perspective of a practitioner" (2009) 20 *European J. Int'l L.* 265

Sohn, L. "Voting procedures in United Nations Conferences for the codification of international law" (1975) 69 *Am. J. Int'l L.* 310

"Implications of the Law of the Sea Convention regarding the protection of the marine environment," in R. B. Krueger and S. A. Riesenfeld (eds.), *The Developing Order of the Oceans* (Law of the Sea Institute, 1985) 103

Stevenson, J. R. and B. H. Oxman, "The Third United Nations Conference on the Law of the Sea: the 1974 Caracas Session" (1975) 69 *Am. J. Int'l L.* 1

Subedi, P. "The doctrine of objective regimes in international law and the competence of the United Nations to impose territorial or peace settlements on states" (1994) 37 *German Ybk Int'l L.* 162

Swan, J. "Decision-making in Regional Fishery Bodies or arrangements: the evolving role of RFBs and international agreement on decision-making processes," FAO Fisheries Circular No. 995, 2004

"Port state measures to combat IUU fishing: international and regional developments" (2006–2007) 7 *Sus. Dev. L. & Pol'y* 38

Swan, J. and B. P. Sastia, "Contribution of the Committee on Fisheries to global fisheries governance 1977–1997," *FAO Fisheries Circular C938*, 1999

Tomuschat, C. "Obligations arising for states without or against their will" (1993) 241 *Recueil des Cours* 195

Treves, T. "UNCLOS as a non-universally ratified instrument," in B. H. Oxman and A. W. Koers (eds.), *The 1982 Convention on the Law of the Sea* (Law of the Sea Institute, 1982) 685

"The General Assembly and the Meeting of States Parties in the implementation of the LOS Convention," in A. Oude Elferink (ed.), *Stability and Change in the Law of the Sea: The Role of the LOS Convention* (Martinus Nijhoff Publishers, 2005) 55

Tuerk, H. "The contribution of the International Tribunal for the Law of the Sea to international law," in E. J. Molenaar and A. G. Oude Elferink (eds.), *The International Legal Regime of Areas beyond National Jurisdiction: Current and Future Developments* (Martinus Nijhoff Publishers, 2010) 217

Valenzuela, M. "IMO: public international law and regulation," in D. M. Johnston and N. G. Letalik (eds.), *The Law of the Sea and Ocean Industry: New Opportunities and Restraints* (Law of the Sea Institute, 1984) 141

Van Reenen, R. "Rules of Reference in the new Convention on the Law of the Sea in particular connection with the pollution of the sea by oil from tankers" (1981) *Netherlands Ybk Int'l L.* 3.

Vasciannie, S. "Part XI of the Law of the Sea Convention and Third States: some general observations" (1989) 48 *Cambridge L. J.* 85

Vierdag, E. W. "The time of the conclusion of a multilateral treaty: Article 30 of the Vienna Convention on the Law of Treaties and Related Provisions" (1988) *Brit. Ybk Int'l L.* 75

Vignes, D. "Will the Third Conference on the Law of the Sea work according to consensus rule?" (1975) 69 *Am. J. Int'l L.* 119

"La valeur juridique de certaines regles, normes ou pratiques mentionnees au T.N.C.O. comme generalement acceptees" (1979) 25 *Annuaire Français de Droit International* 712

Vorbach, J. "The vital role of non-flag state actors in the pursuit of safer shipping" (2001) *Ocean Dev. & Int'l Law* 27

Vukas, B. "Generally accepted international rules and standards," in A. Soons (ed.), *Implementation of the Law of the Sea Convention through International Institutions* (Law of the Sea Institute, 1990) 405

Weiler, J. "The geology of international law – governance, democracy and legitimacy" (2004) 64 *ZaöRV* 547

Weisburd, A. "Customary international law: the problem of treaties" (1988) 21 *Vanderbilt J. Transnational L.* 1

Werksman, J. "The Conference of the Parties to Environmental Treaties," in J. Werksman (ed.), *Greening International Institutions* (Earthscan Publications, 1996) 55.

Wolfrum, R. "Fishery Commissions," in R. Bernhardt (ed.), *Encyclopedia of Public International Law, Vol. 2* (North-Holland, 1989) 393.

"The legal order for the seas and the oceans," in M. Nordquist and J. Moore (eds.), *Entry into Force of the Law of the Sea Convention* (Kluwer Law International, 1995) 161.

"IMO interface with the Law of the Sea Convention," in J. N. Moore and M. Nordquist (eds.), *Current Maritime Issues and the International Maritime Organization* (Martinus Nijhoff Publishers, 1999) 223

Wood, M. "International Seabed Authority: the first four years" (1999) *Max Planck U. N. Ybk* 172

Wright, Q. "Custom as a basis for international law in the post-world war world" (1966) *Texas Int'l L. Forum* 147

Yankov, A. "The significance of the 1982 Convention for the protection of the marine environment – Third Committee Issues," in B. H. Oxman and A. W. Koers (eds.), *The 1982 Convention on the Law of the Sea* (Law of the Sea Institute, 1983) 71

Index

Lightning Source UK Ltd.
Milton Keynes UK
UKOW04f0448290114

225471UK00007B/280/P